THE LEGEND OF SAM PANDOLFO

John Dominik

Minnesota's Pan Motor Company and Its Legacy

John J. Dominik

PRINTED AND PUBLISHED IN THE USA BY:
Park Press Quality Printing, Inc.
Waite Park, MN 56387

ISBN #: 1-892740-01-X

TABLE OF CONTENTS

PREFACE

A LEGEND FROM EARLY Christian times relates that during the reign of Tiberius, coincidental with the death of Christ, pagan passengers on a ship sailing the Aegean Sea heard a voice cry out from an island they were passing: "Tell everyone! The great god Pan is dead!"

The mythical Pan, half-god, half-man, was the link between the Greeks and the gods of Olympus. The legend is presumed to have grown out of the Christians' desire to inform the pagans that a new era had dawned.

No similar legend grew out of the death of the Pan car in March, 1922. Unlike the god-man Pan, the Pan car did exist. From 1917 to 1922 more than 700 of them were produced in St. Cloud, Minnesota.

There are, however, legends surrounding the Pan car, the Pan Motor Company that produced the car, and Samuel C. Pandolfo, the man who founded and promoted the company.

The company, legend insists, was "killed by a conspiracy of the big car companies in Detroit." If true, there would certainly be little evidence left lying around to support the claim, Detroit corporations being no less loath than others to attract attention for such activity. Pandolfo himself originated that legend, claiming that International Harvester was worried about the impact the Pan Motor Company's tank-tread tractor would have on Harvester's farm business in the agricultural Midwest.

But several of the convenient ogres in Detroit, far from conspiring to crush the struggling Pan Motor Company, aided it in one way or another at various times. In addition, if they had taken the time to place obstacles in the way of only half of the hundreds of fledgling car companies then springing up all over the country—many with a far better prognosis for success than Pan—they would have had little time left to pursue their own prosperity.

The seeds of the legend were planted upon Pandolfo's arrival in St. Cloud. At first, only a few people knew of his arrival, and those few knew only his purpose in coming; certainly none of them could have foreseen the demise of the Pan Motor Company nor the unbecoming manner of that demise.

There was no doubting the ability of Samuel Pandolfo. In less than three years, and with the nation involved in a World War, he organized the Pan Motor Company and sold stock to fund it, built a factory complex that was astonishing in its size and capability, and erected a small town of more than 50 homes.

But the shadows that surrounded Pandolfo's origins were sustained, though perhaps not deliberately, until rudely illuminated by a cantankerous judge in Chicago. While the country watched, the court trial bent the man, broke the company, and killed the car.

Nor was the city of St. Cloud itself immune from the effects of the Pan trial. The community's spirit, its derring-do, was overwhelmed and crushed. For a generation following, most of its leading citizens shunned new dreams, especially large and imaginative ones. At first they did so openly; the Commercial Club (forerunner of the Chamber of Commerce) at one time passed a resolution stating that they would not endorse a new rock-crushing company, but that they would "boost a going concern." Eventually, they masked their reticence and perhaps even convinced themselves that they were being wisely conservative.

Not all of the blame for this attitude can be placed on the hood of the Pan car; after the company's collapse, several local industrial attempts on a scale that was only slightly less grand met with disaster, driving despair deeper into the city's soul.

But perhaps the impact of the Pan Motor Company's failure was so deep, so pervasive, so long lasting, because its future at one time was so big, so bright, so promising. And so many in St. Cloud were so totally committed to the success of Pan.

At the center of it all, where he wanted to be, was Pandolfo, the creator, organizer, salesman, promoter, driver—in short, the brains and guts of Pan. It seemed everything he put his hand to was a dazzling success—initially.

In St. Cloud, in 1917, Samuel Conner Pandolfo brought his genius to splendid bloom in the Pan Motor Company.

PROLOGUE

CHICAGO, ILLINOIS—SATURDAY, DECEMBER 6, 1919

DECEMBER, BY ONLY the sixth day of the month, had already set record low temperatures in Chicago. This Saturday, rain and snow fell intermittently, and clouds covered the sun all day. From around one o'clock in the afternoon, light fog and an accumulation of smoke combined to make the loop area, already wet and slushy, drearier still.

On the sixth floor of the Federal Building, in the courtroom of Judge Kenesaw M. Landis, 13 defendants had spent an anxious day. Judge Landis had charged the jury at 10:20 the night before, following the surprising statement from the battery of defense attorneys that they would make no closing arguments. When the jury did not immediately reach a decision, the judge departed at midnight, leaving instructions that should the jury reach a decision during the night, it was to be sealed and held until ten o'clock Saturday morning, when he would convene court.

At 11:15, Saturday morning, the jury called for the bailiff, but it was only to seek the advice of the judge on a point of law. An hour later they wanted to know if the jury was to impose the penalty or if that was the judge's duty. At 1:30, Landis recessed the court for an hour to let the jury and the contending forces eat lunch in whatever serenity they could muster.

The long, dismal afternoon wore on. Reporters and other onlookers spent some of the time in the corridors outside the courtroom trying to nap on the marble steps or leaning over the railing under the rotunda to watch the customers in the post office six floors below.

At 5:30, a call went out that the jury was returning. Six weeks of testimony and more than a year of preparation would culminate in their verdict. There was a controlled rush for seats of advantage in the courtroom. Landis had instructed the jury to eliminate from consideration several charges in the original indictment, but those remaining were enough to present serious threat to the liberty and well-being of the defendants.

As the scowling Landis, looking as fierce as usual beneath his tangle of white hair, swept into the courtroom, the defendants rose. They were:

Samuel C. Pandolfo, founder and organizer of the Pan Motor Company, now its fiscal agent, president, and general manager; Charles F. Ladner, vice president; H. S. Wigle, former vice president; John Barritt, company secretary; Charles D. Schwab, treasurer; Hugh Evans, Fred Schilplin, George E. Hanscom, Charles Bunnell, Peter R. Thielman,

George Heidman, and Norman Street, all members of the Board of Directors; and Harry C. Ervin, Jr., a former member of the board.

These men, extremely successful and prominent as individuals, now faced corporate catastrophe as they listened to Joseph O'Sullivan, clerk of court, read the verdict. O'Sullivan read the name of Samuel C. Pandolfo, glanced at him briefly, and declared him guilty on four counts of using the mails to defraud, not guilty on five counts including one to conspire to defraud.

Pandolfo sagged slightly. The other defendants waited. Seven weeks ago they had been certain they would reach this point—if indeed the judge did not throw the case out of court—with impunity, even with gratitude for the opportunity to clear the air of the lingering doubt concerning their integrity. The government's withdrawal of similar charges almost a year ago in the district court of Fergus Falls, Minnesota, had buoyed them, made them confident to the point of treating the present trial as a pointless but necessary charade in the process of starting a large automobile company on a prairie in Minnesota. Then the trial started and evidence to the contrary began to grow, presented by men who saw their actions in a different, culpable light. Policies and actions that had seemed normal and easily explained at one time were now described as efforts to commit conspiracy to defraud the stockholders of the Pan Motor Company.

They waited, then, as the clerk read their names in alphabetical order. "John Barritt, Charles Bunnell, Harry C. Ervin, Hugh Evans, George Hanscom, George Heidman, Charles F. Ladner, Fred Schilplin, Charles Schwab, Norman Street, Peter Thielman, H. S. Wigle." The clerk paused and then read, "Not guilty on any count."

Color returned to their faces and several of them wept openly. In the moments following, while the judge thanked the men of the jury and dismissed them, while the attorneys and defendants added their own thanks, and while the judge congratulated the vindicated men, Samuel Pandolfo moved slowly among them, shaking hands and giving some of them a strong embrace. "It might have been worse," he said repeatedly. "I'm certainly glad you fellows were cleared."

Carl Cummins, Pandolfo's St. Paul attorney (he had three, including one from St. Cloud and one from Chicago), immediately moved that the verdict on Pandolfo be set aside. When Landis denied the motion, Cummins moved for a new trial. After consulting his calendar, Landis set the hearing on the motion for December 15.

So they were free, with the exception of Pandolfo. They could return to St. Cloud and, one of them said, "make good on promises for the Pan Motor Company."

But how had they arrived here? What had transpired in the past two and a half years that could bring some of the city's most distinguished, respected, and capable men before a bar of justice in Chicago accused of fraud? How had these men allowed themselves to be placed in such jeopardy?

CHAPTER I

THE BEST SALESMAN I EVER KNEW

FIRST GENERATION AMERICANS in the early 1900s, if they had high aspirations for success, liked to claim royal connections for their family line. If they could find none they added as much romance as they could to the reason their parents left their homeland.

Samuel Pandolfo combined both approaches. A Pandolfo, he said, had been a member of the Spanish royal court of Ferdinand and Isabella at the time Columbus discovered America. More recently, his father, Anthony A. Pandolfo, born in Palermo, Sicily, May 14, 1825, was an only child of devout Catholic parents who were pressing him to become a priest, a vocation for which he knew he was unsuited. Anthony ran away from home and country in 1842, at the age of 17, to seek an uncle in America who was in business in Natchez, Mississippi.

Following a short stay with his uncle, Anthony went on to New Orleans, where he began his own mercantile business, achieving the kind of initial success his son Samuel would later duplicate. In a short time, according to his son, Anthony owned two freight boats and one passenger packet that regularly traveled the Gulf of Mexico between New Orleans, Mobile, and Cuba. One after the other, however, all three boats were destroyed by hurricanes, and Anthony gave up naval commerce to confine himself to a land-based mercantile business in Mobile.

During the Civil War, Anthony joined the Confederate Army, attaining the rank of captain by the time he was released from duty. His primary duty appears to have been tracking down deserters and slackers in southern Alabama and Florida. Lee's surrender, in 1865, left isolated pockets of resistance active in the South. One such pocket attracted a massive Federal cavalry attack that destroyed $500,000 worth of cotton and turpentine in a swamp of the Big Dog River outside Mobile. That cache had been Anthony Pandolfo's inventory. How his father had managed to gather that much materiel in the South at the end of the war, Samuel never explained, but its destruction meant starting over.

Anthony moved to Meridian, Mississippi, to begin yet another mercantile business and here met Kate Miller, a child of Dutch immigrants (who had changed their name). Kate was living with her brother Pole after the death of their parents.

Despite the difference in their ages—he was 15 or 20 years older than she—Kate married Anthony Pandolfo.

In a log cabin on the banks of the Tombigbee River, about a mile out of Macon, Mississippi, Samuel Conner Pandolfo was born on November 22, 1874. When Samuel was five, his father gave up the mercantile business and purchased a plantation three miles out of Starkville, near the eastern border of the state. There Samuel grew up, attending both the country school at Starkville and later, the public school at West Point, about ten miles northeast of Starkville.

The main crop on the Pandolfo plantation was cotton. Samuel, when he was old enough, knew the hard work of a Southern farm: splitting rails, cutting crossties, and following a walking plow behind a mule.

In 1891, when Samuel was 17, his father moved to Bessemer, ten miles southwest of Birmingham, Alabama, then just beginning to boom as a southern steel town. The family followed later. Samuel had already received more schooling than many southern children, but he not only finished high school in Bessemer, he also attended Southern University, a Methodist college then at Greensboro, Alabama, for two terms, in 1893 and 1894. He might have completed his college education, but the death of his father, on June 29, 1895, meant he was the sole support of his mother and his sister Lena.

His education and his temperament inclined him to teaching and he began in southeastern Alabama schools. In 1896 he became principal of the high school in Lindale, in eastern Texas, and remained there for three years until he moved on to Las Cruces, New Mexico, to become superintendent of schools. At the time, New Mexico, Arizona, Oklahoma, and Indian Territory (eastern Oklahoma) were not yet states. In his second year at Las Cruces, Pandolfo also became an agent for the New York Life Insurance Company on the side. It is possible that his growing family responsibilities caused him to seek more income; in addition to his mother, he was now supporting a wife, Sallie Phillips, and son, Egbert, born 19 December 1897, in Lindale, Texas.

(There is no evidence to indicate whether his first wife died in childbirth or divorced him. He was free to marry again five years later. When he married the third time in 1926, he stated that his first wife was now dead.)

Pandolfo soon discovered that his life as a salesman was more fulfilling than his life as a teacher, not only in personal satisfaction but—the deciding factor—in the wealth it brought him. He said later that he made more money in three months selling insurance than he did in three years teaching school.

In 1902, Pandolfo left Las Cruces for Tucumcari, a town just coming into being in northwestern New Mexico. The Chicago, Rock Island

and Pacific Railroad ended beside a construction camp near Tucumcari Mountain; a settlement was founded, and it became the division point for the railroad. When Quay county was founded in February, 1903, Tucumcari was made the county seat.

Pandolfo had given up his career in education by now, but in addition to his insurance business, he also became the head bookkeeper for the M. B. Goldenberg Company, a large general merchandise store in Tucumcari. However, within a year his insurance business consumed so much of his time that he quit his job at Goldenberg's to devote full time to the career that eventually earned him his first real wealth.

In a short time he represented 23 of the oldest and largest legal reserve fire insurance companies, and his territory was all of northwestern New Mexico; in March he became agent for the Missouri State Life Insurance Company of St. Louis and his territory covered all of New Mexico, Arizona, and Texas. This larger sphere of operations required a second office, and he opened one in El Paso, at the juncture of the Texas, New Mexico, and Mexico borders.

He later claimed that at this time he owned the first water works in Tucumcari and erected the first 25 good buildings there; most of them were residences, but three were business and office buildings. He also had a homestead adjacent to Tucumcari. He was investing his new wealth in land and buildings.

There was other evidence of his prosperity. He is remembered as having a rather courtly manner. Some thought it affectation, but it was as much a part of his nature as his high appreciation of good food—especially wild game and fish—drink, and women. His clothes—diamond stick pin, gold watch chain stretching across his ample stomach, boutonniere when proper—reflected his affluence. His one possible lapse in fashion, although it certainly was not that in the Southwest, was his hat. When other men changed to a fedora, or a derby, or a straw boater, or a homburg as the style or season required, Pandolfo retained his Western slouch hat, a large-crowned, narrow-brimmed, sand-colored one, pinched and dipped at the front and always with a thin, leather band, not the more fashionable broad silk one. Not until late in his life did he submit to a more urbane mode.

From his first day teaching school, Pandolfo had been sure of himself in manner and in fact. Except for frequent lapses into an abruptly direct manner, he was judged to be a cultured, even cosmopolitan man. He had more education than average and was well-read in the business literature of the time, if not in classical literature. But with remarkable ease and speed he could drop his refined manner and lash out at enemies with blunt and stinging sarcasm of some invention. The more successful he became, the more enemies he gathered, and the more frequently he struck out at them.

Even as a young man Pandolfo had a tendency to stoutness. Now that he could afford richer meals and was not getting the exercise of hard farm work, he became portly. At five feet seven inches, he was below average height, and this exaggerated his plumpness. His instincts as a salesman would have compelled him to neatness if it had not been his natural inclination, inherited most likely from his tidy Dutch mother. Pride in his appearance included his personal grooming: his black hair was neatly trimmed and combed (and in later life he hid the gray that appeared with a touch-up pencil); his soft, full cheeks were regularly barber-shaved and talced; the nails on his short, round fingers were clean, clipped, and polished. The one distraction in his appearance was his strabismus; his brown eyes did not both look in the same direction. This was more of a problem for others, for it was difficult to tell if he was looking directly at you or over your shoulder. He was, of course, doing both. Formal portraits were usually retouched to bring both eyes to conjunction, and where retouching was not possible he usually turned to present his profile to the camera.

Some time in 1905, Pandolfo married Anna Wayne, a Texas beauty in any time and place. They had two children, a daughter Vivian, and a son, given the impressive name Samuel Conner Parker Pandolfo, Jr., but usually called Sammy.

Pandolfo's insurance agency grew rapidly as he added lines. One of them, the United States Health and Accident Insurance Company of Saginaw, Michigan, insured the El Paso Northeastern Railroad and this franchise allowed Pandolfo and his agents to travel through the eastern half of New Mexico on passes, which they used regularly.

Life, health, and accident insurance was handled from Pandolfo's El Paso office; the Tucumcari office was confined to writing fire insurance policies. His large real estate holdings around Tucumcari added to his reasons for maintaining the New Mexico office.

By 1907, the Missouri State Life Insurance Company made Pandolfo the field superintendent of all agents west of the Mississippi river. The responsibility soon required a city with a larger population base for office headquarters, and in 1910 the El Paso office was closed and a new one opened in San Antonio. A year later, when Missouri State Life was sold to an Ohio insurance combine, Pandolfo left the new syndicate to become general agent for Cherokee Life Insurance Company of Rome, Georgia, his territory to include Texas, New Mexico, and Oklahoma. Within a few months his agency was writing over a million dollars of new insurance business a month. Because of the time and expense involved (each applicant for a policy had to be examined and the inspection report filed), the company was not able to immediately absorb all of the business Pandolfo's agents generated.

When his agency sold two million dollars worth of new business that Cherokee could not immediately accept, Pandolfo went to the main offices in Georgia to work out an agreement. The company proposed limiting him to seven million dollars in new business yearly. Pandolfo gave them a counter-proposal: If he gave them all the new business they could handle he should be allowed to place the surplus with other companies. Cherokee accepted.

(Twenty-five years later, Lloyd Dameron, vice president and general manager of Cherokee at the time Pandolfo became an agent, recalled that Pandolfo's agency had written 20 million dollars worth of insurance in three years and that 97 percent of his first-year policy holders renewed.)

One of the companies absorbing some of Cherokee's overflow from Pandolfo was the Independent Life Insurance Company of Nashville. Pandolfo, through James Dunne, publisher of *Dunne's International Insurance Reports* in Louisville, had met Paul Roberts, president of Independent Life. Roberts traveled to San Antonio to see Pandolfo and a contract was signed whereby Pandolfo's agency would produce two million dollars a year in new business for this company. He was also requested to come to Nashville to direct the drafting of three special policies. He hired an Indianapolis actuarial firm to prepare the calculations on which the policies were based and also got the policies approved by the insurance commissions of the states in which they were to be sold. The royalties earned on these policies, which his agency had the exclusive right to sell in his territory, were handsome.

There seemed no limit to what his agency could produce; Pandolfo also signed a contract with Great Republic Life of Los Angeles calling for five million dollars a year in his territory.

If this seems an impossible amount of business, especially for the early 1900s, some insight into Pandolfo's sales methods may provide the answer. W. H. Vernor, who later founded the Texas Motor Car Association, which produced the short-lived Texan car, described Pandolfo's sales procedure in his autobiography, *A Rugged American, W. H. Vernor*:

> The best salesman I ever knew was a man named S. C. Pandolfo .... My brother had been working for Pandolfo for some time and suggested to him that he get me on his staff. Pandolfo came over to my house one Sunday morning and we talked it over. He sold me. That afternoon, we drove to Sabinal, Texas, about 90 miles west of San Antonio and within 20 miles of so of where lived a famous man named John Garner, who was afterwards to become vice president of the United States.
>
> We spent the night at the hotel in Sabinal, and the next morning drove to the bank. Pandolfo's introduction to the bank was direct, as usual, and very effective. He said to the banker: "My name is Pandolfo, and I would like for you to give me the names of some of the men who live around here whose notes you would buy."
>
> In those days, every sale of an insurance policy was a case of simple assault and no money ever changed hands but a note was always accepted as the first year's premium, and the man who was selling the policy usually made arrangements in advance to sell these notes to the bank.
>
> "Here are some names of people whose notes we will

> buy," said the banker.
>
> "Thank you," said Pandolfo, and we walked out and got into the car. Pandolfo said to me, "We will first go out and see this man, George Heims," which we proceeded to do. We found old George out in the lot, messing with his horses, and Pandolfo said to him, "Let's go up to the house and sit down in some of your chairs."
>
> We went up to the house, but there were no chairs on the porch. "Go in the house," Pandolfo said to George, "and bring out some chairs that we can sit on." Thus making George obey his command, which was the first step in selling him. We sat down and Pandolfo reached in his bag, brought out the insurance policy which was the popular one of the day, and, beginning at the top, he read it all to Mr. Heims, including the fine print and the receipt for the first year's premium which was attached by perforation to the bottom of the policy. He then reached in another pocket and brought out a pad of promissory notes, made out to himself for the amount of the premium, which must have been something over $400. He handed all of this over to Mr. Heims and commanded, "Sign here!" pointing to the bottom line on both the insurance application and the promissory note.
>
> Mr. Heims graciously signed everything as instructed before he woke up. He handed the papers back to Pandolfo with this statement: "I didn't intend to buy any insurance."
>
> "Well, you have bought some," Pandolfo said as he folded up the papers and we took our departure.
>
> We made two more calls, and sales, that same day, and as the commission to the salesman was 80 percent of the first year's premium, it made pretty good money for the day's effort. That night we went back into San Antonio and Tuesday I purchased a car and continued to work the territory alone around Sabinal and Uvalde.

The amount of business Pandolfo was doing in this vast territory required extensive traveling, and he later said that he had been the first salesman in the Southwest to use an automobile as a regular means of transportation. Early in 1909 he bought his first car, a 4-cylinder Rambler made by the Thomas B. Jeffrey Company in Kenosha, Wisconsin. It was shipped to him in Deming, New Mexico, arriving in crates, unassembled. Pandolfo and his chauffeur/mechanic had to put the car together on the railroad platform before they could drive off.

Because of the scarcity of filling stations in the Southwest, Pandolfo was required to ship gasoline and oil ahead by rail to the various cities he planned to visit by car. This ponderous procedure prompted the idea he later patented and installed on Pan cars: the Pandolfo Combination Compartment Tank that carried not only extra gasoline, oil, and water, but also had a compartment for tools and an ice-cooled section for beverages and food.

That Rambler was the first of many Ramblers and other makes that Pandolfo claimed to have owned between 1909 and 1916; he later recalled having had at least 37 cars during this period, and his interest in what he thought a car should be began to grow.

By 1916, Pandolfo's enchantment with the insurance business was fading. Despite his large force of agents (one of his men estimated that there were at least 500 agents working for him at one time), he found it increasingly difficult to meet the commitments made to the companies he represented. Crop failure in many areas of the Southwest was causing many business failures, and many of the policies the Pandolfo agency had sold were lapsing for non-payment of the premiums.

There was an additional problem: Pandolfo, for one reason or another, had fallen into disfavor with one of the insurance commissioners for the state of Texas and his license to sell in that state was taken away. He decided to abandon the insurance business and to initiate another project his fertile brain had been contemplating: a high-class, medium-priced automobile produced by a company organized on a unique basis.

In a somewhat complicated maneuver, Pandolfo sold his agency's commissions to banks in Dallas, San Antonio, and El Paso, and then borrowed against the commissions from the insurance companies themselves. His contracts with the three main companies he represented called for 90 percent of the first year's premium (not the 80 percent Vernor remembered), 15 percent renewal commission for the second year, and ten percent thereafter for the premium-paying period of the policy. In addition, he had the use of the entire first premium until the policy was 60 days old; then the ten percent owed to the company would come due and he would be charged six percent interest on it until it was paid to the company.

In his own vague explanation, Pandolfo said he owed $137,750 to banks in the Southwest from whom he had borrowed, using his future commissions as security. More precisely, the indebtedness was against his renewal account, and when it was paid off, less than two years later, the commissions were then paid directly to him until he sold them outright to the respective insurance companies for a cash settlement.

Pandolfo's decision to abandon insurance and enter the automobile business may have been prompted by some economic news. Manufacturing wages were going up. By 1917 they would be twice what they were in 1914. Farm income, apart from the Southwest, was going up. People were buying almost everything they wanted and paying for it in cash, installment buying not being introduced into the general economy until 1923.

But to Pandolfo the most significant statistic was auto sales; they tripled in the two years from 1914 to 1916. In its early days the automobile had been a novelty. It had been said that three things were needed to transform the automobile from a plaything of the rich into a popular necessity: an inexpensive, but reliable car; a network of good, all-weather roads; ready accessibility to fuel and repairs. All three were developing rapidly—and nationally—at the outbreak of World War I.

A profit picture like this was certain to catch the eye of a man as astute as Pandolfo. By the spring of 1916, he and H. S. Wigle, one of his ex-insurance salesmen, were selling stock in the Pan Motor Company.

Despite the obvious connection with his own name, Pandolfo at first insisted that the company's name was a shortened version of "Pan-American." (There was some slight basis for this. He had formed a company in Texas called the Pan-American Trust Company whose purpose was to borrow the money he needed to keep his agency afloat in its last days. The proposal failed and the money was returned to the investors.) The mention of Pan-American was made only once, very early in Pandolfo's activities for the company; from that time on Pandolfo did not disturb the presumption that Pan referred to Pandolfo.

Although no formal corporation had yet come into existence, Pandolfo and Wigle went through New Mexico, Colorado, and Wyoming, selling stock, taking names and addresses, leaving simple receipts for subscriptions to the stock of the Pan Motor Company. In 1944, Pandolfo referred to a Dr. E. M. Fisher of Roswell, New Mexico, as "stockholder number one in the Pan Motor Company." Dr. Fisher bought three shares in the early summer of 1916.

By the middle of the summer of 1916, Pandolfo and Wigle were active around Clovis, New Mexico, a small town a few miles from the Texas border. Pandolfo had secured the tacit support of several bankers in the area, including one of the bankers in Clovis. But Alex Shipley, president of the Clovis National Bank, disagreed with Pandolfo's methods and ideas and said so frequently and publicly. Pandolfo finally proposed a public debate where their differences could be aired and discussed openly. The meeting was scheduled for Wednesday evening, July 19, 1916. Either Shipley had never heard Pandolfo speak, or he had an exaggerated opinion of his own ability; most men who knew Pandolfo, then and later, preferred not to engage him in open debate before an audience.

The debate itself was never fully reported, but following the meeting Pandolfo claimed that Shipley had tried to stampede the audience with his own henchmen, and Shipley claimed that Pandolfo had tried to start a run on his bank. The following day Shipley filed a suit asking $35,000 damages; Pandolfo promptly filed a counter-suit for $50,000.

A month later an agreement was reached canceling both suits and both participants agreed to make no further comment. The case was dropped . . . for the moment.

Pandolfo believed ever after that this disagreement with Shipley was the beginning of all his later troubles at the Pan Motor Company. He claimed that Shipley, or someone encouraged by him, wrote an anonymous letter to the Arizona Bankers Association stating that "one S. C. Pandolfo was heading for Arizona, and that he was organizing some kind of automobile insurance company." The letter, which went on to list several uncomplimentary descriptions of Pandolfo's character, was read at the Bankers Association meeting in Phoenix in October, 1916, and was later published in the association's magazine.

Despite the after-the-fact importance Pandolfo gave to this letter, it did not have any substantial effect on sale of Pan Motor "stock" in the state. It did inspire a later law suit by Pandolfo and might have instigated the investigation which led to his indictment in connection with the Pan Motor Company.

Pandolfo was selling stock, really in the basic idea of the company, fast enough to start gathering a sales force, and many who joined were former agents from his insurance agency. He also recruited John Barritt. Barritt was the founder and president of the Cheyenne (Wyoming) Business College when Pandolfo met and recruited him for the Pan Motor Company. Born in England in 1879, Barritt had studied accounting and worked for an engineering firm in Colne, England, before coming to the American branch of an English company in 1908. Barritt's cultivated manner and appearance lent an air of continental polish to the new Pan Motor Company.

In the early fall of 1916, Samuel Pandolfo, H. S. Wigle, and John Barritt headed for Chicago to formally incorporate the Pan Motor Company.

Dr. Louis A. Bean, of Denver, Colorado, whom Pandolfo identified as the first Pan car owner, with friends. Dr. Bean may also have been a Pan stock salesman, according to his sister, who testified at Pandolfo's Chicago trial.

This interior view of the Experimental Shop, which was also called Factory No. 1, shows the crowded space in which the engineers had to modify the Model 10 Pans supplied by Reed & Glaser, Indianapolis engineers.

CHAPTER II

HURRAH FOR THE PAN MOTOR COMPANY

THE FIRST OFFICES of the Pan Motor Company were in the Venetian Building in Chicago, on Washington Street between State and Wabasha. With Barritt and Wigle, Pandolfo settled down to get the company incorporated. He hired a secretary, Marie Cadieux, to assist in keeping up with the flood of correspondence he would produce.

Several inquiries concerning incorporation led Pandolfo to the offices of the Corporation Trust Company where William R. Watson agreed to handle certain aspects of the incorporation of the Pan Motor Company. He also gave Pandolfo a list of several law firms specializing in corporation law who could complete the procedure. One firm on the list, Heidman and Street, also specialized in patent law and trademarks; Pandolfo, with several patentable ideas of his own in mind, sought out the offices of Heidman and Street in the Peoples Gas Building.

The qualifications of Heidman and Street were impeccable. George Heidman had attended the Law College of Cincinnati (incidentally four years behind Kenesaw M. Landis), graduating and being admitted to the bar in 1895. Heidman had his first law office in Cincinnati and later worked in New York before settling in Chicago in 1907 and specializing in patent law.

Norman Arthur Street was born in Chicago in 1876, the son of Charles A. Street, a partner in the Street-Chatfield Lumber Company. Street earned a bachelor's degree at Yale in 1898 and got his law degree from Northwestern in 1901. He was admitted to the Illinois bar the same year and joined George Heidman in legal practice in 1907. He was listed as a Republican, and his clubs were the University, the Saddle and Cycle, and the Yale.

Heidman was not in the office when Pandolfo called, but Street listened to Pandolfo outline the plan of the Pan Motor Company. Street's enthusiasm and liking for the short, dapper westerner grew despite his natural caution. Street recommended that the company should be incorporated under the laws of the state of Delaware. That state's law would allow a charter with a broader scope for the company and lower corporation taxes.

Pandolfo had not yet selected a location for the company so there was no reason to consider any other state.

The first meeting of the directors of the Pan Motor Company was held in Chicago on January 5, 1917, three days before the charter was granted in Delaware. Present at the meeting were Norman Street, George Heidman, H. S. Wigle, John Barritt, Marie Cadieux, and Samuel C. Pandolfo. Norman Street was elected president, George Heidman secretary-treasurer, and Marie Cadieux (without her knowledge, she later said, although Pandolfo claimed she was present) was elected vice-president. Street, Heidman, and Wigle were named to the executive committee. Pandolfo, for the moment, was content to be employed by the company solely as fiscal agent. There was little to administer at this point. Until the company had some tangible assets or at least a location and a staff, all of the action would be in the money-raising department, and that's where Pandolfo wanted to be.

Transfer of the stock from the Delaware agent to the executive committee was accepted and the Pan Motor Company was officially born. "Hurrah for the Pan Motor Company (short for Pan-American)," Pandolfo wrote to the early stockholders, giving them the news of the incorporation and enclosing their new stock certificates. It was his final mention of the longer name, possibly because there were rumors around Chicago of another automobile to be called the Pan-American.

Its corporate charter now allowed the Pan Motor Company to manufacture not only automobiles but also trucks, tractors, airplanes, balloons, railroad cars, and other gas-powered vehicles; it could also acquire steam railroads, oil wells, and refineries, and "sell the products therefrom."

Apart from the officers of the company and the stockholders, the rest of the public received news of the incorporation with equanimity. The *Automotive Trade Journal* for March listed the news of Pan Motor Company's incorporation along with eight other car companies, four truck companies, and several parts and specialty companies that were entering the new and lucrative automotive field.

The articles of incorporation stated that the Pan Motor Company was capitalized at five million dollars, but the arrangement under which Pandolfo sold stock in the company allowed him to collect ten million dollars if all the stock was sold. Five dollars of the ten-dollar price per share was labeled "Capital Fund," and this amount was banked for later corporate use in capital expenditures. The other five dollars, labeled "Surplus," was to be used "at the discretion of the Board of Directors."

It is surprising that neither Heidman nor Street was able to persuade Pandolfo that this discretionary power was too broad, allowed too much freedom; but Pandolfo could be obstinate and also convincing in such arguments, as he was throughout the rest of his life. He was frequently able to talk people into letting him control their money.

The surplus fund was, in effect, Pandolfo's to do with as he pleased.

He was limited in a sense and for a while; he was required to pay all the expenses of the company from the surplus fund until the company had habitation—that is, a location—and had $30,000 in the capital fund. Thereafter he still paid all expenses involved in advertising and further sale of the stock. What made this arrangement particularly lucrative for Pandolfo was that the surplus fund received the first five dollars that came in for payment of the stock. Stockholders received their shares only after the entire subscription price was paid. Some shareholders, therefore, preferred to buy their stock in small lots. When the company became the target of bad publicity and some larger stockholders stopped paying on their stock, they discovered that they had less equity in the company than they had thought because most if not all of the money they had paid had gone for "surplus."

The general terms were pointed out on every stock sale agreement the company printed, and no one ever complained about the practice. In fact, several prospective buyers said they were pleasantly surprised to see the arrangement so plainly stated. And if 50 percent was a large share to be specified for this purpose, it was also the limit that could be so used.

Pandolfo and his small staff kept in touch with their growing army of stockholders through a blizzard of correspondence, some of it so hastily written and with such bravado—and with such little knowledge of the time necessary to produce an automobile—that it would form the basis for the indictment to be drawn up two years later.

Pandolfo was busy during those first months of 1917. He continued to recruit and boldly encourage an increasing number of stock salesmen; he sent out inquiries to cities in central and western states seeking a site for the company; he located and hired the nucleus of the engineering, design, and production staffs; he arranged for the first Pan cars to be built by an independent engineering firm, assembled from standard parts because he felt he needed something immediately to show to potential stockholders.

The Indianapolis engineering firm of Reed & Glaser was selected to build the first Pan cars. William S. Reed and Charles F. Glaser had formed their company only a short time earlier, specializing in automobile design and parts. Pandolfo came to their offices in the Merchants Bank Building bringing pictures of the Oldsmobile and Mercer cars and several ideas.

His instructions were to build a "handsome car, rugged enough to withstand the Western terrain, with a ten-inch clearance for the hog-back roads it would have to travel, with a seat that folded down to make a bed, and to sell for less than $1500." Reed & Glaser were given an initial order for four Pan cars. (Six more would be ordered later in spite of problems with the first four.)

The engineering staff for the Pan Motor Company was recruited in an unorthodox but direct manner: Pandolfo simply approached several major manufacturers and asked them to recommend the best men they knew. A location for the company was found in the same direct way: Pandolfo wrote to dozens of Chambers of Commerce or Commercial Clubs asking if they were interested. One of the letters was received by the Commercial Club in St. Cloud, Minnesota.

St. Cloud had been settled in 1853 on a site the Indians called O-za-te, meaning "the forks of the trail." In the city's early days, the Red River Trail, on which ox-carts hauled beaver pelts and other commerce from the Northwest to St. Paul, passed through and around St. Cloud. By 1917, when Pandolfo's inquiry was received, St. Cloud was a city of 16,000 residents. The National Parks highway, or Red Trail, from New York to Seattle, and the Jefferson Trail, from Winnipeg to the Gulf, both passed through St. Cloud, as did the Minnesota Scenic Highway. (The Red River ox-cart traffic had ceased long since.) The city had two rail lines, the Great Northern and the Northern Pacific, both with transcontinental connections.

Minnesota had greater funds for education at that time than any other state in the Union, and there was evidence of it in St. Cloud. The State Normal School, with a faculty of 42, had already graduated over 2,000 students. In 1917, the city had just completed the construction of Technical High School, at a cost of $240,000, and the Catholic population, shortly before, had just spent $75,000 erecting Cathedral High School. The Public Library, built on a Carnegie grant in 1903, had over 15,000 volumes. Two daily newspapers, the *Journal-Press* and the *Daily Times*, served the city. St. Raphael's Hospital, a modern, four-story building, was on the northern fringe of the city.

Ten miles of streetcar lines ran from the southern residence area, through the downtown business district, and out to the Great Northern car shops in Waite Park, west of St. Cloud; they also tied Sauk Rapids, across the Mississippi to the east, to the larger city.

St. Cloud's industrial base, except for the Pan Motor Company, would be insignificantly touched by the boom brought on by World War I. The town had had a fairly stable growth; its largest single business in 1916 was the railroad car shops. Seven freight cars a day were produced at the shops and although located in adjacent Waite Park, St. Cloud was the commercial center for the shops. The several granite companies in the area, encompassing quarrying, finishing, and tool supply, were the other large employers.

A 1914 inventory of industry in St. Cloud listed 77 different manufacturing businesses including flour mills, foundries, machine shops, wood-working factories, cement works, breweries, a broom factory, printing plants, cigar makers, bakeries, woolen mills, brick factories, and wagon and sled factories. Seven miles north of St. Cloud in Sartell, on the Mississippi, was the Watab Paper Mill. Labor in the St. Cloud area was therefore familiar with manufacturing techniques.

A better indication of the industry in St. Cloud was the fact that between 1910 and 1914 the number of wage earners in the city grew by 128.3 percent, more than three times the growth of St. Paul or Duluth, more than four times that of Minneapolis, more than 20 times that of Winona, Minnesota, and more than 30 times that of Mankato, Minnesota. It may have been this growth record that triggered Pandolfo's inquiry. Or the fact that St. Cloud supported six banks. Two, the First National and Merchants National, had federal charters; Zapp Bank, Security Bank, Farmers Bank, and St. Cloud Bank were state chartered.

The true wealth of the area, though, was in the rich farmland surrounding the city. The St. Cloud agricultural district had never known a crop failure. Farmers in the area raised blooded stock and had won international recognition for their pure-bred Shorthorn cattle as well as for their Clydesdale horses.

Apart from this litany of civic and economic achievement and growth, St. Cloud was not as curious a choice for destiny in the form of the Pan Motor Company as it may seem. Before most of the automotive muscle concentrated in the Detroit area, there were manufacturing companies springing up to build automobiles in such far removed places as Enid and Tulsa, Oklahoma; Rock Hill, South Carolina; Waterloo, Iowa; Pueblo, Colorado; Gresham, Oregon; Shreveport, Louisiana; Hannibal, Missouri; Hyattsville, Maryland; Omaha, Nebraska; Little Rock, Arkansas; Tiffen, Ohio; Atlanta, Georgia; Sydney and Staten Island, New York; Bristol, Rhode Island; and Moose Jaw, Saskatchewan, in Canada.

Between 1900 and 1916, Minnesota itself had seen 16 automobile companies start up. There is some dispute whether the Whaley-Henriette or the Davenport Steam Stage was the first one in St. Paul. Before Pan came to St. Cloud, Minneapolis had ten companies and St. Paul three that produced vehicles. None of these had survived to the time Pan arrived and, except for the Fords still assembled in St. Paul, the Pan was the last vehicle manufactured in Minnesota. The clatter of automobile production, therefore, was not foreign to the state in 1917.

But still . . . why St. Cloud?

In his later advertisements for the company Pandolfo answered the question with this list of reasons:

> BECAUSE:
>
> Eighty percent of the iron ore of the United States is produced in Minnesota, within 150 miles of St. Cloud.
>
> The Pan Motor Company is from 1,000 to 2,000 miles nearer the mines, from which practically all steel manufactured in the United States is produced, than the automobile factories of the East . . . .
>
> St. Cloud is on the Mississippi with several power dams above and below it, and a great many power dam sites near St. Cloud not yet harnessed up.
>
> The coal situation will require that water power be used to develop electricity in the near future, as the electrical process is the best, and because most of the material that steel is made of

> is in Minnesota we think the future steel manufacturing center is in the Pan's back yard.
>
> Transportation by water by the Great Lakes and Mississippi provides cheap transportation to most parts of the world, Duluth having one of the best and deepest harbors in this country.
>
> St. Cloud is in the center of a giant hardwood belt of timber. . . .
>
> Much lumber is used for automobile building.
>
> An immense steel plant, said to have cost $25,000,000 is located at Duluth, 125 miles distant.
>
> St. Cloud is the center of a rich farming and dairy country.
>
> St. Cloud is on two transcontinental railroads, the main lines of the Great Northern and the Northern Pacific, giving direct routes to all parts of the country. . . .
>
> St. Cloud is far removed from the seat of labor troubles in the East.
>
> It costs from 10 to 25 percent less to live in St. Cloud than it does in Detroit or the automobile manufacturing territory of the East.
>
> St. Cloud is located in one of the most beautiful districts of the world with beautiful rolling prairies, farm lands, hillsides, clear streams, lakes with gamy [sic] fish and excellent roads.
>
> A thorough investigation shows that St. Cloud has better facilities and a location that cannot be equaled in any other part of the United States.
>
> WE DON'T SEE ANY REASON FOR LOCATING AN AUTOMOBILE PLANT ANYWHERE ELSE

This was published in February 1918 in *Pan Siftings*, a promotional magazine published by Pan Motor Company to keep its stockholders informed, and any reasons it gave for anything must be looked at in the light of that purpose and Pandolfo's zeal for selling stock.

Pandolfo's reasons for selecting St. Cloud had nothing to do with free land or tax-exempt status. Neither was given. What did possibly sway him was the fact that several leading bankers and businessmen, hearing of his interest in locating here, offered him their support.

NUMBER 6462

SHARES *ONE*

Incorporated under the Laws of Delaware

Pan Motor Company

CAPITAL STOCK, $5,000,000.00

This Certifies that ********JOSEPH HASTREITER******** is the owner of ***********ONE*********** Shares of the Capital Stock of **Pan Motor Company**, fully paid and non-assessable, transferable only on the books of this Corporation in person or by Attorney upon surrender of this Certificate properly endorsed.

IN WITNESS WHEREOF, the said Corporation has caused this Certificate to be signed by its duly authorized officers and its Corporate Seal to be hereunto affixed at ST. CLOUD, MINN. 17TH day of DECEMBER A.D. 19 17

SECRETARY PRESIDENT

SHARES $5.00 EACH

SPECIAL AGREEMENT ON OTHER SIDE.

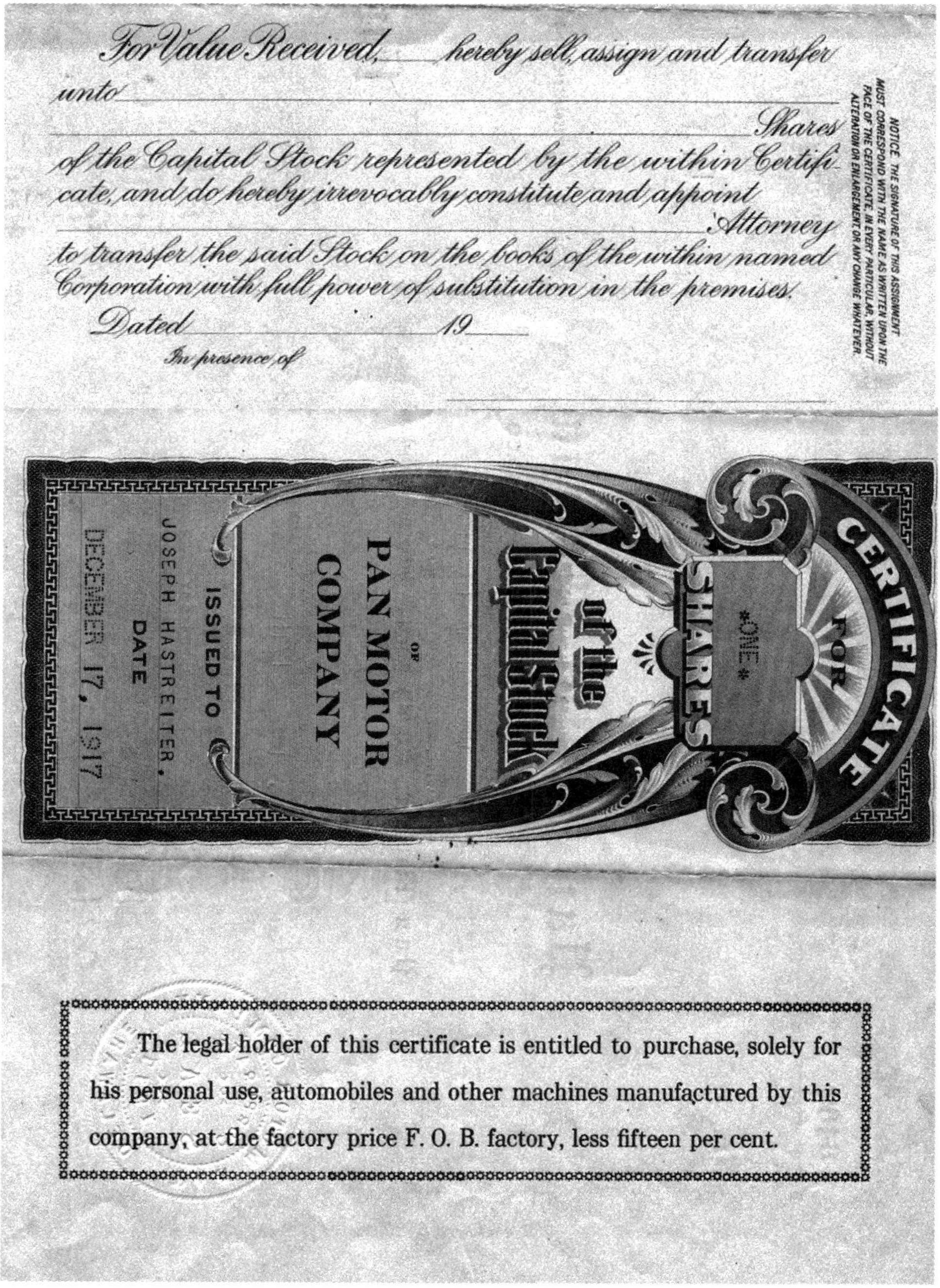
For Value Received, ________ hereby sell, assign and transfer unto ________________________________

________________________________ Shares of the Capital Stock represented by the within Certificate, and do hereby irrevocably constitute and appoint ________________________________ Attorney to transfer the said Stock on the books of the within named Corporation with full power of substitution in the premises.

Dated ________________ 19____

In presence of

____

NOTICE. THE SIGNATURE OF THIS ASSIGNMENT MUST CORRESPOND WITH THE NAME AS WRITTEN UPON THE FACE OF THE CERTIFICATE, IN EVERY PARTICULAR, WITHOUT ALTERATION OR ENLARGEMENT OR ANY CHANGE WHATEVER.

CERTIFICATE FOR *ONE* SHARES of the Capital Stock OF PAN MOTOR COMPANY

ISSUED TO JOSEPH HASTREITER.

DATE DECEMBER 17, 1917

The legal holder of this certificate is entitled to purchase, solely for his personal use, automobiles and other machines manufactured by this company, at the factory price F. O. B. factory, less fifteen per cent.

CHAPTER III

PAN MOTOR COMPANY IS DOING THINGS!

THE RESIDENTS OF St. Cloud and vicinity received the first news of the Pan Motor Company from the *St. Cloud Daily Times* and the *St. Cloud Journal-Press* on Friday, March 2, 1917. Headlines read: AUTOMOBILE FACTORY TO LOCATE IN ST. CLOUD.

Initially, Pandolfo contacted Peter J. Seberger, secretary of the Commercial Club in St. Cloud. Seberger, encouraged by Charles Schwab, president of both the Commercial Club and the Farmers State Bank, invited Pandolfo to St. Cloud. Seberger and Schwab were probably the two men best qualified to answer and expedite Pandolfo's inquiry. Seberger had served two terms as mayor of St. Cloud under the old form of city government, was chairman of the committee of three that drafted the new commission-form charter, and was then elected as first mayor under that charter in 1912. He had also been president of the Commercial Club and was elected secretary in 1915. Schwab's banking experience and contacts in the St. Cloud area made it easy for him to canvass the bankers and businessmen and get their positive reaction to Pandolfo's proposal.

Pandolfo came to St. Cloud in January, 1917, shortly after the Pan Motor Company had started to incorporate, to meet quietly with local officials and businessmen. Pandolfo provided his references for the St. Cloud men, candidly admitting his difficulties in the past, particularly in Texas, and describing the debts he had incurred with his previous insurance business. He explained his own financial arrangement with the Pan Motor Company.

The reaction of the Commercial Club to Pandolfo's frankness was favorable; one of the men remarked to a friend after the meeting, "He told us what we wanted to know, and he looked and talked like a man who knows how to handle large sums of money."

Pandolfo admitted to some of the men, semi-confidentially, that he expected to make a million dollars in selling the stock of the Pan Motor Company, and they agreed that a million dollars was fair compensation if all the stock would be sold.

After Pandolfo returned to Chicago, the St. Cloud men launched their investigation of his references. Schwab made inquiries in the Southwest through his own banking sources, independent of the Commercial Club's survey. All answers agreed: Pandolfo was honest, industrious, a born promoter, but he had had a run of bad luck lately.

The last week of February, 1917, the officers of the Pan Motor Company held another meeting in Chicago. With Wigle, Street, Heidman, and Pandolfo present, Pandolfo was elected to the Board of Directors to replace Marie Cadieux, whose resignation the Board accepted. Wigle was elected vice president in her place, and the by-laws were amended to permit 12 directors instead of five. The fiscal agent was then empowered by the Board to look into the matter of property for the factory, specifically a 16-acre tract in Stearns county, value not to exceed $4300.

This was the last meeting of the Pan Motor Company in Chicago. The offices in the Venetian building were closed and all subsequent Board meetings were held in St. Cloud, first at the Farmers State Bank, later at the Elks Club, until offices at the plant were available.

Pandolfo now put his promotional genius to work in earnest. From March, 1917, when the first headlines appeared, the names of Pandolfo and the Pan Motor Company appeared in the *Daily Times* on a daily basis and only slightly less regularly in the *Journal-Press*. (The greater frequency for the *Times* may be explained by the fact that the secretary-treasurer of the *Times* Publishing corporation, Fred Schilplin, was a member of the Pan Motor Company's Board of Directors.)

The factory, the first news stories declared, would consist of three large units, costing almost the entire capitalization of five million dollars. The first building unit would be used to build pleasure cars, the second would make popular-priced trucks, and the third would produce farm tractors. Pandolfo claimed that orders were already on hand for more cars than could be built in a year. "We have dozens of agents at work selling our stock in various parts of the country," he said, "and we already have 1,159 stockholders." The office force, consisting of Pandolfo, John Barritt, auditor Edward J. Gorman, and two others, were housed in the Farmers State Bank building for the moment.

On Wednesday, March 21, the first meeting of the officers of the company was held in St. Cloud. Attorneys Street and Heidman resigned as president and secretary; this had been agreed to at the time of incorporation. They offered to resign from the Board as well, but Pandolfo persuaded them to stay on because of their familiarity with the patents and trademarks of the company. Pandolfo was elected president to succeed Street, and Barritt succeeded Heidman as secretary. Taken on as new directors were Charles Schwab, who became treasurer, Hugh Evans, Fred Schilplin, George Hanscom, Charles Bunnell, Peter R. Thielman, and H. C. Ervin, Jr. St. Cloud needed no introduction to the local members of the Board; the rest of the world was soon enlightened by Pandolfo. To their embarrassment, he referred to them as "The Twenty Million Dollar Board," with only slight exaggeration.

CHARLES SCHWAB had started his business career in 1888, at the age of 16, when he had charge of a general store in Clear Lake, Minnesota. By the time he was 24, he had organized the First State Bank of Clear Lake; 15 years later he started the Farmers State Bank of St. Cloud. He was president of both of these banks, president of the Farmers Loan and Investment Company of St. Cloud, and a dealer in real estate.

HUGH EVANS, born in South Bend, Minnesota, in 1859, had come to St. Cloud in 1900 to organize the St. Cloud Grocery Company, a wholesale firm serving the central section of the state. Evans had also served two terms (1908 and 1909) as mayor of St. Cloud.

FRED SCHILPLIN was born in nearby St. Joseph, Minnesota, in 1868. The Schilplin family, as early as 1545 in Bern, Switzerland, had been referred to as a "very honorable family whose members were frequently learned men, students of philosophy and theology." Schilplin's father, Frederick, had translated Rousseau, among others, from the French, and this literary inclination was evident in Fred, who at one time or another filled every position on the *St. Cloud Daily Times* and was now secretary-treasurer of the corporation. He was also active in Democratic politics in the state and had served four years as sheriff of Stearns county. (Schilplin was appointed postmaster of St. Cloud while he was on the Pan Board.)

GEORGE HANSCOM was born in Eden Lake, Minnesota, in 1872, and took several commercial courses as a young man. He was president of the Merchants National Bank of St. Cloud, and was an officer or director of the First State Bank of Stewartville, the State Bank of Mayer, the State Bank of Watertown, the State Bank of Maple Plain, the State Bank of Long Lake, and the Farmers and Merchants State Bank of Sedan. He was, obviously, a banker.

GEORGE BUNNELL, born in Canada in 1857, had come to St. Cloud when he was 20 years old to work for Nehemiah P. Clarke in the lumber and stock business. He was now a trustee for the Clarke estate, which included lumber, banking, mining, and other state-wide real estate interests.

PETER R. THIELMAN, born in St. Cloud in 1872, started dealing in real estate in 1900. His marriage, in 1903, to the sister of Charles Schwab brought him into closer contact with the banker, and Thielman became a director of the Farmers Loan and Investment Company. He also ran a large and successful stock farm.

HARRY C. ERVIN, JR., born in Philadelphia in 1886, came to St. Cloud with his parents two years later. His formal education was concluded at the University of Minnesota, and he joined his father's milling business as an accountant in 1907. With his brother Thomas, he enlarged the business following the death of their father. Harry was a director, secretary-treasurer and manager of the St. Cloud branch of the H. C. Ervin Company, a director and vice president of the Beltrami Elevator and Milling Company, Bemidji, Minnesota, and a director of the Merchants National Bank of St. Cloud.

These men constituted the "Twenty Million Dollar Board."

On April 6, 1917, the United States entered the European war. But with the excited activity surrounding the Pan Motor Company, in St. Cloud it was one more event in many event-filled days.

The offices on the second floor of the Farmers State Bank on Fifth avenue were soon crowded and additional space, on the second and third floors of the First National Bank Building on St. Germain street, was rented. Before the company could move out to offices in the factory building they also took over the entire Board of Education Building, a small structure at 218 Fifth Avenue South, primarily used for the storage of envelopes and brochures and to handle the mailings being sent out to stockholders and prospects, and for the architectural and engineering staffs.

A printing salesman from St. Paul, making his first call on the Pan advertising manager, was astonished at the activity in St. Cloud. The salesman, Richard L. Daggy from the Webb Publishing Company, had come to bid on a magazine the Pan Motor Company wanted to print. It was to be called *The Stars and Stripes*, but after the first or second issue the Army requested use of the title, Daggy recalled, and the magazine's title was changed to *Pan Siftings*. (The new title was explained by a couplet on the masthead: "Sifting the Sand from the Pay-Dirt Land, And Leaving the Nuggets True.")

With his business concluded, Daggy was ready to return to St. Paul. "As I waited at the depot for the train, I saw a large, chauffeur-driven Pierce Arrow drive up. A man and woman got out, and I heard a buzz go through the crowd: 'There's Pandolfo!' 'That's Pan!'

"It was a chilly evening in spring and Mrs. Pandolfo was wrapped up in an expensive collection of furs, but I could still see plenty of jewelry sparkling." Daggy boarded the St. Paul-bound train and made for the smoker car. When Pandolfo entered later, Daggy introduced himself and in a short while the conversation turned to general topics. "I have never heard a man so well-versed on almost any topic that came up. He must have read volumes to be that well informed, and later, when I got to know him well and knew how much time he put in at the office, I often wondered where he got the time to read."

The limitation that Pandolfo had received earlier from the executive committee in Chicago regarding a site for the factory—16 acres at a cost not to exceed $4300—was soon seen to be unreal. A 47¾-acre tract in Cooper's Addition west of St. Cloud was purchased from Ted Bolsom for $11,000. The Pan property was bordered on the east by 33rd Avenue, and it straddled an east-west road that was an extension of Cooper avenue north but, after it crossed 33rd Avenue, was called the St. Joe Road. The main Great Northern line paralleled the long south limit of the property and made getting a spur track onto the plant site a simple matter.

But Pandolfo faced other difficulties. The housing situation in St. Cloud was, in Pandolfo's view, critical. The growth of the town had been steady, without serious economic setbacks. As a result most homes were owned and there were few for rent or sale. By the middle of April, Pandolfo announced that he would have to build 100 homes for the employees of Pan Motor. He attempted to interest the city in making houses available, but municipally funded housing to benefit a private business was out of the question in 1917.

Strictly speaking, this was not a Pan Motor Company project, and Pandolfo quite correctly would not commit any company funds to building the homes. The money would have to come from local investors. So 20 local businessmen among others joined Pandolfo to form the Pan Addition Company and Pan-Town-on-the-Mississippi was born.

Located at the edge of the city near the Pan plant, Pan Town (the full name was used only in advertising) was not like the usual company or row house project. Only 52 were built, not the hundred that Pandolfo had wanted, but they were of 25 different designs and in several sizes. The best material and the best workmanship was used, and most of the houses are still in use almost a century later

Apart from his investment in Pan Town, Pandolfo also purchased property in the business section of St. Cloud for his own use. One parcel, on the northwest corner of 6th avenue and 2nd Street South, already had a building on it being used as a veterinary hospital. Immediately after Pandolfo's purchase of it, machinery began to arrive and a sign went up announcing PANDOLFO MFG. CO., AUTO PARTS AND ACCESSORIES. In addition to aiding with incorporation, one of the tasks Pandolfo had assigned to Heidman and Street had been to secure a patent on his compartment tank for automobiles. Filed in Pandolfo's name on January 22, 1917, the patent was granted on December 18. When the bids from several factories for construction of the tank were too high to suit Pandolfo, his compartment tank became the prime product of his manufacturing company for the next two years.

On May 9, 1917, ads in the local papers were trumpeting the news: "PAN MOTOR COMPANY IS DOING THINGS!" The company now had over 400 local and enthusiastic stockholders, another 2200 throughout the country. The ads claimed the company had orders for 2500 automobiles, and, at an intended profit of $100 per car, it anticipated a profit of a quarter of a million dollars.

There was evidence at the factory site that the company was "doing things!" An experimental workshop, erected on the east side of 33rd Avenue, became headquarters for the growing engineering staff. Taking war-time conditions into account, the construction that took place in the first 15 months was phenomenal: A total of 211,902 square feet was distributed among the main factory, the drop forge plant, the die shop, the heat treat building, the forge warehouse, the main power house, and a host of peripheral and support buildings. The main factory plant was planned to grow to three times its original size. Plans were also drawn for an administration building, a hospital, and a test track on land north of the factory.

The news the public had been waiting for was finally released in June 1917: The first Pan cars were due to arrive in St. Cloud. Pandolfo, Victor Gauvreau, the chief design engineer, and a third man identified only as Duncan, went to Indianapolis to drive the cars back. (Reed & Glaser were unable to complete the fourth car on time.) Pandolfo wanted to publicize the arrival of the cars in St. Cloud at a giant barbecue, and invitations went out by the thousands.

The cars left Indianapolis on June 26, and on Saturday, June 30, Pandolfo telephoned from Minneapolis to report, "The car is standing up wonderfully in view of the grueling test we have given it."

The first cars reached St. Cloud at 11:00 Saturday night. The drivers reported that one had been driven from Milwaukee without a fan on the motor. However, it was of little consequence since all major parts in the cars were standard parts and only few would remain on the final Pan design.

Preparations for the barbecue, meanwhile, had been going full blast. It was planned for the Fourth of July and the celebration was remembered long after fireworks displays were forgotten. Anyone with a room to spare for visiting stockholders and guests was asked to contact the Commercial Club, there being only one sizeable hotel, the Grand Central, in town.

Bread—8,000 loaves of it—was ordered. But the big item was meat. Joseph Hunstiger & Company, a local butcher, arranged through Swift & Company in St. Paul to have 15,434 pounds of baby beef shipped in. The beef, in 136 quarters, arrived by train Monday evening, July 2. It was immediately taken to the prairie east of 33rd Avenue, spitted, and placed over the fires, in trenches, to begin 40 hours of slow cooking. On Tuesday the newspapers printed an appeal for pickles and other garnishes. The program for the day was simple: In the morning there would be a dance and speeches by the Reverend Joseph F. Busch, Bishop of the St. Cloud Diocese, and Ripley B. Brower, local attorney, and sandwiches of the barbecued beef; in the afternoon there would be tours of the plant site and the buildings under construction; in the evening the visitors were invited to watch the city's fireworks display. And, of course, the Pan cars would be on display. It was not officially a listed part of the program but stock in the Pan Motor Company would be sold also.

By 7:00 on the morning of the Fourth, 3000 people were already on the grounds. Technically, the Pan plant was outside the city limits, but St. Cloud Police Chief Ed Brick sent six men out to the barbecue site to direct the parking of more than 5000 cars during the day. Eleven visitors reported to police their pockets had been picked. Estimates of the total number attending the barbecue went as high as 70,000. One of the visitors was Charles Hood, manager of Swift & Company in St. Paul; he made the trip, he said, "just to get a look at the crowd that would eat all that meat."

The lines formed up ahead of the men cutting the bread and wound past the pits where slabs of beef were placed on huge platters. By 2:00 in the afternoon only the bones remained of the 15,000 pounds of meat.

Whatever they thought of the free meal, most people were there to view the Pan cars, and platforms were erected to raise the cars above the crowd. In honor of the holiday, the cars had been painted red, white, and blue.

The eating, the dancing, the speeches—even viewing the cars—was secondary to Pandolfo; he had salesmen circulating in the crowd selling stock, and he had motion picture photographers filming the spectacle; the film would be exhibited later in August at the Miner Theatre in St. Cloud.

In the weeks following the barbecue, more and more machinery began to arrive at the plant, and early in August, the Great Northern ran a spur track from the main line onto the plant grounds. Steel for the main building and other material could now be off-loaded directly at the construction site.

The immediate need of the company was still cash, cash to finish the buildings and to pay the engineering staff. So, on August 4, when the last of the ten cars ordered from Reed & Glaser arrived by train, they were dispatched quickly to stock salesmen in the field. There were two exceptions. In mid-August Pandolfo agreed to give a Pan car to the Women's Guild, a Catholic charitable organization, to be delivered in November; and a Catholic parish in Duluth was to be given a car in October that they could raffle off to raise money. Pandolfo made it clear that he, as fiscal agent, was paying for the cars, not the stockholders of the company.

The engineering staff in the experimental building now took over assembling the cars and had the opportunity—or chore—of getting rid of the bugs in the hastily built early cars. They had been put together from stock parts, thus had ill-fitting components that made them somewhat dangerous in certain situations. As they re-assembled these early models, called the Model 10 simply because there were ten of them, the staff was also working on the design of the ultimate Pan car, the 1919 Model A. The engineers had finally shown Pandolfo that a new car could not be conceived, tested, and built in a matter of months. In fact, there would be an interim model, the Model 250, between the early Reed & Glaser cars and the final model.

The people in St. Cloud and the immediate area knew about Pan, but it was nice to see notice was being taken in other areas. *Western Magazine*, a St. Paul publication, noted the growing enterprise in an article titled "Pan Town."

> It has been truly said that if a man knew how to do one thing better than any other man, the world would beat a path to his doorway, even if he built his cabin in an inaccessible place.
>
> For nearly a year the people of this country have been beating a path toward St. Cloud, the Granite City of Minnesota. No other northwestern community has been so widely heralded, has been so much in the limelight of public observation, has had so

> much of constructive publicity, and has had so thorough an awakening as St. Cloud.
>
> Drop into St. Cloud, any day, and at once you will be impressed with a new atmosphere. Pan is in the air. Every citizen wears a Pan tap, a Pan fob, or a Pan badge. Men, women, and youth all strive to preach the doctrine of Pan, as if some wizard had inoculated the entire population with a virus of industrial revolution.

Adding to this panegyric, Pandolfo placed an ad in local newspapers early in October, 1917, to publicize several items: 1) More than 9,000 people, living in 37 states, owned Pan stock; 2) Every physical asset the Pan Motor Company had was paid for; 3) The company was paying the St. Cloud Post Office from $30,000 to $40,000 a year (this was more than half of the local office's yearly revenue); 4) Pandolfo owned more stock than the three next largest stockholders together; 5) The company's freight bill with the Great Northern was averaging $2,000 a week; 6) Pandolfo had personally invested $150,000 in real estate in and around St. Cloud.

Not everything was going smoothly for the company, however. Water and sewage lines could not come immediately to Pan Town, despite Pandolfo's urgent demands. In the middle of October, Pandolfo opened round one in a battle with the city when he presented the city commissioners with an alternate plan. He would lay his own lines, furnishing the Pan Town addition with water from the Pan Motor Company water tank, which was supplied by artesian wells. The city could hook up to his lines when it was in a position to do so. He would also put in his own sewage lines to run the short distance to the Sauk River, into which the raw sewage would be discharged. The city commission agreed to the plan but the State Board of Health vetoed the idea.

Round Two, a little more characteristic of Pandolfo's methods and manner, began with two stories in the newspapers of Saturday, October 20. Pandolfo was calling a public meeting in the Nemec Theatre for Wednesday night. "Those who want a red hot time should come to this meeting," he was quoted as saying. "Let us start the fur flying!" Special invitations were tendered to Mayor D. H. Freeman, the city commissioners, and A. G. Whitney, St. Cloud Public Service Company president.

The second news story initiated the city's habit of referring to the company and to its founder by the single term, Pan. The headline stated: PAN, LIKE TIME AND TIDE, CAN WAIT FOR NO MAN. The story went on to reveal that Pandolfo had contracted with a St. Paul firm to put in sewer and water lines at a cost of $45,455.76.

Round three was the city's reply to Pandolfo. In a semi-official statement in the newspapers on Tuesday, October 23, full of "Whereases" and "Therefores," Mayor Freeman and Commissioners George Magnuson and Henry Maybury informed the city that Pandolfo was being given the same treatment as any other citizen. They stated that the city would repay Pandolfo when they connected to his lines, at the going rate of $1.56 per foot of frontage.

The fourth and final round was reported in Thursday's paper under the headline, PAN WANTS SEWERS AND HE WANTS THEM NOW. More than a thousand people had crowded into the Nemec Theatre to hear Pandolfo castigate the city fathers for forcing him to lay his own lines. He went after the power company, too. Whitney had promised him, he said, lower power rates than any automobile company in the country. Pandolfo had written to several companies and determined that Ford was paying $.01 per kilowatt hour, Hudson from $.009 to .01, Haynes was paying $.0175, and Dodge $.01. "The Pan Motor Company has been paying the St. Cloud Public Service Company five cents per kilowatt hour," Pandolfo roared. And Whitney had recently quoted him a rate of $.0222 per kilowatt hour. Pandolfo was not pleased. "Well, old top, the Pan Motor Company has purchased an electric plant and we will make our own power . . . ."

The city agreed to install sewer and water lines.

In November 1917, the prestige of the Pan Company was enhanced by acquiring a new vice president: Charles F. Ladner. Born in Pottsville, Pennsylvania, in 1857, Ladner had come with his parents to St. Cloud in 1886. Six years later he bought a hardware store and made it extremely successful. He was one of the organizers of the Hardware Mutual Insurance Company; he was also a vice president of the St. Cloud Iron Works and the Miner Theatre Company; and he was a director of the Security State Bank. One of the city's leading citizens, Ladner was a member of every Liberty Bond, Red Cross, and other philanthropic drive in the city in the days when such drives were frequent.

By the end of the year, Pandolfo had begun to shift some of the promotional emphasis from selling stock to showing cars. Late in January 1918, the company exhibited the Pan car at the National Auto Show at the Hotel LaSalle in Chicago. An added attraction in the Pan exhibit was John Smith, an Indian who claimed to be 130 years old. His Indian name, Ka-Be-Naw-Way-Wence, meant Wrinkled Meat, and he sat, in a chief's feathered bonnet, in front of a tepee and conversed with visitors.

Early in February the exhibit moved to the Minneapolis Auto Show at the Hotel Radisson, and later in February took its new unconventional tractor design to Kansas City where it was described as "the hit of the show!"

Some notion of the activity of the company can be judged by examining the St. Cloud post office revenues and the effect the arrival of Pan had on them. In 1915, post office revenues had been $49,172.57; in 1916 (the year before the Pan Motor Company was incorporated) they had increased to $52,471.99; in 1917, although the company had located in St. Cloud only in March and did little early business, revenues were $73,507.56. But for the first six months of 1918, during the full flurry of stock-selling activity at Pan, revenues totaled $54,536.79, a gain of almost

50 percent when the national average for increase was only six percent.

The people of St. Cloud were "pushing for Pan," or at least one resident was. He sent the following letter to the editor of the *St. Cloud Daily Times:*

> Having noticed in the *Times* of February 4th the item in regards to new Auto for Police Department, I note bids were received from the Ford, Buick, Dodge and Maxwell agencies, as well as from the Pan Motor Company. The price of the Pan being above the $800 limit.
>
> Now, Gentlemen, does it not seem that it would surely please every resident of the City of St. Cloud to see our police department using a new Pan car? It seems to me that our Chief of Police is surely entitled to have in his department one of these fine cars.
>
> Does it not seem a shame to even think that every businessman in St. Cloud who is able to do so would not gladly donate part of the additional amount necessary to provide our police department with a fully equipped Pan car, a car made in our home town, and a car which all must admit has quality and quantity for the price?
>
> Why not have a real car for this Department? Is it not possible in some way to get the ball rolling in that direction?
>
> Yours very truly,
> A. E. Bakeman

The police department did get a Pan car, but it had an unhappy and mysterious accident some time later.

Throughout the winter, construction at the Pan plant and on the homes in Pan Town was keeping St. Cloud the most active city in the state. On March 1, 1918, the company noted its first anniversary in St. Cloud with a recapitulation printed in the *St. Cloud Journal-Press:*

> Pan Motor Company, who located in this city one year ago, has had a remarkable period of growth even discounting wartime conditions . . . . The company had three employees when it came here: S. C. Pandolfo, John Barritt, and E. J. Gorman. Pandolfo was accompanied by his wife and children, Vivian and Samuel, Jr.
>
> The company was located in three rooms in the Farmers Bank building. Today there are more than 350 employees of the company, and they are rushed with the ever-increasing business being done.
>
> One year ago there were 1100 stockholders; today there are 23,000 stockholders, 1,113 in St. Cloud alone.

> Today the Pan Motor Company occupies the entire upper two floors of the Farmers Bank building, the Hayward Building, using two floors and the full basement for advertising purposes, and the former Education building, comprising two floors and a basement, for the engineering and architectural staffs. . . .
>
> More than 50 homes have been started or completed in the Pan Addition; many of these homes have been occupied by Pan employees. More are moving into them every week as fast as homes are completed. . . .

Without a showroom of its own, the Pan Motor Company was obliged to exhibit its car and the Tank Tread Tractor in the newly redecorated quarters of the Commercial Club on Fifth Avenue South. In addition to the Model 250, then being assembled by the company, they also displayed a hand-built Model A or "Perfected Pan." Engineers and designers were on hand for several days to explain the features of the cars and the tractor to the local and out-of-town stockholders who wanted to see what their investment was producing.

The Commercial Club joined in promoting the company by sponsoring an essay contest, the subject of which was "Why St. Cloud Should Be Proud of the Pan Motor Company." Prizes were shares of Pan stock and War Saving and Thrift Stamps. Other promotional efforts included running a Pan car onto a theater stage during an intermission of "Johnnie Get Your Gun," and a ladies' day tour of the Pan plant to watch a paint spraying machine put "a high enamel gloss on a large automobile body in less than four minutes."

But Pandolfo was less than pleased with the amount of stock being purchased by St. Cloud citizens. Early in March 1918, at a testimonial dinner given by local businessmen to thank him for the prosperity and fame he had brought to the city, he reminded them of their one-sided use of the Pan Motor Company.

"No man ever appreciated more the kind of reception I have been given here tonight," he said. "But I need more than that. Money comes here from all over the country, but not much comes from St. Cloud. Make no mistake, we're proud of the fact that we have 1100 subscribers for stock in St. Cloud, but when we're asked how much money those 1100 have invested, that's an entirely different story. Only 100,000 dollars has been corkscrewed out of the St. Cloud businessmen, laborers, clerks, and every type of citizen.

"You have all shown confidence in Pan Motor stock and boosted it, but we need cash. If St. Cloud never buys one more cent of Pan Motor stock, the company is going to be a big success. But if St. Cloud does not come through quickly they are going to lose the greatest opportunity they ever had or ever will have. The more rapidly our stock is sold, just that much sooner will we be in a position to help St. Cloud. Through the Pan Motor

Company and my own efforts we have increased property values in St. Cloud more than six million dollars, yet you have subscribed only 100,000.

"I am honest. You know that. I have had opportunities to make great sums of money by being dishonest. But even if I made ten million dollars by a crooked deal, I would never enjoy the benefit of a nickel of it. There are property owners whose property value has been increased by thousands of dollars, and yet some of those property owners have not bought a damn cent's worth of Pan stock.

"We want big subscribers who are able to buy large blocks of stock. The men with big businesses and large property are the men who are reaping big profits from Pan locating here."

I. J. Doke, a Denver lawyer and businessman who had come to St. Cloud to inspect the company on behalf of Denver stockholders was a guest at the dinner. It was a growing custom with distant stockholders, especially when the fiscal agent, Pandolfo, paid their way. Doke, asked to speak at the dinner, said his report to his Denver friends would be favorable, but pointed out that while distant stockholders only received dividends on their stock (dividends, by the way, that the company had not yet paid and never would), St. Cloud residents got dividends and increased property values in addition.

Pandolfo's invective precipitated the Commercial Club into passing a resolution, which it promptly published, finding Pandolfo "not only honest to a fault, but a man of great capabilities." It also recommended "to the entire citizenship of this city that they cease to do business with any foreign enterprise, rating company, or commercial agency antagonistic to the Pan Motor Company and S. C. Pandolfo as president."

It was the first overt indication that trouble was over the horizon.

A few weeks later a small incident demonstrated an advantage of the promotional efforts at Pan Town. A small brush fire, whipped by the wind, swept in from the prairie west of Pan Addition and threatened to destroy the St. Cloud baseball park grandstand and also Pandolfo's Motor Hotel, which was nearing completion. It was put out by people from the Pan Addition who beat out the flames using the FOR SALE signs real estate dealers had staked out on nearby property.

Five days later the water system to Pan Town was turned on and the area was assured of an adequate water supply to fight future fires.

George Heidman Norman Street

The Chicago lawyers Pandolfo hired to form his corporation and secure his patents. They became board members of the company.

The Venetian Building, on Washington between State and Wabash, in Chicago, where the first offices of the Pan Motor Company were located. *(Photo courtesy Chicago Historical Society)*

The Pan Motor Company Board of Directors

Samuel C. Pandolfo Charles Ladner

John Barritt Charles Schwab

Hugh Evans Fred Schilpin

George Hanscom Charles Bunnell

The Pan Motor Company Board of Directors

Peter R. Thielman

H. C. Ervin, Jr.

Pan Engineering Staff

Victor Gauvreau

Leroy R. Brown

Alfred Krieg

Ray J. Fitness

Ray A. DeVlieg

Edgard DeSmet

First home of the Pandolfo Manufacturing Co. Located on the northwest corner of 6th Avenue and 2nd Street South. It later became the showroom and garage of Hornibrook Hudson Essex dealership.

Construction begins on Factory Building No. 2 of the Pan Motor Company.

In the meantime, design and assembly took place in the Experimental Building across 33rd Avenue from the main plant.

The Fourth of July barbecue to celebrate the arrival of the first hand-built "Pan" cars from Indianapolis drew visitors to St. Cloud in record numbers from hundreds of miles around. Speeches and eating—and selling stock—was the order of the day.

PANDOLFO

PAN MOTOR COMPANY

CAPITALIZED FOR

$5,000,000.00

PAN

S. C. PANDOLFO, PRESIDENT

PAN-TOWN-ON-THE-MISSISSIPPI
SAINT CLOUD, MINNESOTA

ADDRESS REPLY TO
DEPT.

The company's letterhead seemed more interested in its capitalization than in the car it would produce.

Before Factory Building No. 2 was built, offices of the Pan Motor Company were spread among three buildings in "downtown" St. Cloud.

General Offices were in the First National Bank building on St. Germain Street.

Additional offices dealing mainly with stock sales and record keeping were in the Farmers State Bank of which Charles Schwab was president.

(Left) Much of the company's advertising material was prepared and stored until use in the Board of Education building between 2nd and 3rd Streets on 5th Avenue. (This building no longer exists.)

Offices of the president *(above)* and sales manager *(right)* of the Pan Motor Company. Note the window decoration in the sales manager's office, not yet applied in the president's office.

The Pan Motor complex of buildings was remarkable considering the restrictions imposed by World War I conditions and the short time in which it was achieved.

DIE SHOP

HEAT TREATING PLANT

This is the only building of the Drop Forge Complex still standing.

The Drop Forge and some of its equipment.

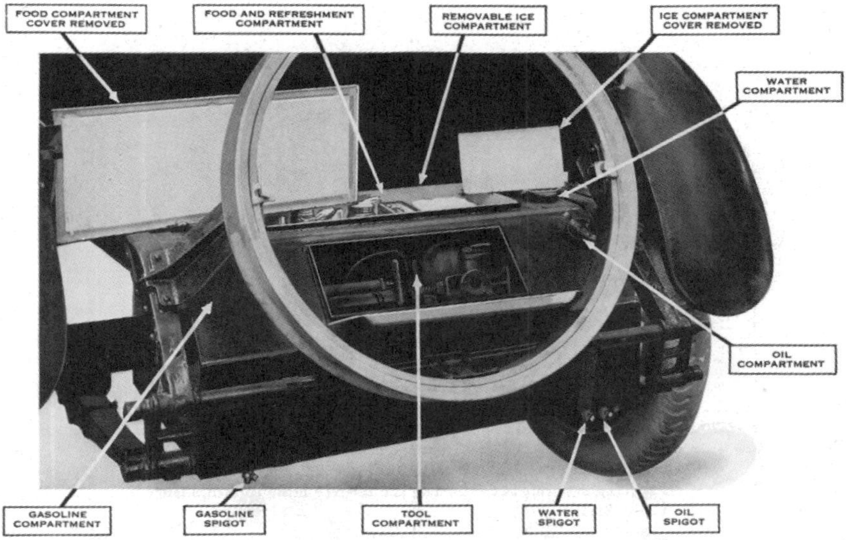

The Pandolfo-patented Combination Compartment Tank.

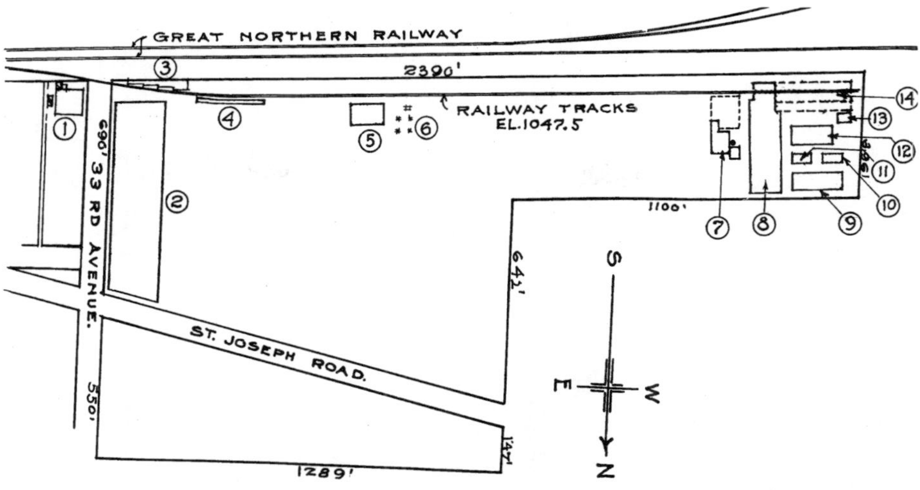

This property map locates (1) the Experimental Engineering Building and Blacksmith Shop; (2) Factory Building No. 2; (3) Works Department Warehouse; (4) Shipping and Receiving Platform; (5) Main Power and Light Plant; (6) Water Tower and Pump House; (7) Drop Forge Power House and Coal Storage; (8) Drop Forge Hammer Shop; (9) Drop Forge Die Shop; (10) Drop Forge Office Building; (11) Oil Storage Building; (12) Heat Treat Building; (13) Metallurgical Laboratory; (14) Drop Forge Warehouse site (never built).

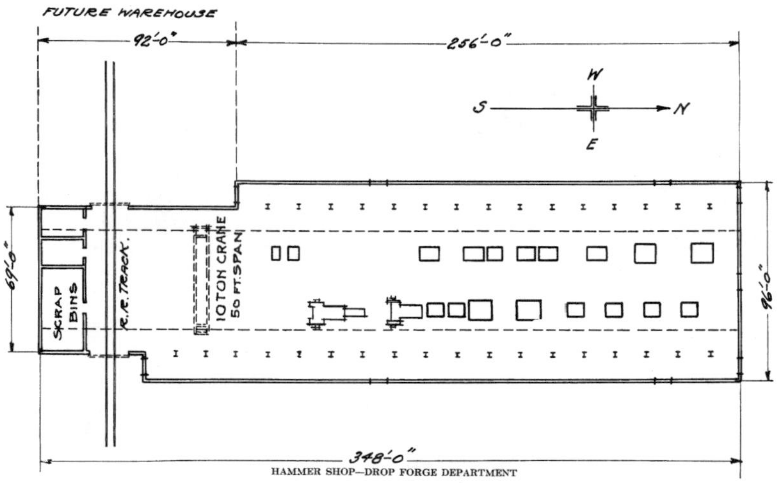

Drop Forge Building Plan

The Assembly of a Pan

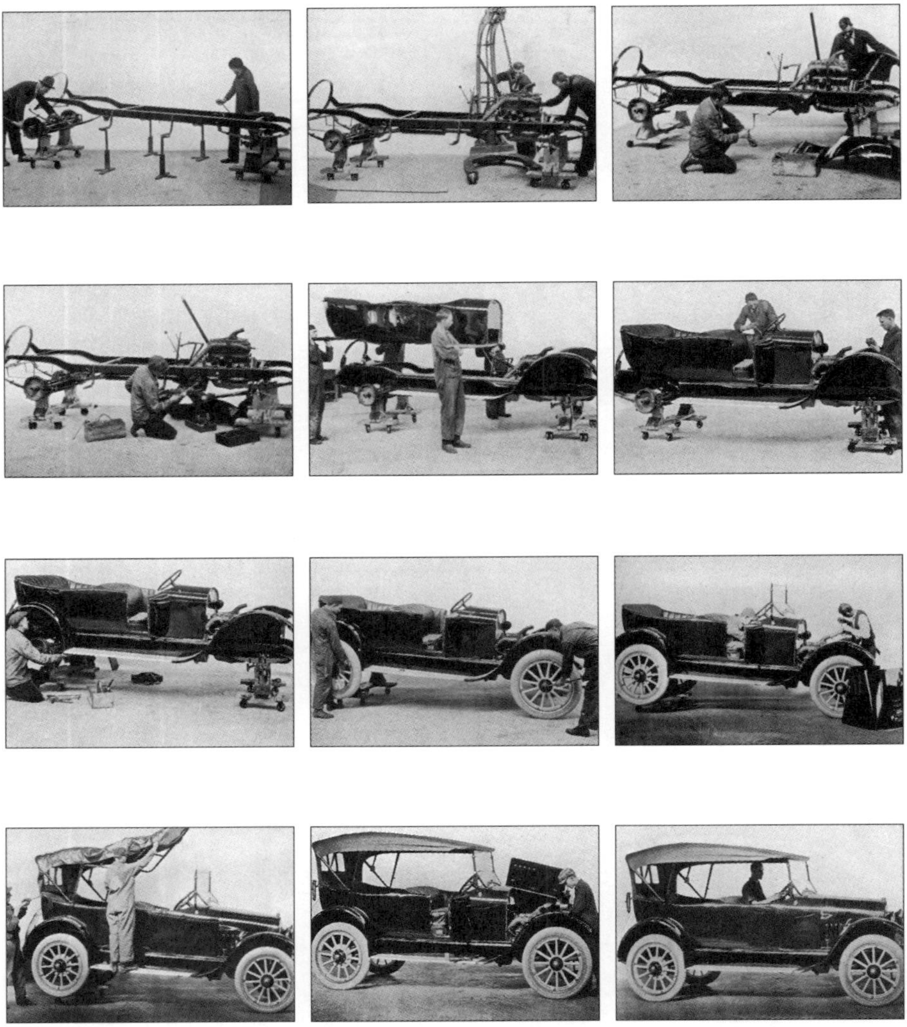

Factory amenities for the workmen were excellent.

CHAPTER IV

EXPERIENCED SPECIALISTS ARE IN CHARGE

ONE OF THE FIRST MEN hired for the technical staff of the Pan Motor Company was the chief automobile designing engineer, Victor Gauvreau. Born in France in 1888, Gauvreau, as a boy, wanted to become an artist but his parents' practical advice persuaded him to turn to engineering, and he graduated from the Portiers Technical High School in 1907 and then attended the *École Nationale des Arts et Métiers* from which he graduated in 1909 at the age of 21. He came to America for the first time in 1908 during a school vacation, and after his graduation and a short stay at Peugeot in France, he returned to the United States and worked as a mechanical engineer for Mercer Automobile Company in Trenton, New Jersey. He remained in this country a year, then returned to France to serve a year in the French army. He was still in service in 1911 when he received a letter from his friend Louis Chevrolet asking him to return to America when his enlistment was up and help with the design of a car.

Gauvreau came to Detroit and worked on the first Chevrolet, but when the company, consisting of 75 men, moved to Flint, Gauvreau quit to remain in Detroit and court the girl he later married in 1913. They honeymooned in France, and when they returned to America, Gauvreau took a job as assistant chief engineer on the first Dodge. By 1915 he was back with Louis Chevrolet, helping in the design and construction of the Frontenac racers. Chevrolet had hired an experimental engineer, Joseph Nelson, from Maxwell, and when Gauvreau later went to Buick, Nelson went along to assist in building the Buick racing cars. Gauvreau, however, was not working for Buick but for Walter Chrysler, then president of Buick but looking forward to the day when he would produce a car bearing his own name. Gauvreau was doing research for Chrysler on an engine that would not be a copy of Buick's.

Pandolfo, searching for a staff in his direct fashion, wrote to the chief engineers of the leading automobile manufacturers asking them to recommend young design engineers for the new company he was forming. Either Gauvreau's name appeared several times or the recommendation he got was overwhelming. Pandolfo asked him to come to Chicago for an interview and hired him. Walter Chrysler at first tried to dissuade Gauvreau from the Minnesota job but eventually let him make his own decision.

Following the hiring of Gauvreau, and perhaps with his advice, the staff grew rapidly and by late 1917 included the following:

RAY J. FITNESS, hired as assistant designing engineer, had experience with Cadillac, Packard, Studebaker, Dodge Brothers (where it is possible he met Gauvreau), Continental Motors, and Nordyke and Marmon.

L. A. LaFOND, tractor designing engineer, had come from the Dakota King Tractor Company where he was chief designing engineer. In 1908, he designed one of the first successful tractors, and he spent the next two years designing and superintending the building of a grain-shocking machine at Dallas. He was chief designing engineer for the Diamond Tractor Company and later with the Hi-D Company. Farm tractors were thought to be a significant—and locally important—product for the Pan Motor Company.

MAURICE STAHL, tractor engineer, was a native of Strasbourg, Alsace, and graduated from one of the best engineering schools in Europe, the Zurich *Technicum* in Switzerland. He worked for the Benz Automobile Company in Germany before joining the Pioneer Tractor Company in Minneapolis in 1909, where he designed the Simplex Tractor, a four-plow machine, and later was chief engineer for Beeman Garden Tractor Company.

RUSSELL T. WING, assistant electrical engineer, was a typical example of the attraction the Pan Motor Company had for mechanically gifted men in the area, but he was typical in no other way. He had a wide range of interests and was a practical inventor. Several of his theoretical designs later received recognition, including one for a helicopter, for which he received acknowledgment from the United States Aeronautical Advisory Committee to whom he had sent it as an idea for protecting United States shipping from German submarines. He also received a patent on a headlight lens for automobiles, pioneered several ideas for car design—including a camping car—and patented the fountain pen feed later incorporated into the Parker 51 pen. Despite his capabilities, Wing did no work on the design of the Pan car, possibly because the technically educated and experienced senior engineers did not relish working with an untrained inventor, however gifted. Wing's work was confined to construction of the Pan buildings.

EDGARD DeSMET, body designing engineer, graduated with honors from the Industrial College in Ghent, Belgium. He studied body designing with Vanden Plas in Brussels and worked for Locomobile and Dodge Brothers in the United States before coming to Pan.

GEORGE BOOTH, works managing engineer, was born in England and had served seven years as an apprentice with Markham & Company, engineers in Chesterfield, before moving on to Davy Brothers in Sheffield and then Hick-Hargeaves & Company in Bolton. In the United States, he worked for Buick and the Welch Motor Company of Pontiac.

PAUL REUTER, works engineering department, was born in Germany. He started his technical training in 1903 at the Technical College in Elberfeld, in Europe. He had 15 years practical experience in architectural and mechanical engineering in Europe before coming to the United States and working for Chas. Leffler & Company, Brooklyn; Otis Elevator Company, New York; Exceter Machine Works, Pittston, Pennsylvania; Dodge Brothers, Detroit; and Belden Manufacturing Company, Chicago.

ADELBERT R. SMITH, general superintendent of the drop forge unit, had been with the Waverly Electric Car Company of Indianapolis and the Erie Foundry Company, manufacturer of much of the equipment the Pan Motor Company was installing. He had been the general superintendent of the five forge plants of the Maxwell Automobile Company and general superintendent of forging for the United States Motor Company.

ARTHUR L. CRAMP, assistant general superintendent, was the third native of England in the employ of Pan. He had been foreman of the grinding department of the Buda Company, Harvey, Illinois, and for a time was assistant foreman of the Continental Motor Manufacturing Company at Muskegon. He came to Pan after seven years as shop foreman for the Rutenber Motor Company of Marion, Indiana. (Buda, Continental, and Rutenber all supplied engines to the Pan Motor Company before work on the Pan engine was completed.)

H. L. DAVIES, inspection department, had worked for Pierce Arrow, had also been with J. W. McGuire Company, and was the American service representative for the Rochet & Schneider Automobile Company of Lyon and Paris. His other experience was with the Kent Motor Car Company and in the experimental motor department of Hudson, assisting in developing the Super Six. He was thus possibly the reason for Hudson's later claim that the Pan was a copy of their new Essex.

"Experienced specialists" were in charge in the front office, too. Personnel turnover in the new company was rapid, as it was in most of the automobile companies of the time, but the following people stayed long enough at least to be featured in an issue of *Pan Siftings*.

JOHN B. McGOLRICK, director of sales, was described in the magazine as coming "to Pan from New York, where he handled traffic matters for Senator W. A. Clark of New York for his three large copper mining companies in Montana and Arizona, the Butte Electric Railway, the Montana Hardware Company, Butte; Waclark Wire Company, manufacturers, Elizabeth, New Jersey; Henry-Bonnard Bronze Company, manufacturers, Mt. Vernon, New York, and other interests. He held important traffic positions with the Erie, North-Western and Salt Lake Route Railroads

MRS. FLORENCE COLEMAN, company postmistress, had nine years of experience as a postoffice clerk at Clovis, New Mexico. What probably assured her job at Pan, however, was the fact that Mrs. Coleman was the first woman to buy Pan stock. (Although no direct evidence was found, it is possible Mrs. Coleman was related to Mrs. Pandolfo; she lived with the Pandolfo family for a time.)

F. S. MILBERG, secretary to the president, had been the official court reporter for the Alberta (Canada) Supreme Court for several years, and he was later associated with the largest law reporting firm in the world, Central Law Reporting Company of Chicago. He had also been a reporter for the House of Representatives and Senate for the State of Illinois.

BENJAMIN FRANKLIN FORSYTH, advertising manager, had experience in automobile advertising and as the automotive editor of the *Minneapolis Daily News*. He had been advertising and business manager of the Virginia *Daily Enterprise* in northern Minnesota and started doing publicity work in 1909 on the *Minneapolis Journal*. Forsyth, second only to Pandolfo, became most identified with the Pan Motor Company locally, because his position required that when Pan was mentioned the information came either from Pandolfo or from Forsyth.

JACK HAMMOND, director of publicity, had long experience on newspapers. He had been managing editor and editorial writer for the Daily Virginian of Virginia, Minnesota (thus was in competition with Forsyth who had also worked in Virginia, although not at the same time). Hammond had studied law for three years at the University of North Dakota, had held editorial positions on the *Fargo Forum* and the *Grand Forks Herald*, both of North Dakota, and the *Duluth News-Tribune*. Later he had been a headline writer for the St. Paul News and the *St. Paul Pioneer-Press* for several years.

This was the nucleus of the design and office staffs of the Pan Motor Company. As construction continued on factory facilities, additional men were added. By March 1918, the hammer shop of the drop forge complex was closed in, and machinery was immediately installed. By July, the peripheral service buildings—the power house, die shop, oil storage, and heat treat buildings—were completed and the drop forge unit was in full operation.

Whatever may be said about the rest of the Pan Motor operation, the drop forge was a success from the start. It was the most completely equipped plant west of the Mississippi, and no plant, east or west, had equipment that was as completely modern. Here on the Minnesota prairie, far from any other industrial activity of similar capability, stood a drop forge complex that six years later, after all the construction spurred by World War I, was still the fifth largest drop forge in the United States!

Part of its success stemmed from the fact that Pandolfo hired the best men for the job by paying the best salaries. In addition to those men already mentioned, the drop forge plant work-force, by the fall of 1918, included the following:

F. F. TAYLOR, sales manager of the drop forge, had 15 years of experience in the steel, automobile, and drop forge business. Pandolfo claimed Taylor had "made, bought, and sold steel."

JOHN D. BOYLE, metallurgist and heat treat expert, had studied mining and mechanical engineering in the Mining and Mechanical Institute at Freeland, Pennsylvania, backing his courses with practical work in the blacksmithing, forging, and heat treating departments of Coxe Brothers & Company at Drifton, Pennsylvania. Boyle was in the heat treating department at Bethlehem Steel where he worked on heavy gun forgings. During his nine years with Bethlehem, he spent almost three years in government service in the Panama Canal zone as master mechanic and mechanical inspector. He joined Anderson Forge & Machine Company, where he was foreman of the laboratory and heat treating department and chief metallurgist before coming to Pan.

HENRY RADEMAKERS, superintendent of the die and forge shop, was born in Holland, and took a three year course at the Academy of Fine Arts and Technics at Rotterdam. In the United States, he took special courses in mechanical engineering in the American School of the Armour Institute of Chicago, taking the courses at night and working during the day. He became a die sinker with the Chicago Drop Forge & Foundry Company at Kensington, Illinois, and later foreman of the experimental department of the Vaughan-Bushnell Tool Works at Chicago. He had also worked at the Waverly Electric Automobile Company in Indianapolis, Fenkle & Sons in Chicago, Whitman & Barnes of Chicago, and the Anderson Forge & Machine Company in Detroit before joining the mass transfer to Pan.

AL C. PETTERS, tool maker, was one of the few local men with the experience to work in this area. Petters had received his training as a machinist for the Minneapolis Steel & Machinery Company, the Grundman Auto Company, a car dealership in St. Cloud, and the McCadden Machine Works, manufacturers of pistons in St. Cloud.

There was no doubt in St. Cloud—at least in west St. Cloud—that the drop forge had started production. The thunderous clank of the massive hammers shook the area day and night.

During the latter part of 1918, the staff of the Pan Motor Company continued to grow as new jobs were created in the expanding company.

ALFRED KREIG, tractor designing engineer, had spent four years, following college, in practical shopwork in various engineering fields, including gasoline engines, ship building, and locomotive works. He had worked for the Westinghouse Air Brake Company a year-and-a-half as a draftsman, with the Twin City Rapid Transit Company in St. Paul a year-and-a-half as a draftsman and designer, and he spent a year with Fawcus Machine Company of Pittsburgh as draftsman and estimator. Krieg came to the Pan Motor Company from the Emerson-Brantingham Company, where he had been for over seven years, the last three-and-a-half as chief designer. He was hired to replace LaFond, the first tractor engineer at Pan, and while his coming kept the company active in an area they had been promoting with some effort, it was also the cause of some later embarrassment. Krieg did not share LaFond's enthusiasm for the tank-tread principle applied to tractors, and he scrapped all of the preliminary work on this design, including the prototype, to concentrate on a more conventional four-wheel design. Later, when the trial of Pandolfo and the other directors neared, last-minute attempts were made to put LaFond's tank-tread model into action. They did, finally, get it operating, but the prototype of Krieg's newer design was never built.

LEROY R. BROWN, manager of manufacturing, came to Pan late in 1918 from Detroit where he had been supervisor of production of the Ordnance Department for the government. He had experience in almost every phase of the automotive industry: He had been in charge of special sales for the Seager Engine Works at Lansing; superintendent of the Neway Motor Company, general superintendent and assistant factory manager of the Duplex Truck Company of Charlotte, Michigan; and general superintendent of the Republic Truck Company, Alma, Michigan, where he tripled production in one year. The last accomplishment was exactly what the Pan Motor Company needed. Brown was bright, forceful, and friendly. He not only saw the Pan Model A into production at a perilous time for the company, but after leaving Pan he was hired to run a local company meant to produce off-road trucks for the granite industry.

RAY A. DeVLIEG, methods engineer, had been a toolmaker for the Olds Motor Company at Lansing, a toolmaker and mechanic for Burroughs Adding Machine Company in Detroit, a draftsman for the Universal Motor Truck Company in Detroit, and a tool designer for Cadillac Motor Company. For four years he taught machine shop practice in Detroit evening high school classes. He had been chief engineer in charge of the machine and tool designing department of Kearney & Tracker Company in Milwaukee. He had also worked for Dodge Brothers as a checker in the engineering department of the ordnance division, later becoming assistant chief draftsman, still later chassis engineer, and finally chief engineer.

Out of the entire staff in late 1918, Gauvreau, Fitness, Krieg, DeVlieg, and H. E. Lambert were members of the Society of Automotive Engineers. DeSmet, the body engineer, later joined the SAE and served in several elected positions many years after his association with Pan had ended.

Model 250 Pan cars were being turned out slowly and irregularly, and in preparation for full scale production on the Model A Pan, additional experts in various fields were hired.

F. A. GUSTAFSON, superintendent of the paint shop, had experience going back to carriage days; his first employers had been Monroe Brothers, carriage builders in Illinois, and he later worked for some of the oldest carriage firms in Chicago. In St. Paul, he had worked for the Thomas Scott Carriage Company and in St. Louis for the Mansor Tibbet White Elephant Buggy Company (which later changed its name to Deere and Mansor). In St. Louis, Gustafson had been assistant manager for five years and foreman of the paint shop for two years. He was a striper and ornamenter for Pope Toledo Car Company in Toledo, and later went to Moline, Illinois, where he laid out and installed the paint shop for the Velie Motor

Car Company and was superintendent of the paint shops.

C. W. ROGERS, body finisher and striper, had also been a carriage painter, working for the D. F. Isaacs Carriage Company of Coffeyville, Kansas. He had worked at the Kansas City Southern Railroad at Pittsburg, Kansas, the Packard Missouri Motor Company at St. Louis, and the Jones Motor Car Company of Wichita.

GEORGE STONE, chief automobile inspector, born in Franklinville, New York, started his own garage in 1909 and joined the Packard Motor Car Company in 1912 in the inspection department. He came to Pan from the newly formed Elgin Motor Car Corporation of Argo, Illinois.

MARK N. SCHNETTLER, foreman of automobile assembly, was another of the few local men well qualified to hold a position of responsibility at Pan Motor. He had graduated from Rahe's Automobile Training School in Kansas City, and had worked at Hupp Motor Car Corporation in Detroit and the Velie Motor Vehicle Company in Moline before coming back to St. Cloud to work at Pan.

The extensive work histories are given here to indicate that experienced and able men were working at Pan, and not the "window dressing" crews that some critics later claimed.

If there was any question whether the Pan Motor Company was a valuable asset to the economy of St. Cloud, it was answered by an article in the *Twin City Trade and Labor Review* of St. Paul. So that it would not be missed in the light barrage of criticism the company was beginning to attract nationally, the article was reprinted in *Pan Siftings* for August 1918.

> St. Cloud, Minnesota, has opened to the nation's workers a door of opportunity such as few cities of twice to three times the size have made accessible to the "men behind." The establishment of the gigantic Pan Motor Company project in St. Cloud is the reason. This big, new infant of the Motor industry is attracting the attention of the nation because of the opportunities it presents to both the investor of money and the investor of labor.
>
> Established a little more than one year ago, the Pan Motor Company has already placed itself on the map in capital letters and it is a question whether any similar project has ever made as rapid progress as this new Minnesota giant. Attesting to this fact are over 42,000 loyal, boosting stockholders located throughout the nation.
>
> The Pan Motor Company, through its able leader, S. C. Pandolfo, the president and founder, has taken care of the labor question in a manner that will appeal to the better class of workmen throughout the country. This fact is already testified to by the hundreds of employees now on the ground who, after all, are

> the most accurate judges. With hardly an exception, every man and woman of the hundreds employed have manifested their intention of staying with the company and becoming factors in the civic and commercial life of St. Cloud by buying homes, or otherwise establishing themselves in a manner that indicates their desire to make their stay permanent. Another fact testifying to the desire of labor to come to St. Cloud is that over a thousand applications for various positions in one department have been received.
>
> There are several reasons for the Pan Motor Company's popularity with labor: first, only the best class of loyal workmen are considered for employment with the company; second, wages are right—the man is worth his hire; third, with the rounding out and completion of the giant plant, wage earners are to be placed on a profit-sharing basis; fourth, the right social environment and home life is provided for. . . .
>
> There will be other features which enter into real common fundamentals. A hospital to care for the sick; a community house for the entertainment and club life of the hundreds of employees; an athletic field for the indulgence of many sports; all will have their part in this great whole, which to the careful investigator looks about like the last word in industrial development of our times
>
> Last, but not least, the thorough-going Americanism of the company and the man at its head is rapidly making the organization felt as a dominant factor in the efforts of this territory to place herself on a basis of efficiency such as will enable her to contribute to the cause of the nation, and through her, to the cause of the world.

It wasn't until January 1919, however, that the Pan Addition Athletic and Social Club came into being. The members elected Edward J. Gorman, Pan auditor, president of the club; Ben Forsyth and C. W. Williams, both from the advertising department, were elected vice president and secretary-treasurer. These three, plus Ray DeVlieg and Victor Gauvreau, made up the Board of Directors. The first activity of the group was a dance, using the factory as a ballroom, on January 18. It was admitted that the athletic side of the club would have to develop more slowly, but they planned on a gymnasium and "a swimming tank with all modern fixtures."

The glowing article in the *Twin City Trade and Labor Review* notwithstanding, Pan Motor did have occasional labor problems. A dispute arose in the second-last week of July 1919, when the basis of overtime was the point of a short walkout at the plant. The men were not associated with any larger industry-wide or even state-wide union. Pan Motor paid time-and-a-half for overtime, but wanted the overtime to start only after 48 hours for the week had been worked; some of the men in the machine shop felt that overtime should begin after an eight-hour day had been put in. When the company would not change its policy, the men walked off the job.

A meeting between officials and the disgruntled workers was arranged at the St. Cloud Institute by Bishop Joseph F. Busch, who spoke in Pandolfo's behalf, strongly upholding the president's character and ideas and reminding the men of the company's interest in their welfare in the matter of housing and eventual sharing in the profits. Union organizers from Minneapolis were allowed to speak at the meeting, and they urged the workers to join a union to avoid such problems.

When Pandolfo spoke, he offered the men two alternatives: overtime pay based on the 48-hour week, or no overtime work at all. He did not receive the idea of a union in the Pan plant with open arms, but neither did he reject it. "It makes no difference at all to me," the president said "whether a man is a member of a union or not. The Pan Motor Company is paying for work, and men who wish to work under the conditions, which are the best in the state, are welcome regardless of their affiliation. The wages paid by the Pan plant are exceeded by only one firm in the state." At the time, the Pan payroll was $60,000 a month. "A standard working day is in force and the men have Saturday afternoon off. This will continue until September 1, when the full six day week will again be in force."

Although Pandolfo was loudly cheered by the men, who appeared to like him personally, the majority of them favored the no-overtime-work option.

LeRoy Brown was asked to explain the status of the men who had walked out rather than do overtime. "These men were not discharged," he said. "They merely left their work, and if at any time they wish to return to the Pan Motor Company, they will be accepted."

Thus ended the only serious labor dispute the Pan Motor Company had.

Until the main factory was completed and necessary parts were received for the Model A Pan, the Model 10s and the Model 250s were assembled in the Experimental Building across the street from the Main Factory building.

Model 250 Pans ready for delivery.

CHAPTER V

. . . a meritorius small car . . .

WHATEVER THE ADVANTAGES of Pandolfo's organizational plan for the Pan Motor Company, and whatever his ability to sell the stock in that company, success depended ultimately on the car the company would design and produce.

A car does not spring, Athena-like, from the brow of the designer but is planned in a long series of compromises; a change in one element of the design starts a chain reaction necessitating corresponding adjustments in many other elements. Its design and production stack one complication upon another; today computers help to sort out the intricate process.

Pandolfo needed a car immediately, something in finished form to display to prospective investors; he could not wait for the engineering staff to evolve a design through a year or more of give and take. In fact, he would not even wait until he had hired a staff. Reed & Glaser, Indianapolis consulting engineers, were hired to produce the first Pan cars. There were some specifics in the instructions Pandolfo gave the firm. Remembering his days of traveling by car in the Southwest, he ordered the designers to give the Pan car some of the facilities of a camping car. Hotels and gasoline stations were widely scattered in the Southwest at the time; the first drive-in gasoline station had been erected by Gulf Oil Company in Pittsburgh only four years before the Pan Motor Company was formed. The Pan car, therefore, was to be equipped with the Pandolfo Combination Compartment Tank. This metal box, bolted on the rear of the frame (and on the running board of cars other than Pan), carried an extra supply of gasoline, water, and oil for the car, and food and beverages, with an ice compartment to keep them cool, for the passengers. Tools and a jack were also carried in the tank.

The second design feature, an indication of the prescience that Pandolfo exhibited at various times, was the "Tourist Sleeper" body. Something similar had been tried in the Spaulding car, manufactured in Grinnell, Iowa, in 1914. The Pan Tourist Sleeper body had a front seat on which the back could be folded down to allow passengers—two of them, at any rate—to sleep in shelter, if not in comfort, inside the car.

With this much to go on, Reed & Glaser assembled the first three Pan cars that arrived in St. Cloud on Saturday, June 30, 1917, to be exhibited at the giant barbecue on the Fourth of July. None of the cars produced by Reed & Glaser, however, had the Tourist Sleeper body; this feature was not incorporated into the design until a body designing engineer had been hired. The Reed & Glaser cars were prototypes of the Model 250, although these first cars were called Model 10. They were similar in size to what the final Pan would be, but there was little to distinguish them from a dozen or more other makes on the market at the time. In fact, after the Hudson Essex was introduced in 1918, the Pan engineers claimed their design had been copied by Hudson engineers, and the Hudson group claimed there had been a leak of their plans to Pan.

A month after those first three cars were driven to St. Cloud, a second shipment of four more touring cars arrived by rail from Reed & Glaser, with the last of the cars produced by the Indianapolis engineers coming still later. Some thought had been given to ordering 54 more cars, but by then the experimental building was completed, and late in 1917 or early 1918 the local car was being turned out locally. That is, they were being assembled in St. Cloud.

There were technical differences between manufacturing and assembling automobiles. Automobile manufacturing, as distinct from experimental building, began around the turn of the century. In the days before 1906-08, many companies thought there was an advantage in advertising that they made many of the parts for their own product. With slightly lifted nose, the Maxwell-Briscoe Company stated in an ad in a 1904 issue of *Motor World*, "The Maxwell plant is not an assembly plant, but one where every part of the Maxwell automobile is actually made under the direct supervision of the designer, Mr. J. D. Maxwell." The makers of the Rambler, in Kenosha, Wisconsin, were advertising, "Excepting only the body, tires, and spark coil, every part of the Rambler touring car is made in our own factory."

The development of large parts-making firms, many of them better known than the car manufacturers they were supplying, brought an end to the practice (and snobbery) of total "one-roof" production, and car makers began to advertise their use of a Continental engine (as in the Model 250 Pan), Brown-Lipe gears, Timken-Detroit axles (as in the Pan), or Hyatt roller bearings. After 1910, manufacturers did not disguise the fact that they assembled some units made by outside companies.

Pandolfo's stated intention to become completely free from suppliers, including tire manufacturers, was in the future for quantity producers of cars, which he certainly intended the Pan Motor Company to become, but he was starting out, as most of them had, as an "assembler."

The car the Pan Motor Company was assembling in early 1918, the Model 250, was still novel despite being an assembled car and sharing many components with other makes. It had a four-cylinder Continental engine, with a 3½ inch bore and a 5 inch stroke, that produced 34 horsepower. The carburetor was by Zenith, and the ignition, a closed-circuit type, used a Remy distributor and a six volt Gould battery. The transmission was a selective type manufactured by Detroit Gear & Machine Company, and had a Borg & Beck clutch. The rear axle was by Adams, the front axle was a Pan-made drop-forged I-beam. The Model 250 featured Hotchkiss drive with semi-elliptic springs front and rear, and a frame of high-carbon pressed steel. The brakes, service and emergency, were Raybestos-lined and the two sets were internal expanding and external contracting respectively. The special drive shaft had Spicer universals. The wheels were artillery type, second-growth hickory, with Firestone tires, 34 × 4 with non-skids on the rear on demountable rims. The car had a wheelbase of 116 inches and a clearance of 11 inches. The convertible top was called a "one-man type, with jiffy curtains," and the double-cowl body was painted Pan green with cream running gear. The standard equipment included a Boyce Motometer, Stewart-Warner speedometer, rim-wind dash clock, electric horn, a set of tools, tire pump, jack, tire carrier, and special Pandolfo Combination Compartment Tank. The car weighed 2800 pounds (some specifications list 2100), and was advertised to sell at $1250 f.o.b. St. Cloud, Minnesota, "subject to change without notice." While working ahead on the 1919 or Model A Pan, the engineering staff was still testing the Model 250.

And Pandolfo was still promoting it. On March 6, 1918, George Magnuson, superintendent of the Department of Finance and Accounts for the city of St. Cloud but acting mayor for the week, wrote a letter to the mayor of El Paso, Texas, to be delivered by Ray Fitness and George Stone, who would drive 2,038 miles from Minnesota in a Model 250 Pan. The letter, terse almost to a fault, stated:

> My Dear Mayor:—
>
> St. Cloud, Minnesota, sends you greetings via the "PAN," the car you have been waiting for.
>
> The PAN is a St. Cloud product, we are proud of it.
>
> The PAN will carry you through sand or mud and over any kind of hill.
>
> The car left St. Cloud at three o'clock P.M. Wednesday, March 6, 1918, on its first test run.

According to a story of the trip that appeared in the April issue of Pan Siftings, Pandolfo had asked Fitness and Stone to make the trip on one day's notice. "I want you to take a trip of at least two thousand miles," he said. "I want you to drive the car every way you can think of and under every kind of road and weather conditions possible. Punish it, make it do work that will break it if it is weak at any point. I want the truth about this car. If there are any 'bugs' in it, find them."

Fitness and Stone drove to Minneapolis and then headed straight south to Albert Lea, Minnesota, Des Moines, and Indianola, Iowa. They crossed into Missouri near Blythedale and out again at Kansas City, went west through Emporia, Kansas, on their way to La Junta, Colorado. In Nevada, they went through Las Vegas, west to Santa Fe, New Mexico, then south to Albuquerque, Hot Springs (now renamed Truth and Consequences), and Las Cruces, following the Rio Grande into El Paso. The Pan Siftings described the completion of the trip:

"The entire trip was made in 99 hours and 40 minutes of actual driving time. From an endurance standpoint, the trip proved to be a record-breaking test. No car that was not right in every respect could possibly hold up in a grind such as the Pan went through. The Pan lived up to its royal title of "Queen of the Highway"—it showed no respect for any road."

Fitness and Stone left the Pan to be sold in Texas and returned by train, arriving in St. Cloud on March 23 with a letter from the El Paso mayor.

My Dear Mayor:—

I have just had the pleasure of a call from Mr. R. J. Fitness and Mr. George Stone, who drove the "PAN" test car from St. Cloud to El Paso, arriving here on March 18, 1918. They report a very enjoyable and successful trip, not having had an accident or trouble of any kind.

I assure you I am very much gratified that these gentlemen have seen fit to visit our city, that I highly appreciate your good wishes, and desire that Messrs. Fitness and Stone extend to you cordial greetings from the City of El Paso.

Very Sincerely,
CHAS. DAVIS, Mayor

The Pan was beginning to be noticed by the trade press as well. The Pan Motor Company exhibit at the Chicago Automobile Show in January 1918 was visited by the *Automobile Trade Journal*, which reported the exhibit in their March issue.

Many Interesting Features on the New Pan Car

Visitors to the Chicago Automobile Show who happened to visit the La Salle Hotel were introduced to a new car that was exhibited for the first time in the lobby of the aforesaid hotel. It is a feature car because of the many little innovations that have been worked out upon it, its "uptodateness" and the fact that it is a five-passenger car with 108 in. wheelbase, designed to sell for about $1000.

The article described the technical features of the car in detail and then concluded with the following general comment:

> One little feature that seemed to cause more comment by the user than any other on the car was the emergency supply compartment at the rear of the chassis. In the place of the conventional gasoline tank at the rear of the chassis is mounted a compartment tank containing all the necessities that one needs on a tour, 3½ gallons of gasoline, 2 gallons of water, and 3 quarts of lubricating oil. Then, in between these, are a couple of compartments, one for the tools and the other surrounded by an inch of felt so that it retains the cold and can be used as an ice box when touring to carry sandwiches and cold refreshments. A small box is provided to carry the ice so as not to wet the edibles in the box.

At the end of the 1918 Chicago show, the Pan Motor Company moved its exhibit to the Hotel Radisson in Minneapolis for the local auto show and also took its novel tractor to the National Tractor Show in Kansas City, February 11 to 16.

The tractor was the outgrowth of a wartime weapon. The British Army, on September 15, 1916, at the Somme, introduced the tank into modern warfare.

Although it was some time before the use of the tank as a cover for attacking infantry would evolve, its use of an endless track for locomotion quickly became synonymous with unlimited power and traction. Within a short time several machines intended for farm use tried to adapt the principle.

The Pan Motor Company had hired L. A. LaFond from the Dakota King Tractor Company where he had been chief tractor designing engineer. His specifications for the Pan Tank Tread Tractor called for a Buda engine burning a mixture of kerosene and gasoline. The engine, with a bore of 4½ inches and a stroke of 5½ inches, delivered 12 horsepower at the drawbar, 24 horsepower at the power takeoff. The tractor had one reverse and three forward speeds and a turning radius of 12 feet. The steering column and clutch and brake levers telescoped to permit steering and operating the tractor from the seat of a plow, binder, or other machinery being towed.

On paper, and perhaps even in the field at times, there was no denying the appeal of this tractor. The company received inquiries on it from many foreign countries and even reproduced in its magazine a cablegram from Paris requesting "the lowest distributor price and schipping [sic] delay one Pan Tank Tread Tractor."

But when a stockholders' committee visited the company in December 1918, they were shown a new design for a tractor that was being developed, the first one of which was supposed to be in operation for experimental purposes early in the spring of 1919. It was to be a conventional four-wheel machine with a 12-to-20 horsepower rating. No mention was made of the Pan Tank Tread Tractor.

The change had come about when Alfred Krieg replaced LaFond as the chief tractor designer late in 1918. All work on the tank tread design disappeared from the drafting boards when LaFond left Pan, and the prototype was put in storage.

Limited by a small staff and by time, the Pan Motor Company never did work on the design for a Pan truck, although it was the third item in the priorities Pandolfo had listed for the company.

Assembly of the Model 250 Pan cars was sporadic at best and never faster than one a day. The late delivery of parts was given as one reason for this, and with the war-time conditions it is reasonable. Although production of automobiles had increased every year in the United States from 1900 until 1917, when 1,170,000 units were produced, the first reduction took place in 1918 when, due to the time and material given to war production, only 703,000 automobiles were produced. The Pan Motor Company was not alone in finding volume production difficult to achieve.

On June 1, 1918, the first hand-built Model A Pan was driven into St. Cloud from the Pan plant by Pandolfo and Victor Gauvreau. The body was only slightly different from the Model 250, but the car now had the Gauvreau-designed Pan engine. For the rest of the year, Gauvreau spent much of his time behind the wheel of that Model A between Minneapolis and St. Cloud, probing for weaknesses, refining the design. Several times, when the wind was right and the sky was clear, he covered the 75 miles in one hour and 55 minutes, and this at a time when parts of the highway were still unpaved.

By the end of 1918, the Pan Motor Company was the third largest industry in St. Cloud, ranking behind the Great Northern car shops and the granite industry. Because the car shops were not strictly local, and because the granite industry had to total all of the employees of many companies to outnumber Pan, it could be argued that Pan was the single, largest, totally local business in the city . . . and it was only two years old!

Production of the Model 250 Pan car was not sufficient to make a profit for the company; in fact, the company lost about $1000 on each car it sold (an economic fault that would plague Pandolfo for years). The drop forge, which started production in the fall of 1918, cut the losses but not significantly. Earlier in the year, priority orders for the equipment needed in the drop forge had been obtained from Bernard Baruch, director of the War Industries Board. On May 27, 1918, the first of 17 large drop forge hammers arrived in St. Cloud. The hammer alone weighed a ton, and the base and other parts added another 45,000 pounds. The unloading drew a crowd of onlookers, although they grew more blasé as other units arrived in the following weeks.

Even while the drop forge was in the planning stage, the sales staff had solicited business, and in the last half of 1918, to the consternation of those who felt the Detroit companies would put Pan out of business, the drop forge was making parts for Chevrolet: 22,500 crankshafts, 90,000 connecting rods, 12,500 camshafts, and 50,000 clutch forks. It had other work, too. It was making 10,000 connecting rods for the Buda Motor Company to be used in Nash Quad trucks; 5,000 connecting rods for the Emerson-Brantingham Company; 100 steering arms for the Winther Motor Truck Company; 10,000 units of a patented hoe, rake, and cultivator combination tool for the Schoener Manufacturing Company of St. Cloud; 200,000 hammock hooks, 5,000 galvanized chain plates, 5,000 three inch pad hooks; 5,000 1¼-inch foot rail stanchions, and 5,000 guard line stanchion heads—all for the United States Navy Department.

The drop forge also had an internal contract from the Pan Motor Company for parts for the Pan cars.

In September 1918, three Pan Model 250 cars made a trip of 11,000 miles through the Southwest, stopping at fairs and exhibits, giving the local stock salesmen a chance to sell Pan stock. Bill Bettenberg, an inspector-mechanic at Pan, W. A. Furlong, a "front-office" man recruited for the trip, and an engineer, whose name was not recorded, were the drivers. They carried a fourth man, Tommy Wood, who was used to draw a crowd if the appearance of the Pan cars themselves didn't. Wood, 23 years old, from Brainerd, Minnesota, was six feet four inches tall and weighed 500 pounds. He played the ukulele, and that small instrument all but disappeared in his large hands.

During the week of September 22 the cars were demonstrated at Pueblo, Colorado, in the usual way; the men would arrange for the use of an important crossroad in town, tie down the steering wheel, set the hand throttle, and let the car circle in the intersection, unattended, in high gear.

On Saturday, September 28, they drove up to Colorado Springs at the foot of Pike's Peak. They were told that they'd never make it to the top of the 14,110-foot climb without special equipment. According to Bettenberg, nothing extra was done to the Pan cars to prepare them for the assault on the Peak Sunday morning except to make certain the Combination Compartment Tanks were filled with water, oil, and gasoline. They went up in low and second gears, and as the radiators boiled it away water from the extra supply was added. They reached Summit House at the top without incident, and prepared to eat lunch. They had been told not to shut off their motors because it would be difficult to start them again in the high altitude, but when they were ready to descend the engines fired up easily and they started down.

Tommy Wood was the extra passenger in Bill Bettenberg's Pan, and if Bill had worried about making it to the top with the extra weight, he was more worried about coming down. He and Furlong took it easy, braking with the engine and easing the car down the grades. But the engineer wanted to give the car a good test, and he started down full tilt, hitting the brakes on the sharp bends and opening the throttle on the straights.

When Furlong and Bettenberg reached the bottom they found the engineer crouched beside his Pan, checking for damage. He discovered a nut missing from a fender brace and all of the paint burned off his brake drums, but there was no other damage, according to the reports Pandolfo promptly gave wide circulation.

But the resulting publicity in the Colorado Springs newspaper stirred up more activity than anticipated. Congressman Edward T. Taylor, from the fourth congressional district in Colorado, and the Grand Junction Daily Sentinel started an investigation of the Pan Motor Company and Samuel Pandolfo. The company had been receiving good and bad publicity in Colorado as the result of the reports from committees investigating it, and this local performance of the Pan car added more pressure to the controversy.

(It may have been all gold for Tommy Wood, however. Following his trip with the Pan cars, Wood went to Hollywood and made a movie with Charlie Chaplin. In June 1919, the people of St. Cloud, then slightly numbed by the indictment of the directors of the Pan Motor Company, could forget their troubles momentarily by stopping at the Nemec Theatre to see Charlie Chaplin and "Fatty" Wood in *Sunnyside*. Wood's Hollywood career was brief, however; he died of pneumonia a short time later.)

When the Armistice ended the World War in November 1918, and also ended the Pan Motor Company's direct contribution to the war effort, Pandolfo stepped up the publicity. The February 1919 issue of *Automotive Engineering* contained a six-page story on the new car titled, "The 1919 Pan, A Meritorious Small Motor Car." The article was so complimentary that it might have been written by the Pan advertising manager, except for the existence of a letter received by Victor Gauvreau from Morris Hall of Gallon-Hall, publishers of *Automotive Engineering*.

> Dear Sir:-
>
> In preparing the description of your Pan 1919 Car for our printer, I made an interesting discovery and thought I would pass it on to you.
>
> First I would like to say that this was the earliest opportunity I have had to go over the car in detail, but as a result of this detailed examination, I wish to congratulate you upon the car you have produced.
>
> I do not know exactly what the price is, but at any rate, it is an unusual small car, and your company should be unusually successful with it.
>
> The thing that I have discovered is that your motor has an

> output for 1 cubic cylinder capacity of .3074 hp. As it stands, this is only a string of figures, but I happened to be interested enough to figure out the same item for our supposedly very efficient Liberty motor, and on the basis of its maximum hp, attained only in approved tests, fuels, and under very successful circumstances, of 526, the figure is only .3189; that is, the Liberty motor surpasses your motor by only 3.6 percent.
>
> Another way to put it is that if you had a 12 cylinder motor, the same size as the Liberty 5 × 7, and used the same construction, and were able to obtain such an efficient engine, the output would have been 507 hp, as compared with the Liberty maximum of 526.
>
> I consider this a great achievement and thought that possibly you might not have happened to figure it out in this way, so that these figures might interest you.

They also interested Pandolfo who made a mailing piece out of the letter.

The year 1919 was the peak year for the Pan Motor Company. Its stock selling methods were successful enough to attract the attention of several investigating committees, both official and unofficial. Its running start would be enough to carry it for some time, but indictments brought against the Board of Directors in April 1919 were beginning to have some effect on the sale of stock.

Meanwhile, almost every day some new piece of equipment was put into production at the drop forge, and the future looked promising. In fact, the future success of the Pan operation appeared so obvious that it was attracting a number of other would-be tycoons to St. Cloud. One, R. J. Harris, had a device that he guaranteed would keep the lights of a Ford Model T at constant brightness whatever the speed of the engine. Another inventor, H. E. LeRoy, was seeking financial backing for the manufacture of the LeRoy Grand Orchestrion, an elaborate player piano.

They were not the only ones seeking riches in the industrial environs of St. Cloud. On July 14, 1919, articles of incorporation were filed in St. Paul for the Minnesota Motor and Warehouse Company of St. Cloud. This company planned to manufacture and sell automobile parts and accessories. The incorporators were F. M. and Albert D. Wright, H. J. Limperich, J. B. Dunn, Walter W. Murphy, Albert H. Kendall, Peter J. Seberger, and J. C. Lindt, all of St. Cloud, and Reuben A. McMillian of Minneapolis. In September, the Minnesota Motor and Warehouse Company announced that it would build a three-story building covering a city block on Seventh Avenue North, east of the railroad tracks. The company offered 1,000 shares of its capital stock for sale at $100 a share, with an extended period in which to pay the full subscription price. They expected to sell it all in St. Cloud in ten days.

The offering was ill-timed. Although the Pan Motor Company was steaming along, it was under the threat of a grand jury indictment with the trial only a month away. People seemed assured that the Pan Board would be exonerated, but they were going to wait before investing in a similar business. (When Pandolfo was convicted, the Minnesota Motor and Warehouse Company sank out of view from lack of public interest and support.)

Probably unaware of any special significance of the date, the Pan Motor Company placed an ad in the St. Cloud newspapers on April 1, 1919:

> USED CARS—WITH A VIEW TOWARD CLEANING UP THE FEW REMAINING MODEL 10 AND MODEL 250 PAN CARS IN ADVANCE OF PRODUCTION ON THE 1919 PAN, WE OFFER FOR SALE AT ATTRACTIVE PRICES THE CARS WHICH HAVE BEEN IN USE IN OUR SERVICE AND COURTESY DEPARTMENTS. WE WOULD SUGGEST THAT YOU TAKE ADVANTAGE OF THIS OPPORTUNITY TO SECURE ONE OF THESE BARGAINS—SOME AS LOW AS $500. THEY MAY BE SEEN ON THE FACTORY FLOOR. ASK FOR MR. CATER, COURTESY DEPARTMENT.

Even with the country returned to a peace-time basis, production on the Model A Pan automobile started slowly. Whether it was lack of steel or simply a precautionary measure, not wanting to stockpile parts that might have to be changed later, orders to the drop forge indicate that a first run of only 30 cars was planned. By the first of August it was announced that production would soon be "many cars a day." (For comparison, Ford was turning out 3,200 Model T cars a day and falling behind the demand.) But this proposed limited production schedule was never reached. Along with this announcement, another stated that an increase in the price of Pan stock, from $10 to $12.50 a share, was contemplated. It never occurred either.

Because it was assumed that the local manufacture of its parts would be cheaper than buying them from outside manufacturers, the Model A Pan was most often advertised to sell at $1058, $200 less than the final advertised price of the Model 250. But in fact, production costs remained at about $1300 per car so that the 300 Model A Pans, apart from the 50 or so Model 250's, produced during 1919 lost around $75,000. Other losses, perhaps on the Model 250, brought the total 1919 deficit of the Pan Motor Company to $100,000. The company now carried a three year net loss of $500,000.

One of Pandolfo's last large promotional/testing efforts for the car was a trip for five of the new Model As. It began in St. Cloud on October 25, 1919, after all of the company's officers and directors had left the city for the trial in Chicago, and it covered 2,000 miles of the roughest driving that could be found. Five cars were selected and the bodies were removed and replaced with a seat for a driver and observer. A 350-pound concrete block, fastened to the frame in the rear, made up for the weight of the missing body and passengers. One of the five cars had a huge tool box bolted on in place of the concrete weight, and it served as the traveling service center during the trip.

Nine of the men making the trip were Pan engineers or mechanics; the tenth was St. Cloud Police Chief Ed Brick. The Pan men were paired in the cars: LeRoy Brown paired with Victor Gauvreau; Ray DeVlieg was with Ray Salter; Ray Fitness went with Ed Gliszinski; Hiram F. Humphrey paired with Mark Schnettler; and Charles Carney had Chief Brick as a passenger.

Four days—and 650 miles—later, the *St. Cloud Daily Times* reported on part of the trip in a casual story.

> "Say, that little car is a wonder. You may think cars have been tested out but one never was until the Pan went on this trip," were the words of L. C. Brown, manufacturing manager of the Pan Motor Company on his return from the test trip which was started last Wednesday.
>
> The cars were driven from here to Brainerd and it was just a little beyond this point that bad roads were encountered. From there to Walker the mud was hub deep in most places and Walker was made the night control. The following morning the trip was resumed with Cass Lake as the objective. Over a foot of snow had fallen and the cars plowed away although most of the distance had to be traveled in low gear. A distance of 30 miles required eight hours time but the little car worked away and never gave up for a second.
>
> "Of course," said Mr. Brown, "you understand that all of this distance was not traveled on roads. We might see a sand pit at one side of the road and made a detour through that; if we heard of a bad mile or so of roads we would hit for that. Plowed fields were our favorites and that Pan car seemed to thrive on work. At no time during the entire 650 miles did I have to stop to look at my motor. It never missed a shot and even when I drove into St. Cloud last night it was humming away as smoothly as when we left on Wednesday."
>
> Cass Lake was made the night control on the second day. Here the cars were checked over and it was found that none needed any attention. The snow had been falling fast and the cars were covered with mud and snow. It was here that Mr. Brown learned that he must leave the party and return to the factory. The rest of the men tried to persuade him to take the

train back and return for the car in better weather, but Brown stated that he had driven out of St. Cloud and he was going to drive back, so he left Cass Lake at 3:30 p.m. and drove until 11:00 that night, landing at Park Rapids. He left Park Rapids at six o'clock the following morning and arrived in St. Cloud that evening at 7:00 (last evening) having covered about 650 miles.

When Mr. Brown left the party they had but one accident. Brown was driving at a high rate of speed through the snow. The snow and sleet made it impossible to see and the car jumped the road and over a ditch. When the machine was brought to a stop the lower part of the left front wheel was above the top of the right rear one. In removing the car from the ridge, the frame was broken. The severe twist failed to break it and it was not until it was being removed that it snapped. The frame was braced with heavy timbers and the trip was continued.

"I could tell you many interesting incidents," said Mr. Brown, "but I know you wouldn't believe them, but when the remainder of the party returns I will show you pictures and let you judge for yourself. There was one stretch of nine miles that was being graded. When we approached, the foreman of the job told us it was impassable but we told him that was just what we were looking for so we went to it and covered the entire nine miles on our own power.

"Another thing you may not want to believe until I show the pictures is the fact that the ice formed so rapidly around the wheels and spindles that we had to stop and chip it off with an ax before we could turn the wheels. If we stopped in the snow-covered road for a minute, we had to chop the tires out of the ice to get started again."

Those who know Mr. Brown know that he gives any car a real test on a good road and they can imagine what would happen with him at the wheel on a test of this sort. A "hard driver" doesn't begin to describe the man. "I had those guys scared to death most of the time," said Mr. Brown, and this isn't a bit hard to believe.

One would never recognize that car as a Pan this morning. There is not a spot of paint to be seen, just mud and sleet. After the car had been parked in the warm factory building from seven o'clock last night until nine this morning there was still snow and ice on it. There was a puddle of water about it that told the tale.

"The rest will continue the trip," said Brown, "and expect to return to St. Cloud early next week. I don't know where they are going any more than I knew where I was headed for when we left here, but I know that that bunch of drivers will give those cars some test."

> In speaking of the performance of the Pan Mr. Brown said to a *Times* representative this morning, "You know something of my career in the automobile game. Well, I have tested out many a car in my day and among them were some of the leading makes in the country, but I never knew what a real test trip was until we started out with these Pans. I have never seen roads or weather conditions such as we went through; I never drove a car with as wonderful a little motor as has this same St. Cloud product." Mr. Brown has been with some of the leading motor companies of the United States and has seen some of them grow from a little shack for a factory to the largest and he has had occasion to test out many cars during his career.

By this time, however, all of the publicity concerning the Pan Motor Company was centered on the trial just getting under way in Chicago, and no more was heard about this last test trip.

Sam Pandolfo in front of his house in Pan Town.

CHAPTER VI

THERE IS MONEY IN PAN FOR YOU!

THE PAN AUTOMOBILE Victor Gauvreau and the staff brought into production was well conceived, carefully designed (discounting the haste and the earlier Model 10, which the subsequent model was somewhat committed to), thoroughly tested, and sturdily made. But there was argument—muted within St. Cloud and vociferous outside, at that time and up to the present—about Pandolfo's method of selling Pan stock and the remuneration he took for it. Some felt that his methods were too flamboyant for a corporation of the size and intent of the Pan Motor Company. They also felt that his methods attracted the small, non-professional investor, one likely to panic and fade away at the first sign of trouble. It was these same small, non-professional investors who not only stayed with the company through its troubled days, they were the ones who organized its resurrection when the large stockholders—the hard-headed businessmen with more sense—were ready to leave it for dead.

Then there were those who said that flamboyance was the only way to get a company of that size and kind started in that era. They pointed out that the large investor was not going to invest in the kind of proposition Pandolfo was selling in the early days of the Pan Motor Company. Pandolfo was no engineer, he had no previous experience in the automotive business nor in any business related to it. He knew nothing about the production of automobiles, although he learned as he went along, and quickly too! He was really a salesman, a super-salesman and promoter.

What large investor, many said, having exhibited the acumen to accumulate some amount of capital, would entrust it to the likes of Pandolfo? Nobody but the little people, he argued. He realized that from the beginning. His first sales of stock were to people who might not have been able to invest large amounts, but for whom the dream of wealth that Pandolfo promised was something so possible that they invested what little they did have in hopes of great returns. They had heard the stories of fortunes made in the automobile industry; Pandolfo's early advertising had recounted several of them.

One of the first brochures produced for the Pan Motor Company, a booklet of more than 60 pages, devoted 15 of the first 35 pages to a description and photos of the Pan Model 250, the specifications and chassis photos of the Model A, the scope of the Pan plant, Pan-Town-on-the-Mississippi, and the reasons for locating such an enterprise in St. Cloud. The rest of the booklet, 25 pages, was devoted to the reasons why the Pan Motor Company was not only a sound investment, but probably the best one around at the moment and for some time to come. The section was titled "How Can I Make Money If I Buy Pan Motor Stock?" The message was unadorned, basic, and direct:

> Suppose I strain a point to buy 50 shares of Pan Motor stock. . . . I would have to invest $500.00 in order to buy these 50 shares of Pan Motor stock.
>
> The Pan car will be the car that everybody sooner or later ought to buy, and at some time or another no doubt will buy. The Pan will perhaps be the best car for the price on the market. . . . In fact, I think the man who does not buy a Pan will lose money and also make a mistake. . . .
>
> Every Pan Motor Company stockholder is entitled to buy from the Company, for his own use, an automobile, or any other machine manufactured by it, so as to save the middleman's profit or dealer's commission of 15%. Suppose the price of the Pan be $950. 15% of that will amount to $142.50. The stockholder would get his $950 car for $807.50. Suppose I have 40 neighbors, acquaintances, relatives, and friends who would want to buy the Pan or some other machine manufactured by the Pan Motor Company. I should easily be able to sell at least 40 people one share each. I should be able to get at least $50.00 for each share. My neighbor could well afford to pay me $50.00 for one share, and on the basis of this calculation he would then be $92.50 to the good on buying just one car, and still have his share of stock, which would forever afterwards entitle him to this special discount, so long as he was a stockholder.
>
> Suppose I sell these 40 shares to 40 different people at $50.00 apiece. These 40 shares would bring me $2000.00, for which I had paid only $400.00. That would represent a profit of 500% on my money invested in these 40 shares. In other words, it would return to me on this basis of calculation, my $500 originally invested in Pan Motor stock and $1500 cash profit, and I would still own ten shares of Pan Motor stock, which I would keep, and these ten shares would be enough to make me, or my family, rich in the course of time. . . .
>
> In conclusion, I am not only glad that I have the opportunity to subscribe for at least 50 shares of Pan Motor stock, but I can safely recommend that every other right-thinking man, who

> has the opportunity to subscribe for Pan Motor stock, do so immediately: Because, Opportunities do not Hang Around and Linger and Constantly Knock at the Door for Admittance.

Perhaps an elaborate and flamboyant selling campaign was necessary. There had been an early reluctance to invest in the automotive industry, and it was still evident. In 1904, the Horseless Age, the oldest trade journal in the industry, warned investors not to succumb to "promoters' gilded dreams of 5000 men in a single factory, making automobiles." Selling automobile stock, therefore, required a heavy hand writing the advertising, and Pandolfo certainly supplied it.

The earliest known figure for the number of stockholders in the Pan Motor Company was given out by Pandolfo on March 2, 1917, when he stated that the company at the time of its arrival in St. Cloud had 1159 stockholders. Twenty days after the St. Cloud offices opened the number had jumped to 1500.

This did not mean that the company had, therefore, $15,000 in its treasury. Because the stock could be purchased on a subscription basis—and it was most often sold to the small investor who purchased it on that basis—it was never possible to count the number of shares sold and multiply by $10 to determine how much money the company had.

All over the United States, but especially in the southwest and midwest, the sale of Pan stock began to accelerate at a rapid rate. By May 1917, there were 2600 stockholders, 400 of them in St. Cloud alone.

Once the company had located in St. Cloud, Pandolfo retained John D. Sullivan, state senator from St. Cloud, who had been co-author of the state's new blue-sky law regulating the sale of stock in Minnesota. Sullivan was hired to obtain from a reluctant state Securities Commission a permit for the Pan Motor Company to sell stock in its home state. On September 10, 1917, a license was granted. (This does not mean that stock sold in the state previous to September 10 was sold illegally; since the law had been passed by the last legislature, this was the first year in which permits were required.) There were by this time over 1000 local subscribers to the stock.

Pandolfo had good reason to hire Sullivan. The Pan Motor Company was having difficulty obtaining its license from the Securities Commission with the problem centering on the commission paid to the fiscal agent (Pandolfo) for sale of the stock. It wasn't until the amount was more precisely accounted for that Sullivan was able to tell Pandolfo that the license would be granted. In spite of Sullivan's guidance, which Pandolfo either frequently ignored or only partially accepted, the company's relationship with the Securities Commission continued to be marked by tension.

Pandolfo never mentioned publicly how many stockholders were added to the rolls of the company on the day of the giant barbecue, July 4, 1917, but it was disclosed on October 3 that the company now had over 9,000 stockholders residing in 37 states.

On March 1, 1918, on the first anniversary of its arrival in St. Cloud with 1159 stockholders, the company announced with considerable pride that it now had 23,000 stockholders, 1,113 of them living in St. Cloud.

Nevertheless, Pandolfo was never satisfied with the local response to the sale of Pan stock. At a testimonial dinner given for him on March 4, 1919, he complained of what he considered a lack of total support from St. Cloud people; but at another public dinner one week later he pointed out that there were Pan stockholders in 42 of the 48 states and some in Africa as well. At this same second dinner, given by Pan officers for the employees, he gave the first hint of the difficulties the company was beginning to experience with the sale of its stock.

"If an attempt were to be made," he said, "and would succeed in prohibiting the company from soliciting subscriptions for its stock in the United States because of the war, the company will forward its efforts to other countries to sell stock there. We *will* get the money necessary to promote this business and keep it going until it is on a dividend-paying basis. Have no fear of that!"

A few nights later he called a public meeting at one of the local theatres. The *Journal-Press* reported the affair succinctly. "Pandolfo is not refined," the reporter wrote. "He was not introduced to his audience last night. He calmly walked on stage, placed his cigar on the table, cast a glance at his audience, spat on the floor, took a drink from a glass of water, and proceeded to talk for an hour and a half."

The speech covered not only the affairs of the Pan Motor Company, but touched his personal life as well. "I don't condemn a man who differs with me, or even one who doubts my ability to do what I say I will do. But I have no use at all for a man who carps at me only because I am apparently successful. Some of you here tonight said I would bleed the area of as much as I could get and then pull out. Well, I'm still here!" He slapped the table with his open palm.

"Some of you here tonight said I was doing the same thing in an Illinois city. Well, the Pan Motor Company of St. Cloud and the Pan American Motor Company of Decatur are two different breeds of pup, let me tell you."

He paused for a sip of water. "I've gotten to where I like criticism. I feel uncomfortable if I don't hear it every day. I'll stick around just to hear what in hell they are going to say next. The latest story is that I am in favor of prohibition." The audience, rapt and silent to this point by his outburst, erupted in a roar of laughter. "That is a lie," he shouted above the laughter and jabbed a plump forefinger in the air. "A damnable lie!"

When the laughter died, he continued. "I also heard it said that I haven't put any of my own money in Pan Motor stock. Let me tell you that I have, as of right now, 19,000 dollars invested in Pan stock, and I am investing more from month to month. I have borrowed 150,000 dollars from banks in the city to buy real estate. I believe that property values in this city will increase four-fold because of Pan, and I want to make a little of this money myself. I think I have the right. I'm responsible for it."

Then he touched on a subject that had been the topic of heated debates within and without the company. "It has been said that Pandolfo receives half of the money turned into the office from the sale of stock." He paused, looking out over the audience. "Well, that's right," he said softly. "That's right." A little louder. "But with that money," he went on in a rising crescendo and began ticking the items off on his fingers, "I pay postage—10,000 dollars a month; literature and printing—ten thousand dollars a month; salaries in the fiscal agency department, salaries in the secretary's department, salaries in the sales department, salaries in the advertising department, and all other such expenses. And I have been paying them from the start of this company.

"Actually, I receive about a five percent commission on the stock that is sold. And I want to point out here and now that this has nothing to do with the par value of the stock. That value has to do with the actual buildings and the producing activity of the firm. And I want to tell you that this company is being organized and its plant is being built for less money than any other automobile plant in the country

"The trouble with many of you here is that you are used to conducting a small business in a small town. You cannot grasp the immense proportions of this proposition. Now, let's be fair! No man should be anything but friendly to the Pan Motor Company. And the only way to be really friendly to the company is to invest money in it. Money talks!"

He gave a candid outline of the plans for the immediate future of the company. "We intend to invest about two million dollars in buildings and equipment within the next six months. We only have 652,000 of this amount pledged to come into the office the next few months from the sale of stock. The rest—1,350,000—has to be raised by the sale of more stock.

"The drop forge plant will be started next week. Frankly, the money to complete it is not in our hands. It must be raised. Now, with the completion of this plant—and it will be the only one in the northwest and the largest and best equipped in the United States—we can do enough work for other firms to pay a neat dividend on our stock even if we never make an automobile.

"Remember, the Pan Motor Company has a 100 percent unimpaired capital. We now have cash deposits for more than a million dollars worth of automobiles. If that doesn't make Pan stock a sounder investment than anything else you ever heard of, I don't know what does.

"It comes down to this: Money is an absolute necessity. Why don't you people come across and buy stock?"

It was the kickoff for a stock sale campaign in the city and throughout the state. The usual procedure was to get a delegation of prominent citizens from out-state cities to visit the plant and use the resulting publicity to promote stock sales and more delegations.

On Monday, March 25, 1918, for example, a news story covered the visit of a delegation from the Iron Range area of Minnesota. They had come to inspect the plant as the guests of John Hesse, Pan Motor representative on the Iron Range. The delegation included Mayor Louis Bower of Crosby, E. B. Brown, editor of the Crosby Crucible, Municipal Judge William Brady of Hibbing, and Newt Randall, Ray Edwards, and William Wilson, said to be former big league ball players then living in Hibbing.

By April 1918, Pandolfo, as good as his word concerning foreign sales of Pan stock, hired a foreign secretary, Charles T. Lazzari, who was fluent in French, Italian, and Spanish. The Pan Motor Company shortly had subscribers of its stock in Canada, Alaska, England, and Italy, in addition to Africa.

The ubiquity of Pan stock salesmen is revealed in an incident related by Glanville Smith, the son of W. W. Smith, cashier of the Farmers State Bank of St. Cloud. W. W. Smith, at the height of the Pan mania in St. Cloud, received a letter from the king of Siam, Rama VI, or Vajiravudh. Bangkok had been visited by Pan salesmen seeking to sell stock, and the king was inquiring about the wisdom of such an investment, whether for himself or for individual Siamese people he did not make clear. W. W. Smith had been recommended by some American missionaries in Siam as one who would be close enough to the situation to be knowledgeable and fair enough to give an impartial answer. After thinking it over carefully, Smith advised the king to be cautious.

This prudent answer committed Smith's brush with Siamese royalty to secrecy for many years, for if he had exhibited the king's inquiry to anyone outside of his own family they would certainly have wanted to know what advice he had given the king. And the answer would have alienated a large segment of St. Cloud's citizenry from Smith's bank. Certainly Smith himself would have found his position at the bank awkward, for the president of the Farmers State Bank was Charles D. Schwab, secretary of the Pan Motor Company; privately Schwab might have applauded Smith's prudent banker's reply, but he would have found it difficult to live with publicly.

It is almost certain that Vajiravudh took Smith's advice and waited; if he had bought stock there is no doubt that Pandolfo would have broadcast the news to the world in every medium available.

If Smith had let the contents of his letter to the king be known, there is also little doubt what the result would have been. Indeed, an example is available. On Thursday, July 11, 1918, the following ad appeared in the *St. Cloud Journal-Press.*

> SO THAT EVERYONE IN ST. CLOUD MAY KNOW
>
> There are a few pinheads in St. Cloud. There are also a few snakes, lizards, tarantulas, scorpions, vinegaroons, gila monsters, parasites, and human leeches in St. Cloud. All such are commonly known as knockers. A knocker is not human but only an

escaped imp from hell. The Pan Motor Company has quite a few hammers but they are all in its big drop forge plant.

We have just received a letter from Mr. Ben K. Duffy, one of our special representatives in Denver, Colorado. The letter is self-explanatory. Every right-thinking man in St. Cloud should make it his business to spot the knockers and give them just so many minutes to get beyond the city limits. We cannot build a city and allow the fork-tongued human snakes to crawl around in the city. We do not know of any Pan Motor stock for sale at less than $10.00 a share. And any man offering his stock for sale for less than $10.00 a share is an enemy to the up-building and development of this city, and is an undesirable citizen. Here is the letter that we received from Mr. Duffy in Denver. Read it and then locate the knocker.

"A man from Parker, Colorado, named Henry Haltimer came to St. Cloud a short time ago to look over the plant with intentions of investing $2000 cash in our stock. Mr. M. J. Casey has already sold this man and his family $600 worth of stock, and ribbed him up to come there and buy $2000 more cash. Unfortunately he arrived in St. Cloud on Sunday and went to some restaurant there and the man who runs the restaurant told him he would sell him all he could carry away at $8.00 a share. This killed him dead. He took the next train for Colorado and has been some knocker ever since."

All Pan Motor Company employees and friends are respectfully requested to report to me the name and address of any knockers in this city. And I offer a $50.00 cash reward for the name and address of the knocker named in Mr. Duffy's letter

S. C. Pandolfo

So much for Pandolfo's statement that he wouldn't condemn a man who disagreed with him. With this exhibition of quick and violent reaction to criticism, it was obvious that little open resistance to the company would be voiced in St. Cloud by those of faint heart.

The kingdom of Siam was a small loss to Pandolfo's agents. Many of the salesmen hired by his fiscal agency had previously worked for Pandolfo in what he called "my gigantic Life Insurance Agency." They were, therefore, familiar with Pandolfo's techniques, which meant that they sold hard. In April 1918, for example, his force of 396 agents sold a total of 43,059½ shares of Pan stock. With the addition of 929 shares that came in directly through mail solicitation, sales totalled almost $440,000 for the one month. During May, 393 salesmen were active and they accounted for

48,141½ shares with another 1071 shares coming in by mail. One day alone, May 6, 1918, the company received more than $30,000 in payments at the St. Cloud offices. Minnesota-based salesmen were doing well too; the company now counted almost 9,000 stockholders in its home state.

On that day, May 6, Pandolfo wrote a letter to appear in the back of the *Pan Stock Sales Record*, published by the fiscal agency of the company and listing the sales records for the month of April. In bold type at the top of the first page was the statement:

> UNTIL FURTHER NOTICE, WE WILL ACCEPT LIBERTY BONDS AT PAR FROM THOSE SUBSCRIBING FOR PAN MOTOR STOCK—PROVIDED ALL THE NOT-DUE INTEREST COUPONS ARE ATTACHED. WE WILL NOT ALLOW ANY ACCRUED INTEREST ON THESE BONDS, AND ANY NOT-DUE INTEREST COUPONS WHICH MAY BE DETACHED WILL BE CHARGED AGAINST THE AGENT SENDING IN SAME.

The rest of the letter indicated how enthusiastic Pandolfo could be about the sale of Pan stock when writing to his "men in the field."

> There never was more money in circulation than there is now. Everybody has some money. The weather is fine—the roads are good—and everybody is happy and prosperous.
>
> Get out among the farmers, the ranchmen, and the small interior places and crowd for results. I want every salesman to do his level best in May. . . .
>
> At the close of business May 2, we had 31,206 subscribers and stockholders—and 8513 of them live in Minnesota—our Home State. We have subscribers and stockholders who live in 42 states, Canada, England, and France. We have more subscribers and stockholders in Minnesota than in any other one state—Colorado coming second with over 7000. The best way to judge any proposition is how it is regarded at home.
>
> If conditions should develop so that the passenger [car] industry should be seriously handicapped during the war, the Pan Motor Company will be able to make a great success for its stockholders out of their immense drop forge plant, which should be completed and in operation by July or August, this year, and also by devoting a great deal of its attention to the manufacturing of Tractors—so come what may, the Pan Motor Company is going to make for its stockholders a big success and I believe will show a substantial dividend earning for its stockholders this year. All we need is sufficient capital to carry out our plans. We are counting

> on you—the stock sales organization—our friends in the field, to get this capital for us without delay, thereby benefitting both the Pan Motor Company and yourselves.

It is impossible to predict how fast the sales would have spiraled had not the Minnesota State Securities Commission called a hearing on May 13, 1918, to determine if the sales methods of the Pan Motor Company needed closer scrutiny and better control by the Board of Directors.

There are several versions as to why the hearings were held. It began, according to one interpretation, when a representative of the Minneapolis Advertising Club visited Pandolfo to discuss the advertising being circulated by the fiscal agency. After a heated discussion, according to a witness, Pandolfo grabbed the man by one shoulder and the seat of his pants and rapidly guided him to the door. The witness, Richard Daggy, the printing salesman from Webb Publishing Company in St. Paul, watched in astonishment and with misgivings. He later advised Pandolfo he shouldn't have done it; only trouble could result from such a display of temper. Pandolfo replied angrily, "No 50-dollar-a week bastard is going to shove me around. He came in here to tell me we were lying in our advertising!"

The Associated Advertising Clubs of the World, the loosely-knit forerunner of the Better Business Bureau, was then in the middle of a campaign promoting "Truth in Advertising." In the May 1918, issue of their magazine, *Associated Advertising*, the association broached its attack on the Pan Motor Company and Pandolfo. Under the title, "Flowery Statements Describe Motor Stock," it published a few paragraphs which, while not finding anything specific to condemn, left little doubt as to what the future references to the Pan Motor Company would be like in that publication.

> There is a world-wide demand for an automobile that has no respect for bad roads, mountain passes, gullies or any other kind of road difficulties—opportunity is now knocking at your door.
>
> These and many other flowery statements were embraced in a letter to Des Moines people from one Johnson, a stock salesman for the Pan Motor Company of St. Cloud, Minn., and Frank Armstrong, secretary of the Associated Vigilance Committee of Iowa, investigated.
>
> He was informed the company was licensed under the Minnesota blue sky law and that the stock, of $5 par value, was being sold at $10, $5 of which, he was informed, was going into the treasury and $5 into promotion expense. The authorized capitalization is $5,000,000.
>
> The president of the company, Mr. Armstrong was informed, is a former insurance man who at one time went through bankruptcy, but the investigation showed that several St. Cloud

> bankers were stockholders in the enterprise. The president of the company, as a personal venture, has laid out a 40-acre subdivision at St. Cloud, Mr. Armstrong was informed, and has announced that he is going to build himself a $15,000 home there.
>
> The possibility that the Government might put some restriction upon the building of passenger cars, Mr. Armstrong found, apparently had not bothered the promoters of Pan Motor.
>
> Mr. Armstrong's report on the case was not of a character that would be likely to help Johnson, the stock salesman.

The article contained several errors of fact, yet it presented a rumor—the Government restriction on construction of pleasure cars—as a fact, one that should have bothered the company.

Pandolfo fought back. He began to give wide circulation to a letter written on the stationary of the St. Cloud Advertising Club, the local affiliate of the Associated Advertising Clubs of the World. The letter was dated May 11, 1918.

> TO WHOM IT MAY CONCERN:
>
> I have received and read the literature issued by the Pan Motor Company and its Fiscal Agency, and there are no misleading or untrue statements in same.
>
> The Pan Motor Company stands well among the representative people of its Home Town.
>
> Any attack on the Pan Motor Company or its President, Mr. S. C. Pandolfo, on account of their advertising, is unwarranted, unjust, unfair, and malicious, and when this attack comes from unfriendly sources, it seems to me to be inspired by those seeking to destroy this Company.

The letter was signed by the secretary-treasurer of the St. Cloud Advertising Club, Daniel J. Fouquette.

A second version of the reason for the attacks on the Pan Motor Company, one occasionally endorsed by Pandolfo himself, although he supported any and all versions at one time or another, was that they were motivated by the jealousy of Minneapolis businessmen who disliked seeing an enterprise with the potential of Pan out of their reach. For some reason, Pandolfo did not attribute the same attitude to the business community of St. Paul. In any case, naming Minneapolis as the source of the attacks had about the same validity as did the later stories that sought to blame Detroit auto makers for the Pan Motor Company's ultimate demise. They were the ones who would benefit most by the failure, the reasoning ran, therefore they must be the culprits.

The night before the Minnesota Securities Commission hearings were to start in St. Paul, a meeting was held in St. Cloud. At the meeting Pandolfo claimed that if the Pan Motor Company was going to be in quantity production by July 1, it would need $75,000 immediately. Volunteers at that meeting subscribed $14,500, enough to assure the continued life of the company but not the quantity production of the Model A Pan, still undergoing tests.

The Pan Motor Company had been informed of the meeting of the Securities Commission by a notice asking it to appear before the commissioners and show cause why its permit to sell stock in the state of Minnesota should not be revoked. More than 200 St. Cloud people journeyed to St. Paul for the first day of the hearings. It was expected the hearing would be short, but it continued for a week and a half. On the first day, May 13, 1918, in addition to the general delegation from St. Cloud, Pandolfo had the support of his legal counsel, state Senator John D. Sullivan, former senator Ripley B. Brower, both of St. Cloud, and St. Paul attorney Carl W. Cummins. Also attending and testifying in Pandolfo's behalf was Bishop Joseph F. Busch of St. Cloud.

Ostensibly, the complaint against the company concerned a report that they were paying a 50 percent commission on sale of the stock; it should have paid no more than 25 percent. But before the hearing ended much of Pandolfo's personal history had been aired, most of it by Pandolfo himself, and the Pan Motor Company's advertising was closely scrutinized.

Most of the testimony during the first day of the hearing came from Leland Duxbury, state representative from Caledonia, Minnesota, and Ira B. Henthorne, Minneapolis representative of the Associated Advertising Clubs of the World. Both men said they had visited Texas in their investigation of Pandolfo. But when they were asked by Pandolfo's counsel if they had made any effort to check carefully into 73 of the 75 sources of letters endorsing Pandolfo, they admitted they had not.

Brower and Cummins then read into the record of the hearing the history of Pandolfo's insurance business in Texas. The cotton crop in Texas failed, and Pandolfo's notes were not paid. His insurance business failed, and, heavily in debt, he left Texas, started another business and paid off his debts.

As the hearing progressed during the rest of the week, Pandolfo had reason to be pleased. Henthorne said he had been employed by the National Vigilance Committee of the Associated Advertising Clubs of the World, headquartered in Indianapolis, and he had spent several weeks investigating the Pan Motor Company and Pandolfo. Pandolfo smiled broadly during an exchange between lawyer Cummins and witness Henthorne in which Henthorne admitted that his investigation of the Pan Motor Company, which had taken him to Texas, had not taken him to St. Cloud, only 75 miles from Minneapolis.

Henthorne would get another chance under more favorable conditions a year later in Chicago, but for now the nature of the hearing changed when the next witness testified. He was Charles J. Andre, secretary of the commission, and his testimony indicated that the investigation of the Pan Motor Company resulted when reports reached the commission that the company was spending more on promotion than was thought proper for publicly owned corporations under Minnesota law. To the direct question, "Who brought in those reports and suggested the investigation?" he replied, "The Associated Advertising Clubs of the World."

With that answer, the hearing's complexion changed from that of a probe of serious wrong-doing to one of meddlesome interference in a corporation by a quasi-official private organization with the somewhat unwilling assistance of a state agency. It was apparent that the commission was neutral concerning the Pan Motor Company; they had been supplied with information and had been requested to make an investigation. As a regulatory agency of the state, they complied.

Quite obviously, without the evidence of the factory complex then burgeoning at St. Cloud, the promotional efforts of the company could easily have warranted an investigation. An enormous amount of money was pouring into the treasury of the Pan Motor Company and pouring right out almost as fast, and the flamboyance and pressure of Pandolfo's sales campaigns sounded alien in an industry where most of the money came from conservative sources. Here was an automobile company being promoted among small investors, most of whom had never invested ten cents in any large business before and who were as ignorant of the financial aspects of the automotive industry as they were of international commerce. The approach to such investors had to be different, and it was, Pandolfo's attorneys explained. Only a certain amount of the income from stock sales was being spent on promotion, they said. A five-minute walk around the factory grounds at St. Cloud would show where the greatest share of the money was going. Every building was substantially built, equipped with the most modern facilities, and the machinery in the plant was ample and expensive. And of the money earmarked "surplus," a substantial part of this was being directed to promoting the car as well as the sale of stock.

The officers of the company were called to testify, and they corroborated the statements of Charles Schwab, Pan Motor treasurer, that 50 percent of the revenue from stock sales went to the capital fund while the remainder was put into the surplus, used to pay the sales expenses, commissions, and various other promotional expenses. Schwab pointed out that this arrangement was not hidden, that it was, in fact, a part of every contract form the company used in selling stock, and it was frequently explained in detail as a major part of the unique organizational plan of the Pan Motor Company. J. B. Sanborn, chairman of the commission, closely questioned each Board member on the nature of their work as director of the company.

Near the end of the hearing Pandolfo was called, and he proved to be as interesting a speaker under the trial-like atmosphere of the hearing as he was when freewheeling on the stages of the local theatres. He claimed that most of his trouble stemmed from his hot temper and the state of Texas. "If I can be frank here without sounding too boastful," he said, "I conducted the largest insurance agency in the country from offices in Texas, and frequently my office wrote over 1,500,000 a month in insurance. In fact, my success led many people to be against me for that reason alone. Many made efforts to discredit me. J. F. Patterson, the Texas insurance commissioner at that time, was against me. But he was a wanted man; he had killed someone. He was an appointee of Governor Ferguson, who was later impeached. It has been said that my license to sell insurance in Texas was revoked. The truth is, I abandoned it. It was not worth the fight that crooked administration would have put me through. I was doing all right outside that state until the cotton crop failed. I had been out of Texas for two months when I was informed that my license had been revoked.

"In January of 1917, when I went to St. Cloud, I told the directors to investigate me. For their peace of mind, as well as my own, I wanted them to hear everything that would be said against me. They know the truth. They completed a searching inquiry, not only through the people I had told them to contact, but also through their own sources. They asked me to come back and answer some questions. The result is that the people of St. Cloud have full confidence in my honesty and my sincerity."

His face reddened when he was asked about the Associated Advertising Clubs of the World. "In that short article in their magazine they have lied several times. Since December, 1917, I have been living in the house they say I plan to build. They say my Texas license was revoked; it was not, really. They say I went through bankruptcy; I did not. If they were so eager to conduct a fair investigation of the Pan Motor Company why didn't they come to St. Cloud and ask us what they wanted to know? Or why didn't they trust their own St. Cloud branch of the Association?" He read the letter Daniel Fouquette had written concerning the company's advertising. "Now, why didn't they ask this man? He was right on the spot. Or didn't they trust him on a local matter? Then why trust Mr. Armstrong in Des Moines? Or Mr. Henthorne in Minneapolis? Mr. Fouquette is not a member of our company; he would have no reason to lie about us. He is a banker and he knows business matters. Why didn't they ask him? I'll tell you. Because someone in Minneapolis wanted this organization to do their dirty work for them."

Brower asked Pandolfo about the price of Pan Motor stock. "We're capitalized at five million dollars, but we will realize ten million dollars from the sale of the stock. Now, I don't see anything wrong in that. We state it very plainly whenever we well the stock. We're taking out the expenses of organizing the business right at the beginning. Any other corporation would say they were going to capitalize at five million and then spend one million or more in the effort to set up a corporation, which can only be worth four million after that. We say we'll be worth five million dollars, and we'll be worth twice that much. Now, what's wrong with that?"

The hearings finally closed on Wednesday, May 22, 1918. The Securities Commission directed the company to modify its bookkeeping methods to permit the directors more power in conducting the affairs of the company, and it strongly suggested a new contract with the fiscal agent, reducing the commissions paid for sale of the company's stock.

The formal report of the commission was issued the following Tuesday, May 28. The last section of the report contained the meat of it.

> 17. The evidence presented does not support the charge that the company has placed before the public deceptive and misleading advertising regarding its securities.
> 18. There is no evidence to support the charge that the company did not furnish to the Commission all of its prospectuses, circulars and advertising used by it in conjunction with the sale of its securities.
> 19. The evidence does not justify a finding to the effect that the plan of business of the company as now proposed and modified by the resolutions and contract of May 23, 1918, is of such a nature that the sale of the capital stock of the company is likely to work a fraud upon the purchasers thereof, that the stock of the company is not fraudulent, and that the sale thereof is not, in the opinion of this Commission, in violation of Chapter 429, General Laws of Minnesota, 1917, and as conclusion
>
> That the order to show cause should be vacated
> and discharged. Dated May 23, 1918
> State Securities Commission of Minnesota

The order was signed by Andrew E. Fritz, president of the Commission, John B. Sanborn and M. J. Brown, Commissioners, and attested by Charles J. Andre, secretary.

On August 1, 1918, the Pan Motor Company was issued a new license by the Commission. It was numbered 100,035 and carried the typed-in notice: "This license is issued in extension and in lieu of license No. 100,035 issued September 8, 1917." The license stated that the "Pan Motor Company has been and hereby is authorized to offer for sale in Minnesota and other states not to exceed 1,000,000 shares of its capital stock at not to exceed $10.00 per share on the condition, however, that from and after August 15, 1918, the commissions and all selling expense incidental to the sale of said stock shall not exceed 20 percent of the selling price."

This was the only public reference to a meeting that attempted to change Pandolfo's control of the company and which, introduced during the trial in Chicago, became known as "the resolution of May 25."

In the middle of June 1918, Pandolfo wrote a newsletter to his salesmen, detailing their May sales records, and under the headline YOUR TIME IS YOUR CAPITAL—MAKE IT EARN DIVIDENDS, he started off, "Well, Boys, congratulations to you on your May record. It is very gratifying to note that our May sales amounted to almost one-half million dollars." He pointed out that when the mail sales were added in, a new monthly record had been achieved: 49,212½ shares. The salesmen were all invited to attend the Fourth of July celebration and the first annual stockholders meeting in St. Cloud on July 4th and 5th, and to bring any prospects who were "Bell Wethers," [sic] not only to sell them stock on the grounds but to use their influence when they returned home. The letter closed with a reminder and a bit of metaphorical advice. "Please bear in mind that in my opinion, you are all conferring a great favor on everyone whom you induce to buy Pan Motor stock and that I believe Pan Motor stock is one of the safest and offers more possibilities for profit than any other investment the people ever had a chance to buy. Get your steam up to a thousand-pound pressure and keep it there—get in high gear and throw your throttle wide open and stop only at stations where you take on business."

Only slightly vexed by the state Securities Commission hearing and more buoyed up by the continuing gain in stock sales, the company was host at its first stockholders' meeting on July 4th and 5th. More than one thousand stockholders were present in person in the main assembly building, and a majority of the outstanding stock, then around 38,000 paid-up shares, was represented at the meeting. Minnesota, Iowa, North and South Dakota stockholders were generously represented, but there were also shareholders from as far east as Ohio and as far west as California.

They gathered in an assembly room at the north end of the factory building where a large platform had been erected and surrounded by bench seats. Pandolfo, on a motion by C. S. Bunnell, seconded by William B. Mitchell, was elected temporary chairman of the meeting. The Board of Directors was unanimously reelected for the following year, and Pandolfo called upon C. F. Ladner, Fred Schilplin, and R. B. Brower for brief statements in regard to the conduct of the company's affairs. Brower's short but stirring address received a tremendous ovation when he complimented the management for offering the government the use of the factory for war production.

The stockholders, again unanimously, passed a resolution that described their feelings concerning the recent difficulties the company had gone through.

> RESOLVED, by the stockholders of Pan Motor Company, in annual stockholders' meeting assembled, that a careful review of the advertising matter of this Company as heretofore issued, does not, in our opinion, do full and complete justice to the development and progress of the Company, as we have familiarized ourselves with the same upon the ground. We congratulate

> the management of this Company upon the business ability and capacity displayed and the progress that has been made in the development of the plant and property of the Company. The literature and advertising matter of this Company does not, in fact, in our opinion, fully reflect the entire progress made during the past year in the building, equipment and development of the Company's work and property.
>
> The Advertising Department of this Company is to be commended upon its conservative statements in respect to the Company's progress and development. In fact, the advertising matter of the Company, could, in our judgment, accurately and legitimately present greater claims of development and progress.

Near the close of the meeting Pandolfo reviewed the company's progress and outlined the future business policy. "The first duty of this company, I'm certain you will agree, is to serve the government of the United States in this time of crisis. Whatever we are called upon to do, that we will do. Our second duty is to protect the interests of our stockholders and earn for them a fair dividend on their investment. I am confident that our business policy is one that will accomplish our objectives in a most satisfactory manner.

"Despite the recent difficulties we have had in connection with the sale of our stock, I appeal to all of you, and through you to your friends, not to dispose of your stock. The investment you have made in the Pan Motor Company is as good a one as it is possible to make, and a better one now than it ever was."

For the first time, in public at least, Pandolfo made reference to the fact that it might take several years to fully "develop and round out" the company.

The financial statement of the company was handed out to stockholders and contained no surprises except, perhaps, for the figure assigned to intangibles: $1,585,632.05

Pandolfo's letter to his stock sales force, written on August 6 to accompany the July sales record, carried his usual sales pep talk: "The country is universally prosperous and we have a bountiful crop, which is now mostly harvested, and it is bringing a big price, and weather and road conditions are good." During July, 405 salesmen had sold 46,808½ shares of Pan stock, and the addition of 781 shares sold by mail made the total for July 47,589½ shares.

One paragraph in Pandolfo's letter seemed to hint at events to come, and while it may not have struck those who read it at that time, it seems to be the whole point of the letter when read in the light of later events.

> The Pan Motor Company is a good faith proposition from start to finish. It was conceived in good faith, and the efforts of all the people connected with it from the beginning up to now have

> been strenuous and in good faith along the line of trying to make this company a success for those who have put their money in it. We want all our salesmen to learn all about the Pan Motor Company and the people connected with it. Our salesmen should carefully read and study all literature that we send them. We want all of our salesmen to be conscientious in their work and to be on their guard in regard to any statements they may make concerning the company and the people with it. In other words, Pan Motor stock can be sold more quickly and more readily by telling the absolute truth about this company. Sincerity carries conviction.

Pandolfo closed with a somewhat uncharacteristic wish. After hoping that they would make more money for themselves in August than ever before, he added, "And I hope you have the courage and foresight to save it."

A month later, the subdued tone of his letter written to accompany the August sales record was apparent in the first sentence: "Everything considered, the August sales record was very good." With 366 salesmen, and the mail sale of 460 shares, 44,943½ shares were sold. Even though the letter was going out near the end of the month, salesmen were cautioned that while they should sell hard in September, they should keep in mind that the fourth Liberty Bond Drive would be starting soon, and they should not infringe on it unduly.

> EVERY SALESMAN SHOULD EXERT EVERY EFFORT THAT HE IS CAPABLE OF BETWEEN NOW AND THE COMMENCEMENT OF THE FOURTH LIBERTY LOAN DRIVE; because after that drive begins, and during the drive, selling securities other that those offered by the Government will be somewhat different than at other times. We want all of our Salesmen to cooperate with the Government, in every way possible, in helping put over the Fourth Liberty Loan. I think it the proper thing for them to do. Of course, in the meantime, it may be very convenient, now and then, for you to make a sale without in any way reflecting on or detracting from your own proposition. We want all of our Salesmen to use good sense and discretion during the Liberty Loan Drive. Those who are alive to the situation will be able to not only help the Government, but also lay the foundation for a very satisfactory business for themselves later.

In retrospect, it sounds as though Pandolfo knew exactly what was in his immediate future when he wrote those lines.

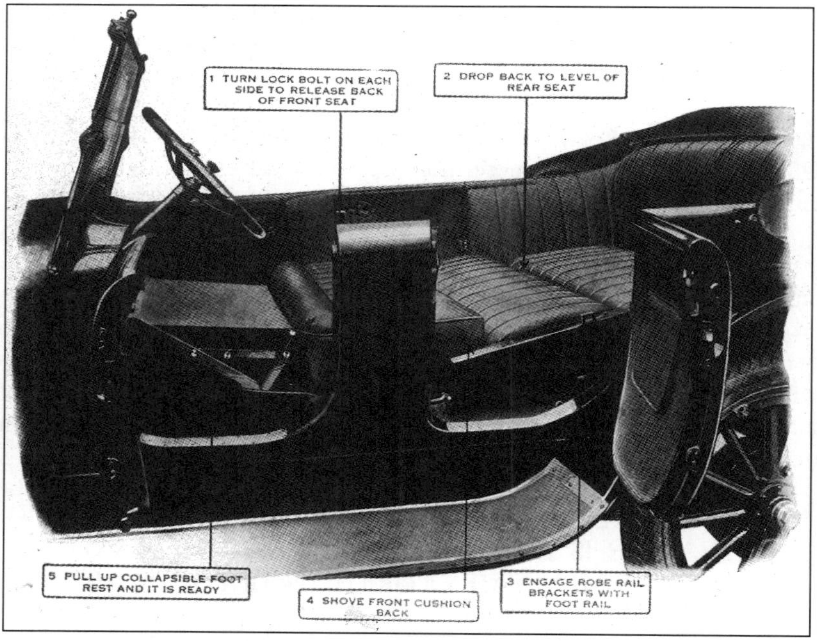

The convertible bed feature for the Pan Model A was a talking point for Pandolfo, but by the time the car reached the production stage, he no longer was president of the Pan Motor Company.

CHAPTER VII

PICTORIAL PROOF OF PROGRESS

PAN SALESMEN SOLD stock not only in competition with Liberty Bond drives but also under increasingly direct attacks from several groups, some definitely known, and others shapeless and shadowy. The aggressive tactics used by many of the stock salesmen were certainly responsible for some of the attacks, but the concerted efforts of other groups—the Associated Advertising Clubs of the World (who had not given up after their bout with the Securities Commission), a western bankers' group, and the securities commissions of several other states—were driving the Pan Motor Company into a serious confrontation with the Capital Issues Committee, the securities investigating branch of the United States Congress.

One of the first groups to separate from the murky miasma of investigative stockholder groups was identified as the Monte Vista (Colorado) Stock Sales Investigation Committee, its name already suggesting the conclusion it would reach.

Pandolfo was convinced that the "committee" was simply a front for the bankers of southern Colorado who he said had been feeling the pinch of the withdrawals made in order to buy Pan stock. He offered a $50 reward to anyone who could show him that any member of this committee was also a stockholder in the Pan Motor Company. There were no takers. He claimed that the committee had sent only one man, C. H. Kohler, to St. Cloud to investigate.

"When Mr. Kohler was in St. Cloud his attitude was one of antagonism from the very beginning. I asked him if there were certain things that he saw and certain buildings that he was in and went through, and he said 'No.' I then insisted on having him stay overnight until the following day so I might have someone go with him through all of our buildings and offices. He told me he had looked through the windows of some of these buildings and that he had seen all that he cared to see."

Kohler's primary objection to the Pan Motor Company was that some of the Pan stock agents had sold notes at big discounts. "I made it plain to him," Pandolfo said, "that we pay some of our agents 15 percent to sell Pan motor stock and that frequently an agent will take a note for the first payment, amounting to five percent or ten percent more, as a general rule, than his commission on the sale would amount to, and that it is universally customary for all agents to sell such notes. If the agents were blocked in selling their notes to the local banks, they were driven to selling them to other people, and as long as the company got what was coming to it out of the proceeds of those notes, it is nobody's business how much of the agent's commission he is losing by discounting notes."

The *Monte Vista Journal* had printed a second story on Pan Motor in which they stated that the company had outstanding obligations of $500,000. Pandolfo's ire was highly visible in his criticism of this statement. "I wonder what kind of 'dope' the Monte Vista Investigation Committee takes, or what kind of opiated tobacco they smoke."

His more formal answer was the May 31, 1918, Statement of Financial Condition that had been presented at the annual stockholders meeting in July. He also quoted the resolutions the stockholders had passed and noted that the stockholders themselves seemed satisfied with the conduct of the company. It was only the Monte Vista Committee, none of whom held stock in the company, who seemed upset. Pandolfo's tendency to write himself into a lather when he warmed to his subject is apparent in the following:

> Old Tops, I suggest that you back up, lay off, and from now on attend strictly to your own business, and confine your playing altogether in your own backyard. If the bankers in the Monte Vista district do not bury their hammers and lay off interfering with the Pan Motor Company's business in that territory, I shall immediately take steps to organize a bank in that territory that will be friendly to the Pan Motor Company, and will lend money not to exceed 6%, and we will make it the people's bank. If the merchants in that district continue to use their hammers, I shall furnish the avenues for the bulk of outside capital to put up a large general store, to be run on the cooperative plan.

He invited any and all interested in either proposition to write to him, and he continued his attack on a new line.

> Old Chaps, we have the 'dope' on you, and we know all about your little conspiracy, and we might make your eyes bulge out and your hair stand up if we are forced to show your hole cards and if we are compelled to open up your little play house and let others look in.

The ferocity of Pandolfo's rebuttal may have slowed further attacks from the Monte Vista sector, but there were more springing up in other quarters. Pandolfo found it advantageous to circulate a letter from Isaac B.

Stevens, Secretary of State from Tennessee. Some time in July, Pandolfo had received a wire from Stevens advising that he (Stevens) would have to revoke the company's permit to sell stock in Tennessee on the basis of information that had come to him. Pandolfo immediately requested a more thorough investigation, and Stevens came up to St. Cloud to conduct it. His decision, after visiting the plant, was expressed in a letter to Ira Henthorne, and Stevens graciously sent a copy to Pandolfo.

August 24, 1918

Mr. I. B. Henthorne, Sec.,
Vigilance Committee Minnesota Adv. Forum
Minneapolis, Minn.

My Dear Sir:

I have just this morning returned from a trip to St. Cloud for the purpose of inspecting the Pan Motor Co., also for the purpose of investigating their use of our letter dated Oct. 24, 1917, and, pursuant to my promise to you, I desire to advise you of my findings.

In the first place I discover that Mr. S. C. Pandolfo, the President and General Manager of the Pan Motor Company, is most an elegant and substantial man. Further, that he is honest, diligent, and without any desire whatsoever to secrete any material fact concerning the upbuilding of his enterprise.

I also find there one of the most splendid industrial developments in the entire Northwest, and I must say that it was a very pleasant surprise. I find that in the management of the affairs of the Pan Motor Co., that Mr. Pandolfo has surrounded himself with the very best talent obtainable; that many of his workmen have held the highest positions with other concerns of similar character in the United States. He has a splendid organization and a most unusual and searching system of accounting, which makes it possible for him to reach in that particular the highest state of perfection.

I went through every department and over the entire plant, and it seems to me that everything is looked after in scientific detail, and that the plant and machinery which is being installed are most progressive and up-to-date. The plant is being equipped so that if he should at any time decide to depart from the manufacture of cars, that there are many other lines of mechanical operation to which the plant will be adapted. The very remarkable part to me is that he is able, when many other institutions are suffering for lack of priority, to get any and everything he needs for the equipment of the plant. He is now

> about to enter upon contracts for the government which will no doubt prove very profitable and certainly will be a great aid in winning the war. If Tennessee had such a man as Pandolfo and such an industrial enterprise as he is building in Minnesota, it would be distinctly proud of him and in every way co-operate with him to make it a great success.
>
> As to the use of the letter, I came readily to the conclusion that the limited use he made was altogether justified, and I advised him if a further use of the letter would be valuable to the institution, which would necessarily be valuable to the commonwealth, he was at liberty to use it. It seems to me that St. Cloud is ideally located for the establishment of a concern like this, and I observed that the substantial people of that city and community were very enthusiastically behind Mr. Pandolfo. I am sure you will be pleased to have your own citizens and your own institution so highly lauded, but the facts justify even more than I have said.
>
> Very truly yours,
> Ike B. Stevens,
> Secretary of State

Of course, the letter was not what Henthorne was looking for, but late in the fall of 1918 he found the news from St. Cloud more to his purpose. On November 16, 1918, five days after the Armistice ending World War I had been signed, S. C. Pandolfo and John Barritt appeared in United States District Court in Fergus Falls, Minnesota, to plead not guilty to an indictment brought three days before by the grand jury; the indictment charged the men with using the mails in furtherance of a scheme to defraud.

The floodgates were opening.

Specifically, the indictment charged that Pandolfo and Barritt had, on July 1, 1916, devised a scheme to defraud consisting, in short, of the Pan Motor Company. The four counts in the indictment all involved letters written to stockholders or prospective stockholders of the company. The first letter was dated March 14, 1918, to Victor Bourg of Watson, Colorado, and in it Barritt and Pandolfo congratulated Mr. Bourg on becoming a stockholder in the Pan Motor Company. He was informed that despite the fact that the certificate stated that the par value of the stock was $5.00, it was actually worth what he had paid for it, $10.00.

The second count consisted of a letter to William S. Atwood of Minneapolis, written on March 15, 1918. Mr. Atwood was again asked, as he apparently had been several times before, to buy stock in Pan. He was advised that the company was at that time manufacturing automobiles in its first building and was starting construction of its drop forge. The letter went on to claim that "The Pan-Powered-Tank-Tractor, the Farmers' War Tank, together with our passenger car, took the visitors by storm at the

Denver, Chicago, Minneapolis, Kansas City and Des Moines Shows." The specific charge here was that the Pan engine was never used in the tractor.

The third count consisted of a letter written on November 5, 1917, to G. S. Humphrey of Tyrone, Oklahoma. The letter began by telling Humphrey the number of stockholders in the company and then stated that Liberty Bonds would be accepted for payment of stock subscriptions the same as cash "if delivery of the bonds can be made now."

A letter written on June 5, 1917, to Roscoe M. Collins of Eaton, Colorado, constituted the fourth count of the indictment. Collins was asked to send in his unpaid balance of $50 at once. The letter continued:

> Our first car will be completed and on exhibition about the 15th of this month. It will be "Some # car!" We now have nearly four thousand subscribers and stockholders in 28 states. We are doing things. . . . We have orders for nearly three thousand automobiles, and by making a net profit of only $100 per car, we have in sight approximately 300,000 dollars of profit right now, which we should receive just as soon as we can make deliveries and gather in the money.

At the prelininary hearing in Fergus Falls, state Senator Ripley B. Brower, appearing as attorney for the Pan officers, asked for an immediate trial. "Government contracts worth three to 400,000 dollars will be jeopardized if the charges are allowed to stand any length of time," Brower insisted. "There are certain interests opposed to an automobile manufacturing concern in the Northwest that have been trying to hamper the Pan Motor Company for some time."

United States District Attorney Alfred Jacques asked that the trial be deferred. He required more time to make a more extended examination of the company's books and to summon witnesses from almost every state in the Union to properly present the case.

Judge Page Morris weighed both arguments, then stated that if it was the government's intention to warn prospective investors in the company by seeking an early indictment while not yet ready to go to trial, the warning was now given. On the other hand, if the company were to be found blameless it would be unfair to deny them their opportunity for due process as quickly as possible. He set January 3, 1919, as the date for the trial.

Before the end of November, Pandolfo was in Minneapolis testifying before a subcommittee of the Capital Issues Committee of the federal government. This committee, created by the War Finance Corporation Act, was authorized "to investigate, pass upon, and determine whether it is compatible with the national interest that there should be sold or offered for sale or for subscription any issue. . . of securities. . . ." The object of the senate committee was to conserve the financial resources, labor, and material essential to the prosecution of the war.

When Pandolfo applied for permission to sell an additional 360,000 shares of Pan stock, the committee notified the company that the officers would have to appear and give testimony. Pandolfo appeared before a subcommittee in Minneapolis and later before the whole committee in Washington, D.C.

On November 29, the committee disapproved the company's application to issue the additional stock. In its formal report, issued in mid-December, the committee stated that the company had been formed by men who had no experience in automobile production, that it could not fulfill the claims it had made in its literature, that its financial plan was suspect to put it temperately, and that it had no immediate possibility of getting into quantity production and repaying its investors.

On the whole, Pandolfo had sufficient reason to label the report "damnable lies," which he did. In its first conclusion, the committee made an assumption when it stated that "the enterprise was conceived by an individual having no previous experience in the business and without models, designs, or definite plans for production." Pandolfo had never indicated that he would play a great part in the design of the Pan car to any great or technical extent. His experience had been in management, promotion and sales, and if there was any doubt of his ability here one had only to look at the rest of the committee's report wherein it found the success of the company to that point "remarkable."

The committee also complained that the original concept of the Pan car had not advanced beyond the experimental stage in nearly two years. This statement displayed an ignorance as profound as Pandolfo's when he first stated that starting with nothing he would produce Pan cars within six months. If the interruption caused by the war were not in itself enough to create a delay, the fact that the Pan Motor Company, starting with an empty prairie only 17 or 18 months earlier, was now about a year away from production start-up on its own design should have been the basis for compliments, not a cause for complaint.

That Pan stock was sold in the face of the "Government's efforts to conserve the Nation's wealth," would have been a valid charge if it did not seem to strike only at the size of the Pan Motor Company rather than at its existence. In point of fact all of the Liberty Bond drives had easily met and most had exceeded the quotas set for them where they were competing directly with Pan Motor Company's stock-selling drives. (Some of the Pan directors were responsible for the success of the Liberty Bond drives in St. Cloud.)

However, the complaint that Liberty Bonds were accepted as payment for Pan stock did point out a breech of patriotism by the company because it rightly presumed that the bonds were cashed as soon as they came into the fiscal agent's possession.

The committee's abbreviated statement of Pan Motor's financial plan belied its neutral posture. If dedicated enemies of the company could have dictated the exact wording they wanted to appear in the committee's report, they would not have had to change a word. It was incongruous that this same plan had attracted so many investors who were otherwise astute businessmen.

Finally, in stating that the factory as it stood could be utilized only as an assembling plant and that it could have been built for a fraction of the cost, the Capital Issues Committee displayed a complete lack of judgment or at least a high degree of incompetence. It appeared to deliberately overlook the chronological sequence of the design and construction of the buildings.

In the end, the only other legitimate complaint the committee could make concerned the commissions Pandolfo was paying to the salesmen, in short, the disposition of the surplus fund. And this seems to have been only their complaint; no stockholder, before indictments began to descend on the company, ever registered a complaint about the way the surplus was spent.

What disappointed Pandolfo most perhaps was that his most lavish promotional piece did not convince the legislators in Washington—at least not the ones on the committee—that the Pan Motor Company was a viable enterprise.

Earlier, during April and May 1918, the advertising department of the Pan Motor Company planned a brochure to answer complaints that the company was not moving forward in the production of automobiles. It would detail the progress of the company during the year and a half of its existence. Webb Publishing Company of St. Paul was the low bidder on the early form of the brochure, but during the summer, as the company became the butt of more and more criticism from various sections of the country, the brochure was expanded again and again. Eventually it became one of the most extravagant publications ever produced by any automobile company. It was more than a catalog, although it contained one; it was more than a history of the company, although it included that too, and a brief historical overview of St. Cloud as well.

The brochure grew into a book that was a total presentation of the Pan Motor Company, its officers, its staff, its labor force, its buildings, its machinery, its product, its homes, its home town; it contained everything the Pan Motor Company touched upon and what it hoped to become. One thing about it, however, remained the same during its genesis: from the beginning the name was *Pictorial Proof of Progress.*

The brochure grew into a 270-page book in a 9½ × 12½ inch horizontal format. By the fall of 1918, the book was ready to commit to the printer. The addition of extra pages, color inserts, maps and map pockets, and embossed, padded covers had boosted the price from the original $9500 for 5000 copies to $14,750. This included a special run of 300 copies with gold-leaf added on the cover; these were to be sent to every senator and congressman in Washington and to the governor of every state.

The Capital Issues Committee's unfavorable report had, by now, been sent by congressional representatives to their hometown newspapers, especially in the areas where Pan stock sales had been heavy and the resistance to the company active. In Colorado, on December 7, 1918, the *Grand Junction Daily Sentinel* headlined its story:

> HUNDREDS OF LOCAL PEOPLE HOLD STOCK IN COMPANY WHOSE AFFAIRS ARE BEING PROBED BY GOVERNMENT
>
> Sentinel Urges that No Further Payments Be Made on Pan Motor Stock until Legal Advice Is Secured; Startling Report Made to Congressman Taylor by Government Committee Concerning the Operations of the Company; Sensational Disclosures Are Certain to Follow

The story under these headlines absolved local Pan stock salesmen concluding that they could not have been aware of developments in the St. Cloud-based company. It went on to state that "the operations of the president and high officials of the concern have been reprehensible to say the least." Congressman Edward T. Taylor, of Colorado's Fourth Congressional District, was cited as the source for the news item.

The following week the *Daily Sentinel* printed a statement by publisher Walter Walker "in further reference to the Pan Motor Company and Samuel Pandolfo, its president."

> The Sentinel has no reason to modify in any way the statement it made on Saturday concerning the Pan Motor Company. . . . President Pandolfo, who is now under federal indictment, or none of his insistent representatives can work any bluff on us in this matter.
>
> Neither are we inclined to take a junket trip at the expense of Mr. Pandolfo for the purpose of doing a "white wash" job to please Pandolfo and his associates.
>
> The Sentinel's statement of last Saturday has attracted far more than state-wide attention, and the Sentinel is the first paper in the country to publicly call attention to the affairs of the Pan Motor concern and to warn the people to be sure their investments are safe before making further payments.

The attacks by this and other western newspapers injured the company, but the official warnings from federal and state agencies had a deeper and more lasting effect.

On December 16, 1918, the Minnesota Securities Commission, having granted the company a license first on September 8, 1917, and having revised and reissued it on August 1, 1918, now finally revoked the Pan Motor Company's license to sell stock in Minnesota. (It would never be reinstated while Pandolfo was an officer in the company.) The reason for the revocation, apparently, was the release of the report of the Capital Issues Committee in which it cited the Pan Motor Company as an example of the type of promotion scheme that should be suppressed by the enactment of a Federal Blue Sky law to protect small investors.

The company was not entirely without defenders. The St. Cloud Journal-Press, in reporting the loss of the company's license, blamed the conclusion of the Capital Issues Committee on "Minneapolis interests who went to the limit to injure the company." They added their own sidebar to the story that came over their news wire:

> Senator Knute Nelson and Congressman Harold Knutson had demanded and got the government to send one of its most expert men to investigate the company and his report is said to be most favorable. . . .
>
> There is a belief in St. Cloud that the true cause of the report of the Capital Issues Committee is one of jealousy in Minneapolis. They wanted the plant located there, and certain big businessmen there saw the possibility of buying the plant up cheap if it can be destroyed now. A suspicious circumstance is that the report of the only government official to visit the plant was not given out. However, Pandolfo is a good fighter and will go to the mat with his enemies.

Around the middle of December, Pandolfo called a public meeting to be held in the auditorium of the St. Cloud Institute. In the packed audience were representatives from Minneapolis. J. J. Hilbe, president of the St. Cloud Commercial Club, opened the meeting. "We, as business people of St. Cloud, resent the attitude of animosity so plainly betrayed to us by certain outside interests, which reflects upon the character not only of the Pan Motor Company as an organization, but upon Mr. Pandolfo, its president, and upon the city as a manufacturing center.

"It has been suggested that the Pan Motor Company is a joke, a huge swindle to extort money from people for our own personal gain; that we had no city in which an industry could ever exist; that our railroad facilities are inadequate, our housing facilities far below requirements, and that the labor situation would prove to be insufficient to meet the demands of industry.

"Well, as you all know, St. Cloud is located on two of the largest transcontinental railroad lines in the country. The labor situation must be adequately fulfilled, for we have been supplying labor for the Great Northern shops and the granite industry in a manner more than adequate, and what is more, this labor is high class, much more so than average. We have been building homes at an average of 65 a year, and are in a position to increase our erection schedule."

But Hilbe's generalized, generally mild statements did not suit the mood of Pandolfo and in response to a quick gesture he introduced the motor company president. Pandolfo quickly brought the audience up to date on the company's imbroglios with various regulatory agencies, official and unofficial.

"Last March, Richard H. Lee, of the Associated Advertising Clubs of the World, came all the way from New York City to Minneapolis. What for? To confer with the small peanuts and take a leading part in the activities against the Pan Motor Company. He consorted with Ira B. Henthorne and they both went to see Charles J. Andre, secretary of the Minnesota Securities Commission.

"Andre and Henthorne went to Chicago and called on the *Merchant, Banker and Manufacturer* magazine and passed themselves off as oil people and asked how they might get a write-up in the magazine. They wanted to establish that we had paid for articles which we had reproduced and not got them legitimately.

"Now, who paid their expenses to Chicago? Why—and I want Minneapolis to answer—why did they go to Chicago? The Vigilance Bureau of the Minneapolis Forum is supposed to look after advertising within the limits of Minneapolis. That's where their funds come from. We are not in Minneapolis. We are not in conflict with the Minneapolis parties or any member of that Forum. Why did they go to Chicago in the early part of this year, spend that money, and misrepresent themselves? Now it doesn't take a smart man to guess. And that ain't all!"

Interrupted frequently by shouts and applause, Pandolfo related how Henthorne and Leland Duxbury of the state legislature traveled to the Southwest to interview people who had vouched for him.

"This Duxbury and this Henthorne had a list of over 90 people who had given me letters of endorsement. They called upon seven of those people and tried to get them to retract their statements. They called those people liars. They misrepresented the facts to those people for the purpose of inducing those people to write the state securities commission and demand that their names not be used any further by me and by my salesmen."

Pandolfo was warming to his topic and to his audience. "The First and Security Bank of Minneapolis told Hal Ervin that as long as he remained on the Board of Directors of the Pan Motor Company he need not expect much in a business way from them, and while they could not refuse him credit, it would be much better if he severed his connection with Pan Motor. And Mr. Wold, president of the Federal Reserve Bank, told Ralph Olson, of the St. Cloud First National Bank, that as long as the bankers of St. Cloud were supporting the Pan Motor Company they need not expect any business courtesies from him. Mr. Hanscom and Mr. Schwab, both bankers and both directors, were told practically the same thing.

"You should go through my files and see the evidence I have. I have not fought back because I thought I would give them as much rope as they wanted. Now is the time to call a halt. The Minneapolis Credit Men's Association, Traveling Men's Association, and the Advertising Club and other similar organizations and the big bankers have got to stop. If they do not stop, I am going to stop them by law. I am going to sue the hell out of them."

Several members of the audience came up on stage by invitation and told of their experiences. A doctor from Georgia had bought $30,000 in stock and also had secured a dealership in Georgia. Hearing rumors of trouble for the company, he started back to St. Cloud. On the way to Chicago, a Minneapolis furniture dealer on the train advised him to have nothing to do with the company. The plant was small, the climate was not good, and the fuel situation was worse, the doctor was told.

Another member of the audience told of asking a Minneapolis banker his opinion of the Pan Motor Company; the reply was that it was unreliable.

When Pandolfo demanded a response from the Minneapolis delegation in the audience, Howard Strong, secretary of the Minneapolis Civic and Commerce Association, mounted the stage white-faced and shaken, certain of the response he would get from the pro-Pandolfo crowd. "I have been intensely interested in what Mr. Pandolfo has said, and I must tell you, on behalf of my association and the city of Minneapolis, I resent the charges he has brought against us. I must be one of the arch criminals he talks about; that is, I am a member of the Minneapolis business community. But I find this a unique experience—one town indicting another."

Strong yielded the stage to E. J. Fairfield, vice president of the Minneapolis Civic and Commerce Association. "I want you to know why I came to the platform," Fairfield began. "We have been accused in Minneapolis of being everything under the sun, pretty nearly, and I suppose the accusation was brought to include that of being cowards. But I came up here to show you that we are not cowards. I know that I speak to a very prejudiced audience, so I shall present our case briefly. I couldn't say anything tonight that would influence you to our side.

"Yesterday was the first time I had heard of any trouble between our cities. I was shown Mr. Pandolfo's remarks, which he made at a previous meeting, implying that there was a conspiracy among Minneapolis businessmen to damage the Pan Motor Company. Nothing could be further from the truth. When I came up here I was met at the train by a group of very courteous gentlemen and enjoyed the privilege of going through the Pan plant. It is a magnificent plant. I have visited a large number of factories in my life and time, and this is one of the best I have ever seen. I could find no evidence but what the plant was up for honorable purposes. And I hope that a big success will be made of it.

"I have attended many meetings also, but I have never heard of anything detrimental to the Pan Motor Company being discussed at them."

He went on to say that if one or two or three businessmen of Minneapolis had said or done anything to harm the reputation of the Pan Motor Company they had done so as individuals, not as representatives of any group or as members of any conspiracy by the Civic and Commerce Association.

Fairfield's remarks were received in the stony silence he had predicted. Pandolfo concluded the meeting by asking all in the audience who were with him to rise; the response was unanimous.

The character of the meeting was so bizarre that Chicago newspapers carried reports of it.

In the wake of this turmoil, on Friday, January 2, 1919, Pandolfo, John Barritt, and attorney Ripley Brower returned to Fergus Falls and the district court of Judge Page Morris. In spite of the judge's last warning, District Attorney Alfred Jacques asked for further postponement, citing difficulties in examining the company's books, and getting interviews from numerous stockholders in order to present the case properly. When Brower again demanded immediate trial, Judge Morris agreed and ordered the government to proceed at once. Rather than risk dismissal or a directed acquittal, Jacques withdrew the case.

Brower publicly treated the withdrawal as a complete vindication of the company. With the war in Europe over and the trials in the United States behind them, there was only success in the future of the Pan Motor Company.

The euphoria was short-lived. By January 16, Federal Judge Carpenter quashed a subpoena directing the company to bring all its records to Chicago for examination by another grand jury. It would place too much of a hardship on the company, the judge said, to operate in St. Cloud while all of its corporate records were in Chicago.

But Pan Motor Company's rapid financial growth died that winter.

Pandolfo's efforts to bring in financial help for the company began to sound and look desperate. In a brochure directed to stockholders in Colorado, he asked them to pay the balance of their subscription whether it was due or not. He enclosed three subscription blanks for them to use in getting others to buy stock. "You will observe," he noted, "that there will be no commission paid to any agents on any subscription that comes in on this form."

The brochure—actually another stockholders' committee report—was purported to have been written by men from the area around Grand Junction, and included the editor of the *Grand Junction Daily News*, a rival newspaper to the *Daily Sentinel*, Pandolfo's nemesis in that area.

The report went into such detail that it remains the only source for some information about the company. For example, the Pan Motor accounting department at the time of the committee's visit employed 35 people and occupied the northeast corner of the main building; the total number of employees varied from 319 to 343 and the daily payroll was about $1500.

The report mentioned documents in the committee's possession that, for lack of space, they were unable to include. One such document was the report of the J. G. White Engineering Company of New York. White had examined the company at the government's request and gave the company what the report labeled a "100 percent endorsement."

But even the White report's glowing summary could not combat the bad publicity the company was receiving. The "Colorado Stockholders Report" was sent only to those people concerned with the company; *World's Work*, a nationally distributed, New York-based publication concerned with industry and labor issues, spent much of the space in its January 1919 issue "exposing" confidence men of the period. In an article titled "Pirates of Promotion, Methods of the Industrial Promoters," the authors, Louis Guenther and John K. Barnes, covered the careers of Nova Adolphus Brown, Nicholas Field Wilson, Giles P. Cory, and Samuel C. Pandolfo among others. The final sentence of the article's handling of Pandolfo may be the best clue to its credibility: "As a possible explanation of this promoter's apparent success at St. Cloud, it might be explained that he is generally considered to be a hypnotist."

If he could do it through the mails he was some hypnotist.

Pandolfo was not without other defenders in Colorado. George A. Levy, chief of the Industrial Bureau of the City and County of Denver, was dispatched to St. Cloud to investigate the company. Levy's highly favorable and voluminous—but shallow—report on the company may have gained back some of the stature it had lost, at least in Colorado.

But retorts were too slow for Pandolfo. And even his rancorous vituperation couldn't satisfy his hunger for revenge. On January 5, 1919, two libel suits against the Associated Advertising Clubs of the World were filed in Indianapolis. Filed by the Pan Motor Company and by Samuel C. Pandolfo, they each asked damages of $250,000. On January 7, a million dollar libel suit was filed in Phoenix against the 63 member banks of the Arizona Bankers' Association for publishing in their magazine a letter from an unnamed Texan who cast reflections on the integrity of Pandolfo. On January 22, a million dollar damage suit was filed in Minneapolis against the 50 members of the Minneapolis Advertising Forum. (Among the more prominent members of the Forum were Dayton's, Leader Mercantile Company, Hartman Furniture and Carpet Company, Minneapolis Tribune Company, Journal Printing Company, Russell-Miller Milling Company, Maurice L. Rothschild Company, M. W. Savage factories, F. W. Woolworth Company, and Young-Quinlan Company.) Later, in February, a $400,000 libel suit was filed against the Grand Junction, Colorado, *Daily Sentinel.*

The Pan Motor Company, or rather its Board of Directors, was also on the receiving end of a suit. On the first of February, less than a month after the dismissal of the Fergus Falls indictment, the government sought and got another indictment in Chicago. In addition to Pandolfo and Barritt, the entire Board of Directors, along with recently-resigned H. C.

Ervin and former vice president H. S. Wigle, were accused of being conspirators in a scheme to use the mails to defraud.

St. Cloud, through its Commercial Club and its newspapers, immediately sprang to the defense of the Pan Board. An editorial by Alvah Eastman in the *Journal-Press* claimed that Congressman Taylor of Colorado had stated that the trial had to be moved to Chicago because a fair hearing could not be obtained in Minnesota. Eastman considered the statement an insult to the judges and citizens of the North Star state and concluded his editorial with, for him, strong language. "The indictment is an outrage, and it is humiliating to see government officials doing the dirty work of the pirates of big business."

Legal maneuvering on all sides took up the next several months. In Minneapolis, on February 10, Judge Wilbur Booth ruled that the charge in the Pan Motor suit against the Minneapolis Advertising Forum was too broad; he ordered the company's attorney, J. M. Bradford of Murphy, Bradford, and Cummins, to be more specific. A month later the company filed new charges detailing six causes of action and including Ira B. Henthorne among the indictees.

In the middle of the legal flurries, Pandolfo kept mailing a stream of favorable reports, letters, copies of indictments and his responses, and pleas for financial support. Concerning the Chicago indictment, he commented that if the letters he wrote to stockholders constituted criminal acts, the gentleman who drew the indictment were very charitable, "because he could just as easily have made it eight million instead of only eight."

During the March grand jury term, new evidence was presented in the case against the Pan directors, and the first week in April the grand jury, at the request of District Attorney Charles F. Clyne, dismissed the original eight count indictment and issued a new one of 11 counts. Was this in response to Pandolfo's boast?

As spring melted into summer, the company argued for an early trial date as each day brought more evidence that little additional stock could be sold, nor would present subscribers continue to pay on their accounts, until the problems facing the company were resolved favorably.

The trial was set for November 3, 1919, but on May 8 it was announced that an immediate trial had been granted. Then, on June 6, Judge George A. Carpenter transferred the case to the court of Judge George T. Page and set September 22 as the date. In a short autobiography he published in 1959, Pandolfo gave this version of the events surrounding placement of the trial.

> Just a few days before the Fergus Falls indictment, in the lobby of the St. Paul Hotel, Herman Moeller, then clerk of the [Minnesota] State Supreme Court, overheard two strangers say that if they did not hurry the indictment against me, that in a

few months I would be so far along that nothing would stop me or blow me up. . . .

Just before Christmas a newspaper reporter from Duluth, a friend of mine, made a special trip to St. Cloud to see me and to warn me that if I insisted on going to trial on the first Monday in January, 1919, at Fergus Falls . . . the case would be dismissed and later another indictment would be brought against me in Chicago and that Judge Landis would finally get the case and that I had no chance of victory in the court of Judge Landis. On a previous trip to northwestern Wisconsin, a short distance from Duluth, Judge Landis had made the remark that he didn't need evidence to convict Pandolfo.

Pandolfo then described the two indictments returned by the Chicago grand jury and continued his version of how the trial was finally given to Judge Landis.

Remembering the warning of the newspaper reporter, I went to Chicago and got the case in Judge Carpenter's court. My attorney and I looked over Judge Carpenter's desk and saw Better Business Bureau [Associated Advertising Clubs of the World] propaganda against the Pan Motor Company and S. C. Pandolfo all over his desk. We called Judge Carpenter's attention to those things and he threw the case out of his court. Then we undertook to dodge Judge Landis and to have the case placed in Judge Page's court.

Since filing the libel suit against the Arizona Bankers Association, we had filed about 3½ million dollars of libel against the World's Work, other newspapers, and the Associated Advertising Clubs of the World, and the Better Business Bureau . . . including Congressman Taylor from Glenwood Springs, Colorado. In the meantime, we had employed the Burns Detective Agency. When Congressman Taylor was visiting Boston in the summer of 1919, a Burns operator in Boston casually contacted Congressman Taylor and jokingly brought up the matter of Pan Motor Company and the suit against him. Congressman Taylor confided in him that when he went to the same high school in Peoria, Illinois, that Judge Page went to, they became good friends and that he could handle Judge Page. When we received this information from the Burns Agency, we had our attorneys relay this information to Judge Page. He quickly threw the case out of his court.

It had no other place to go except into the court of Judge Landis.

Landis set October 23 as the date for the trial.

In January, 1918, J. D. Kowalkowski, the postmaster in St. Cloud, had died, and the man appointed to succeed him on February 9 was Fred Schilplin, secretary of the St. Cloud Times Publishing Company and a member of the Pan Motor Company Board of Directors. In April 1919, as the St. Cloud men went to Chicago to post bond for each other—$10,000 for Pandolfo and $5000 for each of the others—Schilplin commented on the incongruity of his position. He, the postmaster of St. Cloud, was awaiting trial on a charge of using the mails to defraud.

Official Washington found the circumstance not only incongruous but untenable. On May 19, Schilplin was asked to resign the postmaster's office. After an appearance in Washington on June 2, he announced the matter of his removal had been continued, but on August 4 an order was sent removing him from office.

Schilplin was not the only Pan officer affected by official Washington; the Federal Trade Commission cited Pandolfo to appear before it. The unfair methods the company was ostensibly using in interstate commerce consisted of using the word "manufacturing" in their literature when in fact they were only "assembling" a car. It was a fine distinction.

In Chicago, Pandolfo found himself outgunned when it came to getting publicity during the summer of 1919. Henry Ford had sued the *Chicago Tribune* for libeling him and had asked one million dollars in damages. In the middle of August, the verdict was returned in favor of Ford. The *Tribune* was ordered to make payment in the amount of six cents. Both Ford and the *Tribune* announced their satisfaction with the decision—Ford with the verdict and the *Tribune* with the judgment.

The Pan Motor Company badly needed some good publicity, and it got some, along with a dash of humor, from Dan B. Shields, the Attorney General of Utah. Shields had investigated the company on August 27 and 28 and wrote his report to the Securities Commission of his state on September 18. Gordon Snow, Secretary of the Commission, sent a copy to Pandolfo who promptly turned it into a mailing piece.

The report is reproduced at length here because of the comments Pandolfo made on its contents, because it is one of the last quasi-official statements on the company's condition, and because of its own interesting and candid presentation.

> Gentlemen:
>
> Upon the suggestion of your Commission, and the request for such visitation from the Company, the undersigned on the 27th and 28th of August of this year, made a rather comprehensive examination of the assets of the Pan Motor Company of St. Cloud, Minnesota. As you will remember, and your records will confirm, this Com-

pany has already been denied authority by the Utah Securities Commission to offer its stock or securities in Utah, upon the representations made to the Commission that the institution was financially unsound, that its stock sales were made upon misrepresentation, and, generally, that the allowance of an authority to sell such stock in Utah would be subversive to public good, and finally, that the Company was and is officered by men in whom confidence could not be placed.

The request of the Company that the Commission make an examination, and its offer to defray the necessary expenses, apparently seemed such an offer of good faith, that it was concluded that the least that could be done in fairness was to see the plant and go over the institution from end to end, and, accordingly, I presented myself and credentials at the Pan Motor Company plant on the morning of the 27th of August, and requested authority to make the examination. At the outset, it is only fair for me to say that my treatment at the hands of the officers of the Company was at once courteous and considerate, and that every effort was made, without the slightest apparent attempt to conceal the facts, to put me in complete possession of all information connected with the business, and I am conceited enough to think that what I gathered were the facts.

. . . .

At the time of my visit, the stock balance sheet showed 801,903 shares of stock in the "sold" column, although this amount may be modified somewhat when the entire issue has been sold as a result of forfeiture and failures to complete contracts on the part of some of the purchasers. . . . [Shields discovered that there were already 1765 stockholders in the state of Utah.]

A balance of the Company's books, taken on July 1st of this year, indicates the following conditions in figures:

Assets, current	$891,071.32

Which contains cash on hand, bonds of the United States, accounts receivable for work of manufacturing; material and machinery; purchase expense, which is a small amount, not more than $25 or $30 and refers to overpayment of freight, or something of that sort; materials and supplies, which will be well over $200,000; work in progress, which means stock or material upon which any work has been done; insurance, unearned; notes receivable, etc.

> Assets, fixed $1,769,666.45
> Which includes land upon which the property is located, and it may be well to observe in passing that this land is carried at $11,400, or the exact amount at which it was purchased some two or more years ago; buildings, machinery and fixtures; dies; patents, tools, etc.; service cars and tractors; furniture and fixtures and miscellaneous property.
>
> Assets, deferred $324,974.33
> Which includes experimental cars and tractors; plans, blueprints and specifications; freight and express, undisputed; patents and patent rights; including the actual expense in applying therefor; and production expense, which includes labor accounts, etc.
>
> Unpaid balance from subscribers belonging to the capital stock $1,281,620.93
>
> Unpaid balance from subscribers belonging to the surplus or premium $477,265.99
>
> Or a grand total of $4,744,599.02
>
> These assets are considered by the Company as tangible or concrete assets. In addition, thereto, is shown a good will or intangible assets, which represents expenditures from the surplus account and not charged to the assets, amounting to $3,132,131.18 which when added to the tangible assets, makes a grand total of assets amounting to $7,876,730.20.
>
> On the same day, the balance sheet showed liabilities, exclusive of the capital stock account, amounting to $350,075.20.

[Shields then explained that the intangible assets consisted of the advertising the Company had produced and the publicity it had received. He reviewed the sales contract that Pandolfo had with the Company and that had been revised at the order of the Minnesota State Securities Commission. Then he went on to describe the plant.]

> The assembling portion of the plant is equipped with the most modern machinery in all particulars, lathes, dies, cutters, presses, jiggs [sic] etc., which are now working upon the production of Pan cars for the trade. I had the experience of riding in one of

the new cars which had just been assembled, and while not posing as an expert upon car manufacturing, I have no hesitancy in saying that the Pan car will be a rather vigorous competitor for cars of its class, if the one I rode in is to be the criterion for judgment of the future work of the plant.

The Company had expected to have its foundry work done by a Cleveland company, and to that end it made patterns and designs, and sent its material to that plant. The Cleveland foundries are no exception to the general rule, and for more than two months now this material has waited for the adjustment of a strike. But this experience gained was useful to the Company, in that it, by this condition of affairs, made evident the necessity for a plant of its own, and, accordingly, the Pan Motor people bought a small foundry located in St. Cloud, and at this plant they are now turning out some 12-15 cylinder blocks per day. A Company foundry is being constructed as rapidly as men and material can put it in place, and I would judge that 60 days at the outside would see all foundry work for the Pan cars done on the premises.

[Shields went on to describe some of the staff, misspelling some of the names, and then closed his report with a description of the location of the plant and of the Grand Central Hotel, mentioning the Breen Hotel, which was then in the process of construction.]

The hotel at St. Cloud, however, is one of the things about which very little should be said, but I desire to remark in passing that it seems to me impossible that there should exist in the heart of civilization such an establishment as the Grand Central Hotel of St. Cloud, Minnesota. This is an American plan institution, but I think it is an American plan upon which the patent must have expired. Comfort, consideration and courtesy are lacking in all departments, but until you approach the dining room, you are not entirely impressed with the atrocity of the situation. One meal is sufficient to emphasize your desire that your stay shall be brief, and your determination to fast grows as your meal progresses. The only encouraging thing about this hotel is, as you sit in the dining room aforesaid, that you can look across the way and see the workmen laying the foundation for a new hotel, and I think that the wish was universal, at least on the part of those who were fellow diners, that the work might be pushed to a speedy conclusion.

After having made the examination herein reported in brief, it seems to me that many of the statements made by those opposing the Pan Motor Company are in no way borne out. My

> conviction is that while from a solid financial standpoint, the original plan of financing, so far as the promoters of the enterprise are concerned, might be considered unfair to the stockholders and purchasers, yet, the stock was sold by the Company and purchased by the subscribers only after the full knowledge of the facts, and acquaintance with the application to be made of the money paid, to the extent, at least, that the purchaser agreed that the first money went for the advertising and selling expense of the Company.
>
> Unquestionably, this Commission was not in possession of all the facts connected with the Pan Motor Company when its recent order was made, and I feel, in fairness to the corporation, if the request for a rehearing be made, the least that the Securities Commission of Utah can do will be to grant the same, and I so recommend.
>
> Respectfully submitted
> Dan B. Shields
> Attorney General of Utah

Pandolfo used quotations from Shields' letter to try to prove his contention that a "gigantic conspiracy" was afoot to discredit the Pan Motor Company and himself. At the conclusion of his comments on Shields' report Pandolfo stated the following:

> The Pan Motor Company has been examined by many different investigating committees from different Blue Sky or State Securities Commissions. We have failed to find where one single report has been other than very favorable to the Company. . . .
>
> In conclusion, the people who are stockholders seem to be quite well satisfied. The Pan Motor Company is already a big success. It is going to be a bigger success. Regardless of all the malicious attacks, prosecutions and persecutions the Pan Motor Company is going right along—getting bigger and stronger every day—and day by day—and is going to be, in a very few years, one of the biggest, strongest and most powerful industrial enterprises in the United States.

The mailing piece was one of Pandolfo's last major efforts for the Pan Motor Company, but it did nothing to slow the judicial process. On Friday, September 26, 1919, Judge Kenesaw M. Landis demonstrated how the trial of the Pan Motor Company officers and directors would be handled. He issued a court order warning Pan Company attorneys against intimidating or communicating in any way with government witnesses called in the case. It was too late; the communications had already been sent. By Pandolfo.

Fletcher Dobyns, a Chicago attorney retained by Pandolfo had appeared in court requesting that District Attorney Charles F. Clyne turn over the list of more than 100 government witnesses. Clyne was reluctant to do so, stating that the Pan defendants had already hired a detective agency to follow him and his assistants, and further attempts at intimidation would result if the list of witnesses were known. Landis ruled that the prosecution must supply the list but issued the court order about contacting the witnesses.

Monday evening, October 20, several hundred people gathered at the Northern Pacific depot in east St. Cloud, offering their support to the first contingent of Pan directors leaving for Chicago. Mr. and Mrs. Pandolfo boarded the train with Mr. and Mrs. John Barritt, Mr. and Mrs. John McGolrick, Mr. and Mrs. Edward Gorman, and a number of office workers. Two carloads of office equipment, including many of the company records, were being shipped out, and much of the administrative duties of the Pan Motor Company would be done in Chicago for the next several weeks.

Additional office crew left Tuesday evening, accompanying directors Charles D. Schwab, Charles S. Bunnell, Peter R. Thielman, Hugh Evans, George Hanscom, Hal C. Ervin, Fred Schilplin, and attorney Ripley C. Brower. In St. Paul they would be joined by attorney Carl Cummins, part of the Pan legal defense. Charles F. Ladner, vice president of the Pan Motor Company, was in Milwaukee and would go directly to Chicago from there.

Pandolfo had taken over the entire sixth floor of the Atlantic Hotel as headquarters for the company's defense. The hotel, at 316 South Clark Street, had been called the Kaiserhof but was renamed during the war. A few blocks to the north was the Federal Building, on the sixth floor of which the trial would take place.

On October 22, Pandolfo and the other company officials spent the day completing their arrangements at the hotel. Conferences with attorneys went on all day, the last one at eight o'clock in the evening. The northwest corner of the sixth floor was converted into a business office; phone lines from the St. Cloud office were kept open to this Chicago "branch office" during business hours. Downstairs, in the lobby of the hotel, the Pan Tank Tread Tractor was prominently displayed. In another side room were the new Pan wheel tractor, both models of the Pan car—Model 250 and Model A—and eight framed displays of drop forgings made by the Pan Motor Company for use in the new Pan car.

An air of quiet confidence permeated the sixth floor of the Atlantic Hotel the night of October 22. The trial would begin the following morning.

Special bus every hour to Pan Motor Company's grounds.

Street cars run to the plant.

CHAPTER VIII

. . . into the mouth of the cannon

OCTOBER 1919 SET new weather records in Chicago. The number of days with rain and the amount of precipitation were both the highest ever recorded. It was also the warmest October since 1900 and the first one without snowfall since 1902. Thursday, October 23, the first day of the Pan trial, the temperature was in the high 50s and low 60s, the day was clear, and in Judge Landis' courtroom some of the windows were opened to the breezes.

The Federal Building housed the main Chicago post office on the ground floor. Only eight stories, capped with a rotunda, the building was not unusually tall but was impressive for its sprawling bulk.

The sixth-floor courtroom, 40 × 90 feet, was two stories high, the upper part lit by small clerestory windows. The lower half of the walls, in the architectural style of the time for federal buildings, was marble; the upper reaches were decorated with frescoes featuring biblical characters and appropriate quotations.

Shortly before ten o'clock, the Pan Motor Company defendants entered the courtroom with their battery of defense attorneys. The lawyers opened their bulging briefcases, sorted out papers onto the tables, then settled down to wait for Judge Landis. Most midwestern Americans knew him by reputation; they knew his unusual names, Kenesaw Mountain, and some of them knew that the judge's father, Dr. Abraham Landis, had been a surgeon with the Union forces in the Civil War and had suffered a leg wound at the battle of Kennesaw Mountain in northwestern Georgia. Somewhere between Georgia and Millville, Ohio, where his son was born in 1866 and named after the incident, the doctor's memory buckled and his son went through life with a name one "n" shy of the mountain.

Landis had studied law at the University of Cincinnati and the Union Law School in Chicago. Shortly after admission to the bar in 1891, he was appointed private secretary to Grover Cleveland's Secretary of State, Walter Q. Gresham, in Washington, D. C. On Gresham's death two years later, Landis returned to Chicago and practised law for 12 years until 1905, when he was appointed a judge for the Northern District of Illinois by

President Theodore Roosevelt.

His major claim to judicial prominence came in 1907 when he adjudicated the trial of Stantard Oil of Indiana in a rebate case. Landis found the company guilty of accepting rebates from railroads and imposed a record fine of $29,240,000. (The fine was appealed and removed by the Supreme Court, but the memory lingered on. In 1944, less than a year before his death, Landis, then Commissioner of Baseball, tried to supplant the Spink's Official Baseball Guide with one of his own devising. Columnist Red Smith commented: "Judge Landis is a fool. And if that be treason, let him go ahead and fine me $29,000,000!")

At precisely ten o'clock this bright Thursday morning Landis entered the courtroom and disposed of minor details in whispered conferences with lawyers and court officers. The Pan defendants had a chance to observe him in person for the first time. Though he was still comparatively young (he would celebrate his 53rd birthday during the trial), his white hair and stern mien made him appear older. His habit of riffling his hair with a quick motion gave him a frazzled look that contributed to the aura of age about him. His movements, like his mind, were quick and impetuous and attorneys soon learned that his opinions, formed quickly, were set in concrete.

An hour after he entered the courtroom Landis announced the case of the United States *versus* Pandolfo *et al.* District Attorney Charles Clyne began with a motion to separate the indictments against Pandolfo from those against the Directors. The defense objected strenuously, arguing that they had been combined in the first place at the insistence of the government. When Landis upheld the defense objection, but dismissed a part of the indictment as redundant, the trial proper began.

Jury selection proceeded quickly, the defense using only three of its ten challenges and the prosecution only four. The jurors were all from northern Illinois: Charles S. St. Clair, a druggist from Dandee; J. B. Goodman, a barber and home builder from Oak Park; Charles C. Lawson, a former barber in Chicago, but now a salesman with the Ford Motor Company; A. W. Jenkinson, a Chicago insurance man; W. W. Hood, a plasterer from Harvey; James H. Marks, a Woodstock farmer and farmland realtor; Peter J. Duell, owner of a summer resort at Grays Lake; William J. Brown, a Waukegan grocer; Max Finke, a steam-fitter from Morton Grove; William Barnard, a retired farmer living in Chicago; Charles Long, an Ottawa farmer; and Lincoln Pettis, a Deerfield well-driller.

Judge Landis laid down his ground rules when attorneys on both sides requested Saturday recesses. "No," Landis replied, "I don't want to waste the time of these jurors. I'm sure they have other things they'd rather be doing than sitting idle on Saturday. I know I have.

"And you might as well hear the rest of the bad news now, too. Unless otherwise instructed, we will begin each morning at ten o'clock and run to one o'clock. We will take a one-hour lunch break and commence again at two o'clock. Our late recess will depend on circumstances, but I strongly suggest that none of you make permanent plans for any evening entertainment. This trial is the most important thing concerning you men at the moment, and you might as well get used to that until it's over.

"One more thing: I want everyone—lawyers, defendants, and spectators, too—to remain in this courtroom until the jury has left the building each night. If my rules are obeyed, gentlemen, we will get along just fine." The jury was sworn in at 5:30 in the afternoon, and Landis recessed the first day of the trial.

In spite of Landis' instructions, court was delayed a few minutes Friday morning because prosecuting attorney Sylvester Rush, scheduled to make the opening statement, was late. Judge Landis fidgeted until Rush finally appeared and then sternly cautioned him and the others that it was not to happen again. "There is only one person entitled to come late in this courtroom: the judge. That is because I have more to do than any of you." Landis was conducting other trials concurrently.

To acquaint the court and jurors with the principals in the case, each defendant was asked to rise as his name was called. The prosecuting attorneys—District Attorney Charles Clyne, and his assistants, Benjamin Epstein and James R. Glass, and Judge Sylvester Rush of Omaha, an assistant attorney general—were introduced. Then the defense attorneys were asked to indicate their clients. Fletcher Dobyns of Chicago stated he was representing Norman Street and George Heidman, the two Chicago patent attorneys; George H. Peaks of Chicago was representing Pandolfo and H. S. Wigle; Carl Cummins of St. Paul was representing Pandolfo and John Barritt. All eight of the St. Cloud directors were represented by Ripley Brower of St. Cloud. (Although he appeared only once or twice in the news stories of the trial, a third attorney, Charles Revelle, also represented Pandolfo.)

Rush prepared to make his opening statement. (District Attorney Clyne retired to the background after the first day and was seldom in attendance in court.) A quiet, dignified man of 59, Rush had considerable experience in prosecuting fraud cases for the government. He gave the general history of the Pan Motor Company since June 1916, when Pandolfo launched his plans at a meeting in Clovis, New Mexico, and sold the first three shares of stock.

"People were admonished to keep the great business opportunity in confidence and to act—meaning to turn over their money to the promoter and his stock salesmen. This Pan Motor Company, at that time when its stock was being sold to people, was without habitation other than that which existed in the minds of these roving stock sellers."

Rush listed several points he said the government would prove in its case: that prospective stockholders were told that half of every ten dollars subscribed for stock went into the treasury as capital, and the other half as surplus; that in reality half of the money subscribed for stock was paid to

Pandolfo, who spent a great portion of his share for advertising and promotion; that the company represented no promotional fees would be paid from a practical standpoint; that from the time the corporation was organized until May 1918, $2,500,000 had been taken in and that after paying promotion fees, etc., Pandolfo had $355,000 left; that the company had represented to Blue Sky boards in several states not more than ten percent was being allowed for promotion of the stock; that the mails were used to spread statements the stock was really worth more than was paid for it and would soon pay big dividends.

"We will introduce testimony to prove that the first stock sold in Chicago was by a prospectus on a car that was to sell for 500 dollars, and that stockholders were to receive a 15 percent reduction on each car, the company would make a profit of 50 dollars on each car, the promoter claimed, and 1,000 cars would be made the first year, it was promised. Eventually the company was represented as to be operated on a production schedule of 30,000 cars a year. Evidence will show," Rush continued, "that no cars have been sold to the public at 500 dollars, and scarcely any at other prices. Not a single car was manufactured by the Pan Motor Company during the year 1917. Despite this, bales, literally bales, of advertising matter on the car was sent from one end of the country to the other."

Rush then touched on the Pan Tank Tread Tractor. "Here was a machine," he stated, "that was widely advertised as `the tractor that will win the war.' We will show that this much-heralded tractor was assembled by the company for exhibition and stock-selling purposes only. At the time, the company did not have a tractor it could commercially produce and sell to farmers of this country. Even this one model was discarded and abandoned. Up to May, 1918, the books of the company will show that not one tractor was sold to a farmer."

The government's version of Pandolfo's income was traced. "In January 1917, with the help of Norman Street and George Heidman, a contract was completed whereby Pandolfo was to get 50 percent of all funds received. In September of the same year, in order to get a license from the securities commission of Minnesota to sell stock in its home state, the company amended the contract to read that Pandolfo would receive only 25 percent as president. He would be given the other 25 percent as advertising and sales manager." Rush claimed that from June 1918, up until the time of the indictment, Pandolfo received more than $27,000 a month—a total of $124,000—under this arrangement.

During the rest of his statement, Rush indicated how the government proposed to prove each count of the indictment.

Representing Heidman and Street, Fletcher Dobyns spoke first in defense. Dobyns had attended Harvard, graduating in 1898, and was admitted to the Illinois bar in 1901. In addition to serving as assistant state's attorney in Cook County in 1901, and instructor at John Marshall Law School in Chicago, he had also been a special district attorney general in

1911. He had been a candidate for attorney general in Illinois on the Progressive ticket in 1912. He was a partner in the law firm of Dent, Dobyns and Freeman.

In his opening statement Dobyns charged that the government's case had been inspired by business enemies of Pandolfo. The company's plan to sell automobiles to its stockholders, designed to take advantage of the sales opportunity present in such a large group of ardent supporters, had aroused the enmity of competitors, Dobyns claimed.

Dobyns made reference to the bitter dispute between Pandolfo and the Associated Advertising Clubs of the World. "As a matter of fact," Dobyns said, "all of the charges made in this case have already been investigated by officials in Minnesota. . . on the scene. . . and by Tennessee, and by other states, and they have been disproved. In every state where the company was given an opportunity to disprove these malicious charges, a license has been issued to sell the company's stock. We will show that these gentlemen, the defendants in this case, acted in good faith, with scrupulous honesty and without criminal intent." The development of the Pan Motor Company had been interfered with seriously by its enemies, by the war, and by the postal inspectors, Dobyns said, and despite the factors blocking its advance the corporation was at present manufacturing and selling superior automobiles.

Carl W. Cummins, the St. Paul attorney retained by Pandolfo and Barritt, pointed out that Pandolfo had received no bonus from the St. Cloud directors for choosing to locate in their city. "Nor did they receive any special consideration for joining the company. They paid dollar-for-dollar for their stock, just as every other stockholder. There is no preferred stock, no awards, no gratuities." He circled the table and approached the jury. "They charge us with misappropriation and misapplication of funds. Now, the government was invited to send an auditor to look over the bookkeeping department. Every dollar of par value of the stock," he slapped the rail of the jury box, emphasizing every word, "has gone into the treasury of the company. We will prove and account for all of it."

As he had through Dobyns' opening remarks, Judge Landis followed Cummins' statement closely, head tilted to one side, resting on the tips of his bony fingers.

"We will also show," Cummins said, "that Mr. Pandolfo could not have met the heavy cost of starting a venture of this magnitude without the percentage he received. And we will also disprove the charge that he served himself first and the company second." Cummins pointed out that the main error in the prosecution's case consisted in assuming that the company could pay a dividend in its first few years of operation.

Cummins then took up some of the specific charges made by Rush in his opening statement, explaining that the company had not promised to turn out a specific number of cars in its first year, or in its second year. "You must remember that only three months after this company was incorporated, it was faced with the situation of a nation at war. All plans made before its existence had to be altered. Intent on building pleasure cars, the company was now faced with the request by its government that such manufacture be curtailed.

"Now these are patriotic men. They have spearheaded bond drives in their community; they have given their sons into the services; they have seen an enormous investment, not only of their own money, but that of their friends and neighbors, jeopardized by this curtailment of immediate production. But they not only supported this curtailment, they supported it with a resolution passed at their annual stockholders meeting. Now they find themselves victimized by the government for agreeing to such patriotic action."

Cummins claimed that lies had been spread about the company. "This plant is not a myth, gentlemen. It is one of the best in the country, designed by experts and equipped with the latest and best machinery available." Cummins completed his statement with comment on one point that Rush had mentioned: that Pandolfo, after saying so often that no one could buy stock at less than ten dollars a share, had arranged a deal whereby he was allowed to purchase 100,000 shares for five dollars a share. "The government has indicated that there was something illegal about a 500,000 dollar note which Mr. Pandolfo had given in exchange for 100,000 shares of stock. We will show that there was nothing illegal or sinister in this, only the efforts of a man trying desperately to save a company, and with it the savings of tens of thousands of stockholders. He is still making that fight. In the end, the note was withdrawn and the shares never delivered.

"Let me point out to you that Mr. Pandolfo, with his own money—not that of the Pan Motor Company—has built homes for employees of the company, individually designed homes with every modern convenience. He will realize only about three percent on this investment. He is also building an independent manufacturing plant near the Pan factory site. Does this sound to you like the actions of a man who wants to get his hands on all the money he can before he clears out?"

Cummins and Dobyns had Landis' attention during their opening statements, but Ripley B. Brower, when he warmed up, had the judge spellbound. Brower knew the St. Cloud defendants best, and his remarks were closely followed. He was a large man, accustomed to speaking before audiences not only from his legal experience but also from two terms as a state senator. Although he had frequently been urged to run, he had consistently refused state-wide endorsement for the office of governor of Minnesota.

Brower began his remarks quietly, almost diffidently. But within two or three minutes his large head came up and his chin came out. The lofty room boomed with the echo of his voice. "I represent," he began, "the eight defendants from St. Cloud. I cannot, as Mr. Rush has, call them wealthy. But they are the leading men of the city. A useful, good, sturdy lot, the backbone of their community in times of stress. And men upon whose reputation there has not been cast any stain . . . until this time. During the war, as you have heard, the sons of some fought for their country. Others donated their services in different ways, in whatever ways they could best serve. After all, in the last analysis, the case will come down to this: did they act in good faith? The government does not, cannot, punish a mistake in judgment, if mistake there was. So what is on trial here? The good faith of these men. That alone. No complaint has been issued by the stockholders in this concern. If they are satisfied with the way things are being done, although they have as yet received no dividends, whose affair is it otherwise? And are they satisfied?" He spread his arms wide. "They have come individually and in groups from all over the country to visit the plant, and they went away saying they were proud of it and would back the company to the end."

Brower launched into his version of the history of the company; he told how Pandolfo had come to St. Cloud without special urging or solicitation on the part of the city. "Doubtless many businessmen in other cities, had they known of Pandolfo's interest and plans for a business, would have offered him special concessions and inducements to get him to select their city. But you have been told—and it is the truth!—that St. Cloud gave him no special consideration of any kind. Nor did he ask for any. Except for the cooperation of the community and their good will, he told them he wanted nothing until he showed them what was to be done. Then he would ask for their help, but in terms of an investment in which they would reap benefits larger than his, because as a newcomer to St. Cloud he had no large real estate holdings that would appreciate in value, no business whose original investment would be doubled or more by the activities of the Pan Motor Company, not to mention the direct benefits in the way of sales to or business with the Pan Motor Company itself. In short, he asked for nothing more than an opportunity. And he was given that—and only that!"

After reviewing the background of the St. Cloud directors, Brower concluded his statement by denying that the business had failed or was on the way to failure. "What company do you know of that has 100,000 dollars business in advance? Does this sound like a failing company? The completion of this business awaits only the successful settlement of this suit."

Judge Landis made notes for a moment or two after Brower concluded at five o'clock, then looked up brightly and said, "Let's all be here on time tomorrow, gentlemen. Ten o'clock sharp." He gathered his papers and left.

Saturday morning there were no delays and the government called its first witness, John H. McQuerry, the second vice president of the Pan Motor Company. McQuerry identified the contract between company officials and Pandolfo as fiscal agent by which Pandolfo was to manage five out of every ten dollars received in the sale of stock. Dated January 16, 1917, the contract was to run two years; Pandolfo then had the option of renewing it for one more year. The contract was signed by Norman Street, George Heidman, and Samuel Pandolfo.

Attorney Benjamin Epstein then called Gertrude Bean, a school teacher from Littleton, Colorado. She had bought five shares of Pan stock in February 1917 and five more in March; the salesman had been her half-brother, Louis Bean. She testified that one line in the company's literature had induced her to buy: "Purchase ten shares of our stock and you will be immensely rich."

Miss Bean, with the clear organization of a teacher's mind, told of a trip she had made to St. Cloud to inspect the Pan plant in August 1919. Asked by Epstein who had paid for the trip, she replied, "My brother Louis, as far as I know."

In cross-examination Cummins asked Miss Bean if she thought that she had been given any special treatment in her tour. She did not think so. "Everyone was most courteous and open, but it seemed to be the general policy of the staff and not something done for my benefit."

Cummins asked her what she had done concerning her trip after returning home, and she said that because of the great interest in the Pan Motor Company in that part of the country and because of conflicting reports about it, she had been asked to write an article about the company for the *Castle Rock Record-Journal*. Because the article had not been mentioned in direct examination, Landis would not allow Cummins to have Miss Bean read from her story. "If you want it that bad, call her as your own witness later." And Landis recessed for the weekend.

On Monday, October 27, Cummins had Miss Bean back on the stand, identifying documents she had turned over to postal inspectors but which the government had failed to introduce as evidence. Cummins was able to indicate to the jury that each of the documents was favorable to the company, but every time he attempted to get one introduced as evidence he was blocked by Landis' admonition, "Call her as your own witness, counselor."

During one loud clash between Cummins and Epstein over this evidence, Landis cut the argument short. "No more of that cheap stuff," he snapped. "If you want to go on with the argument, I have a side room and a set of boxing gloves at your disposal."

The prosecution's next witness, Alexander Shipley, was president of the First National Bank of Clovis, New Mexico, and within a few minutes even Landis was smiling. Shipley described the running feud he had been conducting with Pandolfo ever since June 19, 1916, when the promoter first disclosed his plans for an automobile company at a public meeting in Clovis. During direct examination Shipley was asked how he felt about Pandolfo now. "I bear him no malice," he replied. But he later described Pandolfo as "the dirtiest man in the United States," and said "Pandolfo hasn't had an honest thought in 30 years."

In answer to a question about a doubtful issue, Shipley insisted, "I'm telling the truth! I know how to make Pan lie down. If he'll waltz into the hall with me right now we'll see who's the liar." At other times during his testimony Shipley referred to Pandolfo as a "hot air merchant," "an impractical dreamer," and "a grandstand stock salesman."

Cummins' first question to Shipley on cross-examination caused an uproar. "Have you ever been indicted for stealing cattle in Texas?" Landis sustained the immediate, shouted objection, but Shipley insisted on answering.

When I was 18 years old," he said, "I was in the cattle business in Texas with my father and brother. My brother and I were indicted for stealing a yearling on complaint of a neighbor. It was all due to a misunderstanding, and the indictment was dismissed without trial. The man who caused my indictment is now one of my best friends."

Shipley was allowed to leave the stand pending the production of some letters to him from Ira Henthorne.

The trial was being given maximum publicity in the St. Cloud newspapers with two and sometimes three full-column stories on the front pages. St. Cloud people passing through Chicago, or nearby relatives and friends of St. Cloud residents, were frequent visitors in the courtroom. This Monday, Dr. Warren L. Beebe from St. Cloud attended both the morning and afternoon sessions, and Mrs. Grove C. Dunn of Chicago, the sister of Mrs. Hubert Gans of St. Cloud, came for the afternoon session.

The next morning Judge Landis, impatient with the long examinations being conducted by both the prosecution and the defense, told the lawyers, "Make it snappy!"

Several witnesses who had been approached to buy stock in the Pan Motor Company testified during the morning session. C. F. Hafley of Montrose, Colorado, said that W. R. Crowder and his brother had used a patriotic approach in trying to sell him stock, and when he refused to buy, they asked, "Aren't you patriotic?"

"I told them I was just as patriotic as they were and invited them to get out of the house."

A similar story was told by S. H. Kettle, a Colorado pioneer and rancher. "You see, these two boys—nice appearing boys, too—came out to see me in Colona. They said they were cousins of General Crowder and relatives of the late General Grant. They told me all about the Pan Motor Company and wanted me to take stock in it. When I sort of hesitated, they said the company was working hard on war contracts for Uncle Sam. They said our soldier boys over there didn't have enough steel helmets like the Germans, and they was fighting our battles in wool caps. The company was speeding up to make helmets and had other war contracts. Well, I went in for 500 dollars worth of stock and gave them boys a hundred-dollar Liberty Bond for the first payment. I didn't send them no more money, though."

Most of Wednesday morning was taken up by the testimony of Benjamin Idelman, a Cheyenne stock salesman and Pan stockholder. Idelman had first met and started working for Pandolfo in Cheyenne in November 1916. Much of his testimony consisted of verifying letters Pandolfo had sent to salesmen—the prosecution called them "ginger letters"—which were read into the record.

The next prosecution witnesses caught Judge Landis' attention in such a way that he considered initiating a sweeping investigation of trade journal publications. Paul V. Hyde, a Chicago publisher, told of assigning an article favorable to the Pan Motor Company written for his publication, *The Banker, Merchant & Manufacturer*. Before publication, the article was sent to Pandolfo for checking, with the suggestion that he could use extra promotional copies of the publication. When Pandolfo ordered extra copies, $450 worth, the complete article was scheduled for publication. Hyde admitted that the article would have been curtailed if Pandolfo had not been willing to buy extra copies. He candidly admitted that most of the magazine's income came from the sale of extra copies to people or companies covered favorably by such articles.

Judge Landis sent the jury out of the courtroom at this point and asked the witness, "It is true, isn't it, that you would not have printed the article at all if Pandolfo had not ordered the extra copies?" When Hyde admitted that it was probably true, Landis asked, "What did you do to find the truth in that article about the Pan Company?" Hyde claimed that the literature dispensed by the company was the basis for the article and that a representative of the magazine had been sent to St. Cloud to look at the plant.

With that, Landis thundered at Rush, "Why wasn't this man indicted by the grand jury?"

"The jury chose only to select the officials of the Pan Motor Company," Rush replied quietly.

"Very well," Landis said, "let him be turned over to the grand jury now." Before leaving the stand, however, Hyde first assured the court, in answer to a defense lawyer's questioning, that Pandolfo had not known that the magazine was not bona fide.

E. J. Seymour of Chicago, the next witness, was the author of the article, "Queen of the Highway," that had appeared in *The Banker, Merchant & Manufacturer*. He claimed he had received help from C. W. Williams, who had later gone to work for the Pan Motor Company.

Before leaving the witness stand both witnesses were advised to hold themselves ready for further questioning.

The last witness of the day was Miss Ida Jarger, now of San Francisco, who had worked for Pandolfo when the Pan offices were in the Venetian Building in Chicago. Her testimony was mainly to confirm the government's contention that the mailings out of Chicago in the early days of the company had been deposited in the United States post office. Landis adjourned for the day before she could be cross-examined.

Thursday morning Miss Jarger was cross-examined not only by Ripley Brower but by Judge Landis. She had seen no set of books for the Pan Motor Company because no money was spent for the company as such. Pandolfo kept a strict set of books for the fiscal agency, she said, detailing every expense paid by him from the surplus fund. The Pan Motor Company was carried as an account on this set of books in the same way other accounts were before the company was incorporated.

When she explained that Pandolfo, as fiscal agent for the company, always received the first half of the stock payments, she gained Landis' undivided interest. "Now, suppose a man subscribed for $100 worth of stock and paid the salesman $25 down. What would be the agent's commission?" the judge asked.

"Twenty dollars, usually," Miss Jarger replied.

"Did he take that much out before sending in the rest with the application?"

"Yes."

"Then there was five dollars left to put in the bank. To whose account was that placed, Miss Jarger?" Landis asked.

"Pandolfo's."

"Well, what happened when the buyer of the stock failed to send in further payments?"

Miss Jarger thought for a moment. "I don't know. It never happened when I was with the company."

Landis' quizzical expression lasted until E. J. Seymour was recalled to the stand. He had with him a copy of the article he had written for *The Bankers' Journal*. Titled "Royalty on Wheels," and similar to the one written for *The Banker, Merchant & Manufacturer*, the article compared the Pan automobile to a beautiful woman. "I only wish," Epstein quoted from the article with mock emotion, "the showman had touched whatever was necessary to give life to the mechanical Galatea that I might ride in the upholstered lap of the highway queen. She had all the graces and curves of a beautiful woman in a tailor-made gown." Responding to the amused smiles in the audience, Epstein lowered his voice to a more intimate level. "Extremely responsive to the touch of a man, she may balk at times, as all queens do."

Everyone in the courtroom, including the usually stern Judge Landis, laughed loudest at Epstein's final quote from the article. "In the rear of this double-lapped beauty, in her bustle, so to speak, is another special feature, a tool box and provision for spare oil, gas, water, and food."

When the fading laughter allowed, Judge Landis asked Seymour, "Do you mean to say you got only 60 dollars for that job of writing?" Seymour replied that he usually got 25 percent of what was paid, but as Pandolfo had bought extra copies for $150, he had been given a bonus.

Landis asked Seymour where he got his information for the piece. Seymour had used company literature on the car in the main. "But I also saw the car at the LaSalle Hotel, at the auto show," he added.

Hugh S. Stewart, managing editor of *The Bankers' Journal*, then testified that he had suspended publication a short time ago when informed by federal authorities that he had been violating postal laws. Asked exactly when he had stopped, he said, "Last Friday." He freely admitted that the journal had only 50 regular subscribers and got its revenue from the extra copies it sold

The display advertising of various reputable concerns was run without charge—and without the company's knowledge, in many cases—to "make the publication more legitimate." Landis sent the jury out for 30 minutes while he continued to question the editor, who answered openly and at length. Stewart described how the journal sought prospective buyers of this kind of publicity. He insisted that the companies to be written up were always investigated, and if they were not sound they were not dealt with.

"Did you know to what use the Pan automobile article would be put?" Landis asked.

"I thought they would use it in selling cars, not in selling stock in the company," Stewart said. "That's why we only investigated the car, not the company."

With the hint that he might be called to the stand again later, Landis finally dismissed Stewart and brought the jury back in. Several former secretaries from the Pan Motor Company's early Chicago days testified next. Marie Cadieux said that until she heard the minutes of the company's early meetings read in court during the first days of the trial she had not known that she was at one time a vice president of the Pan Motor Company.

Laura Ward of Little Falls, Minnesota, a stenographer for Pandolfo in St. Cloud, identified some papers, and her nervousness was evident in the way the papers rattled as she held them and in her noncommittal answers. Judge Landis got the impression that the witness was being evasive, and when a woman arose and left the courtroom with a nod and a smile for Miss Ward, he was certain. The jury was sent out again as Landis demanded of Miss Ward, "Who was that woman with the big hat who went out of the courtroom just now, who paused and smiled broadly at you?"

"Mrs. Pandolfo," Miss Ward answered quietly.

Landis ordered Anna Pandolfo brought before him and waved aside her explanation about encouraging a nervous witness. "Let's have no more of that," he snapped impatiently and motioned the bailiff to bring the jury back.

Alex Shipley took the stand again to identify letters from Texas men who spoke ill of Pandolfo. One letter, from N. R. Morgan, county attorney of Seminole, Texas, stated, "I have been looking for Pandolfo for some time as a result of his swindling people hereabout. He is a past master at the art of swindling the average man, and it behooves everyone to help apprehend him." Shipley produced a letter he had received from John S. Patterson, Texas commissioner of insurance. Patterson had written, "Mr. Pandolfo's license to conduct a general insurance agency has been revoked on account of trouble experienced in his own and his agents' dealings with customers."

A number of letters from the St. Cloud directors were introduced. They stated that Pandolfo's background had been investigated and proved him a sound businessman and "in a class by himself as an organizer." One of the letters, however, was from Norman Street to Pandolfo. "I want to warn you about some of your stock-selling methods," Street wrote. "The 50-50 split of the proceeds of stock sales might be questioned."

Because the letter from Street to Pandolfo, read on Thursday, had sounded as though the attorney was questioning the honesty of the president, the defense introduced other correspondence between the two men on Friday. Pandolfo had written to Street in reply:

> Most of the money put to my account is spent in the affairs of the Pan Motor Company. You knew all about the contract from the beginning. I went over it with you. I don't see why you want to side-step the contract. Stand pat! My contract is not going to be changed. As to the contract of May 1917, they refer to, we have no record of it here. As to the letter to Reed & Glaser, I have no apology to make about it, and I stand pat on everything I said.
>
> I have always played my cards face up. I am entitled to a handsome consideration for my services, and probably much more than I will get. Salesmen's commissions will cost me $2,500,000 if I get the stock placed. Advertising may be $2,000,000 more, with postage, etc. I doubt if I will get $250,000. Please get for me statistics of other companies. I am sure from 60 to 80 percent of every dollar taken in goes for promotion purposes.

Street replied to Pandolfo:

> I only wanted to warn you to be careful, not only because of the magnitude of the Pan Motor Company, but because the public is naturally most interested, and a federal investigation is very strict. As to the attacks made upon you by enemies, you should be too broad-minded to consider them. Once production is started, the Pan car will speak for itself.

The prosecution countered with additional correspondence between the two men, also introducing an article unfavorable to the Pan Motor Company which had appeared in the May 1917 issue of *The Financial & Investment Chronicle.* "If they will retract their statement, we can give them some liberal advertisements," Pandolfo wrote to Street. "Feel them out on the proposition."

Testimony about the Chicago auto show of January 1918 brought up some minor confusion that was left unexplained. The chief house detective of the LaSalle Hotel stated that the company had not exhibited its tractor at the hotel, although trade journal ads said that it would be on exhibit. Asked to identify members of the Pan contingent who were present, he pointed out Ben Forsyth, Pan advertising manager, and "maybe that black-haired man." Fred Schilplin arose to be identified. The prosecuting attorneys took care to point out that the identification was in error. They did not mention that Ka-Be-Naw-Wey-Wence, or Wrinkled Meat, had been at the exhibit, nor did they explain how the hotel detective might have mistaken Schilplin for a 130-year-old Chippewa Indian.

The defense suggested that since the witness had been mistaken about the men at the exhibit, he might also have been mistaken about the exhibit itself.

Ben Forsyth was called as a witness for the prosecution and said he not only worked for the Pan Motor Company but also for the Gopher State Advertising Bureau of St. Cloud, a business wholly owned by Pandolfo and which was set up, frankly, to qualify for the discount allowed to agencies in placing advertising. Forsyth said he seldom submitted advertising matter to Pandolfo or to anyone else before sending it out, but Pandolfo occasionally saw proofs of various jobs and sometimes made changes in them.

"Do you mean to say that you got together all the cuts and articles for this issue of *Pan Siftings* magazine and that Pandolfo never saw it before it was printed?" attorney Rush asked.

"That's right."

Judge Landis leaned forward and asked, "You live in the same town with Pandolfo, do you not?"

Forsyth said he did.

"And your relations were friendly?"

"Certainly."

"And Pandolfo, or the Pan Motor Company, or whoever it was, was paying you good money for the advertising, isn't that so?" Landis persisted. Forsyth said that $6,000 to $8,000 was spent on advertising monthly. "One would think," Landis mused, "Pandolfo would want to know where all that money was going. Didn't you think Pandolfo, as your employer, had a right to see all of this matter?"

"I wasn't working for Pandolfo then," Forsyth explained. "I was working for the Pan Motor Company."

"For whom were you working when you prepared that ad for insertion in the Chicago papers?" Landis asked with some heat.

"The Pan Motor Company," Forsyth replied smoothly.

"Go out in the anteroom and meditate on some of this testimony you are giving," Landis said sternly. "We'll call you back later."

Forsyth returned to the stand Saturday morning, November 1. His testimony was directed to the exhibit at the LaSalle Hotel in January 1918, and to the *Pan Siftings* issue of February 1918. The tractor was not part of the exhibit at the hotel because it could not be taken into the hotel, he said. Pandolfo was in Denver when the ad copy for the Tank Tread Tractor was needed and he and his assistant, Jack Hammond, had prepared the ad. Pandolfo, when he finally saw the copy at the LaSalle Hotel, had only time to look it over hurriedly; a few days later, when he had examined it more closely, he directed that some changes be made in it.

Louis Bean, the half-brother of Gertrude, the first-day witness, replaced Forsyth on the stand and testified that he had been given $110 to come to St. Cloud from Littleton, Colorado, to visit the plant. He came, he said, not only because he owned stock and wanted to see the plant, but also because he had an invention in which he wanted to generate interest. At the conclusion of his testimony he asked if he could return to Colorado because he didn't feel well. Because there was some indication he might be needed as a defense witness, Judge Landis asked him if he would return if he was called.

"I will if I'm not sick, Judge," Bean said.

"Just what kind of sickness do you figure on having," Landis wanted to know.

"Well, I might get the flu, like I did last winter," Bean answered. With a puzzled look, Landis allowed him to leave.

Four Iowa stockholders were the next prosecution witnesses, each testifying about the promises made to them about early dividends and a refund of their money later if they didn't like the deal. But in cross-examination two of the three said they bought the stock knowing that half of their purchase price was to be turned over to Pandolfo for incidental expenses, and the third thought that Pandolfo was to get all the money.

The final witness of the week was Charles Olsen, of Des Moines, who told of a visit he made to the plant on October 20, three days before the start of the trial. Pandolfo asked him if he had spoken to a government postal inspector. When Olsen admitted he had, Pandolfo wanted to know if what he had said about the company was good or bad. "He told me," Olsen said, "that he had the word of two judges that it was all right for him to ask me this." Rush asked if either of the names mentioned by Pandolfo was Landis or Page, and Olsen said, "Page might be one."

"Did you see any finished cars at the plant?" Rush asked.

"No, but there was one nearly finished in the paint shop, and a demonstrator was being adjusted, and there were other unfinished machines in the shop."

On Monday morning, November 3, Roy W. Rogers, of Chillicothe, Missouri, testified in cross-examination that he had subscribed for six shares of stock for his son. "I bought the stock for two good reasons: I had faith in the man selling it and, when he gave a lecture on the company and showed some pictures, I was impressed with the homes they were building for their workmen, not all looking alike like most factory homes, but all different and pretty, too."

Most of the afternoon session was devoted to the testimony of William S. Reed, of the Indianapolis engineering firm of Reed & Glaser. Epstein read literature sent out by the Pan Motor Company describing how road difficulties melted into thin air and the highway met its master as the Pathfinder Pan journeyed gracefully out of Indianapolis and effortlessly covered the 400 miles to Minnesota, eventually soaring into history at the famous Pan Motor barbecue on July 4, 1917. Then Epstein read a personal letter Pandolfo had written to the engineering firm at the conclusion of the trip.

Pandolfo seemed to enjoy hearing Epstein read the letter as much as everyone else. After stating that he had had a hard trip through miles of mud and bad roads and wanted to get these grievances out of his system, Pandolfo went on for four typewritten pages to detail the difficulties encountered on the car. Epstein read:

> First, we were lucky to have allowed ourselves extra time; we needed every minute we had. We had to fix leaks in the engine for an extra day before we were able to start. Then we discovered we couldn't crank the engine until we had removed two pieces of tin from the crankcase, which had sheared off from somewhere. Even then we couldn't start the engine. After everyone was exhausted from cranking, we checked and found the wiring was wrong and the timing was completely off.
>
> All went well after that until we were 29 miles out of Indianapolis and the front axle broke. If we had not been going slow—only 20 miles an hour—and on a smooth road, we could have turned a somersault and killed us all. Except for that I would not be dictating this letter now. . . .
>
> That was the poorest job of casting ever perpetrated on an innocent and ignorant public. The steel was as full of holes as a Swiss cheese is of cavities. If you live to be a million, never again put a cast steel axle in another car. You may unintentionally cause the death of some poor boob. . . .
>
> Sundown with the second day and the machinery stopped moving. A bolt had locked the whole thing. We worked all night. . . .
>
> Noise in the gears the next day developed the interesting fact that the transmission was dry as a bone. The rotten fan belt broke seven miles this side of Milwaukee. . . . The support of the gasoline tank is not sufficient and the roaring is terrific. The brakes are bad. If they don't burn, they don't hold. When the top is up there is a space of about three inches between it and the windshield so that in rain you are about as dry as if you were swimming in the ocean.
>
> I would give $1,000 to have had you along on that trip. . . .
>
> Language is inadequate. . . .
>
> Please redesign that steering gear so it will steer. It would take a man with a strong back and a strong arm and a weak mind to turn the car in a 40 acre field in a day's time. . . .
>
> The strongest argument I can advance in favor of this car

> is that it made an indelible impression on my mind. The cold shivers run up and down my back when I think I might have been silly enough to be making 60 miles an hour when that axle broke, or could have been crossing a railroad track ahead of a fast train. . . .
>
> I gave the biggest barbecue in the history of the world; we had 60,000 people on the Pan factory site. The car was on exhibition and made a hit because it has got beautiful lines and its painting was in harmony with the occasion.

In a second letter to Reed Pandolfo wrote:

> I think you are a nice fellow, but I don't like the automobile you turn out by a damn site. . . . If I had known then what I know now I could have ordered a motor, a steering gear, and some other parts and could have taken them to a country blacksmith to assemble for me. Then I would have had a car. I thought you would at least put a carburetor into the machine that was a carburetor. I have given you about $50,000 worth of publicity as engineers and as far as the public goes, that sticks. But you go ahead and make the rest of the cars contracted for as I want them, and we'll get along all right.

During cross-examination by Cummins, Reed said there had been little time to test the car properly before sending it out. All the major parts were standard, he said, such as the Rutenber motor, which he thought was still used in a small Paige, the Adams rear axle, etc. The front axle, which had caused so much trouble, had been cast to order to meet the requirements of the narrow body Pandolfo wanted. When made in quantity by drop forging there would be no trouble with it, and Reed was sure that the engineering staff of Pan knew that.

Cummins wanted Reed's comments on the cost of the car. In direct examination the engineer had said that the ten cars produced by his firm had cost the Pan Motor Company $12,000. At the time, the prosecution pointed out, circulars were advertising the car at $800. Reed answered Cummins' questions by saying that the price of materials had increased an average of 13 percent, and motors had gone up about 30 percent, so the car could not be turned out as cheaply as originally planned. Later, when it was thought the assembly could not be carried out in St. Cloud as soon as planned, Reed & Glaser had quoted a price of $723 each on an order for 100 Pan cars. Reed said that Pandolfo insisted that they skimp on nothing. "He wanted the cars right, regardless of price, and he wanted them right now."

"Was it at all unusual," Cummins asked, "for Mr. Pandolfo to come to your firm for the first model of the car he intended to manufacture himself?"

"Well, he had no plant at all at that time, and he had a very small staff, and he needed the cars in a hurry. No, it was not unusual at all. It is customary among all manufacturers to order some assembled models from outside engineering firms. Many companies, large companies, do it all the time."

Cummins' final question of the afternoon to Reed was, "Do you know if the Pan Motor Company was designed to continue assembling cars, or were they preparing to manufacture them in quantity?"

The prosecution objected that Reed could not possibly know the intent of the company, but Judge Landis, after a short exchange with the witness, allowed him to answer. "They would have little use for a drop forge of the size they have unless they intended to manufacture their own parts."

When court recessed that evening, many of the defendants and their wives took the opportunity to attend a concert by the Vatican Choir, then touring the United States, at the Auditorium Theatre.

Reed was recalled to the stand on Tuesday morning to testify about additional correspondence from Pandolfo. In one of his letters the auto company president stated that he might want 10,000 to 25,000 additional cars from the Indianapolis firm if he were unable to build and equip the Pan plant properly in the time he felt he should. Phrases such as, "I want the model car to stand up under the most severe tests," and "The main thing is to do a good job," and "You can't make it too soon but don't neglect any vital point," and "I want a practical, common-sense auto that will deliver the goods and stand up," recurred throughout the letters.

At one point Judge Landis joined Cummins in questioning Reed about the first cars made for Pan. "What would these cars have cost each in quantity production if you had made them the way you wanted to?" Cummins asked.

"Around 600 dollars," Reed answered.

"And what would they have cost the way Pandolfo wanted them built?"

"We figured, in quantity, around 725."

Landis interrupted Cummins to ask, "What caused the difference?"

"He wanted a few things included that we didn't think were necessary on a car of that class," Reed answered.

The next witness, Ralph Olson, president of the First National Bank of St. Cloud, got a lesson in elocution from Judge Landis. As Rush questioned him, Olson's voice became progressively softer. Landis finally interrupted Rush to ask the witness politely, "You say you are a bank president?" When Olson replied quietly that he was, Landis said briskly, "Well, then, speak in the same tone of voice you would use in refusing a man credit."

Olson's testimony concerned the block of 100,000 shares of Pan Motor stock mentioned in the opening statements by both sides. The stock was brought to the First National Bank, along with Pandolfo's personal note for $500,000, by John Barritt on May 31, 1918. Olson had been instructed that the bank was to hold the stock in escrow until Pandolfo had paid the note. Again Landis joined in the questioning of the witness. "Just so we understand this clearly, that meant that Pandolfo was to get the stock at half the price everyone else was paying?"

"I can't answer for what others were paying for the stock," Olson replied cautiously. "What it does mean is that the price to Pandolfo under the terms of this agreement would have been five dollars a share."

Rush asked Olson about the termination of the contract. Around the middle of December, Olson said, both Pandolfo and Barritt had independently told him that the agreement would not be concluded; the stock was given to Barritt and the note to Pandolfo. To that time, Olson said, Pandolfo had paid nothing on the note.

"And when were you informed that the agreement would not be carried out?" Rush asked.

"On the 27th of December," Olson said.

"Right after Pandolfo and Barritt were indicted in the federal court in Fergus Falls?" Rush asked, and Olson replied with a short nod.

The next witness revealed a surprising offer Pandolfo had made. The witness was W. T. Maxwell, of Little Rock, Arkansas, the commissioner of banking and insurance and executive officer of the Arkansas Blue Sky Board. Attorney Epstein read correspondence passing between Pandolfo and Maxwell relating to a license to sell stock in Arkansas. Shortly after Epstein began reading, defense attorney Peaks objected that the prosecution was speeding through the parts of the correspondence favorable to Pandolfo. After a nod from Landis, Epstein then read with a flourish bordering on comedy.

Pandolfo's first request for a license had been denied because Maxwell felt the 50 percent taken by the fiscal agent was too large a share. Maxwell still replied unfavorably after being told that Pandolfo's contract had been revised to drop his percentage to 25. The Arkansas Board wanted to know what had become of the surplus—at that time about $159,000—taken in by the company. Pandolfo asked them to send an auditor to St. Cloud to check the company's books.

Pandolfo then made an astonishing offer: He would place in an Arkansas bank ten percent of the price of every share of stock sold in the state; the money would be kept for five years and be returned to the shareholders if they had not received a six percent dividend on their investment by that time.

Despite Pandolfo's unique proposition, Maxwell testified, Arkansas never did license the sale of Pan stock in the state. But Maxwell was followed on the stand by Walter R. Flint, a Peoria lawyer who admitted that he was "the whole Blue Sky law of Illinois" at the time the company's application to sell stock in Illinois was delivered by George Heidman in person. On being shown letters reporting that other states had granted the company license to sell stock, Flint said he had done so too.

The first witness to testify on Wednesday morning, November 5, gave the defense some of its best moments. Sidney Weis, employed in a Chicago jewelry store, testified that he had bought two shares of Pan stock in 1917, and later, after seeing the Pan car at the Chicago auto show, he was so impressed that he bought eight more shares. He had even made a trip to St. Cloud early in 1918 to visit the plant. But the point of his testimony for the prosecution was that on September 5, 1919, a month-and-a-half before the trial, he had been visited by H. D. Lambourne, Pan stock salesman, who offered to pay his fare to St. Cloud to visit the plant and to pay him ten dollars for his time. Lambourne did not mention the trial, Weis said, but spoke of opening an agency in Chicago and suggested that Weis, after his trip to St. Cloud, could be of assistance to him.

When the opportunity to cross-examine Weis came, Cummins approached the witness quickly, holding out a sheet of paper. "Will you identify this statement as one you made to postal inspectors investigating the Pan Motor Company?" When Weis had done so, Cummins asked him to read it, "slowly and carefully, please," to the jury.

Weis read:

> I have on hand a good proportion of their correspondence to me and have read and re-read it several times. There is one thing that stands out very forcibly in all statements: that is the frankness of their accomplishments, their expenditures and their honesty. I made a trip to Pan Motor Company in the early part of this year and without the knowledge of any officer of the company (they do not know that I have been there even now!) and made an investigation of my own on my own account in regards to the developments of the buildings which was true in every detail. Another thing which was very impressive and strong for the name Pan was the confidence in and pride for the Pan Motor Company of the people of the city of St. Cloud. They have seen the company springing up. They know what has been accomplished, and they stand for Pan heart and soul, and a big majority, appreciating their prospects, had stood behind that company as the nation stood behind the Liberty loans. I've been impressed with the organization of the Pan Motor Company.
>
> I'm not far from being in financial straits as regards my capital, but I am a plus subscriber and am heart and soul for the Pan Motor Company. I can't be too enthusiastic for Pan and justice. I have studied carefully all the statements made to me as regards the motor company as to their truth. The statements are absolutely beyond criticism.

At the conclusion of the reading Cummins asked Weis, "When did you make that statement, Mr. Weis?"

Weis pointed to the bottom of the sheet. "The date's right here. November 8, 1918."

Cummins smiled broadly, said, "Why, that's almost exactly a year ago," and dismissed the witness.

Most of the rest of the testimony that day centered on the Pan Motor Company's permission to sell stock in various states and on the statements made to several purchasers of stock.

On Thursday the prosecution and defense argued, through the testimony of several witnesses, concerning the admissibility of the report Pandolfo had written, titled "The Real Truth," in answer to the Monte Vista Stock Sales Investigating Committee report. The door was opened by prosecution witness L. R. Whitted, an architect and superintendent of construction for the Treasury Department at Glenwood Springs, Colorado. After quoting some of the more colorful language Pandolfo had used in his retort, the prosecution introduced a letter Whitted had written to the Pan Motor Company claiming that "the value claimed for the stock is in intangible assets. Too much money paid into the company has been diverted into the promotion of it."

In cross-examination, Fletcher Dobyns attempted to ascertain the witness' qualifications for being considered an expert in the organizational requirements of a large company, and he probed for bias in the witness. "Was Congressman Edward J. Taylor instrumental in securing your position for you?" Dobyns asked. (Pandolfo was then in the process of suing Taylor for libel.) The prosecution objected to the question and Landis upheld their objection, telling Dobyns, "You can try Congressman Taylor elsewhere."

Dobyns was quoting from "The Real Truth" when Landis recessed for the day, and the attorney had to pick up with the following quote from Pandolfo on Friday morning:

> In the beginning, when there was nothing back of the proposed Pan Motor Company except the plan and myself, you will observe that the enemy did not at that time frighten me, nor did he succeed in running me out of the country. . . . We have almost 40,000 subscribers and stockholders who are with us and who are for us, and who will go with us, if necessary right up into the mouth of the cannon.

Dobyns finally released Whitted and the government called its last witness, Wesley Bennett, an accountant with the Department of Justice. Bennett had examined the company's books after the first indictment against the company in Fergus Falls, Minnesota, early in December 1918. When the case was dismissed in January 1919, he had stopped his audit only to take it up again when the second indictment was issued.

Bennett testified that the Pan Motor Company had opened its

books about March 5, 1917. (He had never examined the books of the fiscal agency.) On April 27, 1917, he testified, the company had $30,000 in the bank, at which time Pandolfo was no longer responsible for the company's bills, according to his contract. Up to May 31, 1918, the date of the hearing before the Minnesota Securities Commission and the pivotal date for all subsequent discussion, 373,000 shares of stock had been sold. From that date up to April 1, 1919, 259,450 more shares had been sold. Up to May 31, 1918, $2,500,148 had been received in the sale of stock. The company, Bennett testified, had received $914,518, and the fiscal agency had received $1,585,630.

Following a lengthy explanation of Pandolfo's remuneration under the two contracts he had with the Pan Motor Company, attorney Rush asked Bennett, "This is too confusing for many of us. Do you have a total figure for Mr. Pandolfo's compensation?"

Bennett consulted a small notebook and gave as the total figure $628,513.25. When asked if that was the final figure, Bennett replied, "That's the amount received up to April first. But there is still $133,482 due him under the old contract that has not yet been paid up."

Testimony then turned to the cost of producing cars. Bennett said that the company had made 46 cars up to May 31, 1918, at a cost of $48,887, an average of $1062.76 per car. He testified that $272,950 worth of material had been stocked for production of the Model 250. (He had been told by Everett Jeffrey, assistant accountant at Pan, that the model was so named because it was intended to make only 250 units before starting production on the Model A Pan car.) Up to April 1, 1919, according to Bennett, the company had assembled and sold 174 cars, for which they had received $184,205, or an average price of $1058.64, sustaining a loss of $331 on each car, a total loss of over $57,000. For 1919, the company had purchased enough parts and material for 25 Model A's, Bennett said. Questioned about the Pan Tank Tread Tractor, Bennett fixed the cost of the one model produced at $7733.

In a final question to Bennett, and over the objections of the defense, Rush asked the witness if he knew how many Liberty bonds had been received by the company in payment for Pan stock. As Landis weighed his decision, Bennett quietly consulted his notebook. With the objection overruled, Bennett answered, "$500,000 worth."

Cummins' cross-examination of Bennett was first directed to showing that, despite the discrepancy indicated in the amount Pandolfo received from the sale of the company's stock and the amount the company received, this was according to his contract as fiscal agent. Then, after several questions concerning the company's accounting methods, which Bennett agreed were exemplary, Cummins took up the matter of the cost of materials for the automobiles.

"Of the amount you say was material for the Model 250 cars, did you mean to imply that the full amount—all $275,950—was intended for the Model 250 Pan?"

"No, I did not," Bennett answered, and Judge Landis' head snapped up in attention. "I wanted to explain that. There were parts included in that batch that were ordered for other machines, about $50,000 worth."

Cummins nodded calmly and continued. "You also testified that up to April first of this year the Pan Motor Company had produced only 174 cars of a model they were supposed to produce 200. Do you know for a fact that the remainder were not produced?"

"No, I do not. I only know what took place up to April first."

"Now, and I want you to consider carefully before you answer, you testified that the company bought materials for only 25 Model A Pan cars. Did you note anything further about these cars?"

Cummins stared intently at Bennett as the witness lowered his head for a moment in concentration. "Well," Bennett finally answered, "there was some discussion that these were for demonstration purposes."

"Exactly!" Cummins slapped the rail in front of the jury box.

Following another series of questions in which the expenses of the first tractor were explained, Cummins said, "Now, to clear up any lingering doubts or false impressions that may have been created. . ." the lawyer paused momentarily, ". . .in our first testimony, let's get all of this into some figures we can understand. Up to April first of this year, what were the total stock sales of the Pan Motor Company?"

Bennett consulted his notebook and placed the figure at $6,331,105. "But has the company or the fiscal agent received all the money from these sales?"

"No, certainly not," Bennett answered.

"Well, what were the total fixed assets of the company on the same date—April first, this year?"

Bennett flipped some pages in his notebook and gave his answer: $1,550,768.

"This is apart from continuing overhead, like salaries, heat, power, and the like?" Cummins asked.

"Of course."

Cummins paused for several moments, mentally phrasing his next question. "Mr. Bennett, from the figures you have at hand and which you have verified for the government itself, can you tell me whether or not it is true that Mr. Pandolfo's net share of the sales up to May 31 of last year represented LESS THAN TEN PERCENT of the total shares sold?"

Bennett did some fast figuring in his notebook, flipping pages back and forth as spectators in the silent courtroom watched. Faint echoes from the street, six floors below, were the only sounds in the courtroom until Bennett looked up and said, "That's about right." Cummins turned away, dismissing the witness.

Following a short discussion among the prosecuting attorneys, Benjamin Epstein rose and said, "Your Honor, the prosecution rests."

It was 3:40 p.m., Friday, November 7, 1919.

Judge Landis dismissed the jury until Saturday morning and prepared to hear motions for dismissal from the defense attorneys.

During the brief intermission this required, Edward A. Macdonald, a Marquette, Michigan, attorney, talked with the St. Cloud defendants, particularly Fred Schilplin. Macdonald's father, Colin F. Macdonald, had been editor of the *St. Cloud Daily Times*, and had trained Schilplin in journalism.

On behalf of George Heidman and Norman Street, Fletcher Dobyns took up most of the remaining afternoon in discussion of his motion to release his clients from further hearing. "It has not been established," Dobyns argued, "that a plant was NOT built, nor that stock would NOT be worth ten dollars a share when the company is on a production basis, nor that automobiles of good quality are NOT being built in that plant." As to the conspiracy charge, Dobyns argued that where this charge is made a defendant cannot be held responsible for statements made by another unless it is definitely proved that previous agreement existed between them to commit the specific offense.

In rebuttal, Rush claimed that Heidman and Street had helped Pandolfo and Wigle at the very time that "their iniquitous contract was written, providing that half of the money collected should go to Pandolfo. If there has been fraud in the case, it started then."

Discussing the motion, Landis asked Dobyns, "Did you ever hear of any other company where 50 percent of the cash collected was turned over to the president to do with as he pleased?"

"No, I didn't," the attorney said. "I admit it was a novel plan. But Pandolfo was under some constraints from the Board of Directors."

Landis was aware of only the first part of Dobyns' answer. "Yes," the judge replied, nodding rapidly, "it certainly was *novel!*"

Despite Landis' sarcasm, Dobyns continued earnestly. "But there is nothing illegal about it. A plan like this depends on the honesty with which it is worked. Now, no evidence has been introduced which indicates that anything but the utmost honesty has been used by all concerned. Why, look at the plant and facilities they have built in St. Cloud. Isn't that evidence of their good faith? If they had wanted to be fraudulent, they could have taken the money and left."

Landis was shaking his head before Dobyns had finished. "I would remind you, counselor, one of the worst frauds we ever had in Chicago was the Consumer's Packing Company, yet when they were brought to court they continually pointed to over $300,000 that had been invested in actual buildings."

Landis then moved on to criticize the company's acceptance of Liberty bonds in payment for stock, although this action concerned neither Heidman nor Street directly. From the vigor with which he attacked the practice, Landis' super-patriotism seemed more offended by this act than by any possible fraud. "You think it was right to take the securities at less than par and ask the next man to buy at par? I think *that* is fraudulent."

Similar dismissal motions were made on behalf of all other defendants, and Landis promised rulings on the motions in the morning. Late in the afternoon he recessed the court. But courtroom activity involving the Pan Motor Company was not yet concluded for the day.

That evening Landis was hearing motions in another case running concurrently when a bailiff approached the bench and spoke quietly to him. In the flurry of activity that followed, Landis dismissed the litigants then in court and summoned Miss Florence Schoenbeck to the bench. When she had identified herself as an operative for the Jones Detective Agency of Chicago, Landis, his voice barely under control, demanded, "Now, tell me, what do you mean by bothering the jury in the Pan Motor case?"

Miss Schoenbeck said she had been employed to watch the jurors. "I watch them when they come out of the jury room to go to lunch; I follow them on the street; I watch them wherever and whenever I can. I stay with them until they are taken to their hotel rooms at night." Her calm description of her activities may have soothed Landis, but his next curt question was asked with a stern scowl still evident.

"Who employs you?"

"Mr. John E. Jones."

"Bailiff!" Landis shouted. "Take her into my chambers and have her use the telephone there to summon Jones here at once." Landis fidgeted continually at the bench until Miss Schoenbeck returned and reported that she couldn't locate Jones, only Frederick Lynch, the assistant manager, who did not know where Jones was.

Landis wheeled around to the clerk and gave instructions to issue subpoenas for both men, Jones and Lynch. While he waited for the subpoenas, Landis questioned Miss Schoenbeck. "It is my understanding that two women have been trying to make trouble for these jurors. Was anybody working with you?"

"No, sir."

"Was there anyone with you recently when the marshals chased you down Michigan Avenue?"

"No, but my cousin, Mrs. Ruth Hamrock, was with me in a restaurant once when I was watching the jurors."

Landis got Mrs. Hamrock's address, and the clerk was soon busy on another subpoena. Lynch was brought into the courtroom shortly, and Landis immediately motioned him to the bench. After identifying Miss Schoenbeck as an operative, Lynch said in reply to Landis' question that the agency had been hired by a J. L. Hopkins.

"Did he say he wanted you to work for him, or was he hiring you on behalf of a third party?" Landis asked.

"He said he was counsel for some of the officers of the Pan Motor Company of St. Cloud."

"And exactly what were you hired to do?"

"We were told to watch the jury, that's all."

Landis made additional notes and then asked angrily, "Can't you find Jones?"

"No, sir. I haven't been able to."

"You're a fine detective! Well, we'll all wait for Mr. Jones." When Jones arrived later, Landis went over the same questions for the third time. Jones said he had been hired by S. C. Pandolfo and that he reported directly to him. "What were his instructions to you, exactly?" Landis asked again.

"I was to see that the jurors did not read newspapers and that they were not interfered with in any way."

"What do you think we have bailiffs and marshals for?" Landis snapped. "I told the jurors they might read newspapers as long as they didn't read articles referring to this case. Were you told to get so close to them that they would have to walk over your operatives in going from place to place?'

"No, I gave Miss Schoenbeck instructions that she should never get closer than 25 feet to the jurors."

"Well, she did!" Landis snapped. "Now, how much were you paid for this?"

"We agreed on seven dollars a day."

"Seven dollars a day," Landis repeated, shaking his head. "I don't know that I have the power to prevent anybody foolishly spending his money to protect a jury already protected by my bailiffs, but I can protect these jurors from having to step over the bodies of your operatives. I warn you right now to stop the practice."

Assistant district attorney James Glass, who had entered the courtroom early in Landis' questioning, volunteerd the information that he and Sylvester Rush had been followed and watched for some time. Landis threw up his hands in despair and stamped from the courtroom, shaking his head.

CHAPTER IX

. . . through the valley of the shadow of death.

SATURDAY MORNING JUDGE LANDIS was impatient to start. He convened court a little before the usual ten o'clock starting time. Before bringing the jury in, he called Pandolfo to the bench and asked sharply, "Did you hire a man named Jones in connection with this case?"

"Yes, your honor," Pandolfo nodded.

"What did you ask him to do?"

"I gave him a number of detailed instructions."

Landis said tensely, "I want to know what you told him to do." Pandolfo started to speak and then paused to consider his answer. Landis lost the feeble grip on his patience and wheeled to face the defense attorneys. "I want to say to you counsel that after 15 years of experience in this court I would advise you to look up the character of this man, discover what kind of environment you are working in. I don't know where he got his training but you men have your reputation to protect." He turned back to Pandolfo, who had listened to Landis calmly. "There is another thing: why was a woman employed in this case?"

"I didn't know a woman had been assigned to the case," Pandolfo replied, genuinely surprised.

"Did Jones' agents visit the offices and homes of the jurors?" Landis asked severely.

"I can make an explanation of all that," Pandolfo said, but Landis waved him back to his place.

"I've become impatient," Landis said, closing the discussion for the moment with the understatement of the week. Landis' previous inclination and present mood were against all previous motions for dismissal and they were summarily denied.

The jury was brought in and the defense proper began with the appearance of its first witness, Leroy Brown, Pan manager of manufacturing. Brown testified that the Pan Motor Company was not producing cars in quantity because machinery and material were in extremely short supply during the last few months of the war and immediately following. "Which models were you working on? What cars are you referring to?" Dobyns asked.

"The Model 250," Brown answered. Dobyns had established Brown's competence at the beginning of his testimony with a recital of his previous employment, and he now asked Brown, "What is your estimate of the capabilities of the Pan Motor plant, in the light of the experience you have had at Lansing, Cleveland, Detroit, and Toledo? Would you say that the Pan Motor Company is immediately capable, or in the very near future capable of producing automobiles at a profitable rate?"

"Yes." Brown answered. "We have started production on the Model A, and we will get 30 cars out this month, 60 next month, and 70 every month after that until next July." Asked to characterize the atmosphere of the Pan plant, Brown replied, "The conditions under which the men work are the best. The general cleanliness of the plant is reflected in the attitude of the men; they are proud of it. They help to keep it that way. This is not a particularly clean industry and it is difficult. They are also proud of the homes in Pan Town. I would call the Pan plant a model establishment."

This first short direct examination of Brown was concluded by Dobyns asking Brown what his present salary was.

"Ten thousand dollars a year," Brown said.

"Have you had other offers since coming to Pan?"

"Yes, several. Some at higher pay."

"Why did you refuse them?"

"I believe the Pan Motor Company has a bright future. I'd like to be a part of it."

Cross-examining Brown, Rush avoided challenging the witness' competence and confined his questions to verifying information. "Now, Mr. Brown, if my figuring is correct, the production figures for the Model A Pan car will come to over 550 cars. Is that correct?"

"That's about right. We have placed the order, internally in the company between departments, for 500 engine castings."

"Well, why are you so certain that this schedule can be met? We have heard from other witnesses how, for one reason or another, earlier production promises could not be kept."

"We have between 80 and 90 percent of the parts for the first 100 cars on hand right now."

"Now, let's be specific," Rush insisted. "What is done right now, at this moment? I assume you are in touch with the plant in St. Cloud?"

"Yes, I am, and one car is completed and was in the plant Tuesday night. Fourteen will be in chassis paint by Saturday night, tonight. Starting Monday, production will be one or a little more a day until we get accustomed to the production line. Then it will go faster."

"Why, then, has it taken so long to get production started?"

"This is a new model," Brown patiently explained. "Testing took longer because we couldn't get the parts we needed, and our capacity for our own production was being used on other items."

Brown was excused and Victor Gauvreau was called. Gauvreau's dark good looks and his ease of manner made him an attractive witness; his training and experience made him an expert one. One observer remarked that from the appearance of Brown and Gauvreau, Pandolfo should have built the best car in the country. In his thick French accent, Gauvreau described his education in French technical schools, his employment in France and in America—at Mercer, Chevrolet, Dodge, Frontenac, and Buick. He had first heard of Pandolfo in a letter asking if he would like to be the chief engineer for a new company to be located in St. Cloud. After an exchange of letters and an interview, Gauvreau came to St. Cloud in April 1917. He was told to go to work immediately on a reliable engine and a sturdy car with high clearance, low center of gravity, and whatever other features he thought should be on a quality car. He was limited, he said, by having to follow somewhat the cars that Reed & Glaser were doing, but they had been given the same instructions by Pandolfo so there was no great disparity between the goals, only in the means to reach them.

Questioned by Brower, Gauvreau said it usually took 18 to 20 months to design and prepare a new car for production. He said the designing on the Pan had been completed in May 1919. The design had evolved from three hand-built models in the fall of 1917 and spring of 1918; one of the three was sent out on exhibition, to the LaSalle Hotel in Chicago among other places; another was sent on long road tests, to Texas, for example; he had used the third to test the engine in various ways. He described the tests that were completed only two weeks earlier when five of the new Pan engines had been mounted in stripped-down chassis and sent on test runs in northern Minnesota.

His detailed description of the Pan engine was perhaps too technical for most jurors but served to satisfy them that the witness and the engine he had designed were what they had been claimed to be.

During the noon recess the exhibits of Pan drop forgings were brought over from the Atlantic Hotel, and Gauvreau, in his testimony that afternoon, explained the use of each one in the car. First the attorneys, then the jurors, and finally Judge Landis stood and crowded closer, their interest in automobile design obvious.

Brower led Gauvreau through the process of designing a car and preparing it for production. The generally complicated process was made more complicated, Gauvreau said, by the shortage of critical materials and labor conditions. They had hoped to get the Model A into production by July 1919, but were not able to start until this first week in November.

Concerning the Model 250, Gauvreau said he and Pandolfo had first discussed it in the fall of 1917. The machines turned out by Reed & Glaser just wouldn't do, so in addition to working on the Model A, the engineering staff had set about redesigning the Model 10 into the Model 250. Reed & Glaser were not really at fault. Pandolfo had specified certain features he wanted on the car and the Indianapolis engineers had done their best in the time allowed. Not only were the proper parts unavailable in general supply, there wasn't time enough to produce them in quantity. A compromise was accepted, but the Pan engineer did not want to continue that compromise into quantity production. They had replaced the Rutenber engine with the Continental in September 1917, but these were not immediately available, so there were further delays in the delivery of cars.

Gauvreau was still testifying about the cars when Landis recessed for the weekend.

Landis' humor occasionally rose above his stern manner. He was presiding over other litigation in the hours before the Pan trial opened in the mornings. On Monday, November 10, lawyers in a bankruptcy case he was trying were in court when Landis had to call a halt and prepare for the Pan trial. "When these gentlemen here charter about six trains and go home," he told the lawyers, indicating the participants in the Pan case with a majestic sweep of his arm, "then I'll be glad to see you. I think I'll be lonesome then."

With Gauvreau back on the stand, Brower asked about the Pan Tank Tread Tractor. The engineer showed copies of correspondence with the Buda Motor Company indicating that Pan Motor Company had placed an order for 1,000 motors for their tractor in 1918.

In cross-examination, the prosecution ignored all testimony relating to the Model A Pan car and probed instead the matter of the Tank Tread Tractor and the Reed & Glaser-designed original Pan. Gauvreau said he was not qualified to say much about the tractor's design except that after receiving the first engine, around which the tractor had been designed, they were unable to get delivery on any more. Repeated attempts were made to get engines from Buda and finally from any other source. But Buda engines were needed in Nash trucks for the government, and other engines were similarly committed to the war effort by this time.

Concerning the original Pan car produced by Reed & Glaser, Gauvreau made it plain he did not blame the firm for the car's shortcomings. "I am not trying to say that nothing went wrong with those cars. They were abominable under certain conditions. But it was not the fault of the design; the design, basically, was a good one. When we were able to replace the castings with forgings and redesign a few parts, the cars gave good service. In fact, they are still being used by many of the original owners."

When Epstein asked how they compared with the new Model A's now being built, Gauvreau smiled and said, "Well, I designed the new car, and of course I think it is much better."

Alfred Krieg, the tractor engineer who had replaced LaFond, took the stand following Gauvreau and his testimony took most of the rest of the afternoon. After describing the difficulties in attempting to manufacture the tank tread design because of the unavailability of an engine, he described the performance of the prototype tractor in tests in St. Cloud and at Wichita, Kansas, where the tractor pulled three plows with ease. In an endurance test in Wichita, the machine had plowed seven or eight acres without stopping. "And mind you, this was the first design . . . the first model of the design."

As for quantity production of the tractor, Krieg admitted that it wouldn't have made much difference if they had been able to get the Buda engine. The War Production Board, given the job of policing the nation's industrial production during the war, "limited tractor production to a percentage of what had been done the year before, and, of course, we hadn't had any tractor production the year before. The restriction was relaxed after the Armistice was signed in November 1918, but by then we had abandoned that design and were developing a conventional four-wheel tractor."

"Why did you abandon the design if had shown so much promise?" Brower asked.

"There were several reasons," Krieg replied. "First, while it was promising, the design was not my own and I was not totally familiar with it. When we couldn't get engines from any other source, it seemed best to design a wholly new tractor around our own engine. And then, we were not giving up on the design altogether, only shelving it for a time. I thought that following the war the government would have many new ideas on tread design and the like, based on their experience with tanks, and that would be a great advantage in a new design." Krieg said he started on a new tractor design in September or October 1918 and the first model was ready in June 1919.

A short note in the *St. Cloud Journal-Press* explained that with more witnesses coming in as the defense presented its case, the Pan Motor Company's headquarters in the Atlantic Hotel was becoming crowded, and the eight St. Cloud directors with their attorney Ripley Brower had moved three blocks north to the Hotel Morrison, where Ludwig Ladner, a nephew of defendant Charles Ladner, was assistant manager. A different explanation for the move would be given later by Pandolfo.

Tuesday morning, November 11, Judge Landis arrived 30 minutes late. A few minutes before eleven o'clock he ordered the bailiff to bring the Pan jury in. "Gentlemen of the jury, as you observed, I was a little tardy this morning. It was occasioned by the fact that I was under obligation to visit an Army hospital, which engagement was made in consideration of the fact that this is the 11th of November.

"I assume it requires nothing from me to you to awaken in your minds what I am quite sure you are all conscious of on this anniversary. In view of the fact that it is near the hour of 11:00, which is a tremendous hour, I will dismiss the jury until 11:05 with only this suggestion: It will fit the occasion for each citizen not on dress parade, not for the effect upon other people but for the good it will do the citizen himself, at eleven o'clock, wherever he may be, to come to attention with his face to the east, as a reminder to himself of what he owes to the soldiers living, and of what he owes to the memory of the soldiers dead."

The jury left the courtroom and the spectators, lawyers, and defendants sought quiet corners in the hallways on the sixth floor. The entire Federal Building had a subdued atmosphere on this first anniversary of the day of peace in Europe.

Shortly after eleven o'clock, Landis gaveled the court into session and Ray J. Fitness, the next defense witness, was sworn. Early in his testimony, Fitness said that in July 1918 the Pan Motor Company had joined the War Industries Board in St. Paul to seek war orders not only to do its patriotic duty, he frankly admitted, but "to get some work to keep us going until we could build cars again."

Much of the rest of Fitness' testimony centered on the reasons for delay in production of the Model A Pan. "First we were held up on bodies from Racine Manufacturing; then engine blocks and heads from Interstate Foundry were late; fenders, supposed to come in by June or July, were delayed by strikes. Finally we rented a small foundry in St. Cloud to get the castings we needed. The first bodies came in from Racine a month ago."

Epstein, in cross-examining Fitness, wanted to know the number of parts the Pan motor Company was able to make for its own car. "I would say that Ford, Dodge, and Buick are making more parts for their cars than we do for ours," Fitness said. "But we are on a par with Paige, Saxon, Hudson, Velie, and others."

Although it was late in the afternoon when Fitness' testimony was concluded, the defense placed four more witnesses on the stand before Landis adjourned. All four were from Hannibal, Missouri. The first, a saloonkeeper named R. G. Schwab, had bought stock in the Pan Motor Company early. During his direct examination he insisted he had no complaints concerning his purchase. In cross-examination, Epstein asked Schwab if he knew what Pandolfo was receiving for his services. "No, I was satisfied it was a good company with a future, and I bought stock in it."

"Suppose I were to tell you," Epstein said, "that he has already received 650,000 dollars and he still has more coming to him?"

"Well, I guess he needs it to run the business," Schwab said, apparently undisturbed.

"No. This is money he gets himself. This is the money he gets as salary for running the company."

"Then I think he is a pretty smart man to get that much money."

Epstein passed up the opportunity to cross-examine the remaining Missouri witnesses.

Just before adjournment, Brower said the defense planned on introducing motion pictures taken at the plant, and after Brower described what they would be, Landis permitted the equipment required to show the pictures to be brought in. The next morning the defense called Arthur G. Strom, the photographer who had taken the movies, to verify them. In the course of his opening testimony Strom mentioned that he had taken the films at the direction of Ben Forsyth, Pan advertising manager. Landis immediately reversed his ruling of the day before and would not allow the motion pictures to be shown. The statement he made in denying the films became a pivotal point in the appeals Pandolfo later made on his conviction. "It is a matter of common knowledge, not only to me as a judge," Landis said, "but to laymen as well, that an advertising man does not reproduce a thing as it is. If he did, he would lose his job. I know he will show only pictures that will represent just what he wants to be seen. In consideration of this, I will reverse my ruling of yesterday and not allow the motion pictures to be introduced as evidence." The defense attorneys were astonished; Pandolfo was stunned. Most of the company's advertising, already in evidence, had been produced by Forsyth, and Landis had made no objection to it.

Despite Strom's later statement that Forsyth had only gone along to guide him to the areas he was to photograph and in no way had posed any special scenes or staged any activity for the camera, Landis stuck to his ruling forbidding the films.

Sydney C. Hoel of Grand Junction, Colorado, had been a member of the Colorado stockholders' committee whose report had been referred to in earlier testimony. He had been in government reclamation service for two years and presently was the president of the Noah Ross Business College in Grand Junction. He had seen much literature from and heard a lot of talk about the Pan Motor Company and had written to a brother in Paynesville, 35 miles west of St. Cloud, asking if the directors were good men. His brother's favorable report, not only on the directors but also on the buildings rapidly going up, convinced him to buy Pan stock. He became a member of the Colorado committee because of his familiarity with business methods and his family connections in the area around St. Cloud. The committee had spent four days at the plant in St. Cloud in late December 1918.

During cross-examination, Hoel was led, almost word by word, through the report his committee had issued with particular attention being paid to the part referring to "the gigantic conspiracy against the Pan Motor Company."

"Now, Mr. Hoel, where did you get the idea there was a conspiracy?"

"I had read the articles in a Grand Junction newspaper against the company and articles in magazines, such as *World's Work*. Then when we came to St. Cloud we were shown other articles that had been written against the company. Why, when you stood right there in buildings, which some of those articles said were not built and never would be, what else could you call it but a conspiracy?" Hoel's soft answers, given in an almost timid voice, were in sharp contrast to Epstein's brusque, confident manner.

"What I want to know, Mr. Hoel, is, did Mr. Pandolfo suggest that phrase to your committee?"

"No. At least, I don't recall that he used it. He might have, but we didn't talk to him for long. I think I would have remembered it if he had used it. He makes a very deep impression on you."

A curious legal charade the next day caused the defense to spend most of the morning developing evidence it had hoped to enter into the record with a few questions. The witness was Roy M. Halliday of the Bank of North Dakota at Bismarck, a former deputy of the Blue Sky Commission in North Dakota. He had visited the plant in the spring of 1919, but when the defense attempted to introduce the report he wrote to his committee, the prosecution objected, and was sustained by Landis, on the ground that the report was not official. Landis would not even permit Halliday to use the report as memoranda. The point of Halliday's testimony was that as a result of his investigation the company's license to sell stock was not revoked in North Dakota.

The next witness, William Bell Mitchell, was the first of an interrupted parade of St. Cloud residents called as character witnesses. Mitchell had retired from the *Journal-Press* 27 years earlier, and he had interests in several manufacturing companies in the St. Cloud area. During his testimony, Mitchell mentioned that the fact that "only 50 percent of the money taken in went for sales expense and promotion, and guaranteed the remainder for unimpaired capital" particularly appealed to him. He also testified to the good character of defendant Hugh Evans. During cross-examination, Sylvester Rush ignored the testimony about Evans to concentrate on Mitchell's affinity for Pandolfo's plan of organization. Mitchell said he bought stock first in 1917, then purchased more in 1918 and 1919 when he saw the rapid progress the company was making. "You say you had known companies that used practically all the money they had taken in for promotion purposes," Rush said. "Would you tell us what those companies were, or even about one of them?"

"Yes, I will," Mitchell said with a fervor that reminded older St. Cloud residents in the courtroom of his aunt, the fiery former editor of the St. Cloud Democrat, Jane Grey Swisshelm. Mitchell told about the Fibreware Company of St. Cloud in which he had invested $100. As far as he knew, the company never turned out a single piece of saleable goods. "I never saw the 100 dollars or any part of it again."

"Do you think you would have been better off if you had invested 200 dollars and they had used half of it for promotion?" Rush asked.

Mitchell leaned back in the witness chair. "If the company had used only 50 of my 100 dollars for honest buildings and materials I would not have lost so much." Rush excused the witness.

Part of the testimony of August Thummel, of Parnell, Missouri, ignited Landis' ire late in the afternoon and caused him to send the jury out while he probed for answers to some questions. Thummel, a wealthy farmer, had purchased 2040 shares of Pan stock. He assured the defense attorney that he was aware of Pandolfo's remuneration and that he was satisfied with his investment. But when he stated that on September 27, 1919—less than a month before the trial began—he had been visited by a man named Marles or Marlin, claiming to be a postal inspector, Landis' undivided attention was riveted on the witness. "I'm sure the man was acquainted with the operation of the postal department," Thummel insisted.

"How do you know that for certain?" Landis interjected.

"Because he referred to some blanks I had received from the post office, and he wanted to know why I hadn't filled them out and sent them in," Thummel replied. "He couldn't know about that unless he had some connection with the post office." Prosecution attorneys denied that a postal inspector, real or bogus, had been sent by them. The two postal inspectors in the courtroom were asked to stand, but Thummel failed to identify either man. "The man who called on me was an elderly man, tall and rather gray," he said.

"Let's get to the bottom of this," Landis said with clipped determination, and the jury was led out of the courtroom. The judge drew a number of letters from a file folder. "These are from the wives of jurors in this case. In each of them the wife writes that they have been visited by men representing themselves as federal agents, questioning them regarding the integrity of their husband. Possibly these federal agents were also detectives," Landis said with a sharp look in Pandolfo's direction. "I'll tell you, gentlemen, this is a dangerous situation. It is an attempt to import into the Federal Building methods that would have degraded the north side in its worst days." Landis' reference was to the Illinois criminal court, notorious for its scandals. "I wish I knew who was responsible for this kind of work. I never wished anything so hard in my life." The defense attorneys told Landis they believed that Richard A. Lee, attorney for the Associated Advertising Clubs of the World, was responsible for shadowing people in the case. They pointed out that Lee had been sued by Pandolfo for $100,000. Cummins assured Landis that Pandolfo had disclaimed any knowledge of these activities. "I have no doubt that you as attorneys are acting in good faith," Landis said, "but I am suspicious of what goes on behind your backs."

Brower, Peaks, Dobyns, and Cummins said they had been followed wherever they went since the trial began. The prosecuting attorneys, Rush and Epstein, advised Landis that they, too, had been followed. Landis shook his head in disbelief. "Things are coming to a dangerous state when a woman almost embraces the jurors and has to be kicked out of this deal to keep her from coming into actual physical contact with the jurymen. Naturally this looks bad for the defense."

Pandolfo rose to his feet. "I want to say a word before the jury is recalled. I want to say that Richard A. Lee, counsel for the Associated Advertising Clubs of the World, is directing this prosecution."

Rush stabbed a finger in Pandolfo's direction. "That's a lie!" he shouted.

"It is true!" Pandolfo shouted back.

"Oh, sit down!" Landis thundered at both men and pounded his gavel until they subsided.

With the jury recalled, Thummel, who sat quietly but brightly interested during the discussion, was excused while Landis promised an investigation of the post office inspector's visits and then adjourned for the day.

On Friday, Bishop Joseph F. Busch of the St. Cloud diocese, was called as a witness. Brower asked him to explain in his own words his interest in the Pan Motor Company. He had talked many times with Pandolfo about the plan of organization, the bishop said. He had been hesitant about buying stock and even about supporting the company vocally. He was about to name some of the concerns that made him suspicious when Landis said brusquely, "That kind of detail isn't necessary."

The bishop nodded and continued. "Well, an additional reason for my hesitation was my official position. I would be lending the approval of the episcopal office to a private conviction. But then I watched the company grow and saw the sentiment in favor of it in the whole community. I met Mr. Pandolfo many more times and formed a favorable opinion of him. He had a reputation in St. Cloud, at least to my personal knowledge, for honesty and fair dealing. I bought stock in the company, personally, on three different occasions."

The bishop's cross-examination was handled gingerly. Asked about Pandolfo's high remuneration for selling the stock while stockholders received no dividends, Busch replied that during the formative years Pandolfo's work was most difficult; later, when the company had been established and was earning a profit, the stockholders would reap the benefits of Pandolfo's labor while his remuneration would decrease.

When asked if he was influenced in his decision regarding Pandolfo's character by the donation of a Pan car to a charitable organization in St. Cloud, Busch answered, "I see no reason to rule out such evidence of his character. If he was merely trying to buy our high regard, he nevertheless gave us a worthwhile and useful gift. And if he was being genuinely charitable, it certainly would be uncharitable of me to ignore his generous action. I am quite sure that there are some men who would do such a thing only to gain favor, but I prefer to think it came from his sense of right until it has been proven otherwise."

Brower, in re-direct examination, asked Busch to tell of his association with the other St. Cloud directors, and the witness began detailing how each of them had helped him raise money for the Institute building, erected as a social center for the community. As he listed the efforts of each of the directors, the prosecution attorneys squirmed under the shower of remembered good works, generous gifts, charitable acts. When they finally objected to the litany as being unnecessarily detailed, Brower, after a nod from Landis, asked the bishop if he could testify generally to the good reputations of the men in their community, and Busch said he could do so willingly.

F. D. Phillips of North Yakima, Washington, explained how the dealership arrangements of the Pan Motor Company worked. He had purchased 150 shares of stock, he said, and after visiting the plant in St. Cloud he bought another 150 and signed up as a dealer for the Pan car. After driving over rough roads in the Yakima Valley he liked the car so much he took on the distributorship for the territory between the Rocky and Cascade Mountains. Asked how the discounts on the car were set up, Phillips explained, "The dealer gets 15 of the 20 percent given to the distributor, and when a car is sold to a stockholder, who gets a 15 percent discount, the dealer and the distributor split the five percent distributor's commission."

R. H. Hutchinson, a Spokane attorney who would also play a later role in the company's history, testified that it was the division of the money into capital and surplus that appealed to him. Echoing Mitchell, Hutchinson said, "Such a concern must be sound if they can make a promise like that and keep it."

Asked on cross-examination if he didn't think 50 percent was a lot to devote to promotion, Hutchinson replied, "That depends on the business. Some need more for promotion than others. I know of a Spokane concern that put 75 or 80 percent of the money received into promotion and had nothing left to produce with after they paid the salaries." Asked if he ever received dividends on his stock, Hutchinson said, "I expected no dividends before this time. Until the promotion period is past, no man with any sense would."

Epstein concluded the cross-examination with his usual question. "Does it interest you to know that Pandolfo got more than 650,000 dollars for his services as a fiscal agent?"

"Not a bit in the world."

"Would it make any difference to you if he got two million dollars?" Epstein asked, exasperated.

"There are some things within reason and some that are not," Hutchinson replied smoothly.

The shadowy postal inspector, Marles, was mentioned again by the next witness, W. H. Patten, owner of a grocery store in Denver. Patten said that a postal inspector who said his name was W. J. Marles visited him after he had bought Pan stock and told him, "Pandolfo is one of the slickest crooks that the post office department ever came into contact with as a promoter."

"Did he go into any detail?" Patten was asked.

"Well, he said that Pandolfo took 50 percent of the money that came in, and I said I knew that. Then he said that buildings in St. Cloud were good but that Pandolfo could have got them for at least a third less money."

"Anything else?"

"Yes, when I told him the Denver Industrial Commission had given the company a good report, he said that George Levy, the man who wrote the report, had been given money for writing it. And he said Bishop Busch of St. Cloud had been given a car to get him to talk up the company."

"Did Marles have any comment on other favorable reports about the company?"

"I asked him about the Colorado stockholders' report, and he said those men were all Pan stock salesmen."

Patten was not cross-examined.

John A. Henry took the stand as a character witness for Charles Bunnell, Pan Director. Henry, a St. Cloud druggist and a bank director, said he bought 110 shares of Pan stock, being convinced of the reliability of the company by watching its growth.

Charles S. Olds, in the coal and ice business in St. Cloud, testified to the good character of Fred Schilplin. Olds said he owned 20 shares of stock and that he "plainly understood the use to be made of each share of the money."

Al Tschumperlin, St. Cloud furniture dealer and undertaker, praised the character of George Hanscom and said he owned 50 shares of Pan stock. Asked in cross-examination if he supplied any office furniture to the company, Tschumperlin answered, "About two dozen chairs."

"That's all?"

"That's all. They make a lot of their own desks and things."

Saturday morning the defense sought help from expert witnesses. They called two automobile engineers to verify some facts about the Pan car. The first, N. T. Planche of Flint, Michigan, had been chief engineer with Chevrolet for two years, assistant chief engineer with Buick for six months, and chief engineer for Dort since 1914. He estimated the cost of the 1917 Pan car as originally planned at between $425 and $450. He was asked to fix the final cost to the customer.

"It should have been somewhere between $675 and $700. Taking the usual dealer discount and advertising costs, and a production of 10,000 units or more, the car would have a factory price of around $500 with a profit somewhere around 50 dollars per car."

Planche said he considered the Pan a "good car in its price range, and a good one to enter into production with." Asked about Victor Gauvreau, Pan's chief engineer, Planche said, "Mr. Gauvreau worked under me at Trenton, New Jersey, and I consider him a first class man and one of the most promising engineer-designers in the country today. What he has accomplished with the Pan car in the short time he was given justifies that opinion." Planche had visited the St. Cloud plant and found the buildings and machinery up-to-date. "In fact," he said, "they surpass by far what is being used by many larger and longer-established companies."

The second expert witness, Frank L. Holman, a Chicago consulting engineer who had been at Cadillac for six years, was asked to justify the low price Pandolfo had advertised for the Pan car. "Based on a production of 50,000 units [in 1916 and 1917] with all major parts being made in the Pan plant, the cost should have run closer to 475 dollars."

Leroy Brown, Pan manufacturing manager, was recalled to prove that Pandolfo's statement about producing 100,000 cars a year was feasible. "What would it take in terms of an additional investment to enlarge the plant to permit such production?" Brower asked.

"On the basis of the plans we have, an investment of 2,170,000 dollars would do it."

Brower took the opportunity to make an oblique attempt to qualify the motion pictures of the Pan plant. "By the way, did you order any special situations, or do you know of any that were arranged, for the motion pictures taken at the plant?"

Brown insisted none had been made, but when Rush cross-examined him, his first question was, "Don't you know that men were taken into the drafting room for the purpose of the motion pictures?"

"No, sir, I don't know that. I told the men under my supervision not to make any false representations."

"Were you present at the time the pictures were made, then?"

"No, I was not."

"So you don't know if your orders were carried out?"

"I didn't until I saw the motion pictures. Then I saw they showed our regular routine."

"Isn't it true that a steam engine, a locomotive, was borrowed for the motion pictures?" Rush pressed him.

"Not to my knowledge. But engines are not continually working on our spur. The photographer may have waited until one came on the siding." Brown was excused, but Brower made no immediate attempt to get the movies re-instated.

Witness Abel E. Scharfer, of Kent, Minnesota, said he bought Pan stock after hearing Bishop Busch had bought it. He owned 108 shares, bought at ten different times. His brother had seen the signature of Bishop Busch on a letter of recommendation, and he had talked to the bishop about the company. "The bishop said that what Pandolfo was doing for the workers was what made him recommend the company. I didn't buy stock right away though. I wanted to know more about the directors. So I asked around. A friend of mine said you could give Fred Schilplin 5,000 dollars in his hand and he would not take a cent." While Shilplin smiled, Brower asked Scharfer if he knew what Pandolfo received for his services, and he replied, "I thought first the 50 percent surplus all went to the promoter. But then someone showed me it was for promotion."

Scharfer was followed on the stand by three character witnesses, all from Tucumcari, New Mexico, who had known Pandolfo earlier. E. F. Saxon, an attorney, had known Pandolfo since 1913. C. F. Aldrich, also a lawyer and a state senator, caused a few smiles when he said Pandolfo had promised to make a car along the lines of the Ford, ". . . but a real car." J. A. Street, in his fifth term as sheriff, said he bought two shares of stock from Pandolfo, whom he had known since 1902, in 1916.

Early in the afternoon, the defense called Steve Tenvoorde of St Cloud to testify to the good character of Peter Thielman. Tenvoorde, who had identified himself as being "in the auto business," was asked why he, a Ford dealer, had bought stock in the Pan Motor Company. "I thought the company would help the city by providing jobs, but I also felt they would make a car for which there would be a good demand." [Tenvoorde's agency, now owned by his descendants, is the oldest Ford dealership in the world.]

George Magnuson, a member of the St. Cloud city commission, testified to the good character of Charles Bunnell and also described the civic improvements made as a result of the Pan plant locating in the city.

"Mr. Pandolfo was active in getting a new school built in the west end of the city for the children of people working and living there. He also put a great deal of effort into getting sewer and water connections for Pan Town." Which was a merciful understatement.

State Senator John D. Sullivan was called, and R. B. Brower began to question the man with whom he was frequently associated as counsel. Sullivan explained that he was one of the men who had framed the Blue Sky law in Minnesota. Brower asked him how he came to help the Pan Motor Company secure its license to sell stock in the state. "Mr. Pandolfo came to me in September of 1917 and he retained me. He said he was unable to get a license, and since I had helped write the law maybe I could find out what was holding up his license. I went to St. Paul where I was told that the difficulty lay in the fact that the company was putting 50 percent of the money it collected into promotion.

"I then conferred with you, Senator Brower, and with Mr. Pandolfo and Mr. Cummins, and we reached an agreement on a contract that allowed 25 percent to be spent on promotion. This meeting took place on the morning of September seventh. In the afternoon, after lunch, another meeting was held. I was not present at this second meeting, and I'm not certain if Mr. Pandolfo was, but all of the St. Cloud directors were, and it is my understanding that they approved the change."

Brower asked Sullivan if Pandolfo had agreed with the changes, and Sullivan said, "Yes, he agreed. Mr. Pandolfo uses the English language pretty freely, and I cannot remember all he said, but I got the distinct impression that while he agreed, he wasn't entirely happy about it."

"Was the arrangement then accepted by the Securities Commission?"

"Not at first. They felt that 20 percent was enough to allow for promotion purposes. But I told them I thought a concern of this size required more than that when starting out, and they accepted the 25 percent figure."

"Was there any attempt at all to keep this arrangement secret?"

"No, there was nothing secret about it. It was discussed in the open hearings of the Securities Commission. What reason would there be to keep it secret?"

Sullivan's cross-examination by Epstein was typified by this exchange. "Do you know, as a state senator, that stock has been sold in Minnesota since the license of the company was revoked?"

"I have heard a lot of things, both as a state senator and as a private citizen, that are not pertinent here." The answer brought an uncharacteristic smile to the face of Judge Landis, and Epstein soon capitulated and released Sullivan.

The last three witnesses of the week were Ben E. Schoener, Stearns county sheriff from St. Cloud, who testified to the good reputations of Charles F. Ladner and Fred Schilplin; Colie Guy, photographer, who vouched for the character of H. C. Ervin, Jr.; and William Fischer, president of a St. Cloud farm implement and fuel business (of which R. B. Brower was vice president), who said George Hanscom was as honest as a man could be.

On Monday morning, November 17, Leroy Brown returned to the stand for the third time, this time with blueprints showing the proposed expansion of the Pan plant. In cross-examining Brown, Rush brought up a simple point that took the combined efforts of three lawyers, the witness, and the judge to settle. (The point still bothered Pandolfo when he wrote about the trial 40 years later!) It began when Rush called attention to a circular sent out by Pandolfo in February 1918, containing a drawing of the plant similar to the blue print Brown was testifying about. "Are all the buildings shown in this circular now built, or were they built at the time this circular was sent out?" Rush asked.

"No," Brown explained, "there were no brass and aluminum foundry, no wood-work shop, or coal bunkers, but two-thirds of the factory building and lumber yard were built."

"Then why is it clearly implied that all of this construction was completed at the time this circular was sent out?"

While Brown stared blankly at Rush, R. B. Brower rose and read from the circular. "This gives an idea of the big plant when completed," he quoted, with emphasis on the last two words.

Rush replied with another quote from the circular. "An aeroplane view of the big plant."

Landis asked Brown, "Was this picture taken from an aeroplane?"

"It is not a photograph," Brown said patiently, still unable to comprehend that an explanation was required. "How could it be when many of these buildings shown are still not erected?"

"That's what we're trying to determine," Landis snapped.

Attorney George Peaks made his contribution. "An aeroplane view doesn't necessarily mean 'taken from an aeroplane' any more than 'a bird's-eye view' means what is in the eye of a bird."

Landis was still shaking his head in doubt when Brower called attention to the fact that the words, "aeroplane view," were enclosed by quotation marks and pointed out that the complete sentence was "An 'aeroplane view' which gives an idea of the big plant when completed." Judge Landis and Sylvester Rush seemed unconvinced, but they dropped the point, and Brown, still incredulous over the quibbling, was allowed to leave the stand.

Brower made another oblique attempt with the next witness Robert H. Moth, works engineer at Pan, to get the motion pictures qualified. "What about the charge that has been made here that the Pan buildings could have been erected for much less money. Is that true?"

"Someone can always be found to do a job for less money, so I suppose it is true," Moth said. "But you wouldn't have the kind of buildings we have at Pan for less than we paid for them. They are modern in every respect and completely equipped not only for production but for the safety and comfort of the men."

"Now, Mr. Moth, were you present when Mr. Strom, the photographer, made the motion pictures at the plant?"

"Yes, I was. Most of the time. I was in the area almost constantly. At least in the main assembly building. Mr. Forsyth brought Mr. Strom into the plant and introduced me to him. He told me to help him if he needed help." Moth said Forsyth did not leave immediately but stayed in the background to watch the photographer set up his equipment.

"Did he direct the photographer in any way?"

"No, he did not," Moth said. "In fact, when he left for a while and came back, Mr. Strom had moved to another area, and I had to tell Mr. Forsyth where he had gone." Still Brower did not immediately ask Landis to allow the motion pictures to be shown.

Ira E. James, superintendent of the Pan drop forge and foundry, testified next about the working force he directed. "We usually have around 120 men working an eight-hour shift. At 60 cents an hour, our payroll is close to 600 dollars a day."

The last witness of the day was A. W. Clark, a car dealer from Brighton, Colorado. Clark said he bought 25 shares of stock in the company because "it looked like a good little car for the price." When Brower asked what he had based that judgment on, Clark said, "I know cars. I have sold them all, from Fords on up."

"From Fords on down," Landis corrected.

On the front page of Tuesday's edition of the *St. Cloud Journal-Press* a story appeared, boxed to set it apart from the other wire and by-lined stories on the trial.

> An appeal for a cash subscription of additional stock is being made today to every stockholder of the Pan Motor Company.
>
> This appeal differs from other appeals to purchasers of stock in that it is not made by S. C. Pandolfo, president, but by the factory organization at St. Cloud.
>
> A circular sent out is signed by W. Hagedorn, office manager, Victor Gauvreau, chief engineer, L. E. Perry, credit manager, W. Harper, production manager, C. H. Varney, superintendent of assembly, W. Humphrey, general superintendent, J. H. McQuerry, second vice president, R. J. Fitness, director of purchases, B. Bratter, sales manager, R. A. DeVlieg, methods engineer, I. B. Hoover, traffic manager, C. E. Harris, drop forge department, H. C. Carter, of personnel, and Orazio Rico, foreign correspondent.
>
> "From present indications," the circular states, "we think the case will be ended early in December. In the meantime, the indicted officials are all in Chicago and know nothing of the sending out of this letter. But the factory organization in St.

> Cloud is on the job and the factory is busy as usual. Deliveries of the new Model A are being made; 15 cars are on the assembly line today, and we expect to finish 30 cars this month, and at least 60 cars during December."

The letter went on to appeal to subscribers to finish payments on their stock purchases and to buy more stock if they possibly could.

At the trial the next morning, testimony began to give some of Pandolfo's Texas background. Much of the morning was spent reading depositions from various insurance company presidents testifying to Pandolfo's character and his ability and industry as a salesman. E. C. Cooper, president of the Great Republic Life Insurance Company of Los Angeles, wrote to Charles Schwab early in 1917, explaining how Pandolfo got in debt.

> He developed in Texas one of the largest agency forces in the west. In his contracts made with various companies he represented, he received a first-year and a renewal commission. In order to secure a volume of insurance on which to derive renewals he, in many cases, gave the large-producing salesmen all, or practically all, of the first year's commission. This would have worked out successfully had he not been the victim in many instances of agents who would write business which was later canceled, and the agents would fail to return the settlement they had received. They left this burden upon Mr. Pandolfo. Margin out of the first year was not large enough to stand this strain, and he was not, at the time he severed connections with this company, receiving sufficient renewals to tide him over. The strain became too great for him, and last August he resigned as a general agent.

Twenty-five letters from bankers and insurance men in the Southwest were read, all in response to inquiries from the defense attorneys in the present trial. They were generally in agreement: Pandolfo had been writing a lot of insurance and taking notes for the premiums while advancing his agents cash against the renewals; when the cotton crop failed to sell and when the policies were not renewed, the notes were not paid off; the agents were unable or unwilling to repay him, and Pandolfo absorbed the loss. The assessments of Pandolfo were fairly unanimous: He was characterized as a promoter and a hustler, probably a bad judge of credits, but honest. Some letters added one other characteristic—Pandolfo usually disregarded advice he was given and favored his instincts.

In the afternoon, two officers of the Minnesota Securities Commission testified concerning their survey of the Pan Motor Company. Some of the record was missing, and Charles J. Andre, executive secretary of the commission, the first of the two witnesses, said he was still trying to locate the missing portions. Brower read the record of the commission's decision of May 28, 1918, allowing the company to continue to sell stock in the state to the amount of $500,000, as stated in the license granted the previous September, but with restrictions on the amount of commissions paid and the amount spent on promotion.

John Sanborn, of the commission, testified that after investigating Pandolfo the commission felt that although his business record was not entirely satisfactory, there was nothing in it to show him to be dishonest. In fact, Sanborn said, it appeared that the debts he incurred using his unconventional and radical methods were always scrupulously paid. During Sanborn's testimony, Brower read to the jury the commission report of December 8, 1918, in which the Pan Motor Company's license was canceled. Sanborn testified that the immediate and principal reasons for the cancellation were the indictment of Pandolfo and Barritt in Fergus Falls and the report of the Capital Issues Committee. Against the background of the company's previous hearing, the commission had decided that canceling the license and waiting until the matter had been settled in court was the prudent course.

When court was adjourned late in the afternoon, the defense lawyers, who had read much of the testimony into the record, were the weariest they had been throughout the trial.

The next morning the defense began the introduction of testimony relating to the legal formation of the Pan Motor Company. The prosecution had insisted that it was at this point the conspiracy to defraud was initiated. William R. Watson of the Corporation Trust Company of Chicago explained how the corporation was formed. When Fletcher Dobyns, conducting the direct examination, asked Watson why the company was incorporated in Delaware and not, for example, in Illinois, Watson replied, "There was no reason to do it in Illinois. We knew the company was not going to locate here. And Delaware has more favorable corporation laws. Most states require a fairly high corporation tax compared to Delaware, but the main reason is that the nature of the business to be incorporated must be specifically—and narrowly—set out in the charter in other states. Delaware allows a broader statement so that a business may branch out later and still be within the limits of its corporate charter. For this, and other more technical reasons, Delaware is usually selected for incorporation."

Cross-examining Watson, Rush asked, "The men who allowed their names to be used in Delaware were merely stool pigeons, were they not? I mean, they had no interest in the proposed concern beyond getting their fee?"

Watson's resentment was obvious long before Rush has finished the question. "I resent the term stool pigeons being used to describe employees of our firm. They act in this fashion honorably and entirely within the law, day in and day out. They are no more interested in just getting their fee, as you put it, than any government attorney at that table is interested in just putting in his time."

Rush was beginning to bristle when Judge Landis raised both

hands and with a cautionary shake of his head forestalled further comment. With some edge still in his voice, Rush then asked if having a person as an officer of the company without their knowledge was also a common practice with Watson's firm.

The tone of Watson's reply demonstrated that he was intimidated neither by Rush nor by Judge Landis. "If you were as familiar with corporate law, sir, as you seem to be with criminal law, you might be aware that the circumstances in this case required and the law in general allows this to be. The Pan Motor Company was going to be located in another area, unknown at the time. Mr. Pandolfo had expressed the reasonable desire that the officers of the company be local men. While it might, indeed, have been wiser to have advised Miss Cadieux that she was needed to fill an official position, there was nothing wrong in not doing so. She was present at the meeting; she must have been inattentive. She would be taking no action that affected the company, nor would she be held liable for anything the company might do."

After exchanging brooding stares with Watson, Rush excused him and, late in the morning, Norman A. Street, the Chicago patent attorney and Pan Motor Company director, became the first of the defendants to be called to the stand. Street, a self-possessed man, appeared slightly nervous when he sat down but his agitation disappeared as he gave his background. He had formed a law partnership with George Heidman in 1907, he said. They specialized in patent law, trademarks, and corporate practice. Pandolfo had called on them late in 1916 and gave his own history quite frankly.

During the course of his testimony Street gave an additional reason for not incorporating the Pan Motor Company under the laws of Illinois. "Illinois law does not allow one corporation to hold stock in another of a similar nature. Mr. Pandolfo was not exactly precise about what he had in mind, but we gathered that he might be planning a similar product, a truck or a tractor, which he might want handled by another company for whatever reason. Illinois law would not have permitted the parent company to own stock in the second company, and since the Pan Motor Company was not going to have any further domicile in Illinois. . . ."

"Were you advised by Mr. Pandolfo that you would not remain as officers of the company?" Dobyns asked.

"Oh, yes. That was not only his wish but ours as well. He wanted local men to be involved. In fact, our resignations were drawn up before the company had received its corporate charter."

"Now, Mr. Street, was it ever suggested that anything other than a legitimate business was being organized, that any misrepresentation would be taking place, that it was all going to be a swindle?" Dobyns asked with great deliberation.

Street inhaled deeply before replying. "Of course not. If there had been, I would not have risked my own reputation or that of our firm." Street continued his description of the early days of the company. In March

1917, when he came to St. Cloud, Street said he was pleased with the caliber of men Pandolfo had enlisted in the company and with the location of the plant as well.

"Did you see or hear anything at St. Cloud to cause you to change your impression of the character of the company or of Mr. Pandolfo?"

"No. Quite the contrary."

Street was still testifying later in the afternoon when Judge Landis broke in and adjourned for the day.

Thursday morning the presence of a large bouquet of pink and yellow chrysanthemums in the courtroom had everyone puzzled until the clerk explained that it was Judge Landis' 53rd birthday. Street's testimony was interrupted for a time in the morning while a few distinguished character witnesses gave their testimony. The first was Congressman Harold Knutson, sixth district representative from St. Cloud, who testified to the good character of Pandolfo. Little more was obtained from Knutson on cross-examination beyond the fact that he was the former city editor of the *St. Cloud Journal-Press*.

The second witness was Judge Van Sickle of Alpine, Texas, whose testimony sounded strange as he identified himself as the writer of a letter that contained the statement, "People said Pandolfo was a crook and a liar."

"Pandolfo has paid his bills, and the people whom I quoted in that letter have changed their minds," the judge said. "They now consider him to be honest."

The third witness was Peter J. Seberger, former mayor of St. Cloud, who testified to the good character of Peter Thielman.

The fourth was another congressman, C. D. Hudspeth, representing the 16th Congressional District of Texas and a former district judge in El Paso. He said he had known Pandolfo for nearly 20 years and his reputation had always been good.

Street then returned to the stand to talk about the advertising of the Pan Motor Company. "Did you think that the booklets the company circulated contained true information, or did you consider them just advertising?" Dobyns asked.

"I thought of them as advertising, not affidavits. More peppery than most, but that was understandable when you knew Mr. Pandolfo. He was enthusiastic."

Street described how he, Pandolfo, and Brower tried to obtain permission from the Capital Issues Committee to sell additional stock. Street echoed faintly the loud Pandolfo claim that the committee had made up its mind long before the petitioners reached Washington, D.C.

Once again, as he had throughout the interrogation, Dobyns asked Street at the conclusion of his testimony, "At any time, from the beginning to the present, did you ever find anything questionable about the way the company was being run?"

"I became convinced more and more strongly to the contrary as time went on," Street said firmly. George Peaks then asked if he had ever heard or seen anything in the words or conduct of H. S. Wigle that caused him concern. "No," Street replied. Brower asked if the St. Cloud directors had ever given him cause for concern. "Not a bit," Street said.

At 5:00 in the afternoon Sylvester Rush began his cross-examination of Street. "Would you say that the first directors were bossed by Pandolfo, that he could get any action he wanted?"

"Certainly not," Street insisted, and he cited several instances where Pandolfo had suggested procedures that were vetoed by the attorneys as redundant or impractical.

Apparently eager to celebrate the remainder of his birthday away from the courtroom, Landis adjourned early. Dr. Fred Stangl of St. Cloud, then working at Cook County Hospital in Chicago, visited with the defendants as they waited for the jury to clear the building.

Friday morning the sky over Chicago, which had been clear and bright for the past several days, was gray. Intermittent rain fell, and the day seemed chilly even though southwest winds kept the temperature above normal. Street returned to the stand, and Rush asked, as he plucked an advertising piece from the assortment in evidence, "Do you think the statement, 'We intend to make 100,000 cars the first year,' was truthful in view of the fact that the factory was not yet erected?"

Street said he understood that to mean the first year of quantity production; it was pretty obvious it couldn't be the first year of organization.

Rush shifted the point of his question and asked, "Now, did you really think it was all right for Pandolfo to make 650,000 dollars up to April of this year while the stockholders were getting nothing?"

"Considering that he has built up the value of the company to 100 million dollars, I think that it is all right."

"Oh, come now, Mr. Street, do you really believe that this company is worth 100 million dollars?"

"Everything considered, yes, I do."

"Do you know if Pandolfo has continued to sell stock after the Capital Issues Committee said further sales should be prohibited?"

"I do not know of my own knowledge. But the Capital Issues Committee does not have any legal right to prevent the sale of stock. They can only recommend."

Following Street's testimony, Charles Andre, executive secretary of the Minnesota Securities Commission, was recalled and produced the missing records of the commission. Andre admitted the commission had gone through all Pan literature and had found nothing fraudulent. Brower then read into the trial record much of the testimony given at the commission hearing by E. J. Bishop, public accountant who had examined the company's books at Pandolfo's request in November 1917. Bishop had testified that he suggested to Pandolfo that after September 7, 1917, the expenditures from the second 25 percent above par—the payment that did not go to Pandolfo for sales commission—be transferred to the books of the Pan Motor Company from those of the fiscal agency. The accountant had also declared to the commission that he thought the Pan Motor Company's accounting system for handling promotion expenses had an advantage over many other, "as promotion expenses were usually 25 percent, and other expenses impaired the capital from 25 to 40 percent, while here the capital is unimpaired."

Following a laughing objection from Sylvester Rush about speeches by attorneys being introduced as evidence, Carl Cummins read from the commission record the remarks made by himself and R. B. Brower at the hearing. When Cummins started to read, Landis shifted his chair back from the bench and was nearly hidden from view. During the long readings, first by Brower and then by Cummins, nothing was heard from Landis. The attorneys finally concluded at five minutes to six. There was no word from the judge to break the silence that followed, and it appeared the lawyers' calm voices had lulled the court into oblivion. After a moment Landis leaned forward, admitted nothing, but said, "Your speeches, Mr. Cummins and Mr. Brower, are better at putting a man to sleep than those of Mr. Taft."

The short rest had not been enough for Landis and he adjourned, ending the first day of the fifth week of testimony.

On Saturday morning Cummins continued the direct examination of Andre, establishing that the commission had granted Pandolfo the right to retain a 25 percent commission on stock sales. Cross-examined, Andre admitted that the special consideration had been given to Pandolfo because of the number of letters the commission had received requesting that the license not be revoked.

"Do you know why these letters were sent?"

"Yes, some writers stated they were written in response to a letter from Mr. Pandolfo requesting that they write the commission."

But in redirect, Brower established that the commission's decision had rested not on the letters they had received, but on the evidence that the company was proceeding properly.

George Heidman's testimony concerned mainly his work on patents for the Pan Motor Company. Again, as with Street, Dobyns frequently asked Heidman if he had seen anything suspicious in regard to the head of the company, the methods used, or the directors chosen. Heidman insisted each time that he would not have jeopardized his reputation with any enterprise that suggested anything unfavorable.

The prosecution had frequently referred to the dismissal of the indictment in Fergus Falls, implying that the existence of the indictment alone placed a judgment on the company. Dobyns concluded his examination of Heidman by asking what he thought of the dismissal of the indictment. The attorney replied, "My good opinion of the company was bolstered by the court's action."

Epstein immediately took up the point in his cross-examination of

Heidman. "As a lawyer, Mr. Heidman, were you affected by the fact that the indictment was withdrawn—not quashed, mind you—but withdrawn, when there was no trial?"

"Yes, I was. The grounds for the dismissal was insufficient evidence. That affected me as a lawyer."

Though it was only 5:30, Landis turned to the jury and said, "Ten o'clock Monday morning, gentlemen."

The St. Cloud defendants had telephoned in the morning for the remaining character witnesses from St. Cloud, and 20 or more were expected to arrive on Monday.

Despite the fact that Judge Landis was himself late Monday morning and did not convene court until 11:00 o'clock, and the fact that a juror was taken ill shortly before one o'clock and court was adjourned, more witnesses were heard on Monday, November 24, than on any previous day. The session began with the short conclusion of Heidman's cross-examination, and the parade of St. Cloud witnesses began.

As R. B. Brower questioned them, each witness stated his name and occupation, then vouched for the good character of one or another of the defendants. Edwin F. Moore had lived in St. Cloud for 17 years, was a former president of the First National Bank, had been a grain and stock broker in New York City before coming to St. Cloud, and vouched for H. C. Ervin, Jr., as did Alvah Eastman, publisher of the *St. Cloud Journal-Press* for the past 27 years. John A. Roeser had lived in St. Cloud 39 years, was a district court judge for six years, and had known Charles Schwab for nine years and George Hanscom for 16. Rev. Leo Gans, pastor of the St. Cloud Cathedral parish for nine years, had lived in St. Cloud the greater part of his life, and said there was no finer, more honest man alive than Charles F. Ladner. Frank Fandel had lived in St. Cloud 40 years and also testified for Ladner. Joseph J. Hilbe, proprietor of the Golden Rule store, had lived in St. Cloud for 19 years and testified for Fred Schilplin. Robert L. Gale, of the St. Cloud Produce and Storage Company, said he had known Charles Bunnell for 32 years; A. A. Wright had known Bunnell only 31 years but agreed with Gale that he was trustworthy. H. J. Limperich, mayor of St. Cloud and former clerk of district court, had known Peter Thielman from childhood. H. R. Neide, the Great Northern agent in St. Cloud, had also known Peter Thielman. Dr. Claude B. Lewis, brother of Sinclair Lewis, said he had known Charles Schwab for 15 years and was "well-acquainted with his honesty." J. B. Galernault, president of the National Exchange Bank of St. Paul, said he had known George Hanscom for 15 years and also knew Schwab, but for a shorter time.

As Galernault was testifying, juror Peter Duell became ill, and Landis recessed the court for lunch. When the afternoon session opened, Duell was sleeping. Landis said he would "give the poor man every chance to recover," and he recessed for the day.

Tuesday morning, George Hanscom, the first of the St. Cloud

directors to testify, began by saying that he supported the Pan Motor Company because he felt the city, including his Merchants National Bank, would benefit from the presence of the company. He first heard of Pandolfo when he was called to a meeting of the Commercial Club in January 1917. "When he came to St. Cloud, we asked him what he knew about the auto business and whether he could dispose of ten million dollars in stock. This was a large task, larger than any of us had had experience with. He told us he had no practical experience in automobile manufacturing. He would hire people who had that experience. But he did have experience with the financing of large corporations. None as large as this would be, but few men had that experience. We had the impression he was confident he could dispose of the stock."

"Did he indicate at that time what he felt his own compensation would be?"

"He said he couldn't say for certain because the expenses in a venture like this would be large. He did say that whether he personally made much or little—and he frankly said he hoped it would be much—the capital would be intact."

Hanscom, when asked about the sale of the large block of shares at half price to Pandolfo, said that Pandolfo's reasons for taking the stock were understandable, considering the crisis the company was facing, but when he discovered that the directors were not in agreement with his tactic he canceled the note and replaced the shares.

Hanscom was then asked when he first heard the amount of Pandolfo's remuneration. "In the fall of 1918," the director replied. "The J. G. White Company made a study of the company, and their report stated that up to that time Mr. Pandolfo had received 355,000 dollars. The capital stock of the company had received 275,000 dollars from the surplus since the five percent contract was made, with 500,000 still due."

"Do you think, Mr. Hanscom, that Mr. Pandolfo has received too much compensation?"

Hanscom answered with deliberation. "Considering all the circumstances under which he has undertaken to make it, I do not think it is too much remuneration. He has re-invested the major share of it in the Pan Addition and the Motor Hotel and his manufacturing company."

Epstein approached Hancom's cross-examination with obvious relish, pleased at finally having someone on the stand who could give the precise information he had been seeking. "How much cash has the Pan Motor Company in the bank presently?"

"Around 5,000 dollars."

"How much does the company presently owe to banks?"

"About 175,000 dollars."

"How much has the company collected from the sale of its stock?"

"About 6,700,000 dollars, with 1,500,000 commissions on the subscriptions."

"What is the present payroll of the company?"

"I think it is between 50-60,000 a month."

"What profit does the company expect to make from the sale of 500 cars to be manufactured by July 1, 1920?"

"About 150-200 dollars per car."

"What was the profit from the drop forge in August, September, and October of this year?"

"I have no figures on that," Hanscom answered evenly.

Epstein had been characterized as quick, probing, and merciless in cross-examination. His questions were rapid fire with hardly a pause for the answers. Hanscom's answers, given directly but in a methodical manner, seemed to irritate Epstein on occasion. Many of the prosecutor's questions were prefaced with, "As a director, do you know this?" At one point, after three or four quick questions about the company's finances, Epstein asked Hanscom, "Do you know that Pandolfo got 90,000 dollars this fall in three months, while the company had 5,000 dollars in the bank and owes over 170,000 dollars?"

"Yes, I know about that."

"Well, do you think it is right?"

"Yes, it's according to the contract. He's building for the future of this company and the small amount of current cash does not disturb us greatly."

Epstein had just begun to question Hanscom on the amount of guidance the Board members had given Pandolfo, suggesting they had not done enough to stabilize the president, when Judge Landis broke in to adjourn for the day.

Wednesday morning Epstein read to Hanscom a story from the *Minneapolis Daily News* of October 13, 1917, in which it was stated that the company "is now turning out from two to three cars a day." As had previous defense witnesses from the Pan Motor Company, Hanscom agreed that the statement was not true. Judge Landis thought it was time to settle the issue of the story, which had cropped up in previous testimony. "Was that a news story or an ad?" Landis asked Epstein. When Epstein pointed to the clipping, indicating that it was a news story and said it was later used by the Pan Motor Company as an ad, Landis asked, "Was the story sent out from St. Cloud, or did it originate on the authority of the *Daily News*?" Epstein, unable to answer looked to the defense table for help. None was offered. Landis scanned the court room. "Ask Forsyth. Where's Forsyth? Is he here?"

Brower pointed out that Forsyth was not employed by the Pan Motor Company at that time, and Landis said, "Very well, if no one else will find out about this thing, I will." He turned to the clerk and instructed him to make out a subpoena for the managing editor of the *Minneapolis Daily News* and a copy of the pertinent October edition. "Does anyone know the managing editor's name?"

"John G. Burgess," Pandolfo offered.

Landis gave him a small smile, said, "Thank you, sir," and instructed the clerk, "Issue it." Later, as the cross-examination continued, Forsyth entered the court room but Landis either did not notice him or felt he had a better source coming and did not call him.

Epstein picked up the February 1918 issue of *Pan Siftings* and indicated the ad for the Pan Tank Tread Tractor. "Do you call these statements true?"

Hanscom glanced at the magazine. "Yes, I think on the whole they are true."

Landis broke in. "Read that again, witness, and having regard to the meaning it is meant to convey to others, have you anything to add to your statement?" Hanscom read the ad to himself and said he might add that the company was not then in production but that it was in all good faith working to complete the tractor. Landis was not satisfied but allowed Epstein to continue.

Hanscom was excused in mid-morning and Fred Schilplin was called. Brower's direct examination of Schilplin was completed in two hours. The witness said he had lived in St. Cloud and nearby St. Joseph all his life with the exception of one year spent at school in Switzerland. He had filled every position on the *St. Cloud Daily Times*, finally buying into the corporation. His testimony about Pandolfo's arrival in St. Cloud paralleled Hanscom's. "I felt that the plan was novel but that it would work. I went on the Board feeling that I was not only being identified with an honest concern, but that I was doing a public duty to my home town." Schilplin also agreed with Hanscom on the matter of Pandolfo's note for 100,000 shares of stock. "He willingly agreed to abandon the project when he knew we were against it. But we knew his reason for wanting to do it and we understood."

Asked about Pandolfo's remuneration, Schilplin said, "I suppose if the company were to fail, people will say it was too much. But we plan on succeeding, and then the salary does not seem so much."

Brower asked Schilplin his frank opinion of Pandolfo. "I think Mr. Pandolfo, in the hundreds of decisions he had to make, has made some errors of judgment, as we all have. It happens that Mr. Pandolfo's honest mistakes are a little more public than most other people's. But I believe firmly in his honesty."

Epstein began Schilplin's cross-examination with the publisher's admission that some of the company's advertising was "not exactly right." He had nothing specific in mind, he said, but he did not like the idea of accepting Liberty bonds for stock. "And when we did object to some piece of literature at a Board meeting, it was changed."

"Mr. Hanscom testified that the Board did not review the advertising Pandolfo prepared," Epstein snapped.

"I think he meant that we did not judge its effectiveness as advertising," Schilplin said, "but we all read it for our own information. After it was off the press, however. Mr. Pandolfo acts quickly."

With the next witness, Charles F. Ladner, vice president of the Pan

Motor Company, Brower spent only a short time in direct examination. Because he had not joined the company until November 1917, Ladner had no direct knowledge of the early days of the company in St. Cloud. "But you had, shall we say, outside knowledge of the company?" Brower asked.

"As a businessman in St. Cloud, it was impossible not to come into contact with the Pan Motor Company in a hundred different ways each day."

"Well, from your outside knowledge and your later association with him, what is your opinion of Mr. Pandolfo?"

"I think Mr. Pandolfo, in 1917, was the busiest man in Minnesota," Ladner quietly replied. "He was trying to get the company started; he was working on all fronts at one time. He was supervising construction, not only on the buildings but on the cars and also the homes in Pan Town. And he was trying to get the stock sold. I never believed one man had that much energy."

Asked if he had ever heard of a stockholder complaining about or condemning the company, Ladner responded, "On the contrary, I have heard many, in spite of the fact that they have received no dividend, advising patience in seeing the company through the crisis caused by the war and now by this suit."

Ladner said he and his family were stockholders to the amount of $5,000. Asked about his own plans for the future with the company, he said his health was not good. "It is only because I feel it is my duty to remain a director until this lawsuit is determined that I have not resigned from the Board."

During Ladner's cross-examination, conducted by Sylvester Rush, most of the answers were accepted with easy grace. But at one point Rush seemed incredulous at Ladner's reply. Rush asked why many banks had put a limit on the amount of credit they would extend the company. "I think they were being influenced by gossip and rumors that were circulated concerning the company," Ladner responded.

"Oh, come now, Mr. Ladner! As a successful businessman, president of an insurance company, and a director of a bank, wouldn't you agree that a company listing 3,500,000 dollars in intangible assets was a poor credit risk?" Rush asked.

"No," Ladner stubbornly insisted. "There were tangible assets enough to cover any loan we wanted. There were other reasons for the refusals."

"Well, can you tell me why Clarence Atwood, or Albert Whitney, or even Senator Brower here were not directors?" Rush had mentioned several St. Cloud residents who were on a par, financially or otherwise, with the other Pan directors.

"I don't know why they weren't asked. I do know that Mr. Atwood has changed his opinion of the company. He now thinks there is more to it than he first thought."

At 5:30, when Rush had completed his questions, Landis, instead of adjourning for the night, said, "Call your next witness, gentlemen." H. C. Ervin, Jr., was called, but after only an hour or so of testimony, Landis finally adjourned with his usual, "Ten o'clock tomorrow morning, gentlemen." He had told the participants he would permit no holiday the next day, Thanksgiving; he would, however, allow a two-hour recess at noon, but the afternoon session would then run until 7:00 in the evening.

Ervin's direct examination was completed quickly Thanksgiving morning, and Epstein's cross-examination was directed to one point: trying to show that Ervin's resignation from the Pan Board had been prompted by the company's advertising, which had gone too far. Folder after folder was shown to Ervin and he was repeatedly asked, "Do you consider this to be the truth?" Ervin usually insisted that he considered them to be truthful, occasionally indicating that while some advertising did not disclose all the facts, it did not distort what information it did give. He consistently maintained that his only reasons for resigning from the company were that his milling business was taking more of his time and the fact that a Minneapolis banker had told him that the Pan Motor Company was getting a bad reputation among bankers and continued association with it would only hurt his own credit. "What did the bankers on the Pan Board say to that?" Epstein wanted to know.

"They had heard the same rumors. They attributed them to the enemies Mr. Pandolfo had in the banking business in the Southwest and to the anonymous letter the Arizona bankers had printed in their magazine. They said I was free to make my own decision."

Ervin was asked in re-direct examination if he regretted his decision. "Yes, I have. Especially since this lawsuit was instituted. I don't want people to think I was deserting my friends. My resignation was given on November 19th of last year, even before the Fergus Falls indictment was returned. If I had known it was coming I would not have resigned."

Where the other director/witnesses had been confident about the future of the Pan Motor Company, Charles Schwab, the next witness, was exuberantly enthusiastic. As treasurer of the company, he was able to supply answers to Epstein's questions others could not give. Throughout Schwab's testimony, his faith in the Pan Motor Company was obvious and unlimited. Unable to contain his eagerness and hold to a simple yes or no answer, Schwab frequently said, "I would like to explain that a little more." The prosecution, delighted at the ground this opened for cross-examination, made no objection in most cases.

Near the close of his direct examination, Brower asked Schwab his opinion of Pandolfo. "Well, I'll tell you," the banker said. "I think he is in a class by himself when it comes to work of this kind. I never met a man who is more honest and faithful than he has been. His energy is prodigious. Not only for a period of days or weeks, but for months and, yes, years he has worked hard from early morning until far into the night."

Schwab admitted that he, of all Board members, was the only one who had agreed to Pandolfo's exchange of a note for 100,000 shares of stock. He was emphatic in his defense of it. "Let me give you the background on that. We were in the midst of drop forge plans then. We needed the drop forge to stay alive, since we decided not to press production of pleasure cars during the war. Now, if the Blue Sky commissions had stopped us then in selling stock and money stopped coming in, it would have been fatal. We had to have money. Not to protect our right to get it would have been suicidal, a complete surrender of our stockholders' rights. I think Mr. Pandolfo felt he was fighting for the very life of the company when he thought of selling this stock to himself if necessary."

The long explanations Schwab had given in his answers had carried his testimony on into early evening, and as Landis adjourned the court, the chilly air outside the Federal Building was a hint that the storms of the past week were going to continue to make up for the dry weeks of early November.

On Friday morning, November 28, Chicago got its first snowfall of the winter. Schwab's cross-examination began with Epstein reading a letter written by Pandolfo from Chicago early in 1917 to his subscribers saying that they could help the newly-formed company by writing to C. D. Schwab telling their good opinion of the project and of Pandolfo. Schwab did not remember any letter that might have come to him as a result of Pandolfo's urging. "I don't think anyone who knows Mr. Pandolfo would ever accuse him of modesty about his own abilities." Pandolfo smiled broadly at the answer.

Epstein could not shake Schwab's confidence and closed his cross-examination with, "One final question, Mr. Schwab. Have you canceled your subscription for 200 more shares of Pan Motor Company stock?"

The banker looked down at his hands momentarily. "I thought that might be misinterpreted," he said, almost to himself.

"Just a yes or no answer this time, please." Epstein was stern.

"Yes, I did."

Brower, on re-direct examination, asked Schwab to explain the cancellation. "It certainly was not lack of faith in the company or in Mr. Pandolfo. It was just that with the trial coming up I knew I would need funds, and I didn't want to be tied to more commitments than I could carry."

When Brower sat down, Epstein asked one more question. "Doesn't your contract with the fiscal agent require that he pay the expenses of any lawsuit against the company?"

"Yes," Schwab answered quietly.

On Saturday, H. S. Wigle, former vice president of the company was called. Wigle was an easy-going witness even under cross-examination, and he gave his testimony with an amused, relaxed detachment. He had worked for an Oklahoma oil company and was just closing out that association when he met Pandolfo, for whom he had earlier sold insurance, in Clovis, New Mexico, in June 1916. Pandolfo was trying to organize the Pan Motor Company then, Wigle said, "and the last time I heard him give an explanation of his plan was the same as that first time. He never changed it one bit. I had faith in him and his idea from the start. I began to sell stock in his company around Clovis, and in four days I sold 109 shares. I kept 20 percent commission and gave the rest to Pandolfo."

"Were you present at the Clovis meeting when Pandolfo and Shipley debated?" Peaks asked.

"Yes," Wigle said, smiling at the memory. "Shipley was a typical big shot in a small town. He ran it. Or tried to. He had a gang of roughnecks at the meeting. Pandolfo spoke first, outlining his plan for the Pan Motor Company, then Shipley talked, saying it wouldn't work and knocking it. When Pandolfo tried to talk the second time, Shipley's gang tried to break up the meeting, but everybody told them to shut up and sit down. So they walked out. Pandolfo finally made his second talk, and it went over big." Wigle left Clovis when Pandolfo did and went to Colorado, where he sold stock until December, when he met Pandolfo in Chicago. He had come to one meeting of the company's officers in St. Cloud, but he had gone on to Washington almost immediately, and for the past year and a half he had been in charge of the Washington territory with headquarters in Spokane. He resigned as vice president in August 1917, to make room for Ladner; Pandolfo had told him this would happen when they had formed the company.

Wigle said he owned 368 shares of Pan stock, 115 of which he had bought from a broker at seven dollars a share to protect his salesmen. "Did that clean the broker out?" Peaks asked.

"Yes, thank God. He said there was not more than 500 shares of Pan stock floating in the country. But this was all there was in my territory."

Wigle's testimony was interrupted at a quarter to two when the jury was taken to the Atlantic Hotel to see the exhibit of Pan cars and tractors. Judge Landis cautioned the attorneys for the defense that he was relying on them to see that the room was properly cleared while the jurors were there. Attorney Peaks said they would like to show the jurors how the folding sleeper of the Pan car worked, and Landis acceded, saying, "All right, if you have someone on hand who has the art of keeping still while he sleeps."

When Wigle returned to the stand for cross-examination, Epstein picked up at the meeting in Clovis between the witness and Pandolfo. "Did Pandolfo tell you that he was broke as a result of his insurance troubles, and did you tell him you were also?"

Wigle was unperturbed by the sarcasm in Epstein's question. "If he had been broke, I don't think he mentioned it. I know I didn't. Besides, I knew much of what had happened to him."

Epstein took up Wigle's sales methods. "What commission did you pay the salesmen under you?"

"Fifteen percent, usually. In a few cases, 20."

"What did you get?"

"Five percent."

"On top of the 20?"

"No. My five percent comes from Pandolfo. And then whatever I sell myself, of course."

"How much do you make, what do you earn?"

"I grossed about 40,000, of which I figure about 15,000 is net."

"Now, in describing your sales methods you mentioned a `local plugger.' Could you tell us what you mean?" Epstein put gross emphasis on the term, but it failed to bother Wigle, who answered as if he were instructing a new salesman.

"It means exactly what it sounds like, a local man who helps you plug sales. When you're going into a new territory, somewhere you've never been before, get a man who's well known and respected and have him introduce you around. That's all."

"Well, not quite all. This local plugger . . ." again Epstein emphasized the words broadly, " . . . what does he get for his troubles?"

"I would generally give him five percent of my 20, sometimes as high as seven-and-a-half percent."

"Out of your 20?" Epstein asked quickly. "I thought you said you got five percent from Pandolfo?"

"For the whole territory, yes," Wigle explained patiently, "but when I used a local plugger I was selling direct and my commission is the same as my salesmen, 20 percent."

Late in the afternoon Landis picked a quiet moment in Wigle's testimony to adjourn for the weekend, and some of the St. Cloud defendants visited with St. Cloud attorney J. Arthur Bensen, a spectator in the court room.

The first week in December—the last week of the trial—began with below normal temperatures in Chicago. Whether it had anything to do with Judge Landis' disposition or not, his icy humor became apparent as Monday morning progressed. In a discussion at the opening of the morning session, Landis said he wanted to hear from Lambourne, the salesman, and Burgess, the *Minneapolis Daily News* editor. That left only Pandolfo still to be called by the defense after the conclusion of Wigle's testimony.

During cross-examination that morning, Epstein questioned Wigle about three shares of stock he had purchased in March 1917, and Wigle replied he had paid $15.00 for the three shares. Again there was a sudden change in Epstein as he noted a discrepancy. "Do you mean that's all you paid for these shares."

"Yes," Wigle answered and unleashed Landis' wrath. Further questioning was postponed while the jury was escorted out. Then Landis asked the court reporter to read back part of the testimony Wigle had given Saturday. The stenographer read:

> THE COURT: How did you pay for this stock?
> WITNESS: I paid for half of it at that time.
> THE COURT: Did you subsequently pay the rest of it?
> WITNESS: Yes.

> THE COURT: Did you receive any money back in the way of commission?
> WITNESS: No, I paid full price.

"That's all," Landis snapped and whirled on Wigle. "That doesn't agree with what you've said today, does it?" For the first time Wigle, under Landis' fiery stare, seemed disconcerted.

"I must have misunderstood your question Saturday, judge."

"Yes, I guess you did," Landis said, visibly unconvinced. "I will treat this as perjury, but you will not be taken by a marshal until this evening. Hold yourself in readiness when the jury has left." He turned to the lawyers. "A more unwarranted, unvarnished exhibition of false swearing has never been seen in this court. When I think of Evans, Ladner, and men of their standing being mixed up with men of this class, and their fate resting on them, I can't recall anything more pathetically tragic ever taking place here.

"He hasn't fooled any of you lawyers. There is not one of these men from St. Cloud who didn't recognize the testimony as false. I watched their faces. A man can't do that sort of thing in this court and get away with it." He shook his head sadly. "With all the service these St. Cloud men gave this thing, for them to be classed with this man is pathetic and tragic. And they are going to go through with it. They are going to take their punishment. They are better sportsmen than I think I would be under the circumstances."

Landis called the jury back, and Peaks asked Wigle in re-direct examination about the stock. Much subdued, Wigle said that when he first talked to Pandolfo he had been promised stock at a discount. He reminded Pandolfo of that promise in March. "Well, we'll let it go this time," Wigle remembered Pandolfo saying, "but this is the last time, as no stock is to be sold that way in the company." Wigle left the stand late Monday morning, pensive and quiet.

Following the noon recess, H. D. Lambourne was called and under the guidance of his lawyer, Elwood Godman of Chicago, further fueled the fire of Landis's ire by refusing to answer most of the questions put to him. Lambourne said he lived in Chicago, that he had worked for the Pan Motor Company as a stock salesman and debt collector, that he had spent most of the last three months caring for his wife, who was ill. Beyond that he refused to answer any questions "on the grounds that my constitutional rights permit me to remain silent if I would incriminate myself by replying."

At one point Landis told Lambourne that his rights did not extend to evading questions not touching himself, but the witness remained silent. Landis asked Lambourne if he had been hired by Pandolfo to visit the witnesses who were under subpoena, and again he refused to answer. Finally, glaring first at Lambourne and then at Godman, Landis said, "You have no right to wrap the Constitution around yourself in this fashion when the answers to the questions will not invade your protection." Landis eyed

Lambourne with a stony stare in the silence that followed and finally waved him off the stand and out of the court room.

The defense then called Pandolfo. As the motor company president was being sworn in, Judge Landis, after the frustrations of the morning, appeared to be settling in for an enjoyable—or at least educational—afternoon. Pandolfo took the chair without a trace of nervousness and, with an occasional prompting question from Carl Cummins to fill in the details, told the story of his business life. He looked directly at the jurors when he talked, and when Judge Landis, almost with deference at first, asked a question, Pandolfo would pivot in the chair to face the judge as he answered.

He had sold some insurance earlier, he said, but in 1903 he took up the business in earnest and began to handle 20 old-line fire insurance companies. He found that he enjoyed selling and was an instant success at it. He gave a capsulized history of his associations in the Southwest and was interrupted with a question from Cummins. "By the way, as long as we're leaving Texas now, is there any truth to the story that you were forced to abandon your Packard at the state line as you left?"

Pandolfo laughed. "No. There is no truth to the story. I owed a friend 1,000 dollars on that Packard, which I later paid, and I left him the car because I was not going to ship it in by train."

The details of the present Pan Motor Company formed in his mind as he rode through New Mexico in March of 1916. "I felt that if a man could succeed in the insurance business in the Southwest, as I had until the Patterson mob undercut me, he could succeed at almost anything. And frankly, I had become used to living well. I knew teaching could not pay me a sufficient salary, and I was pretty sure bookkeeping wasn't going to do it either. I thought my talents were best suited to selling and promotion, but it had to be something big." He had first thought of the automobile business in 1910, he said, and he had had a special car made. "Most of the cars built at that time were made for the east or places where they had some kind of road or trail. In the Southwest in those days you were lonely if you traveled by car, and you were lucky if you could find a trail of some kind to follow. Ordinary cars just couldn't clear the roads we had. There were ridges and hog-backs, and if you got stuck on one you could stay there till you just about died.

"Then, the more populated areas out east had cities closer together. You could get from hotel to hotel, or city to city, in less than a day. In the Southwest, traveling men often had to sleep in their cars if they traveled by car, and unless you rode a horse or had a rig, that's the only way you could get to some of the towns. The railroads didn't stop at or even go near some towns. So I built this special car, or had it built for me, with a high clearance. I don't remember exactly how high it was, but it was high. We tried to work out something to make a bed in it, but it was pretty crude. About like sleeping on a board." He had abandoned the car project because it wasn't really working, and the insurance business then was still profitable.

He got the idea for the organizational plan of the Pan Motor Company from the surplus for insurance companies. "Insurance companies have to have an unimpaired capital. It's required by law. I felt this would give the company a stability that most new businesses don't have. I tested my ideas on some friends in New Mexico and they wanted to buy stock in the company before it was really formed. A doctor bought three shares, and two other people bought ten each, and the company was started."

Somewhere, Pandolfo said, he had picked up the information that a Ford car could be manufactured for $107 and a Dodge for $336. "These companies, I was told, bought a large number of their parts, and I figured that since the supplier had to make a profit, I could make more of my own parts and pass the saving on to the car buyers. A car that others had to sell at 7-8,000 dollars I figured I could sell at 500-600 dollars. And I still think so!"

As Pandolfo began to describe his debate with Shipley in Clovis, Judge Landis asked, "How long did you talk?"

"About an hour and a half," Pandolfo said.

Landis rolled his eyes and said, "Just give us the substance of it."

Pandolfo laughed. It was merely a detailed presentation of his plan for the Pan Motor Company and the car he thought it should produce. He told how he intended to finance the company and that's where Shipley objected. He and Shipley had been very friendly, Pandolfo said, but it was the banker's objection to any promotion scheme that started the trouble. The debate and the law suits followed. Shipley and his attorneys called on him and offered to pay all bills and settle out of court. "We agreed not to talk against each other, but Shipley broke his word."

The defense introduced several letters Pandolfo had written to automobile companies in December 1916 in which he asked for the names of engineers, mechanics, and foremen and also for prices on parts for cars and on models, or prototype cars. They were offered as early proof of his bona fide intentions to start an automobile company.

Judge Landis adjourned the court at six o'clock. He reduced the amount of bond for H. S. Wigle from $20,000 to $10,000, and Wigle, unable to arrange the bond, was taken to the county jail to spend the night. Court was delayed the next morning when neither Wigle nor the United States marshal assigned to guard him appeared at ten o'clock. The judge's temper was unraveling rapidly when, 25 minutes late, Wigle and his escort appeared in court. The marshal explained that they had started out at 7:15 but their street cars were delayed by various causes. Landis, in no mood to accept excuses, took the names of the cars and promised to have the matter investigated. The marshal's nervousness increased when the judge said that George Peaks, Wigle's attorney, had understood that his client had not been given supper the night before. "Is this true?" Landis inquired, scowling at the marshal.

The marshal vigorously denied the charge. "He not only had supper, your honor, he also had cigars." Smiling once more, Wigle corroborated the marshal's story, and Pandolfo resumed the stand. He was interrupted in mid-morning when John Burgess, editor of the *Minneapolis Daily News*, testified about the article in the October 13 issue. He did not know of his own knowledge who wrote the article, but Forsyth, whom he had seen last week in the offices of the *Daily News*, had told him that he, Forsyth, had written the article. At the time the article appeared, Forsyth was the automobile editor of the paper but left five weeks later to go to the Pan Motor Company as advertising manager. One sentence in the article read, "In the experimental building cars are being turned out at the rate of from three to ten a day."

Burgess had been released from the stand to obtain more information when Cummins informed the court that the company had had the objectionable paragraph removed from the story as soon as it was discovered, and only a few copies had been sent out as advertising.

"Well, that's pertinent," Landis observed, but the angry look on his face remained while Cummins said he was reserving the proof until the proper time. The prosecution, in the person of Sylvester Rush, admitted they had no copies of the expurgated circular, and Landis let it be known that he wanted to hear more on the matter from Forsyth. "Will he be placed on the stand again?"

"He can be called any time, your Honor," Cummins said.

"We're not through with him as yet," Rush added.

Pandolfo picked up the thread of his testimony, telling of his selection of St. Cloud. He was at his best as a witness when he frankly related information that might have been considered damaging testimony to himself. "I told Street that I didn't want any interference," he said, explaining how the company was started. "I said I wanted to select the site and the engineers and superintendent for the first year. Somebody had to be responsible for the success of the project, and I wanted that job myself. I also wanted the plan worked out in harmony with my first idea of an unimpaired capital and a surplus that would be used to promote the company. I told all prospective associates this before they became connected with me. I laid all my cards face up on the table in my first visit to St. Cloud. I told them to investigate me so that they could trust me; I told them all the worst things my enemies would say about me. From past experience I knew that they would go through the valley of the shadow of death with me, and I didn't want any weak-kneed ones to support me. It has come, and that is why they have stood by me."

Pandolfo said he had told the St. Cloud men that his compensation might reach a million dollars, and George Hanscom had said he did not think that was too much if he put the plan over.

At the opening of the afternoon session, John Burgess reported that he had called the *Minneapolis Daily News* during the noon recess to ask if the paper had received any money from the Pan Motor Company for extra copies, plates, photos or plated matter, and he had been told they had not.

With Pandolfo back on the stand, Cummins took literature issued by Pandolfo in Cheyenne in November 1916 and asked him to go through it point by point. One sentence read, "We expect to begin marketing cars in February 1917."

"How could you hope to do this in such a short time?" Cummins asked, and Pandolfo, using the replies he had received from various automotive companies, indicated that he had a basis for his claim: he would be able to begin marketing assembled cars by that time.

"Its tangible assets will be greater than the capital invested when the stock is all sold," read another sentence. This was based, Pandolfo claimed, on the premium value of good will. "Maxwell, Chandler, and other manufacturers carry good will on their books amounting to over half of their capital value," Pandolfo said. "With the army of Pan stockholders we have, I think the figure I have given is in serious error on the low side."

"What's the basis for that?" Cummins asked.

"Well, for example, we now have on hand orders for our products amounting to 113 million dollars. And there are indications that we could get an additional million dollars worth of work right now if we could handle it. This explains another point in our advertising. We have said there is no promotion fee from a practical point of view. Now, most of the money spent on promotion up to this point has been directed to the sale of stock, not strictly to the products of the company. I have been told, and I believe it, that Dodge Company spent two million dollars in advertising their car before they put it on the market. That kind of expenditure is saved the Pan Motor Company by the market already created in the stockholders."

Pandolfo summed up his difficulties with Reed & Glaser's car by saying, "We just could not go into production with that car. I felt we had been buncoed, or, to put it mildly, robbed. We had to stop work on the Model A and redesign the Model Ten into the 250. We did it in six weeks, and we wanted to get into production in November or December of 1917. But we couldn't get bodies, and then sheet metal, and finally motors. And then our Board of Directors decided to forego automobile production for the rest of the war."

Pandolfo claimed that if the war had lasted from five to ten years, as everyone had been saying, the tractor held the most promise for getting into production. "Was the tractor taken to Kansas City just to sell stock?" Cummins asked.

"Well, we weren't going to refuse to sell stock if they wanted to buy it," Pandolfo candidly admitted. "After all, we still needed capital, but it was not the main reason for taking the tractor. We wanted to show the Missouri and Kansas farmer what we had planned for them. We knew the design was not perfected yet, but we also knew the problems were minor. And we just couldn't wait another year to show the tractor."

"Why didn't you go into production with it?"

"Well, we couldn't get motors from anyone. And then the War Industries Board put tractors in a B-4 class as regards priorities. That meant it was impossible to go on."

"Well, to skip ahead, you are in production on the Model A at the present time, are you not?" Cummins asked.

"Yes, since October of this year," Pandolfo said. "We have on hand most of the parts needed for 500 units. We're able to produce more of our own parts now, and we won't be dependent on so many suppliers who have let us down."

Pandolfo said the other defendants were not the only ones who had lent money to the company; he had given $73,000 in an unsecured loan, which was still not paid back.

"What amount of stock do you own in the Pan Motor Company?" Cummins asked.

"Forty thousand dollars' worth," Pandolfo said, with no special emphasis.

"And what about your investment in Pan Town—the houses and property—has this repaid you?"

"I only wish it was as profitable as it has been represented. I could have made much more money on almost any other investment, but our people needed housing, which just wasn't being erected fast enough. I had to step in. As it is, I have realized only about three percent on the money invested in those houses."

"Now, what about your 500,000 dollar note in exchange for stock, will you explain that?"

"Yes. Unfriendly eyes were turned toward us. At first, when we were beginning, our enemies may have felt we wouldn't succeed, and there was no need to come out against us. But by spring of 1918 we had turned the corner and were well on our way. They began to hamper our efforts to sell stock." He had acted in good faith, he said. He had been informed that he could sell his personal stock to brokers in both Texas and Minnesota even if the company's license to sell was revoked, and he was prepared to do so to protect the company and the stockholders. But the directors insisted that his motives would be questioned. He had finally canceled the note, admitting that he had not done so immediately, but when the Fergus Falls indictment was handed down he had quickly arranged it.

Pandolfo claimed to be as surprised as everyone else by the Chicago publishers who had testified earlier. But he thought it was no reason to claim the stories about the company were also false. "I wasn't paying someone to write those stories. As long as I bought the reprints in good faith, I can't see anything wrong. I couldn't investigate every newspaper and magazine who sold us reprints of articles." Regarding the *Minneapolis Daily News* story, he said he had given orders that the offending paragraph be taken out, but some copies were sent out before that had been done. "We were terribly busy in those early days. I couldn't watch everything myself." Cummins then introduced the corrected version in evidence.

Because of the coal strike, various fuel-saving measures were in effect in Chicago, one of them being the curtailment of the use of electric lights in the court room. Since the day was clear and bright, and the prediction was for a low temperature of just five degrees above zero for that night, everyone agreed that they would prefer to save the fuel for warmth rather than spending it on light, although Judge Landis did not give them the opportunity to choose. Late in the afternoon he adjourned, and Pandolfo, who had been talking most of the day, appeared a little weary.

The trial was already unusual in many ways, but Wednesday morning, Pandolfo, during his testimony, made an accusation that struck Judge Landis, for the moment, as so important that he claimed the present trial was a matter of small import in comparison.

Evidence, in the form of letters from Pandolfo to his salesmen, was introduced to show that he had requested them to conduct themselves like gentlemen; he insisted that since the Pan Motor Company was a clean-cut enterprise he would tolerate only strict attention to business. One letter also forbade the use of any advertising matter by the salesmen that was not first passed on by the company. Shortly after the introduction of this material, Pandolfo made reference to the fact that much of his mail, including letters from his attorneys, had been opened before being delivered to him. Landis immediately demanded that such a claim be followed by introduction of the letters as evidence. A messenger was dispatched to the Atlantic Hotel to pick up the letters. "In comparison with the charge that federal officials have broken United States statutes, the innocence or guilt of the men here on trial is a small matter," Landis said soberly. While awaiting the return of the messenger, Pandolfo charged that some of the government evidence was secured through misrepresentation. He claimed that a postal inspector, Edward A. Schwab, had visited St. Cloud posing as a reporter from the *Financial and Investment Journal* of Milwaukee, a publication that had been critical of the Pan Motor Company.

When the messenger returned from the Atlantic Hotel, the discussion concerning postal inspectors was postponed while a large envelope, which Pandolfo claimed had been opened by the Chicago post office, was examined. The envelope, from the law firm of Wellman, Smyth and Scofield, had been sent by registered mail to Pandolfo in Chicago. Attorney George Peaks said he had been with Pandolfo when this envelope was handed to him, and it had been completely open. Rush contended at first that the flap had never been sealed properly as could be seen, he said, by holding it to the light. The post office had tried to protect the contents by affixing seals. But Peaks claimed that the seals had also been broken. Several other business-size envelopes were produced, and Pandolfo claimed they had all been opened when he received them. Landis wanted to know if this was all of them; Pandolfo said he had not saved the earlier ones.

Landis then wanted more information on the postal inspector who had been checking into the company. Cummins read a business card that had been given to him by Edward Schwab, "Representative and Correspondent, Milwaukee Investment Chronicle." The card gave no indication that

Schwab had any connection with the Post Office Department, Pandolfo said, and when Landis wondered why Pandolfo had had anything to do with Schwab, Cummins explained that the editor of the Milwaukee *Financial and Investment Chronicle* had attacked Pandolfo and the Pan Motor Company several times in his magazine, and Pandolfo had information that led him to believe that the magazine was a spokesman for the Olympian Motors Company, who had offices in the same building as the *Chronicle*.

"I believed he was what he said he was at first, and in order to show him how little we had to fear, we showed him everything and anything he asked for," Pandolfo said. "He went where he wanted to in the plant." They became suspicious of him when he began to frequent the bench outside Pandolfo's office and seemed to be taking notes of the conversations inside. He was followed, and it was learned from a train conductor that Schwab was traveling on a government pass. "I knew then he was an inspector. We found he had called on all the other directors and had given them the same bogus business card." Landis took notes throughout the explanation and seemed to grow more incensed with each new revelation.

Cummins was about to introduce affidavits in connection with letters Pandolfo had sent out on October 5th to all government witnesses in the trial when Peter Duell, the juror who had been sick earlier in the trial, complained of feeling ill again, and the jury was excused for the rest of the morning.

The attorneys used this opportunity to argue the point presented by the affidavits. Several letters from Pandolfo had been offered by the prosecution as evidence that he had tried to influence the testimony of witnesses. The letters began by stating that the Pan Motor Company had secured a list of the witnesses and also had on hand affidavits from stockholders all over the country stating that post office inspectors had made malicious misstatements regarding the Pan Motor Company. "All we want is a square deal," Pandolfo wrote, "and that you tell the truth." The recipient was asked to send the company copies of any statement made to the post office officials and any statements made by the officials. The letter concluded with an invitation to the witness to come to St. Cloud and go through the plant. He would then be in a position to tell the whole truth.

Rush and Epstein objected to the introduction of the letters because the witnesses had not been produced in person. Cummins said he offered them only to show Pandolfo's state of mind at the time he wrote them. Landis was inclined to allow them, but when the prosecution pointed out that some of these witnesses had testified earlier in the trial and had not been questioned about the letters, Landis changed his mind and refused to allow the evidence.

Following the noon recess, the jury was back, and one final effort was made to introduce the motion pictures of the St. Cloud plant in evidence. Cummins, Peaks, and Brower in turn offered opinions why the films were proper evidence, but Landis continued to shake his head in silence. They offered to show the pictures to him alone and let him decide after seeing them if they were bona fide. "I won't watch them," he said stubbornly but pleasantly. "I have had as much experience with moving pictures as anyone in the past 15 years, and I am not to be denuded of the opinion I have regarding them."

Peaks then made the unusual proposal to transport everyone connected with the case—jury, judge, lawyers, and defendants—to St. Cloud to visit the plant. Landis was amused at the offer, but he gave no indication it would be accepted. In resignation, the defense then handed the jurors photographs of the buildings and equipment, the only way left to them to acquaint the jury with the Pan Motor Company's tangible assets.

During the rest of his testimony Pandolfo spent some time talking about postal inspector W. J. Marles. The defense had continually claimed that the trial was prompted by the Associated Advertising Clubs of the World, working with and through post office employees. Pandolfo named two men he said Marles had attempted to intimidate and, because neither man had been a witness in the trial, the defense was allowed to present these affidavits. In substance, they stated that Post Office inspectors had made misstatements about the company.

With the withdrawal of the Fergus Falls indictment, Pandolfo had hired detectives to watch Marles. They followed him to New York several times, where he met with representatives of the Associated Advertising Clubs, and to St. Louis, where he had seen Festus J. Wade, president of the Mercantile Bank & Trust Company and one of the trustees of the fund used by the Vigilance Committee of the A.A.C.W. Cummins then asked Pandolfo what was in his mind when he wrote his letters to the prospective witnesses in October.

"All of our records and our activities had been laid open to the view of people who were conspiring against us. Even the post office inspectors had used subterfuge in attempting to get evidence against us. And they had made false and malicious statements. I felt we had the right to know what would be brought against us."

Landis followed the testimony intently; after hearing Pandolfo's explanation, he said that if he had known this use was going to be made of the list of witnesses he never would have ordered it released to the defense. "I assume you lawyers knew nothing of this. I never heard of such a thing before." He raised both hands and let them drop. "But then, I'm hearing a lot of new things in this trial." Peaks suggested that Landis needn't feel he had made a mistake; the list of witnesses had been published in a Des Moines newspaper as soon as the subpoenas had been issued. The consternation was evident on Landis' face as Peaks prepared to take over Pandolfo's direct examination for the last hour.

Most of this testimony concerned the corporate structure of the company, and Pandolfo reiterated his statement that money from the capital account was used for production purposes only. As part of this testimony, Peaks read more of the J. G. White Engineering Company report made for the Capital Issues Committee but which the committee had not published. The report described the buildings of the Pan Motor Company as "exceptionally high class and solid," and all of the machinery was characterized as "more than adequate in supply and of the latest type and design." Its analysis of the company's future concluded with the statement that failure to allow the company to sell stock would "cause the cessation of its activities, as millions are now needed to carry the initial stage to its completion."

Peaks finished his direct examination of Pandolfo at 4:30 and Epstein began the cross-examination. His first target was Pandolfo's claim about envelopes addressed to him and opened by postal inspectors. The prosecution wanted to see envelopes not already in evidence but others received in St. Cloud. The attorney pointed out that each one had been marked "Opened by mistake," and signed with the initials of the person opening them. Pandolfo protested that simply signing for it was no excuse for the post office to continue to inspect his mail. Landis again asked for additional evidence, and Pandolfo said he had not saved them all. He had written to the postmaster at St. Cloud (the one who had succeeded Fred Schilplin), at St. Paul, and at Chicago protesting the handling of his mail. When Landis asked if he had sent them any of the envelopes, Pandolfo said he hadn't had time, and Landis brusquely told Epstein to proceed.

Epstein's final line of questioning before adjournment centered on the report of the J. G. White Engineering Company. He wondered why the White report, done for the government, was more favorable to the Pan Motor Company than the one issued by Coates & Burchard, a Chicago accounting firm engaged by Pandolfo in the spring of 1919. Pandolfo said he had information from a Mr. Robinson, the accountant in charge of the work for Coates & Burchard, and affidavits from the men working under him that government agents had intimidated them in order to make the report less favorable. "I told Coates and Burchard so and they didn't deny it," Pandolfo charged.

As Landis adjourned, it was learned that a surety company had come to the rescue of H. S. Wigle, and he was freed from the custody of the United States marshal.

The second last day of the trial began with Epstein going back over the later history of the Pan Motor Company. Pandolfo's answers were getting short and petulant as the prosecutor began to probe for the reasons behind certain actions. "No one," Pandolfo said, "worked on the tank tread tractor after LaFond and Stahl left in March 1918 until Alfred Krieg came in June or July." Pandolfo defended this lapse in the development of a promising design by saying, "What could we do? We had no one else really qualified to continue work on the design, and when we got Mr. Krieg, he had his own reasons for not going on with the creeper design."

Epstein shifted his attack and showed Pandolfo a letter written January 14, 1918, in which he stated, "We are now ready to begin shipping automobiles."

"We *were* ready," Pandolfo insisted. "It was on a small scale, and we were making preliminary plans for increased production."

"But you turned out only two cars in that whole month of January," Epstein protested.

"Yes, that's right. But being on a production basis, as I see it, means turning out cars on a schedule, if it's one a month or several a day or a hundred a day. We were kept from increasing our production only by the unavailability of parts."

"Did you ever make a dollar on any car you sold?"

"Well, we did and we didn't," Pandolfo answered with a puzzled look. In his explanation he said that he originally placed the cost of the Model 250 Pan at $906 as he estimated it from the figures given him by A. R. Smith. "That included the cost of the parts plus 20 dollars for labor for assembly. I thought we would make 100 dollars selling it for 1,250 dollars." But he admitted that the profit and loss audit for the period up to April 1919 showed a loss of $351,000 for the company and $59,000 for the drop forge.

In the afternoon session, Epstein pursued the matter of the note Pandolfo had written in exchange for stock. "Why didn't you take this up before the entire Board of Directors before carrying it out?"

"I didn't think it was necessary. I had no idea anyone would criticize it; I thought it was the same as if I had sold the stock myself."

"Do you recall what you told the Federal Trade examiner in April of this year concerning that note?" Pandolfo looked puzzled and Epstein went on. "Do you remember telling the examiner that the Board of Directors had acquiesced in the matter of the note?"

Pandolfo nodded. "Yes, I remember that now. But I was not under oath and talking at random, mainly, as I remember, about something else at the time. I meant that one of them had, and while individuals on the Board spoke against it, they took no formal action. They did not oppose it as strongly at first as they did later. They did not . . . the Board did not learn of it until June fourth."

Landis broke in to ask, "Did you believe in good faith that the Securities Commission would allow you to sell stock that you yourself possessed when the company was forbidden to sell it?"

"Yes, I did," Pandolfo said earnestly, "and I had a letter from a friend to that effect."

Epstein began a series of general questions about the fiscal agency financial report that had been prepared by E. J. Bishop. As the questions become more specific, Pandolfo reddened slightly, and, finally, in response to Epstein's direct question, he admitted that he had made some false entries in the fiscal agency's books in an attempt to show his income as less than it was. He insisted that the purpose was not to avoid paying income tax but to prepare for other troubles. "Such things as salesmen leaving and not giving up the money they had collected in payment for stock. I had that happen to me before in Texas. It was a reserve for bad debts." Gorman, the auditor for the

Pan Motor Company, knew about the entries and so did Barritt, Pandolfo said; he had told both of them the money might be given to them as gratuities but it never was. The entries were later corrected in the books.

When it appeared Epstein had exhausted the subject, Landis sternly asked Pandolfo what amount of money was involved here, and Pandolfo said, "There were various sums involved, but they would add up to about 3,000 dollars." Landis gave Epstein an exasperated look.

The cold temperatures of the first few days of December abated on Friday, December 5, the last day of the trial. The prosecution proposed reading the report of the Capital Issues Committee. All four of the defense attorneys united in their objection, but Landis overruled them on the ground that the report had been brought to the attention of the jury by Pandolfo himself. After the reading, Cummins stated that many of the unfavorable remarks in the report were directly contradicted by the White Engineering Company's report. Cummins then read a statement by John Rich, chairman of the Capital Issues sub-committee, before which the Pan Motor Company had a hearing in Minneapolis on October 2, 1918. Rich stated: "This committee is fully advised that you have in the plant there exactly what you claim. The government knows it is so because they have had their own representatives there and made this investigation."

With the conclusion of this testimony, Pandolfo was finally excused as a witness and various rebuttal witnesses were called.

Late Friday afternoon all witnesses had been heard and all evidence presented. There remained only the final summation by the attorneys and the judge's charge to the jury. Before the last arguments began, the jury was removed to allow Ripley Brower to argue a motion: He requested the court to instruct the jury to return verdicts of not guilty in the case of the St. Cloud defendants. Landis denied it with a smile. "I have some sympathy, because of what you have said, for the eight members of the Board from St. Cloud, but I am not saying this as a juror. As a judge I cannot dismiss their cases. I have in mind just now the action of the salesmen in going around to the homes of patriotic people who had purchased Liberty bonds and telling them the bonds are not worth par." Landis' smile had vanished. "They took bonds in exchange for stock. It does not seem likely the officers of the company did not know this." Brower pointed out that accepting Liberty bonds was not mentioned in the indictment, but Landis was adamant.

The jury returned to the court room and Benjamin Epstein launched into a two-hour review of the evidence. His summation was incomplete; it was to be left to Sylvester Rush to present the final argument after the defense had spoken. One more defense attorney would then argue the final points, and finally Landis would instruct the jury.

There was a short conference at the defense table after Epstein had finished, and then George Peaks announced that the defense would waive all closing arguments.

The move was completely unexpected, and both the prosecution and Judge Landis were caught unprepared. He required a brief recess to prepare his charge to the jury and it took him an hour and a half to deliver it. He directed the jurors to find the eight St. Cloud defendants—Schwab, Thielman, Hanscom, Evans, Ervin, Ladner, Schilplin, and Bunnell—not guilty on the first five of the 11 counts in the indictment; all 13 defendants were to be found innocent of the eighth count. (The sixth and seventh counts had been stricken from the indictment at the opening of the trial.) His instruction left only two counts standing against the St. Cloud defendants: one of conspiracy and one of fraudulent use of the mails. All of the remaining counts applied to Pandolfo, Heidman, Street, Wigle, and Barritt, the judge told the jurors.

At 10:20, the jury, along with 600 pages of testimony taken from more than 200 witnesses, was sequestered.

Landis waited for the jury in the Federal Building until midnight, then departed, leaving instructions that if they reached a verdict during the night it should be sealed, and he would read it in court at ten o'clock Saturday morning. When he arrived in court Saturday he discovered no decision had been reached, but at 11:15 word went through the building that the jury was returning, and defendants, attorneys, and newspaper reporters scrambled with the spectators to return to the sixth-floor court room.

However, the jury only wanted further instructions about a particular point of the indictment. Landis gave them his interpretation, and the jury returned to their quarters only to come back an hour later to ask if they were required to impose the penalty. Landis informed them that it was part of his duty to impose sentence. Some time later the jury wanted to view the exhibits in the court room and it had to be cleared and guarded while they conducted their examination.

At 1:30, Landis announced a one-hour recess for lunch. And from one o'clock on, fog, smoke, and light wind, plus the rain or wet snow that fell through most of the day, combined to make the afternoon, already long and tense, gloomy and depressing as well. Some of those waiting, worn by the vigil of the previous night and the long weeks, found places on the marble steps where they napped at odd moments. The tempo of the activity in the post office below was studied; the architecture of the Federal Building was scrutinized and discussed; the prospects of a settlement in the coal strike were analyzed; the effect of various pieces of evidence on the jury was weighed. The long wait went on until shortly before 5:30, when the third call went out from the jury room.

In the court room, Landis, stern as usual, asked the foreman of the jury if they had reached a verdict. Joseph O'Sullivan, clerk of court, took the envelope handed to him and withdrew the folded sheets. At a nod from Landis he began to read.

Pandolfo was found guilty on four counts of using the mails to defraud and not guilty on all others. The names of the 12 other defendants were read in alphabetical order, and they were all declared not guilty on any count.

The defendants stood in exhausted relief, some of them openly shedding tears, as Judge Landis thanked and dismissed the jury. He assured them that if any were called again for jury duty within the next year and wished to be excused, they had only to come to him for corroboration that they had indeed "been through the mill." Epstein stepped forward to express his thanks, and he was followed by each of the defendants and the attorneys. Landis came down from the bench to offer his congratulations to the freed defendants and was joined in his best wishes by the much-maligned post office officials.

Pandolfo went to each of the other defendants, shaking hands and congratulating them. "It might have been worse," he repeated again and again. "I'm certainly glad you fellows were cleared. I have hopes of vindication in a new trial."

In the more formal moments following, Carl Cummins moved that the verdict regarding Pandolfo be set aside, and when this was summarily denied he moved for a new trial. Landis set December 15 as the date for hearing the motion.

Slowly, jubilation seeped through the directors. One made a brief statement to a Chicago reporter. "It has been a real ordeal, but now that it's over we can get back on the job in earnest and make good on these promises that have been talked of in court."

The court room was beginning to empty, and the early darkness of the December afternoon made it gloomier than ever. To the few spectators and newsmen remaining, Pandolfo read a telegram he had received earlier in the day.

> FROM ST. CLOUD, MINNESOTA, DECEMBER SIXTH. TO S. C. PANDOLFO AND OFFICIALS OF THE PAN MOTOR COMPANY, ATLANTIC HOTEL CHICAGO, ILLINOIS
>
> THE CITIZENS OF ST. CLOUD IN MASS MEETING TODAY ARRANGED FOR SUITABLE RECEPTION OF PAN MOTOR OFFICIALS REGARDLESS OF VERDICT. CITY OF ST. CLOUD BEHIND YOU TO A MAN. SIGNED THE COMMERCIAL CLUB.

Estimates placed the cost of the trial to the government in excess of $100,000. No one estimated the cost of the defense to Pandolfo.

The defendants began to leave Chicago. Mr. and Mrs. Pandolfo and members of their party, having attended to the closing down of the Atlantic Hotel offices, left Monday night for St. Cloud.

An editorial in the *St. Cloud Journal-Press* on Monday, December 8, 1919, reflected the sentiment of many of the people in the city.

> The verdict of the jury in the trial of the officers and direc-

> tors of Pan Motor was to be expected as to the directors, but the verdict of guilty on four counts against the president was not expected and is a keen disappointment. The four counts, as we understand it, relate to the selling of stock before Mr. Pandolfo came to St. Cloud and on these counts the judge charged the jury that the St. Cloud directors could not be held. . . .
>
> To drag men from their own state where there are courts and honest jurymen and subject them to weeks of expensive litigation when any man with an honest sense of fair play would have known that they were not guilty, is certainly a most drastic act. The government has expended an immense amount of money and it had raked the country over with post office inspectors and employees of the so-called department of justice. Over 400 witnesses are said to have been subpoenaed by the district attorney and only 74 put on the stand. One witness was even brought from France whose testimony was not of the slightest value. . . .
>
> Mr. Pandolfo is playing in hard luck, but in spite of the verdict of the jury he came through the fire of the trial as a real man. He was a wonderful witness and a most searching cross-examination by the government attorneys for many hours never caused him the least confusion or to change his evidence in the slightest degree. He did not attempt to evade any of the responsibilities but accepted whatever was coming.
>
> SOME MAN IS PAN!
>
> We congratulate the St. Cloud and other directors on their complete vindication and we regret that it was not also accorded Mr. Pandolfo. And we wish him better luck next time. But for his efforts and his wonderful ability to organize, St. Cloud would not have had this plant and there is not the slightest doubt in the mind of any man who has given the matter fair consideration that he has acted in good faith, honestly trying to make a wonderful success of the Pan Motor plant and to make good every promise to the stockholders.

In the same issue, Miss Irene Dunn, who had covered the Chicago trial for the *Journal-Press*, closed her story of the verdict by writing, "With this, the story of the trial may be brought to a conclusion."

But to Pandolfo, what some took as a conclusion was only a pause.

Pandolfo's experience of travel in the southwest, where hotel accomodations were rare or non-existent, led him to devise the sleeping car body which he also patented with help in the technical aspects from Edgard DeSmet, Pan body designing engineer.

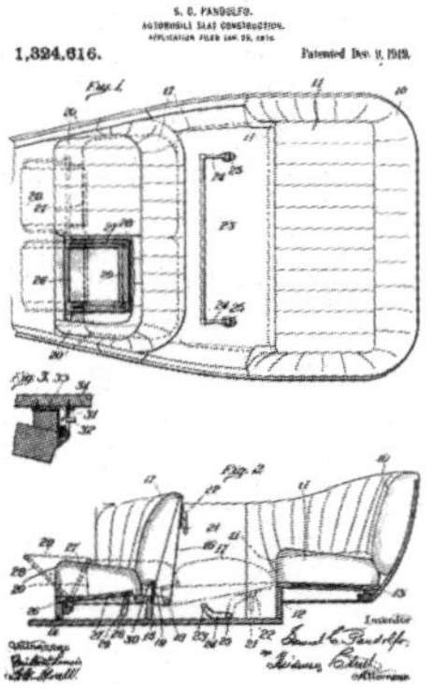

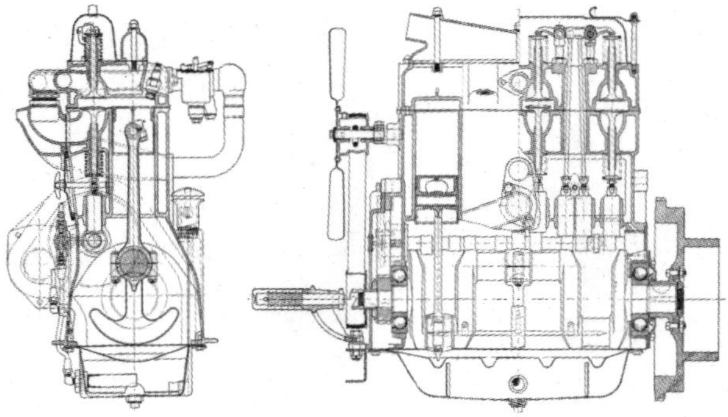

The Gauvreau-designed engine received attention from automotive magazine editors because of its high power-to-size ratio. It was also unique in having a crankshaft running in ball-bearings, a feature usually found in engines for race cars of the time.

Bill Bettenberg, an inspector and test driver at Pan Motor, drove this model up—and down—Pike's Peak in a test Pandolfo gave wide publicity to even though this was not the final Pan Model A.

Pandolfo used every opportunity to give a formal dinner, usually at the Grand Central Hotel. At this one, sitting at the head table are *(from left)* John Barritt, Charles Schwab, Pandolfo, Charles Ladner, Fred Schilplin, E. J. Gorman, Charles Bunnel and unknown. At the next table, Victor Gauvreau is seated between Mrs. Pandolfo on his right, and Florence Coleman, Pan Motor Company postmistress on his left.

(Left) The Federal Court House in Chicago where the board of directors and the president of Pan Motor Company were tried for using the mails to defraud.

(Lower Left) The courtroom in the Federal Building.

(Below) Judge Kenesaw Mountain Landis.

(Left) District Attorney Charles Clyne

(Right) Sylvester Rush

(Photo of Rush, courtesy Nebraska State Historical Society. All others, courtesy Chicago Historical Society.)

(Left) The Atlantic Hotel, the sixth floor of which was taken over by Pandolfo as headquarters, during the trial in Chicago. (The hotel had been named the Kaiserhof but the name was changed during the War.) *Photo courtesy Chicago Historical Society.*

(Above) The much maligned Pan Tank Tread Tractor, with Mrs. Pandolfo, daughter Vivian, and John Barritt attesting to its existence.

Carl Cummins, of St. Paul, was one of three attorneys representing Pandolfo.

(Below) The residence and grounds of the president of the Pan Motor Company in "Pan-Town-on-the-Mississippi."

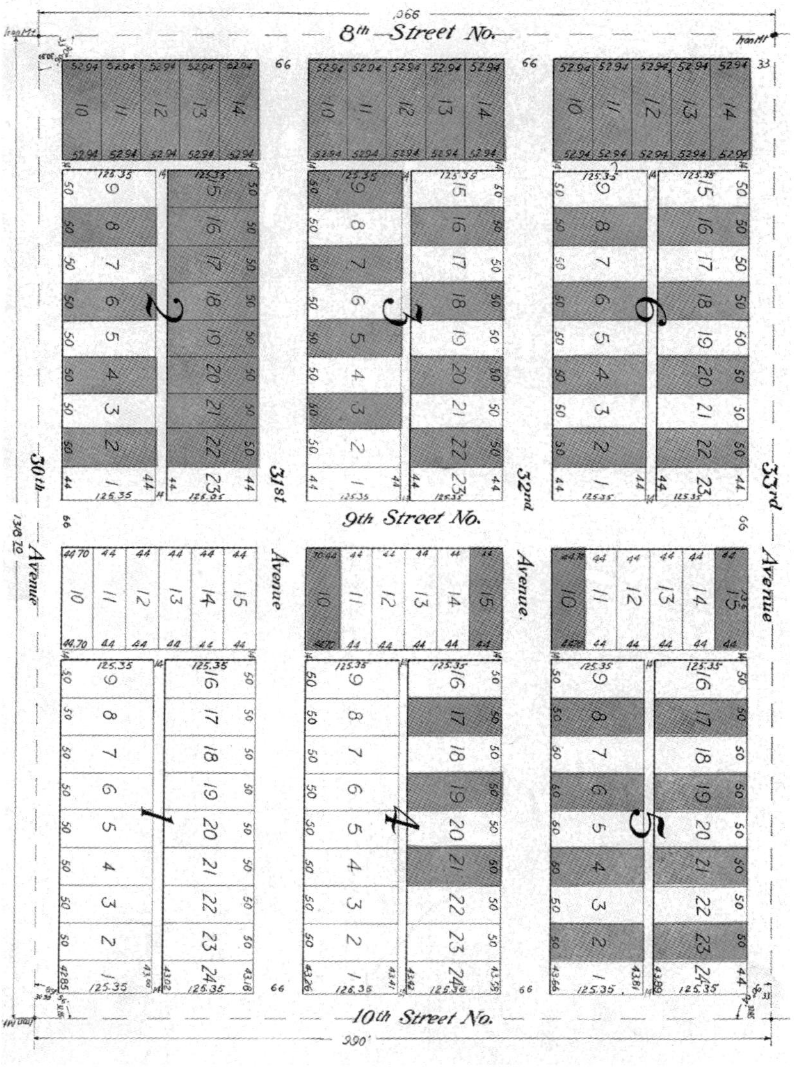

Plot of the homes in "Pan-Town-on-the-Mississippi." The shaded areas indicate those lots on which homes were built.

Lot 14 - Block 2

Lot 21 - Block 5

Lot 22 - Block 6

Lot 13 - Block 3

Lot 2 - Block 5

Lot 23 - Block 5

Lot 13 - Block 6

Lot 12 - Block 6

Lot 21 - Block 2

Lot 19 - Block 4

Lot 10 - Block 3

Lot 10 - Block 2

Lot 15 - Block 5

Lot 22 - Block 3

Lot 11 - Block 2

Lot 2 - Block 2

Lot 19 - Block 2

Lot 18 - Block 2

Lot 4 - Block 2

Lot 15 - Block 2

Lot 10 - Block 4

Lot 19 - Block 5

Lot 12 - Block 2

Lot 20 - Block 6

Lot 16 - Block 3

Lot 7 - Block 3

Lot 4 - Block 6

Lot 12 - Block 3

Lot 20 - Block 2

Lot 21 - Block 4

Lot 10 - Block 5

Lot 18 - Block 3

Lot 18 - Block 6

Lot 8 - Block 6

Lot 17 - Block 5

Lot 16 - Block 6

Lot 10 - Block 6

Lot 6 - Block 6

Lot 15 - Block 4

Lot 14 - Block 6

Lot 9 - Block 3

Lot 2 - Block 6

Lot 2 - Block 6

Lot 11 - Block 3

INCORPORATED UNDER THE LAWS OF DELAWARE

No. 2174 — *5* SHARES

PAN **Pan Motor Company** PAN

Capital Stock $7,000,000

First Preferred $2,000,000 — Common $5,000,000

This Certifies that ********CHARLES H. RICHTER********

is the owner of *****FIVE******* *shares of the First Preferred Capital Stock of PAN MOTOR COMPANY, fully paid and non-assessable, transferable only on the books of this Corporation in person or by Attorney upon surrender of this Certificate properly endorsed.*

Said Preferred Stock shall be a first lien upon the property of this Company after the payment and discharge of liens upon the property of the Company, and the indebtedness of the Company, and, in the event of the dissolution of the Company, or the sale of its property, shall be first retired upon the basis hereinafter stated, before the common stockholders of the Company shall share in the distribution of the assets of the Company properly applicable to their stock. Said First Preferred stock shall bear cumulative dividends at the rate of eight per cent. per annum, from date of issue, with full voting powers and to also share in the dividends to be distributed on the outstanding common stock of the Company. Said First Preferred Stock may be retired by the Company at any time within three years from date of final authorization, at the rate of Eleven Dollars per share, with accrued unpaid dividends, and at any time after three years from authorization, and before five years from authorization, at the rate of $10.50 per share, with accrued unpaid dividends, and at any time after five years from date of authorization, at par, with accrued unpaid dividends.

IN WITNESS WHEREOF, the said corporation has caused this Certificate to be signed by its duly authorized officers and its Corporate Seal to be hereunto affixed this 26TH *day of* AUGUST *192*0*, at St. Cloud, Minnesota.*

E A Cirar — Asst SECRETARY

C D Hemmel — VICE PRESIDENT

SHARES $10.00 EACH

© GOES 177

Preferred Pan Stock was issued after Pandolfo resigned as president of the Pan Motor Company. He dropped his objections when it was pointed out that without more investment in preferred stock the company would certainly fail.

CHAPTER X

A Bit More Capital is Required

ON THURSDAY, DECEMBER 11, 1919, less than a week after the verdict in Chicago, Pandolfo called an afternoon meeting of the Board of Directors in the offices of the Pan Motor plant in St. Cloud and resigned as president and member of the Board. The resignations of James H. McQuerry, second vice president, and George Heidman and Norman Street were also submitted. All resignations were accepted by the Board and Charles Ladner was named Temporary Chairman.

In a statement issued after the meeting, the remaining Board members announced the resignations and stated, "The Company is now in production in a small way and every effort will be made to make that production profitable as quickly as the means at hand will permit. To this end it urgently solicits the cooperation of all stockholders and subscribers."

It was not the announcement Pandolfo would have made. He issued his own statement to the press:

> To the friends, subscribers, and stockholders of the Pan Motor Company of St. Cloud and vicinity:
>
> At the suggestion of the so-called St. Cloud directors and after giving the matter full and careful consideration I concluded that it would be proper under the conditions and circumstances for me to resign as director and president. Messrs. McQuerry, Street, and Heidman also thought it was best for the company for them to resign. This leaves four vacancies on the Board and I discussed with the remaining directors the necessity and advisability of electing four substantial and representative men to take the places of those resigning.
>
> I am confident and hopeful that this will be done and without delay. It is my intention to do all I can in my humble way as a stockholder and outsider to promote the business and best interests of the Pan Motor Company. It is my present intention to continue to make St. Cloud my home. I wish to thank the good people of St. Cloud and vicinity for the assistance, cooperation and support they have given me. I shall always be appreciative of the confidence placed in me by my many St. Cloud friends and supporters.

> The Pan Motor Company is a worthy and meritorious institution. It deserves the fullest measure of your support and cooperation. I urge one and all to support liberally the new management because they can accomplish much more and better results with 100 percent cooperation.

On Saturday, Pandolfo addressed all of the department heads at the Pan plant, explaining the reasons for his resignation. On Tuesday, the motion for a new trial having been denied by Judge Landis the day before, Pandolfo appeared in Chicago for sentencing. Landis reviewed the case at length, saying it would help to explain the sentence he was about to give. "I want the stockholders in the Pan Motor Company to know that the United States government is not a criminal institution whose purpose is to persecute Pandolfo or the company. From some of the allegations made against federal officials, people might be led to believe this. Every United States citizen has the right to throw his money away if he feels like it."

Landis accused Wigle, Heidman, and Street, Pandolfo's associates in the incorporation of the company, of "playing for table stakes and with the greatest luck. It's a shame that Pandolfo should be found guilty and such a creature as Wigle turned loose. Pandolfo was charged guilty by the jury because it was his scheme.

"Now if this court had jurisdiction over a sovereign state, I would call a special grand jury to consider the indictment of the state of Delaware for its offenses as disclosed from time to time in the criminal proceedings in this court. The state of Delaware plays the game because by playing it, it gets money in its treasury to help run the state, thereby relieving its own citizens to that extent from the burden of taxation. Delaware is willing to get it that way and is still getting it."

The several magazines and newspapers mentioned during the trial also came under scathing review by Landis. "Now, the *Minneapolis Daily News*—whose paper is that, Mr. Cummins?"

"It is one of the Clover Leaf Dailies. There is one published in Omaha, one in St. Paul, and one in Minneapolis," Pandolfo's attorney replied.

"Who owns them?" Landis wanted to know.

"The chairman of the Federal Trade Commission is president of the corporation."

"Who is he, what's his name?"

"William B. Clover," Cummins answered.

With a characteristic scowl on his face, Landis said, "If he is the owner of this *Minneapolis Daily News* he had better quit being chairman of the Federal Trade Commission and reform his crooked papers."

"That appointment was in reward for supporting the administration," Cummins volunteered.

Landis turned to Sylvester Rush, a resident of Omaha for 30

years. "Judge Rush, who is the owner of this paper? Is that man the owner of this paper?"

"This is all news to me," Rush unknowingly punned.

"Well, Mr. Cummins lives in St. Paul and he ought to know," Landis mused.

"I did not say he owned it. He is connected with it," the attorney corrected Landis.

"You said he was chairman," Landis claimed.

"I said he was chairman of the Federal Trade Commission. He is one of the officers of the corporation that publishes the Clover Leaf Dailies."

Landis dropped the discussion about ownership to comment on the newspapers themselves. "Now, in the *Minneapolis Daily News* on the second of October, 1917, I find this. 'In the experimental building, just across the street from the main unit, cars are being turned out at the rate of from three to ten a day.'

"Now, there is no more justification for that statement than there is for saying that from three to ten cars a day are being turned out in this room now. But that was in the *Minneapolis Daily News* of October second." Landis proceeded to castigate the *Minneapolis Daily News* along with the *Merchant, Banker and Manufacturer*, Chicago publications whose reporters had written favorably about the Pan Motor Company in hopes of getting advertising later. He touched for a moment on the St. Cloud directors of the Pan Motor Company, whom he characterized as "a fine aggregation of men unwittingly drawn into Pandolfo's plan."

Then, finally, he delivered the sentence. Pandolfo was to serve five years on each of the four counts on which he was convicted, the terms for counts one and two to be served concurrently and the same for counts three and four. In addition, he was fined $1000 on each count. The ten-year term and $4,000 fine was as severe as any attorney in court could recall, although Landis could have made it 20 years and $20,000. Cummins made immediate motion for a writ of supersedes, which would allow Pandolfo his liberty, on $25,000 bond, while appealing the case. (Judge Samuel Alschuler later issued the writ.)

The state of Delaware's reaction to Landis' statement was not recorded. But St. Cloud's reaction to the sentence and fine was predictable, and Alvah Eastman, publisher of the *Journal-Press*, expressed it in a short editorial paragraph titled "The Judicial Equipoise."

> Judge Landis made it clear that the government's action was not intended in any way to influence holders of Pan Motor stock. "The United States citizen still has the right to throw his money away if he feels like it," Landis stated. (I wouldn't for the world say a word against any of my neighbors, but the one next door is the most miserable specimen of humanity that I ever did see.) Anyhow, that honorable judge can claim he was misquoted, and let us hope he was.

The blows to Pandolfo and the Pan Motor Company were coming in series now. While he was being denied a new trial by Landis in Chicago, the Minnesota Supreme Court was affirming a lower court decision that had gone against Pandolfo. Earlier in the year, Mrs. Ruth Stanger had sued Pandolfo for payment for services and expenses due her for management of the Motor Hotel. Early in 1919, Judge John A. Roeser, in St. Cloud, had awarded Mrs. Stanger $518.55. Pandolfo's motion for a new trial here was denied and his appeal was turned down. The verdict stuck.

In January 1920, Pandolfo dropped the one million dollar libel suit against the Vigilance Committee of the Minneapolis Advertising Forum, which by now had changed its name to the Better Business Bureau. Also dropped were all of the other libel suits Pandolfo had pending against various defendants. He made it clear, though, in the suits in which he and not the Pan Motor Company was the litigant, that this was only to conserve his finances for the more immediate and pressing appeal; it was not in any way a capitulation on the merits of the libel actions.

But with the blows there were also back-slaps. On December 30, 1919, a full page in the *Journal-Press* was taken up with a paraphrase of "Invictus," Henly's lyric challenge to fate. The choice was apt.

To Samuel C. Pandolfo

Out of the night that covers thee,
Black as the Pit from pole to pole,
Thank whatever gods may be
For your unconquerable soul.

In the fell clutch of circumstance
You have not winced nor cried aloud.
Under the bludgeonings of chance
Your head is bloody but unbowed.

Beyond this place of wrath and tears
Looms but the Horror of the shade,
And yet the menace of the years
Finds, and shall find, you unafraid.

It matters not how strait the gate,
How charged with punishment the scroll,
You are the master of your fate;
You are the captain of your soul.

Contributed by your St. Cloud friends

In the face of such local loyalty, a merciful government might have felt the urge to offer something more than Judge Landis' backhanded statement about not wishing to persecute any business.

The Pan Motor Company was making heroic efforts to regain momentum and the confidence of investors. In February, Charles Ladner, with the help of Albert Gideon Whitney, president of the Public Service Company, applied for a renewal of the license to sell stock in Minnesota. Whitney and Ladner were not the only powerful influences working in the company's behalf now. Ferdinand Peters of the Cold Spring Granite Company, Cold Spring, Minnesota, identified in a news story as "one of the strongest financial factors in this section," was made a member of the Board of Directors.

But it was clear that with Pandolfo gone much of the steam had gone out of the company. Where three stories a week from the Pan Motor Company ran in the newspapers in the old days, a short paragraph in the editorial column once a month seemed to be all the company could—or wanted to—generate now. One of these paragraphs, appearing early in 1920, crowded it all into one sentence: "The Pan Motor Company has safely emerged from the government attacks and is entering upon an era of active production, and will undoubtedly during the coming year forge ahead and be on a secure foundation of success and will in the near future be one of the great industries of the country."

A banquet late in January featured the business leaders of the community discussing the building projects under way in the area. Ladner reported on the Pan Motor Company, certainly the number one concern. Since the reorganization of the Board, he said, many people of the St. Cloud area had come to the aid of the company and were reducing the immediate liabilities. "A bit more capital is required," Ladner said, "but under the present rate of progress it is hardly likely that grave difficulties will again threaten the welfare of the institution. The plant will be placed on a production basis of 20 cars per day as soon as the new foundry is completed."

How that "bit more capital" was going to be raised was disclosed in a letter that Ladner and the Board sent to the stockholders announcing a meeting on March 31. The Directors proposed to issue preferred stock in the amount of two million dollars with present stockholders given the first chance to buy. They also proposed eliminating the sleeping car feature and compartment tank from future Pan cars. (It would cut the cost, but both of those features were specifically identified with Pandolfo; thus there was the subtle intention of disassociating the company from the founder since the Pandolfo Manufacturing Company, and not the Pan Motor Company, had patents on and produced the Compartment Tank.)

As soon as the letter was issued, the voice of Pandolfo was heard in the land. As the largest individual stockholder in the company he was entitled to a loud voice. His own letter to the stockholders removed any doubts about his resignation being an amicable agreement. The liabilities of the company, he claimed, were now greater than when he was forced to resign, "despite the fact that much material and cars and otherwise which had been paid for when I was president have been turned into cash." He cautioned against issuing preferred stock at eight percent until present outstanding stock subscriptions were paid up and the remaining stock sold. "If this is done, a preferred stock issue will be unnecessary; all the money needed will be available." He urged the stockholders to vote against the amendment at the upcoming meeting.

Pandolfo insisted other mistakes were about to be made in the name of retrenchment. He understood the rights, title, and interests of the Pan Tank Tread Tractor were to be offered for sale. Whether or not this was seriously contemplated is not known. Nor is it known whether the basis for his next objection was real or imagined. "If the management goes through with its plan to change the trademark of the company it will be a grave mistake. Too much money has been spent in introducing and advertising the trademark to the world." Pandolfo's objection had merit, since the onus of the trial was plainly on him, and little if any stigma attached to the company and certainly none to its products.

On Thursday, April 1, 1920, April Fool's Day, the stockholders' meeting convened in the Pan plant and overwhelmingly voted to accept the preferred stock plan. When Pandolfo realized the resolution would pass despite his opposition he withdrew his proxies cast against it.

On April 5, the new issue of preferred stock cleared the Securities Commission in St. Paul. It was stipulated that selling expenses were not to exceed 15 percent and that all proceeds from the sale of the stock were to be used as manufacturing and working capital. The commission's statement emphasized that the permit applied only to 30,000 shares of the preferred stock; the ban on the sale of common stock was continued. The commission felt "the net tangible assets of the company are sufficient to establish a probability that the eight percent dividend will be paid on the new issue."

The day the commission announced its decision, an event occurred that, like so many others connected with Pandolfo and the company, could have been considered an omen. The *Journal-Press* reported it thus:

AUTO PLUNGES OFF HIGH BANK

Police Car Makes Sensational Plunge Over River Bank

> The city police department is today without its official car. The car, a home product, is lying at the water's edge below a 60-foot bluff of the Mississippi River just east of City Hall [which at the time shared the building with the police department and the jail].
>
> The car plunged over the bank at eleven o'clock last night. Whether propelled by the wind, a midnight goblin, a prowler, or set in motion through some other source of power is not known. At eleven, Officers Huhn and Lutgen made a switch of the cars

> in the garage. The Pan was taken out of the garage and Officer Huhn's car put in its place. The Pan car was to be given first place in the garage so it would be accessible during the night.
>
> The officers stepped into the station for a moment and were quickly followed by a boy who said that a car had just plunged over the bank into the river.
>
> The officers went to the scene and found the police car almost a wreck 60 feet below. Two wheels were smashed and other damage done. Officer Lutgen, who took the car from the garage, stated that he had placed the car in neutral and had stopped the motor. The car was in low gear at the foot of the bluff.

Some residents thought the Pan police car had committed suicide.

Within the next few days, an ad in the local newspaper gave the details of the preferred stock plan to Pan stockholders.

> PAN MOTOR COMPANY OFFERS FOR THE PRESENT TO ITS STOCKHOLDERS ONLY $2,000,000 8% CUMULATIVE PREFERRED STOCK AT PAR, $10 PER SHARE, REDEEMABLE AT $11 AND ACCRUED UNPAID DIVIDENDS WITHIN THREE YEARS FROM DATE OF AUTHORIZATION, AT $10.50 AND ACCRUED UNPAID DIVIDENDS AFTER THREE YEARS AND BEFORE FIVE YEARS FROM DATE OF AUTHORIZATION.

The preferred stock, for its security, was said to "bear the relation of a first lien against all assets of the company." The remainder of the ad listed other features of the stock: because of its dividend rate of eight percent and the fact that it also shared in common stock dividends, the preferred stock was said to be "an unusually attractive investment"; the conservative management of the company (in comparison with Pandolfo's) was listed as a desirable feature; for a period of 30 days the stock would be offered only to holders of common stock.

It now seemed as if some god-like hand was propelling obstacles, one after the other, into the path of the Pan Motor Company. Another buffeting came at the hand of the Federal government. The Federal Trade Commission released a "Finding and Order" regarding the company and Pandolfo. The report repeated much of the same material the trial had sifted through, but where the trial had pictured Pandolfo as unfair to the public at large, the FTC accused the company of using "unfair methods of competition in interstate commerce." Pandolfo and the Pan Motor Company were ordered to file, within 60 days, a report setting forth "the matter and form in which they have complied with the order of the Commission herein set forth."

The trial was neither mentioned nor referred to in any way, but the report caught Carl Cummins, Pandolfo's attorney, in a minor error: William B. Clover was indeed a member of the Commission but was not then its chairman.

By itself, the FTC report was not any more damaging than other attacks on the company had been; it did not automatically mean anathema. Other companies receiving "Cease and Desist" orders at the same time included Nestle's Food Company, Sinclair Refining Company, and Standard Oil of Indiana, all of whom survived their slap by the FTC. But the St. Cloud corporation was bearing the burden of other recriminations. The FTC report was simply one more arrow the Federal government had to sling at the outraged fortunes of the Pan Motor Company.

The report was also the final impetus Charles Ladner needed. His failing health, certainly not helped by his constant efforts to stabilize the company, was offered as the reason for his resignation as President of the Pan Motor Company on July 30, 1920. He was just plain tired. He would remain on the Board as Chairman, but in fairness to the stockholders he felt the presidency demanded and should have the services of a younger man. In his place the board elected Charles Schwab.

Schwab was thus in a curious position; he was not only a banker, realtor, and now president of the Pan Motor Company, but also an officer in the St. Cloud Truck Company. The company had been formed early in 1920 by Leroy Brown, former general manager of the Pan Motor Company. Brown had resigned his position a few days after Pandolfo and had been replaced by Ray DeVlieg, the methods engineer. With backing from William J. Bohmer and other men in the granite industry in St. Cloud, Brown began to assemble heavy-duty trucks designed principally for off-highway work around quarry sites. Schwab had been made secretary-treasurer of this company some months before being named the new president of Pan Motor.

As a member of the Pan Board, Schwab was certainly familiar with the problems he would now face as president. Almost immediately there was a two-day shut-down of the plant. No official reason was given for the closing, but it became increasingly manifest that "the little bit of capital" that was required was not coming in easily.

A special meeting of the Commercial Club was called (echoes of the old Pandolfo days!) and all Pan stockholders and "others interested in the future development of St. Cloud" were invited. At the meeting, Schwab indicated that the Pan preferred stock was not selling as rapidly as hoped. In fact, only 20 shares had been sold in St. Cloud. The company had orders for more than $50,000 worth of drop forgings, Schwab said, but to produce these outside orders, as well as continue to manufacture and sell Pan cars, money was needed immediately.

On the motion of William B. Mitchell, a resolution was passed that a committee be appointed to sell $100,000 in preferred stock in St. Cloud. Subscriptions were taken at the meeting that August evening in the amount of $10,000.

It was little consolation but the Pan plant was not the only auto company feeling the pinch of low capital. In Indiana, the plants of Nordyke and Marmon Company, National Motor Car and Vehicle Corporation, and the Stutz Company were laying off workers. The reason: lack of operating capital.

The Pan Motor Company was seeking capital wherever it could, even to offering "the few remaining Pan Model 250 cars" for sale at $850 each, down from $1250.

The Commercial Club began to sell stock 14 days before the third annual stockholders meeting. At 2:30 p.m. on Tuesday, August 24, nearly 1,000 stockholders gathered in the main factory building. Of the 642,921 shares of common stock and 2,186 of preferred outstanding, 14,591 shares were represented in person and 344,762 by proxy. The stockholders returned the Board of Directors—Schwab, Ladner, Bunnell, Schilplin, Thielman, Hanscom, Evans, and Ferdinand Peters—to office. President Schwab, Ferdinand Peters, Ripley Brower, and Samuel Pandolfo addressed the meeting. Pandolfo, awaiting word on the appeal of his sentence, was now urging support of the sale of preferred stock. He also pressed his claim for money due him from the company; a motion was made to pay him but before it could be passed, it was amended and referred to the directors for study.

As the summer of 1920 aged into autumn, the hoped-for relief that the company sought in a boost in car sales or prices was doomed by Henry Ford's announcement that prices on Fords would be reduced about $142 per car. It was followed by an even more significant statement from Ford. Some suppliers had tried to increase their prices to Ford, and he finally balked when a tire company hinted at a price hike. "No," said Henry, "if tire companies raise their prices, I can finance an independent company and make them myself. The time has arrived for a downward trend in prices, but not for a decrease in the scale of wages."

On Saturday, October 2, 1920, the Pan Motor Company unveiled one idea it had for the future: a six-cylinder version of the Model A Pan. Schwab drove the car to downtown St. Cloud, a severely scaled down version of Pandolfo's Texas or Pike's Peak trips, and parked it where the local experts could look it over. Gauvreau had planned this model along the general lines of the Model A. DeSmet's body design lowered the overall height and flattened the lines along the body sides. The car was still called a five passenger model although its horsepower was boosted to 50 and its wheelbase was lengthened ten inches to 118. The compartment tank was gone and the gasoline tank was mounted at the rear. The tool box was at the base of the tonneau and doubled as a footrest. No mention was made of the sleeping car arrangement, but with this model all connection with the Pandolfo-inspired design would be severed. Only one prototype was produced, and it was the last model Gauvreau—or anyone else—would design for the Pan Motor Company. It was not intended to replace the Model A, Schwab said, but to be a companion model. There was no real hope for its production, however.

In spite of a general slowdown in auto production toward the end of the year (in December most major and all minor manufacturers would announce lay-offs and some plant closings), the Pan Motor Company was able to place a dealership in Minneapolis. John Weber and Joseph Gilman, of the Gilman-Johnson Motor Company, drove a demonstrator back to their agency, at 2912 Lyndale South, on November 11. And in the early months of 1921, George F. Brown, identified as the general sales agent for the Pan Motor Company, released some information on the company's activities. "The general belief that the Pan Motor Company is shut down and doing no business whatsoever is wrong. Automobiles are being produced, sold, and driven from the factory nearly every day. One dealer, James Gibson of Rochester, Minnesota, purchased five Pan cars. The city of Rochester has 70 Pan stockholders and every one of them is boosting the Pan Motor Company. H. S. Tallakson of Willmar, another dealer, recently took delivery on five Pan cars. C. W. Simonson, Pan factory representative, has placed a number of agencies recently. We have Steinbering Brothers in Hancock—they just drove some cars out of the factory yesterday. We have Rose and Pearson in Benson; they have the agency for Swift county. Kools and McLoughlin in Donnelly, D. Lyshik in Glenwood, Boe and Wilshusen in Wendell, Howard Bristol in Evansville, W. H. Hill in Fergus Falls, H. G. Hilgers in Barnesville, F. E. Flint in Alexandria, and John Baker in Browns Valley."

All the cars then being sold had been assembled from parts produced the previous year. The Pan Motor Company was no longer producing parts for new car production.

Pandolfo's energy and interest could not be totally consumed in conducting the appeal on his sentence; he had to find another outlet. Since September 1919, even before the start of the Chicago trial, construction had been continuing quietly on the new home of the Pandolfo Manufacturing Company, the business he had organized to manufacture the combination compartment tanks and other metal items. Pandolfo had bought a 38-acre site across the railroad tracks, just south of the Pan Motor Company. He anticipated outgrowing the shop in St. Cloud on the corner of Sixth Avenue and Second Street South. On January 3, 1920, less than three weeks after resigning from the presidency of the Pan Motor Company, Pandolfo made public his plans for a new $300,000 office and factory complex for the Pandolfo Manufacturing Company. The Austin Company of Cleveland, specialists in "standard factories," were erecting three main units: an office building, a main factory, and a power plant.

The office building, red brick and tile, would be 40 × 100 feet and cost $35,000. The factory building would be 110 × 122 feet, white brick and steel. It was Austin's Standard No. 6, a "daylight factory," with six rows of windows in the sides. It was 50 feet high at the center section. With typical Pandolfo enthusiasm the west, or back wall was temporary; it would permit expansion as the business grew. This unit would cost $50,000. Part of the equipment in this building was to be a traveling electric three-ton-capacity crane. The boiler and heating plant, north of the factory, would house two boilers in a 20 × 40 foot area. The plant would also have its own water supply, a 75,000-gallon tank at the top of a 70-foot tower.

One of the principal products of the plant, since the compartment tank was being phased out of the Pan car line, would be the "Simmons Wheel of Steel," an invention of O. G. Simmons. Simmons, who was the chief engineer and purchasing agent for the Pandolfo Manufacturing Company, had worked in the naval gun factory in Washington, D.C., and also claimed to have been associated with Wilbur Wright in "experiments with flying machines." He gave his educational background as "mechanical engineering student, Franklin Institute and Catholic University of America."

The Simmons wheel was pressed steel, made in two parts, and had what Simmons called "tape spokes." With the wheels mounted on his heavy Hudson Six, Simmons had driven over 30,000 miles, including a trip from San Antonio to Detroit to New York and back to San Antonio again before coming to Minnesota.

The compartment tank, although abandoned now by the Pan Motor Company, was still offered by the Pandolfo Manufacturing Company as an accessory for other cars.

At the end of January 1920, news about the Pan Town Addition eclipsed any story concerning either the Pan Motor Company or the Pandolfo Manufacturing Company. The total assessment for the Pan sewer project was announced: $400,000. It was the largest ever levied by the city for one improvement project. One firm was assessed over a fourth of the total amount for the property it owned in the area: Farmers Loan and Investment Company, owned by Charles Schwab and Peter Thielman. Their assessment was $130,000. Schwab and Thielman appeared before the city commission on February 10 to hear city engineer Merton B. Lang explain the assessment. They voiced objection to the levy on only one small plot. They valued the plot, consisting in the main of a water hole, at $100, but the sewer tax on it was $750. Lang promised to review that particular assessment.

Pandolfo was having troubles with the construction of buildings for his new company at the same time he was fighting the preferred stock plan in his old one. During a March windstorm, a healthy gust, gathering strength as it came across the prairie, toppled the east wall of the Pandolfo Manufacturing Company's new factory building, injuring a plumber working on the job. The opening of the plant would be delayed a month while the damage was repaired.

Pandolfo did not try to hide the financial squeeze he was suffering.

For almost a month, from March 27 to April 24, 1920, the following ad ran daily in the *Journal-Press*:

> FARM IN CITY LIMITS FOR SALE
>
> I own a 98-acre farm on St. Germain Street nine-tenths of a mile east from the First National Bank and three-tenths of a mile east of the end of the paved street and white way, and four-tenths of a mile from the Northern Pacific depot. Fifty acres in cultivation and 48 acres in hog and cow pasture. Fine place for dairy farm. Good house, good barn and good fences. I need money and must sell some of my property at a sacrifice. This farm is for sale.
>
> S. C. Pandolfo

This was property he had originally intended for the location of the Pan Motor Company. It's difficult to say whether Pandolfo needed the money for his appeal or for other purposes. While the "Farm for Sale" ad was still running, Ben Forsyth, now advertising manager of the Pandolfo Manufacturing Company, announced plans for the grand opening of the new plant. They were reminiscent, but on a much smaller scale, of the Fourth of July barbecue Pandolfo had given almost three years earlier at the Pan Motor Company. Art Lambert's local 12-piece orchestra was advertised, mysteriously, as an "aerial orchestra," and there was to be other professional entertainment. Everyone in St. Cloud was invited. They were asked to "dress up in clown suits, tramp suits, rube suits . . . anything except dress suits and party gowns." The factory building would provide room for dancing, the host promised, for over one thousand people. Special street cars running right to the front door were arranged for, while those who drove their own car would have ample free parking space next door to the plant with a special watchman on guard. There would be no admission charge.

On the evening of Saturday, May 1, 1920, over five thousand people turned out to attend the grand opening. The Royal Hilo Hawaiian novelty orchestra, recording artists on Edison and Victrola records, returning to Honolulu after a tour of the eastern United States, alternated with Art Lambert's musicians. The mystery concerning the aerial orchestra was solved when the men were discovered seated on a platform suspended from the traveling crane, going from one end of the building to the other, over the heads of the dancers. The society columns reported the event and concluded:

> A good entertainment program was offered during the evening. Miss Bobbie McCadden, whose success as a danseuse is well-known in St. Cloud, appeared in gypsy and Hawaiian dances; the Elks Quartet, comprised of Messrs. Freeman, Cole, Hazlam, and Cooke, entertained with a number of popular songs. The character impersonations given by Miss Gladys Lucille

> Broberg of St. Paul were entertaining; an Irish washerwoman, a Swedish janitress, and other laugh-provoking characters were included. She later appeared in the role of Madame Butterfly.
>
> In a brief address of welcome, Pandolfo outlined the progress of his company and reviewed what it expected to do in the future.

Pandolfo had learned at least one lesson from his trial, and it was manifested in the booklet/catalog he published for the Pandolfo Manufacturing Company. Called "Our Family Album, A Pictorial Presentation of the Plant, Products and Personnel of the Pandolfo Manufacturing Company (Not Incorporated), St. Cloud, Minnesota, U.S.A.," the front page of this booklet carried a disclaimer so inclusive that it might have been invoked to excuse Pandolfo's behavior in the past, as well as protect him in the present and the future.

> Realizing that this volume will be read months—yes, even years—after its publication, attention is called to the fact that the words, figures and pictures printed herein can tell only the story of today—of the present status of our business. Time changes all things and this business can be no exception to the rule. Conditions may arise that necessitate canceling of orders for machinery shown here as now on order or substituting other machines and models, and on the other hand, we hope to add many machines to the list; products we are now making, or propose to make, may be abandoned or changed in design and others may be added; it is proposed to remove all machinery and equipment from plant No. 1 to our new plant at an early date, yet we may find it necessary to continue the old plant and construct additional buildings for the new plant; changes may occur in our personnel from time to time. These and many other things that cannot always be foreseen may occur. But whatever the future may bring, we reserve the sole right to make such changes and do such things as, in our judgment, should be made and done.

If language could prevent it, Pandolfo was not going to be held to the printed word again!

Though the trademark of the Pandolfo Manufacturing Company closely resembled the Pan Motor Company's circular pan emblem, mention of the motor company's name was scrupulously, even fanatically avoided in "Our Family Album"; men who had worked at Pan Motor were identified as having been with "an automobile manufacturing concern," or "a local automobile company."

The new company described its items as "Made-O-Metal Products," and they included a fender-mounted luggage rack (the Handy-

Pandy Luggage Carrier), the Handy-Pandy Metal Folding Chair (advertised as being able to "make a seven passenger out of a five"), and fenders for the Fordson Tractor, which not only contributed to the appearance of the tractor, but also protected the driver from the steel-lugged wheels and prevented the tractor from tipping back on the driver by isolating the rear wheels from the ground if the machine did start to rear up.

Pandolfo's typical foresight was evident in another product, the Handy-Pandy Metal Folding Table, which antedated the TV tray by 25 years. The table was made in two sizes, with or without a painted checkerboard design for use as a game table. "The Coffee-Maker from Sunny Italy" was, the catalog stated, patterned after the genuine Italian pot. What it lacked in elegance it certainly made up in durability.

This tendency to overbuild, coupled with another to underprice and another to over-equip, kept Pandolfo from realizing a profit. Al C. Petters, who worked for Pandolfo at both Pan Motor and later at Pandolfo Manufacturing, recalled a time when the latter company was turning out thousands of simple steel memo pad stands. Petters remarked to the foreman that for the small amount of labor and material involved they should make a good profit on the item. "Are you kidding?" the foreman said. "If Pandolfo's bid would have been high enough to make a profit, we wouldn't have got the order for these things."

Forsyth, in addition to handling the advertising, was also in charge of all marketing matters. But Pandolfo's ability to spend far outstripped the company's ability to make money. On December 22, 1920, another approach was tried. Pandolfo invited more than 200 guests to a beef barbecue, "with potato and all the trimmings," to be held in the plant. Pandolfo's standing in the community was still such that the invited guests all appeared. They ate surrounded by machinery and serenaded by an orchestra, and when the food was gone the speeches began. The main talk, by Pandolfo, was to the point.

"The past is gone," he said, as if it were not haunting him daily. "We have only to deal with the future for good or ill. It takes cooperation to succeed, and no man by himself can ever accomplish much. The building of an industry that gives employment to labor is a benefit to any community, advances the value of real estate, provides more business for the merchants and all of the professions. It may interest you to know that we are shipping our products to India, England, Spain, and other European countries, and to Canada, as well as to every state in the union." He referred briefly to the company's products and to the dealers who were handling them, not failing to mention that orders were "booked for 20,000 dollars' worth of work."

Then he brought up the main point of the evening. "Many of you think I have a motive in bringing so many of you here tonight. Well, you are right. I am going to frankly explain conditions and put a proposition to you that, if accepted, will benefit both you and myself. To tide us over this period of depression when it is impossible to borrow money from the banks, even on government bonds, I need 50,000 dollars. No more, no less. I own this plant; there are no stockholders. I propose to continue to be the sole owner and manager of the business without dictation from anybody because I believe I can make it a great success. I have the reputation of meeting my obligations in full with good interest.

"Now, I want to borrow this money for six months and for a year, at eight percent interest. In normal times I would go to a bank and get such money because I have plenty of assets. But no man can borrow money from the banks these days because they are loaned up to the limit. In addition to the eight percent, I am going to set aside two percent of my sales for the coming year as a bonus for the 50,000, which would be four percent. Four percent added to the eight percent would make 12 percent. If the sales amounted to 500,000 dollars, it would be 10,000 dollars, which would be 20 percent added to the eight percent which would make 28 percent for the use of your money for six months and a year. Half of the loan would be repaid in six months and the rest in a year."

Pandolfo's strange mathematics may have frightened off the more astute investors. Others were given their option in his next statement. "I want no one to make me a loan if he has to make an unnecessary sacrifice to raise the money. But those who do give me money will confer a favor which will be fully and gratefully appreciated." Even though each attending guest received a folding metal table as a gift, none seemed to be willing to make the "necessary sacrifice" in lending Pandolfo the money he required. Nor could any of the other speakers on the program generate interest. They included Freeland H. Dam, Ferdinand Peters, Dr. Warren L. Beebe, Homer McKenzie, Fred Speechly, Martin Molitor, and H. P. Irmeter, all of whom commended Pandolfo for his courage, his energy, and for what he had accomplished for the city. None of them, however, mentioned Pandolfo's contribution to the principles of economics reflected in his manipulation of percentages.

Whatever money, if any, Pandolfo was able to borrow that evening was not enough. It was never enough. A month later he advertised an auction at which the complete furnishings of the Motor Hotel would be sold; he was presiding at the liquidation of part of his empire. There was no doubt that all of the furnishings were being put on the block; the list included 29 mahogany and oak dressers, 29 mahogany and oak chiffonniers, beds, springs, mattresses, pillows, sheets, pillow cases, spreads, comforters, blankets, rockers, chairs, rugs, a National cash register, oak desk, cigar case, quick-meal range (wood or coal), steam table, two three-plate electric stoves, Crescent dish washer, 16 fumed-oak rockers and chairs (Spanish leather upholstered), and many kitchen utensils.

Money from the auction only delayed the inevitable for the Pandolfo Manufacturing Company. On March 26, 1921, court commissioner J. I. Donahue issued a restraining order forbidding a sheriff's sale called for by the Northern Machinery Company of Minneapolis to satisfy judgments totalling over $3,600 against the company. The restraining order had been issued at the request of F. G. Hinze and Ralph Olson, acting as trustees for the holders of Pandolfo Manufacturing Company bonds in the amount of $350,000. The bonds constituted a first mortgage on the real property of the company, and because the first interest payment on the bonds, due March 15, had not been met, the bondholders claimed first right.

Events seemed to gang up on Pandolfo; either he was riding a crest or he was consumed in disaster. He was plummeting downhill now, tossed from one calamitous event to another. At 4:20 on the morning of May 2, 1921, a fire gutted the interior of the Motor Hotel, the dining room of which had been used as a school room by students in the northwest section of the city. Firemen said the blaze, apparently ignited by worn wiring, began in the basement, ate through the floor where the lobby and the dining room joined, burned the stairway to the second floor, and then followed an air vent to the roof, where it burned a four-foot hole. The fire was spotted by a night watchman at the Pan Motor plant, two or three blocks to the north, who turned in the alarm.

Pandolfo did not care to estimate his loss, saying it was covered by insurance, but it was presumed to be more than $5,000. The school children, whose records were the only thing saved from the fire, were transferred to Franklin School for the last month of school; the next fall they would be housed in the new Roosevelt School, built partially to house the children of the anticipated Pan Motor Company employees.

At the end of the month Pandolfo was in Los Angeles attempting to raise money when the federal government, in Fergus Falls district court, filed a tax lien against his property to secure payment of income taxes, which they claimed were due for the years 1917 and 1918. The amount claimed was $414,311.96.

There were additional embarrassments. On June 22, the city commission voted to turn off electric service to the Pan Addition White Way. In lieu of regular street lights, they would leave one light burning at each corner of the three blocks in the addition; 42 of the 54 lights would be dark. Pandolfo, owner of the addition, had not paid assessments for the service since the conclusion of his trial. In mourning for the fading glory of the past, the newspaper headlined the story "PANTOWN WILL BE DIMMED TONIGHT." A few local realtors added, "And damned, too!"

In August, two more former Pan employees revealed their plans. Victor Gauvreau, designer of the Pan car, announced that he and Willard J. Hornibrook were forming the St. Cloud Hudson Essex Company, buying out the Schomer Motor Company. They would locate in what Pandolfo had called plant No. 1 of the Pandolfo Manufacturing Company, at the northwest corner of Sixth avenue and Second street south. Hornibrook had been a chief inspector and superintendent at Pan Motor since the fall of 1918. He had known Gauvreau from the days when they both had worked at Dodge, where Hornibrook had been an inspector.

Hornibrook would be in active charge of the new agency because Gauvreau had also accepted a position as instructor in gas engine and machine design at the engineering college of the University of Minnesota. Another associate from Pan joined Gauvreau at the university; Joseph Nelson, experimental engineer, joined the faculty as an assistant instructor.

(They would be completely at home in the automotive lab; the engineering college at the university had purchased much of the testing equipment of the Pan Motor Company, including the dynamometer.)

Near the end of August, as the time for the annual stockholders meeting of the Pan Motor Company approached, it was disclosed that somehow, somewhere, during the year, an additional 40,000 shares of stock in the company had been sold. This many shares and more had been sold in one month during Pandolfo's heyday, but now the future was bleak, if not blank.

The *Journal-Press*, reporting the meeting on August 24, relegated the story to the back page. If the position was chosen to indicate the relative importance of the story the gesture did not succeed, because both front and back pages of that issue were printed in purple ink, a tribute to the Benevolent and Protective Order of Elks, who were holding their state convention in the city.

William B. Mitchell and Walter Niskern, appointed to determine if a quorum was present at the stockholders meeting, reported that of the total of 684,036½ shares outstanding 349,414½ were represented at the meeting. Ferdinand Peters requested he be allowed to resign from the Board of Directors. (The other members reluctantly agreed to his request, remembering his statement—unverified but reliably reported—when he was advised that the Pan plant was losing $30,000 a month; Peters suggested re-hiring Pandolfo. "He lost only $20,000 a month. We could save $10,000 right there.")

Because the charter of the company provided for 12 members on the Board, the seven remaining directors were instructed to choose five new Directors, one from each state following Minnesota in the number of stockholders. First in this order was Colorado, followed by Kansas, Washington, and Iowa. A large Colorado delegation, led by L. C. Laurent and George Nidy of Denver, heartily endorsed the motion.

Charles Schwab, with next to nothing to describe, had not prepared a written report but summarized the activities of the company in a few sentences. "Conditions are much the same as they were a year ago. The drop forge has been closed down entirely for the past year, and the motor plant was shut down during the winter but has been operating since spring with a reduced force of men turning out two cars a day.

"In August of last year our drop forge was operating on a half million dollars worth of forgings. When Ford reduced the price of their cars and others had to follow suit, our forging orders were either canceled or deferred. We had to close down. The same situation faces not only the Pan drop forge but every independent forge in the country.

"But conditions are brighter now than they have been and in time will get back to where the plant can be operated at a profit. We have had inquiries during the past month on a number of small jobs, but they have not been of sufficiently large quantities to warrant opening the plant.

"When the forge was shut down, the motor plant was operating with orders for seven thousand cars. Then the government put automobiles in the luxury class and banks all over the country began to refuse credit to purchasers of automobiles. Every one of the cars on order was canceled. There was no alternative but to discontinue the manufacture of cars."

What Schwab could not report was that many of the orders shipped by the drop forge were being returned as not to specifications; when the skilled technicians left the company the work had to be done by men unfamiliar with precision work. Schwab did report that 200 cars had been made since spring, and there were sufficient material and parts on hand to produce 69 more before October 1. The outstanding indebtedness had been reduced by $373,853.98 during the past year, he said, and the remaining indebtedness was offset by the raw steel at the drop forge and the unsold cars. "The plant and equipment are therefore, practically speaking, free of encumbrance." (And didn't that sound familiar!)

Schwab's optimism was still evident when he mentioned means for providing approximately one million dollars capital, wiping out all current indebtedness and leaving sufficient working funds to enable the plant to "start making a good profit as soon as conditions make it advisable to get into full production again."

No one mentioned that the car to be produced would be at least three or four years behind competition, since the technical staff had departed some time ago and no new design had been completed. The discussion centered on how to raise the "bit more capital" that was required. Some stockholders favored selling the preferred stock with a fixed goal in mind and asking St. Cloud banks to act as trustees, holding the proceeds from the sale until the goal had been reached and then releasing the money to the directors. If the goal was not reached within the specified time, the banks could return the money to the subscribers. Others claimed this method was not only cumbersome but indicated a lack of confidence in the company and directors.

On the motion of D. J. Lund of Minneapolis, it was voted to sell the preferred stock with the details of the sale and the disposal of the funds left to the discretion of the Board.

S. C. Pandolfo attended the meeting and spoke, in the main criticizing the management since his resignation. Though many of the out-of-town stockholders warmly greeted and embraced the former president, the vote for the policies of the present management was almost unanimous.

It was the last annual meeting of the Pan Motor Company stockholders as such.

Pandolfo, now deprived of a role in the leadership and even an effectual voice in the policies of the Pan Motor Company, rapidly losing control of his Pandolfo Manufacturing Company, and estranged from his wife Anna, turned to revitalizing the Pan Addition as a source of income to support the continuing appeal on his conviction. He had started his own bus line between Pan Addition and the downtown business section of St. Cloud (fare five cents), and he said the new transportation advantage made his Addition the choicest place to live in St. Cloud. "Only a few houses for rent," his ad stated. "If you want to live in the pleasing locality, I advise you to hurry."

On October 8, 1921, the bus line began operating:

> Bus leaves Pan Addition at 7:40 a.m. and will make regular trips every hour until 9:40 at night. From Pan Addition bus will follow Thirty-Third Avenue to Waite Park streetcar line, then will follow street car line to Osseo Avenue, then will follow Osseo Avenue to St. Germain Street, then will go down St. Germain Street to Fourth Avenue South and will circle around Hayward Hotel [the Grand Central] block and strike St. Germain Street at First National Bank and go up St. Germain Street and will wait ten minutes between each two trips across from Post Office in front of Kowalkowski and Vossberg Cigar store.

A few weeks after bus service began, the Granite City Railway Company, operator of the city streetcar line, filed a complaint with the city commission claiming that the bus line was serving passengers that should properly use the streetcars. Pandolfo replied that it was impossible for the Pan Town Bus Line to follow any other route than that which paralleled the street car line for a short distance. At the fare charged, he said, he was making no profit, only providing a service for Pan Town residents. He would be happy to discontinue the bus service as soon as the streetcar company ran a spur track from the Waite Park streetcar line down Thirty-third Avenue to Pan Addition and provided between 30- and 60-minute service.

(There is no indication exactly when his bus service was discontinued, but in January 1923, Steve Tenvoorde sued Pandolfo for $500. Tenvoorde claimed that amount was still due him for the bus. Pandolfo testified he had paid Tenvoorde $300 for the bus, which was all it was worth because it was always breaking down. Tenvoorde said that if the bus hadn't been abused so much by the drivers it wouldn't have needed that much repair, and that was not the point anyway; Pandolfo had agreed to pay $800 for the bus and couldn't change it just because his drivers couldn't properly care for the vehicle. The jury agreed with Tenvoorde and ordered the trustees of the Pan Addition to pay the $500.)

Early in November 1921, the Internal Revenue Service, still pressing its claim against Pandolfo for payment of his 1917 and 1918 income taxes, were auditing his 1919 income; the amount they claimed, with interest and penalties, was given as $437,000. A lien in that amount was placed against him. Pandolfo retained John L. Connolly, a St. Paul attorney, to help him with this tax case, and Connolly, after a trip to Washington and long negotiation, was successful in getting the claim reduced, but by the time the final judgment was made Pandolfo was long past being able to pay any amount.

On November 11, Pandolfo's residence in Pan Town was damaged by a fire. Firemen, who were kept busy with two other fires during the chilly night, arrived at the house at three in the morning to find the inside bright with flames. Four hours later, with the fire out, they determined that the fire had started in the basement laundry room and spread quickly to the second floor. The basement and upper level had suffered the greatest damage, the roof being partly destroyed, while the lower floor suffered water damage. The house was empty; Mrs. Pandolfo had "taken a trip to the south," (permanently, it was later announced, except for her return to look after the children when Pandolfo went to prison), and Pandolfo had stored much of the furniture. It may have seemed like Gotterdammerung to Samuel Pandolfo then, but there was still some time left to him.

In what was only a feeble slap at the difficulties engulfing him, Pandolfo released news of a new household item being produced by the Pandolfo Manufacturing Company. The Spud-Masher was a metal disk, 3½ inches in diameter and punctured with 19 half-inch holes, on a narrow U-shaped metal handle. In early December 1921, he began production with an initial order of 50,000, reporting that he had secured some big orders for his invention from Chicago and Twin Cities dealers. But only worldwide acceptance of the Spud-Masher could now stave off final financial collapse.

In late June 1922, the holders of $350,000 in bonds issued in the name of Mr. and Mrs. Samuel C. Pandolfo were pressing for foreclosure. James J. Quigley, appearing as attorney for the bond holders, said the move to foreclose the bonds had been prompted by Pandolfo's failure to pay any of the interest due on the bonds. The bonds covered houses in Pan Addition and a portion of the Pandolfo Manufacturing Company plant. On Tuesday afternoon, June 27, 1922, Pandolfo met with some of the 200 bond holders and their attorneys in the Commercial Club room in the recently completed Breen Hotel. With every argument he could bring to bear, he fought against foreclosure, telling of his faith in the future and the things he could accomplish if he could only have some extra time. "The company is only now beginning to see daylight," he argued. "Our market is open, our products are developed. We can make it if you'll just give us a little more time."

But as the opposing forces in the bond-holding group became more defined, it was apparent that the group favoring Pandolfo's position was clearly a minority and a weak one. With tears in his eyes, the once proud and jaunty promoter faced the group and pleaded, "Don't crush me like a worm." Stony silence followed his request. He now faced foreclosure of two bond issues aggregating nearly $500,000. Plus prison.

Within a week, Judge John A. Roeser issued a court order preventing Pandolfo from collecting the rents on the property in Pan Addition. The order was issued pending a hearing to determine if a receiver should be appointed. Suit was brought by the bond holders to foreclose the mortgages and trustees of the bonds. Named as defendants in the suit, in addition to Mr. and Mrs. Pandolfo, were 104 others, holders of the property covered by the bonds. The number of defendants made the case unique; there were few civil cases on record in Minnesota where more than 100 defendants were named. The complaint charged that not only was $150,000 in interest on the bonds past due, there were delinquent taxes of $11,585.29 against the property and unpaid insurance premiums amounting to $1,346.45.

Pandolfo repeated in court many of the arguments he had made earlier, but his appeal carried no more weight in court than it did on a personal basis. Roeser appointed a receiver, and Pandolfo promised his full cooperation with the court's choice, Fred J. Schroeder of St. Joseph.

Schroeder's first act as receiver was to agree to allow Pandolfo to retain 40 percent of the gross rent receipts, providing him some means of livelihood.

Twenty days after this case was heard, Pandolfo's picture appeared on the front pages of the St. Cloud newspapers under the headline: PANDOLFO MUST SERVE TEN YEAR PRISON SENTENCE. The headline was correct but premature. The decision of the Seventh Court of Appeals had been pending since January 1922, but this was not yet Pandolfo's final effort to avoid prison. The news was out the next day: Pandolfo was taking it all the way to the United States Supreme Court. Carl Cummins, the St. Paul attorney, now had the help of Chicago attorneys Bernhardt Frank, P. J. Lucey, and Gerald G. Barry, and they obtained a 30-day stay of sentence to prepare a new application.

On September 1, 1922, testimony in the bondholder action against the Pan Addition defendants was completed, and Judge Roeser retired to consider his decision.

In the meantime, the Pan Motor Company was suffering its own death throes. Back in January 1922, the Erie Foundry Company, whose vice president had once praised the drop forge in a letter given wide circulation by Pandolfo, filed suit to recover $64,101, exclusive of interest, which it claimed was due on drop forge hammers and other machinery. It was one more straw to the back of the enfeebled camel; it would totter a few more miles but its strength was fading fast.

In an ad for "St. Cloud's First Annual Auto Show," the Pan Motor Company was still selling cars. The Pan Model A, "A Product of Minnesota Craftsmanship," was one of the exhibits. The auto show was scheduled for February 23, 24, and 25 in St. Cloud's new Armory on Fourth Avenue South, but because a snowstorm limited the attendance on those days, two more days were added to the schedule. On Saturday, February 25, the Pan cars that were exhibited at the show were advertised at the special price of $760, war tax included, to stockholders only. It was the last local advertisement the company would run for its cars.

In March 1922, the last Pan car was assembled in the Pan plant. The building was now used only for storage and sale of parts. During its short life the company had turned out from 735 to 750 cars. The first ten cars, Model 10, had been made in Indianapolis by Reed & Glaser; the next 250 cars, Model 250, were assembled in St. Cloud; parts for 500 engines—the only indication of the total number of Pan-engined cars—had been ordered from the drop forge, and, except for some used for testing, these would account for 500 Model A Pans. Many years later, Pandolfo gave 737 as the number of cars produced by the company and his estimate is as good as any but, given his propensity for promotion, not necessarily better.

Through the summer of 1922 there were periodic blips of activity at the Pan plant, all minor and fruitless, trying to get some production started. On Thursday, September 7, the most noteworthy of the efforts took place when Ralph De Palma toured the plant. De Palma, still driving racing cars though he was almost 40, was one of auto racing's giants. He had been involved, principally for publicity purposes, with the manufacture of parts for automobiles, and he was asked to inspect the Pan plant by a group of Minnesota businessmen interested in reviving the company. De Palma was accompanied to St. Cloud by Messrs. Merril and Wellington of Minneapolis, who drove up from the Twin Cities on a completely paved highway, the last link of which had been completed only the fall before. De Palma toured the Pan plant and pronounced it as fine or finer than any plant in the country. "It should be given over to production without delay," the newspapers quoted him as saying. Then he left for Los Angeles.

The newspapers stated that "neither Schwab nor the other capitalists would make a statement regarding the opening of the plant." The next day, unwilling to give up De Palma's visit and the hope it promised without further comment, the papers stated that company officials had placed information concerning the plant in De Palma's hands and would await word. No further communication was ever made public.

Creditors were now piling up against the Pan Motor Company, and one suit, brought by St. Cloud hardware dealer Ebert Johnson, was the toppling blow. Johnson's suit was for payment of a judgment of $5110.75. R. B. Brower, who was Johnson's attorney in the case, now found himself before Judge Roeser asking that the company be declared in danger of insolvency; three years earlier he had been pleading before Judge Landis to allow the company to continue in business and work out its problems.

Roeser, then, in the fall of 1922, was about to deliver two major decisions of concern to Pandolfo: one affecting his past and the other bearing on his future. The past was taken care of first. On Tuesday, October 10, 1922, Judge Roeser appointed Robert L. Gale and Edward Everett Clark as receivers for the Pan Motor Company. The *Motor World* magazine carried the story in its October 18th issue. (It appeared directly above the story of the Harroun Motor Car Company of Wayne, Michigan, being declared bankrupt. The Harroun story stated that although creditors petitioned to have the company declared bankrupt some years ago, the court proceedings had been delayed because the directors believed they could put the company back on its feet if only they were given the time. It seemed a universal hope.)

Robert L. Gale, one of the trustees selected by Roeser, was a little over 60 years old. He was manager and principal owner of the St. Cloud Storage and Produce Company, which handled eggs, fruit, and dairy products and was a major ice cream producer in the area. (On January 23, 1923, three months after his appointment as trustee, Gale went into his garage to start his car. A small, air-tight stove had been burning in the garage to warm the car, and once started, the engine quickly used up what little oxygen remained. Gale made an effort to get out, but succumbed before he reached safety.)

The other receiver, Edward E. Clark of the Clark Lumber Company, was five years younger than Gale. His parents had been St. Cloud pioneers, and apart from attending the Minneapolis Business College and working in Minneapolis for eight years, he had spent his life in St. Cloud.

Roeser's second decision dealt with Pandolfo's future—or what appeared to be left of it. In the largest judgment ever ordered in Stearns county history (typical of almost everything Pandolfo came into contact with), Roeser awarded the plaintiffs $418,688.13 against the Pan Town property of Pandolfo. The amount covered the entire first bond issue of $350,000, plus expenses and interest. Most plaintiffs would never live to see the judgment fulfilled.

On Wednesday, January 24, 1923, Federal Judge Evans in Chicago denied Pandolfo's request for a rehearing, clearing the way for the appeal to the Supreme Court. In petitioning for the rehearing, Pandolfo's lawyers gave 11 propositions as grounds for reversal:

> (1) There was no evidence to sustain the counts; (2) the evidence for the government was based upon the conspiracy count alone; (3) there is fatal variance between the scheme as charged in the indictment and the evidence adduced for the government; (4) there was error in denying defendants the right to show to the jury moving pictures of the plant; (5) there was error in the comments of the court in making his ruling thereon; (6) the court erred in admitting in evidence representations to prospective stock purchasers by stock salesmen, not parties to the indictment; (7) all the substantial evidence is at least as consistent with Pandolfo's innocence as with his guilt; (8) there was error in conducting an investigation into the affairs of The Bankers, Merchants, and Manufacturers Journal and Bankers Journal; (9)

> there was error in admitting in evidence the report to Congress of the Capital Issues Committee; (10) the court erred in excluding certain affidavits respecting Pandolfo's letter of October 5, 1919; (11) there was error in admitting in evidence applications to "blue sky" commissions of several states and correspondence relating thereto.

Judge Alschuler, writing the opinion, stated that propositions 1, 2, and 7, questioning whether the evidence supported the verdict, necessitated a careful inspection of the trial transcript—which had grown to 3400 pages! In summarizing the evidence, Alschuler stated that since Pandolfo was entitled to the first half of the money taken in for the sale of stock, he received considerably more than half of what was collected. "But this was not all profit to him," the judge wrote. "In fact, agents' commissions were large, and there was much expense involved in advertising. The figures are somewhat involved, but his net personal profit was not less than $350,000, and there is evidence from which the jury could have found it to be over $600,000." The judge then reviewed the early advertising of the company, before incorporation, listing some of the claims Pandolfo had made for the stock as well as those made for the car. He concluded, "When it is considered that at this time the corporation was not organized, its plant not located, no new car had been designed, and not one definite step taken towards building a single car . . . it would scarcely be possible to conclude that in the mind of Pandolfo there was at the time . . . the remotest idea that 100 cars could be on exhibition within two months thereafter, or 30,000 manufactured within the year. And when about the same time he represented to the public that the stock was worth more than it was selling for . . . it cannot be said that the jury was unwarranted in concluding that he knew such predictions and promises could not under most favorable conditions be realized, as indeed they were not."

Regarding Landis' ruling on the motion pictures, Alschuler wrote: "Under the circumstances disclosed, we cannot say that there was error in this ruling. The evidence for defendants consisted very largely in the description of the company's plant. . . . It was in evidence without contradiction that large, substantial, and very costly buildings had been erected at St. Cloud, and these were described with minuteness. . . . The motion pictures would not amplify this. . . and the question of permitting the moving pictures to be displayed was so far within the discretion of the court, that, while it might not have been error to have received it, it was not error to exclude it.

"But a more serious question is not in the exclusion of the offer to show the pictures, but in the comments of the court in excluding it. After having suggested that it was admissible, it developed that Forsyth was present during all the time the photographer was taking it; and thereupon the court in excluding it said:

> I will on my own motion and on the showing that Forsyth

> directed this work, Forsyth the advertising manager, I will rule them out. I will take judicial knowledge of the fact that an advertising manager's prime purpose is not to reproduce a thing as it normally is. That may be a vile thing for a court to know about professionally of advertisers, but I am not going to denude myself of the ABC's of knowledge that I have and everybody has outside.

"It is contended for plaintiff in error that since considerable of the advertising matter in evidence was written by Forsyth this statement of the court in the presence of the jury practically told them that the advertising matter was false; and as the question of the truth or falsity of the advertising was important in the case, this statement invaded the province of the jury and was highly prejudicial. It would doubtless have been better had the remark not been made. Witnesses had testified, and Pandolfo conceded, that in the earlier stages in some of the advertising matter there was 'exaggeration.' The word 'exaggeration' must not be permitted to conceal the real fact. If the jury believed the 'exaggeration' amounted to a materially false representation, made pursuant to a scheme to defraud, followed by the mailing of letters to carry out the scheme, all as charged in the indictment, it would warrant conviction. The conceded 'exaggeration' supplemented as it is by evidence such as above referred to, does not leave room for the conclusion of any very serious harm resulting from the remark of the court, which was not directed at Forsyth alone, but was a general statement, applicable to all advertising managers."

The point raised about the salesmen's advertising being used to convict Pandolfo was disposed of by blaming Pandolfo's "vigorous personality" as the inspiration for his salesmen. Landis' investigation into the affairs of the Chicago "banking journals" was allowable because much of it was conducted out of the hearing of the jury.

The proposition concerning the Capital Issues Committee was more serious, the judge felt. The committee's report on the company was sharply critical, and it was received in evidence over the protest of the defense. Since it was not part of the correspondence between the committee and Pandolfo, it was not contended that it was admissible as original evidence on behalf of the government. But the Capital Issue Committee's report was widely circulated and was the reason for a Colorado stockholders group coming to St. Cloud to examine the Pan Motor Company's affairs. This group issued their own report, referred to by many witnesses including Pandolfo, in the first sentence of which was a reference to the Capital Issues Committee's report. "In view of the fact that these items of evidence, particularly the Colorado report, were induced by and predicated upon and referred to the Capital Issues Committee report, it was not improper to receive in evidence the latter as a part of Pandolfo's cross-examination."

Even if there was impropriety in admitting the report, the judge went on, the reference made to it—"charges of a most serious nature . . . unpleasant publicity"—left a more disturbing impression in the minds of the jury than did the report itself.

Concerning the defense's tenth proposition, the judge wrote:

> Proposition ten involved this feature: pursuant to an order on the district attorney, defendants were supplied with a list of the government's witnesses but cautioned not to communicate with them. Pandolfo nevertheless sent a letter to the witnesses who were stockholders, saying in effect that he had letters and affidavits from stockholders to the effect that post office inspectors had maliciously misstated facts regarding the company and its officers; that all he wanted was a fair trial, and that the facts were entirely different from those represented by the inspectors; that he wished all would go through the plant to know the truth, and requesting that an affidavit be sent him stating what post office inspectors had said to the person addressed. Upon this letter being received in evidence by the government, defendants offered the affidavits said to have been referred to in the letter as the basis for sending it. These affidavits were excluded. The letter was offered no doubt on the theory that it tended to show an attempt on the part of Pandolfo to influence the government's witnesses. As such it in no manner depended on the verity of the assertion therein that Pandolfo had affidavits. The affidavits of themselves were clearly hearsay, and their exclusion was not improper. It appears that many, if not most of the inspectors referred to were witnesses for the government, and their activities among stockholders might have been inquired into as part of their cross-examination, and, if then improper methods were denied, it might have been shown by those who knew the facts, but in no event by affidavits.

On the last of the defense propositions, the judge claimed that correspondence between the various blue sky commissions and Pandolfo was proper evidence since the purpose in offering it was to show that there was withheld from the commissions certain resolutions of the company reflecting Pandolfo's share of stock sales.

Because no substantial error was evident, the judgment of the district court was affirmed and the petition for rehearing was denied.

Within a few weeks there were at least two petitions being circulated among St. Cloud citizens asking President Warren G. Harding and Attorney General Harry M. Daugherty to intervene on Pandolfo's behalf. By noon on Saturday, February 17, 1923, one petition in a downtown location had 250 signatures, and another petition had been started at the cigar stand in the Breen Hotel. For the benefit of women signers, petitions had also been placed at Molitor Drug Store and the Corner Drug Store.

On February 28, Pandolfo returned from Washington, D.C., where he had conferred with his attorneys regarding his final appeal being made to the United States Supreme Court. Coincidental with his return, a meeting was called for the evening of Tuesday, March 6, in the St. Cloud Institute. The news story wisely speculated that the main topic of the meeting might concern a movement among stockholders to take over the Pan Motor Company when it would be put up at the sheriff's sale. Other stockholder meetings, the story said, had been held in Minneapolis, St. Paul, Denver, Fargo, and other western cities.

Eight hundred stockholders crowded into the auditorium of the Institute and, with a speed and unanimity that suggested considerable premeeting preparation, adopted a plan to reorganize the Pan Motor Company into a five million dollar corporation with an initial output of ten thousand automobiles. One of the main speakers at the meeting was H. S. Wigle, the former vice president of the company and one of the defendants at the Chicago trial. He described how the movement for taking over the plant had started in Spokane (his home territory) and spread over the entire West. "Stockholders in Spokane subscribed for funds for this purpose without knowing how stockholders in other parts of the country would regard the plan," Wigle said. After extending a vote of confidence to Pandolfo, the stockholders voted to join the nationwide drive to raise from $400,000 to $750,000 for purchase of the plant when it would be sold April 10.

James R. Bennett, Jr., a St. Cloud attorney, was elected to the central committee to represent the St. Cloud stockholders. The headquarters of the financial committee, Wigle said, would be moved from Denver to St. Cloud. "There have been similar meetings in 11 states so far, and they have all adopted the same plan. If our efforts to purchase the plant are unsuccessful, 75 percent of the subscribed funds will be returned to the investors. We will spend 25 percent on expenses." The explanation of expenses had a familiar ring to most of the audience.

Pandolfo was not present when the meeting began, but when he was informed that the stockholders wanted to hear him, he hurried to the meeting. His entrance was greeted with thunderous applause. He listened as Wigle explained that the first two million dollars in stock in the reorganized company would be sold to stockholders only and would be secured by the physical assets of the plant; an operating capital of three million dollars would remain.

"Where will this capital come from?" Wigle shouted. "What a question to ask! We stockholders of the West want Pandolfo back at the head of the new company. He started on nothing and in a few years had this marvelous Pan plant."

Wigle read a resolution adopted by a Minneapolis stockholder group referring to the charges against Pandolfo as "a prosecution which has proved to be nothing more than a bitter persecution."

"Pandolfo must not go to prison," Wigle insisted. "This vote of confidence is his most impressive vindication. In the face of this confidence do you think officials would imprison him?"

Another roar of approval greeted Pandolfo when he rose to speak. He thanked all of them for their trust in him. "I would like to show the world that I can make a success of that company. Its most difficult years are behind us. We can make a going concern of the Pan Motor Company if we all work and pull together."

If the stockholder movement to buy the Pan Motor Company had started in Spokane, it had been the idea of an idealistic lawyer. Robert Harper Hutchinson had been a member of the first state legislature in Washington and was actively interested in prohibition long before it became a national question. He had been elected mayor of two different towns in Washington and had lived in Spokane since 1911. Hutchinson had testified in Pandolfo's behalf at the trial, saying that he had not been terribly interested in the exact remuneration Pandolfo had received for promoting the company; he was more interested in knowing that a specific amount of the money taken in had been marked for company use. With Wigle's help, Hutchinson had initiated the stockholder takeover and was directing efforts to raise the money.

Shortly after the receivers for the Pan Motor Company had been appointed in St. Cloud, a stockholder committee had been formed in Spokane with Hutchinson as chairman and Lee J. Nance and A. A. De Lamater, both of Spokane, assisting. From what was called "Central Finance Committee" headquarters in the Hyde Building in Spokane, they sent out a brochure with the following letter:

> Dear Fellow Stockholder:
>
> Realizing the critical condition in which our company found itself, after 18 months of idleness, due to the present management, a Stockholders' Committee met in Spokane on August 23rd, to consider a plan to refinance the company. We knew either one of two things was bound to happen in the immediate future. First, the company would go into the hands of a receiver; or, second, some outside interest would buy our plant for a song. (The first has come to pass—the second was contemplated—see enclosed newspaper reprint). So we adopted resolutions setting forth, in brief, these ideas:
>
> We would appeal to other stockholders to join us in refinancing this company. We would urge the reseating of S. C. Pandolfo, who built this wonderful plant for us and had it working full blast, as its guiding genius again.
>
> To these ends, we signed proxies in favor of S. C. Pandolfo, and signed subscriptions to the Refinancing Fund. Seattle, Taco-

ma, Bellingham, Everett, Mt. Vernon, Wenatchee and smaller towns quickly followed with similar resolutions, proxies, and subscriptions. The Georges in every town were putting their shoulders to the task for the benefit of ALL stockholders. Some stockholders, of course, were saying as usual, "Let George do it."

But one of the things we foresaw has happened. A receivership has been named. Our plan has been changed. We still intend to get control of the company and place Pandolfo where he belongs, at the head of this company. But now all the stockholders will not benefit.

NOW, when the Stockholders' Committee buys the plant at the receiver's sale, only the GEORGES WHO PUT UP THE MONEY will be in. All other stockholders will be out. Every last stockholder is being given an opportunity to protect his interest in the company, but we've only got five short months to raise the necessary money; we must act quickly. We fellows who have adopted the name of GEORGE can do it—but remember, only those who join us can benefit.

Read the facts about our plant, and the new plan of refinancing it, on the inside pages. This means money to you—don't pass it up.

The brochure contained several pictures of the Pan plant. Under one view of the drop forge unit was the caption, "Do you realize that this is the fifth largest drop forge plant in the United States?"

Under a picture of the main assembly plant was the caption, "This Plant Cost Us THREE MILLIONS!" The brochure detailed the refinancing plan and expressed the wish to put Pandolfo back at the head of the reorganized company. Also enclosed was a subscription form describing the manner in which payment was to be made and reaffirming that only 75 percent of the subscription was returnable if the plan failed.

It remained only for the United States Supreme Court to reverse Judge Kenesaw M. Landis and the other lower court justices and set Pandolfo free.

In their petition for a *writ of certiorari*, which asked the Supreme Court to call up the record from the lower court, Pandolfo's attorneys, Patrick J. Lucey, Carl W. Cummins, John H. Bradford, E. Howard Morphy, Gerald G. Barry, and Bernhardt Frank, restated the points they felt were the basis for a reversal of the decision:

1) Should a government report—admittedly false—charging the defendant with the offense for which he is on trial be admitted in evidence when the authors of the report were not subject to cross-examination?
2) Should the conspiracy charge, on which the defendant was

> acquitted, with its protracted range of time to include the subsequent operations at St. Cloud, serve as a basis for the substantive introduction of evidence relating to a period two years after Pandolfo had left Chicago?
>
> 3) Did the Circuit Court of Appeal have jurisdiction to determine whether the evidence in a record is as consistent with innocence as with guilt?
>
> 4) Should the trial judge's language, derogatory and prejudicial to the defendant, be allowed to influence the jury?
>
> 5) Can the defendant be declared guilty of fraudulent use of the mails when the advertisements upon which the falsity charge is based were never proved untrue?
>
> 6) Can the court, without admissable evidence, infer that a letter was deposited in the post office?
>
> 7) Should the defendant have allowed the "pernicious activities" of certain postal inspectors to continue without protest or action on his part, and should that action have been identified by the court as "intimidating witnesses"?
>
> 8) Was the defendant guilty of a crime in writing a letter to the government witnesses and calling on them to tell the truth?
>
> 9) Was a constitutional right of the defendant abridged by not presenting certain witnesses for confrontation?
>
> 10) When an alleged scheme is false only in part, can the defendant's conviction be based on the general scheme?

On Monday, March 12, 1923, the Supreme Court answered Pandolfo's plea: It refused to issue the writ of certiorari. The *Journal-Press* headline stated simply SAMUEL PANDOLFO TO SERVE SENTENCE IS HIGH COURT'S ORDER.

When Pandolfo heard of the Supreme Court's refusal to review the case, he said, "I'm ready to take my medicine, and if it comes to a summons to prison, I will go with the hope that I have injured no one and the knowledge that I have done no wrong."

Although all legal avenues had been exhausted, it was not over yet. Stockholder groups, prodded and led by Wigle and others, were beseeching President Harding and Attorney General Daugherty with petitions to grant a presidential pardon to Pandolfo. But both the president and his attorney general were nearing their own denouement involving the Teapot Dome oil reserves, and the plight of Pandolfo was paltry by comparison.

Later in March, a number of St. Cloud men formed a committee to seek a one-year stay of sentence for Pandolfo. Ed A. Murphy, Dr. Claude B. Lewis, Homer McKenzie, Olaf Frick, and Charles N. Beyhan met with judges of the appellate court in Chicago and Indianapolis seeking to obtain the stay. Judges Evans and Geiger heard their pleas. (Judge Alschuler was on his honeymoon.) Evans felt that the case was out of their jurisdiction, but Geiger did not agree. The two judges said they would let the committee know their decision as soon as they could.

As time ran out on Pandolfo, the editors of area newspapers expressed their opinions. William O'Brien, of the *Eden Valley Journal*, came out for Pandolfo. "It is regrettable," he wrote in his March 22nd issue. "Mr. Pandolfo is a capable man, a major of industry, who did not knowingly commit the deed he is convicted of. Justice would be best served by granting Mr. Pandolfo an executive pardon."

But the editorial seeds were falling on arid ground. On Tuesday evening, March 27, the men who had traveled to Chicago in Pandolfo's behalf made their report. They were not too hopeful, they said, "owing to unexpected developments for which we are not responsible." What those unexpected developments were was not immediately explained.

The Chicago judges finally decided that they could not act on the stay of sentence, and another meeting of the local committee was called for Wednesday evening at 8:00 p.m. in the Breen Hotel. At the meeting, Pandolfo spoke with vehemence to his friends. "I am not guilty! What law have I violated? There are 75,000 stockholders in the Pan Motor Company—the very people I am supposed to have defrauded—who say I am not guilty. The press of the northwest knows that I am not guilty." The outburst seemed to have released some tension, and he went on in calmer tones. "I have never really had my day in court. I have been Ku Kluxed—judicially lynched. But I am not going to give up the fight. I'll report to Leavenworth on April sixth on my honor. There'll be no United States marshal on my trail." (Twenty years later these words came back to haunt him.)

Then he read a letter he had sent to the federal judges in Chicago and several state officials giving his reasons for asking for a stay of sentence. He said that his mother, who was 77 years old, was dependent on him for her support. His two children, Vivian, 16 years old, and Samuel Junior, 14, were dependent on him, too. Litigation had exhausted his finances, and he had $500,000 in real estate holdings that would be in jeopardy if he could not protect it personally. His final reason was that the stockholders of the reorganized Pan Motor Company needed his services.

The members of the committee then revealed that this letter had angered Judge Evans; he was a close friend of Landis, and he told the committee members that he doubted if a plea for a stay of sentence even came within their competence. When Judge Geiger told the men that he thought it might be granted, Evans had written Geiger a stern note asking by what authority he had made the statement.

At the conclusion of the meeting, a wet-eyed Pandolfo thanked the committee and everyone who had helped him. "Some day," he said, pausing frequently to retain his composure, "some day, I hope to repay these efforts with compound interest." It could have been a poignant leave-taking; but the conspiracy of fate that now dogged Pandolfo managed to intervene again, this time in the persons of his old friends, H. S. Wigle, and former Pan stock salesmen W. H. Crowder, and George A. Nidy.

Crowder and Nidy, representing themselves as members of the Pan Motor Company Central Finance Committee from Denver, rather vigorously sought an interview with Wigle following the meeting. When Wigle resisted their entry into his hotel room, an argument ensued as a result of which Wigle asked that the two Denver men be arrested on a charge of disorderly conduct. The charge was dismissed the next day for lack of evidence, and, with Wigle's blessing, Crowder and Nidy then told local businessmen that they represented a group of 10,000 Colorado stockholders who wanted to see the Pan Motor Company back on its feet. "Colorado stockholders want this organization to be placed on a strictly business-like basis so that a strong foundation may be laid if the stockholders succeed in acquiring the Pan Motor Company," Crowder said.

Nidy agreed, adding, "There is no doubt that sufficient money to purchase the plant could be raised in Colorado alone. I say this merely to show that these stockholders believe that the plant and the city of St. Cloud are both destined to have a remarkable industrial future." Both men said that the stockholders' first choice to head the reorganization would be Pandolfo, but in the event that he "might not be available, they were prepared to appoint expert managers for the plant."

On Wednesday, April 4, 1923, the newspapers disclosed Pandolfo's timetable for his last few days of freedom. Carl Cummins had wired him that he was not expected in Chicago until the morning of Friday, April 6, so Pandolfo would leave St. Cloud Wednesday evening for St. Paul where he would adjust the $25,000 bond on which he was at liberty. He would then take the train for Chicago.

On Thursday, a new schedule was announced in the newspaper: Pandolfo would take the 8:00 p.m. Great Northern train from St. Cloud directly to Chicago; the stopover at St. Paul was now off the itinerary.

In fact, Pandolfo left St. Cloud by car Thursday at midnight, driving to Minneapolis where he took an 8:00 a.m. train to Chicago. He was to surrender to a United States marshal late Friday afternoon. Before leaving St. Cloud, Pandolfo had placed his daughter in St. Benedict's Academy in St. Joseph, and his son Samuel in St. John's Preparatory School a few miles away at Collegeville. In a last-minute interview he declared that the recent location of a Ford assembly plant in St. Paul had proved his point about locating in Minnesota. "The Ford plant is a harbinger of other good things to come to Minnesota. I believe that this plant at the high bridge in St. Paul will become the largest in the United States if Ford is unable to acquire the Muscle Shoals." (This was property Ford was then trying to obtain from the government.) "I have the greatest faith in the future of the Pan Motor Company, and there is no doubt whatever that stockholders will gain control of it and bring about a successful reorganization. I'm still an optimist, even when facing prison. I still say I have committed no crime, and I never intended to commit one. I am leaving St. Cloud strong in the belief that I will not be gone long. If there is such a thing as justice to the oppressed, I know that I will one day be a free man once more. I retain hope because I do believe that a man is still able to get justice in the United States."

Friday night, as if waiting until he was off the highway, a heavy, wet, record snowfall covered the central part of Minnesota, making travel by car extremely hazardous.

With critical inaccuracies, the *Chicago Tribune* of April 4 headlined a small story with the news that Pandolfo planned to surrender for "FOUR YEARS' PRISON." In the *Sunday Tribune* of April 8 they repeated the error in the headline of a longer story: "$9,000,000 PONZI ON WAY TO SERVE FOUR YEAR TERM." They went on to weave a tale that had little but the names in common with reality. It was stated that when he surrendered to United States marshal Robert R. Levy to start his ten-year term (the body of the story finally got the term correct!) Pandolfo wanted to start for prison immediately, "that not a day be lost in getting his 'stretch' under way. The convicted man who once was one of the best-known individuals both in the northwest and southwest, was tried in 1921 in former Judge Landis' court. . . ." The story claimed that Pandolfo's share of the profits had amounted to $1,000,000. It described his fight to get a rehearing that had taken him to the Supreme Court, and concluded:

> Following the Washington action, Pandolfo was expected to surrender but failed to do so. Finally he was ordered to surrender on or before last Thursday. He failed to do so and arrangements were being made to ask forfeiture of his $25,000 bond when he showed up at the Federal Building yesterday.

On Wednesday, April 11, the *St. Cloud Journal-Press* ran the following:

> Samuel Pandolfo, whose name has been voiced by persons living in every city and town in the United States because of his connection with the Pan Motor Company, today became simply No. 19155 at Leavenworth.

Houses in Pan-Town-on-the-Mississippi, shortly after sidewalks and curbs were put in.

A Model 10 Pan car on display in front of the Zapp State Bank on St. Germain in St. Cloud.

CHAPTER XI

"You Don't Meet a Crook with a Brass Band!"

ONE IMMEDIATE BUT temporary result of Pandolfo's imprisonment was his wife's return to St. Cloud from Texas. She came back to care for the children, Vivian and Samuel Junior, as soon as it was certain their father would not be able to avoid serving his sentence. She had stopped at Leavenworth to visit him and discovered he had been made a clerk in the prison hospital. During most of her estrangement from her husband she had had custody of the children, and now she would not only see to their education but would try to retain the property Pandolfo still owned in St. Cloud and which was soon to be sold for taxes and other debts.

"I visited him in prison Tuesday, April 10th," Anna Pandolfo said. "Even this short time in prison appears to have made him very nervous. His hopes rest with his loyal friends who are attempting to get a pardon for him. I'm here to do what a woman can do in his behalf. I know he has been dealt with unjustly."

The *St. Cloud Journal-Press* published the text of a telegram it had received from Pandolfo in which he requested the paper to be sent to him in Leavenworth. "I do not deserve to be here," he had written, "and while my friends in St. Cloud are enjoying the conveniences that their liberties afford, they must not forget me."

If the circulation department of the *Journal-Press* began his subscription with the back issues for that week, Pandolfo could have read that E. E. Clark, receiver of the Pan Motor Company, would contest only $75,000 or so of the $450,000 in claims submitted against the company.

H. S. Wigle had now set up headquarters for the stockholder group in the Institute Building. Day by day, more responses came in from various stockholder groups throughout the country. Early in May, Wigle went to Leavenworth to confer with Pandolfo about the reorganization of the Pan Motor Company, and he reported Pandolfo was in good health if not in good spirits. "He is eager to be at liberty and promoting the project to which he has deeded his life's work. He still maintains his innocence and is confident that he will soon be released and placed in a position to make good in the automobile industry." The vague generalities of the formal statement left much unsaid.

But Pandolfo's efforts soon fleshed out the statement. He began by enlisting the help of Minnesota Congressman Harold Knutson in Washington and Bishop Busch in St. Cloud. Busch, in writing to Rev. John J. Burke, C.S.P., General Secretary of the National Catholic Welfare Conference in Washington, described Pandolfo as a man who "meant to make a success of his undertaking and had no intention of misleading or defrauding the public. I do believe he had an exaggerated opinion of his ability and was too domineering in his methods and thus aroused needless opposition. He has suffered about all a man can in consequence and I would be glad to see him pardoned."

Some of Pandolfo's confidence was shaken when he saw the ad in the June 18 issue of the *Journal-Press*:

PAN PROPERTY SALE

> The property belonging to S. C. Pandolfo and wife will be sold under mortgage bond foreclosure to the highest bidder on June 22, 1923, at 10:00 a.m. at the front door of the Court House in the city of St. Cloud.
>
> This is your opportunity to get one or more of the following parcels of property at a great bargain. The sheriff will offer the following properties for sale:
>
> 1) the old greenhouse property just behind the Tenvoorde Garage in one parcel;
> 2) the Motor Hotel property;
> 3) the so-called Winslow home across from Empire Park;
> 4) the Pandolfo Manufacturing plant including eight lots of the Schroeder acre lots;
> 5) the balance of the Schroeder acre lots in three separate parcels;
> 6) the houses and lots in Pan Addition in one parcel.
>
> For further information regarding the above property and this sale see Donohue and Quigley, J. B. Himsl, attorneys for trustees.

Strangely, on June 22, no buyers appeared at the Court House. The trustees, bankers John C. Crever of St. Joseph, and Anton Schmitt of Paynesville, were forced to submit a bid in the bondholders' name to retain the property. (Crever and Schmitt had been appointed when Ralph Olson and Frank Hinze, the first trustees, resigned.) The bid of $503,000 covered the indebtedness, interest, taxes, and the cost of foreclosure.

Seven days later another bond foreclosure sale took place. (The advertisements telling of this second sale noted it would take place on Saturday, June 30, but the afternoon paper of Friday, June 29, carried the results of the sale.) For this sale the property, to be sold in three parcels, consisted of (1) a ten-acre tract without buildings located a few blocks east of the Northern Pacific depot; (2) a 14-acre tract with house, barn, and other outbuildings, lying along the Great Northern railroad tracks; and (3) a 98-acre tract, known as the Braun farm, just outside the settled portion of the city along the Great Northern tracks. The last two pieces of property were being sold subject to prior mortgage. The ad for this second sale was signed by Paul Ahles, attorney for the trustees.

Pandolfo's subscription to the *Journal-Press* must have seemed to him the worst investment of his life by the last week of June 1923. Three stories, all in the Friday, June 29 issue, would certainly have caught his eye.

(1) HOLDERS OF PAN STOCK WILL BID FOR AUTO PLANT

Will Attempt To Gain Control Of Property August 1

Drive For Funds Is Successful Fiscal Agent Asserts

Stockholders have subscribed sufficient money to gain control of the auto plant when it is put up for bids according to the order of Judge John A. Roeser, H. S. Wigle says.

When informed by the Journal-Press that the Judge has ordered disposal of the Pan Motor Company in three units on August 1, Pan stockholders have rallied in several states and the stockholders will submit a bid for the property, Wigle said. E. E. Clark will receive bids until 10:00 a.m. on August 1.

Whether eastern auto companies will submit bids could not be determined. Bids will be opened after 10:00 a.m., and the court retains the right to turn down any bids and call for a new letting.

(2) PAN CLAIMS SCHEDULED FOR HEARING IN COURT

A special term of district court will be held during July by Judge John A. Roeser to hear contested claims against the Pan Motor Company.

Roeser arranged a summer calendar that includes 40 cases. These will be heard during July and August.

(3) LOW BIDS TAKE FARM PROPERTY IN AUCTION

Farm property went "for a song" in the second Pandolfo bond foreclosure sale at the Court House. Equity in the 98-acre Braun farm on the road to Foley went to attorney Paul Ahles

> with a bid of $1. Prior mortgages and taxes on the property aggregate $25,000.
>
> Joseph Korte of Luxemburg purchased an equity in a 14-acre tract for $600, and Peter Roth of Cold Spring the equity in a ten-acre tract for $12,000.

As the day set for bidding for the Pan Motor plant neared, it appeared there might be competition. Executive committeemen from the various stockholder groups in several states began to arrive in St. Cloud. Robert H. Hutchinson, Spokane, Washington, and W. W. Hubbard, described as a construction and production engineer from Des Moines, both representing the Central Finance Committee of the stockholder group, were prominent among the bidders, but the identity of other bidders—if there were to be any—was kept hidden. Judge Roeser announced that the property would be offered in three parcels: the first would include the main assembly plant and the experimental buildings, with all machinery and equipment, plus the real estate they stood on; the second included the real estate, buildings, and equipment of the drop forge group (the hammer shop, heat treatment building, die shop, oil storage building, gas house, laboratory, forge office, plant locker room, and other small out-buildings); the third parcel was the empty 10.72 acres of land north of the assembly plant, across the St. Joseph road, as that stretch of Cooper avenue north was then called.

On August 1, Clark opened the bids on the property and discovered, to no one's surprise, that the Pan stockholder group—the "Georges"—had submitted the high bid of $178,000 for the first parcel, which also included the blueprints for the Pan car. A creditor group bid $240,500 for the other two parcels. Pending Judge Roeser's approval of the bids, the stockholder group prepared to announce plans for the plant. Contrary to Pandolfo's original plans, this group saw no great disadvantage in the loss of the drop forge.

The Pan Motor Company—what was left of it—was now finally in the clear. The $418,500 represented by the bids received, plus the $40,000 in cash on hand, was sufficient to satisfy all undisputed claims in full. While the *Journal-Press* did not disclose any of the names of the creditor group that had submitted the high bid for the drop forge and land parcels, both the *Automotive Journal* for August 30 and *Motor Age* for September 6 listed among the incorporators in the new holding company C. F. Ladner, Fred Schilplin, and C. D. Schwab.

The first 15 days of August 1923 were days of "hard news" for St. Cloud newspapers. Following E. E. Clark's acceptance of the bids on August 1, and his recommendation to Judge Roeser that they be accepted by the court, the Judge, on August 2, was prevented from immediately disposing of the matter pending the settlement of the use of the railroad trackage that paralleled the property.

On August 3, all news space in the papers covered the sudden death of President Warren G. Harding.

On August 4, the two groups involved in the sale of the Pan property signed an agreement sharing the rail facilities.

On August 7, the stockholder group paid $175,000 to E. E. Clark, taxes of $25,826.01 to the county, and $11,974.35 for special assessments to the city, and it was given the deed to the plant. The Pan Motor Company was now officially, legally, out of business. It had lasted six years and seven months, less one day.

On August 15, Ralph Olson, former president of the First National Bank, former trustee of the Pandolfo bonds, was indicted on six charges of falsifying bank records and reporting false information to the comptroller of banks.

News couldn't get much harder.

But Pandolfo, reading his newspaper in prison, had not reached the end of the bad news yet. On Tuesday, September 4, 1923, his son was accidentally shot in the right hand while hunting near Pan Town with Max Kern, another 14 year old. On Monday, November 12, Mrs. Pandolfo suffered bruises in a train accident one mile east of Marshalltown, Iowa. When the south-bound Chicago-Great Western train struck a broken rail, one Pullman car turned over, injuring Mrs. Pandolfo, two other passengers, and a porter.

Through the winter of 1923-24, the stockholder group, now led by Robert Hutchinson who had temporarily moved to St. Cloud, completed the reorganization of the Pan Motor Company. The Central Finance Committee had response from 33,000 "Georges" of the Pan stockholders. Though they still retained the old Pan trademark—a map of the western hemisphere overprinted with the name PAN centered in a gold-seeker's pan and surmounted by a top-down touring car—they had changed the name to Mutual Motors & Manufacturing Company, and they had moved the offices from the Pan plant back downtown to the Grand Central Hotel on Fifth avenue south. Hutchinson was president, H. E. Keelor of Denver was vice president, David Saunderson was secretary, W. W. Hubbard was treasurer, and Paul J. Ramstack was retained as plant superintendent.

Ramstack had come from Milwaukee in September 1919 to work in the drop forge department of the Pan Motor Company. He had been made superintendent when the plant was taken over by the receivers.

In April 1924, Mutual Motors claimed to have $32,000 clear, partly in cash, partly in machinery and other personal property. They announced plans for the future at a meeting of the Chamber of Commerce. (The Commercial Club had changed its name, too.) Mutual was proposing to join Diamond Steel Products Company, then at 1414 Marshall Street Northeast in Minneapolis. Diamond had been formed in 1922 by George Bouthinon, an engineer and metallurgist who had come to the United States from Europe. Born and educated in Lyons, France, Bouthinon's early training had been in the steel mills of the district and a later association with Berliet Automobile Company before coming to the United States as a consulting engineer for the American Locomotive Company. In 1913, he entered the auto parts business in Ohio and later moved to Minneapolis where he managed the Arrowhead Steel Products Company before forming his own company.

Diamond Steel was manufacturing piston pins and the company needed additional facilities to keep up with the demand. Three members of the Purity Baking Company of Minneapolis were on the board of directors of Diamond Steel and a Mr. Perie of Purity spoke briefly at a Chamber of Commerce meeting in St. Cloud endorsing the merger between Diamond Steel and Mutual Motors.

The new company would employ additional people to handle the increased production and to replace those Minneapolis workers who would not relocate. All of this would require money, of course, $500,000. St. Cloud was being asked to supply only one-tenth of the amount—$5,000. The Chamber of Commerce, having learned several hard lessons while under its old name, took no immediate action. It appointed a committee to study the proposal.

The news had some effect on Samuel Pandolfo. On May 2, though he had not served the third of his sentence usually required for parole application, Pandolfo got a promise from Robert H. Turner, assistant pardon attorney for the justice department, that a hearing would be held in the immediate future to determine if there was anything to warrant consideration of parole before the regulation waiting period. Even an immediate parole would have been too late for any significant action by Pandolfo.

Exactly how it happened was never explained publicly, but George Bouthinon replaced Robert Hutchinson—Pandolfo's champion—as president of Mutual Motors, and Paul Ramstack replaced W. W. Hubbard as treasurer. On June 20, 1924, the new president of the company sent out notice of a stockholders' meeting to be held on July 15. The meeting was being called to consider an offer from Diamond Steel Products Company, or a new company, to purchase all the assets of Mutual Motors & Manufacturing Company. The Minnesota Securities Commission was still keeping an eye on the company and was going to see that no paper stock trade would be made to organize a new company. It had decreed that proper financing would be necessary before the new company could sell the stock it was hoping to issue to raise additional capital.

This was not the only controversy. W. W. Hubbard, ousted treasurer of Mutual Motors, sent a letter of his own to the stockholders in which he claimed that the proposed sale of the plant to Diamond Steel Products Company for $215,000 was wrong. Stopping short of accusing the new directorate of fraud and conspiracy, Hubbard claimed that the best interests of the stockholders were not being served. He and 24 other stockholders held a meeting in St. Cloud on June 4 during which they explained their position and called for support in the form of proxies.

Bouthinon answered Hubbard's charges on July 11, four days before the stockholders' meeting. He distributed a bulletin to interested parties in which he claimed that Hubbard's letter had been sent "for the sole purpose of falsely and maliciously slandering your present board of directors, mainly Mr. Bouthinon." Hubbard was characterized as "nothing but a questionable stock salesman." (Hubbard had been one of Pandolfo's more successful stock salesmen in the early days of the Pan Motor Company.) His principal activity at Mutual Motors, Bouthinon said, "was to draw his salary." Bouthinon presented a reasoned, detailed accounting of the standing and activities of Mutual Motors and requested stockholders to support him at the coming meeting so that the merger plan could be effected and "prevent the expenditure of your money on an adjourned meeting."

On July 15 the meeting was convened; only 70,000 of the 95,631 shares required for a quorum were represented. Bouthinon's group controlled 40,000 shares, while Hubbard represented 30,850. Both Hubbard and Bouthinon addressed the informal meeting. The stockholders, from such widely separated states as New York and Washington, also heard a nostalgic speech by St. Cloud attorney James Bennett, Jr., in which he eulogized former president Pandolfo, calling him the victim of a nationwide plot and claiming he had never used "so much as a dollar of stockholder money for personal use."

Another meeting was called for August 5.

Most of the St. Cloud support sided with Bouthinon, although not openly. Bouthinon was frequently quoted in news stories; in one of them he cited a recent declaration of the Federal Trade Commission against what was called the "Pittsburgh-plus" practice, and he stated that a midwest company entering the manufacture of auto parts now would have a distinct advantage. "The Federal Trade Commission's recent action removed the one factor that gave Eastern suppliers an advantage over Middle Western firms who may enter the specialty field. If we can get our steel from Duluth plants, we can manufacture to meet competition from anywhere, and we will have a decided advantage in the midwestern field.

"We have a plant lying idle, and we have a chance to merge with a plant which cannot manufacture enough to meet present demand. Legal technicalities require nominal sale of the plant to a new company before we can sell stock to re-equip our present holding and take over the Minneapolis concern. It is this plan we are asking our stockholders to ratify, and if they do it we hope to be able to resume manufacturing this year, possibly.

"In case that the stockholders ratify sale of the plant back to themselves under a new name, negotiations will no doubt be made to secure other buildings which were not purchased by the stockholder group originally."

It was an unfortunate prophecy.

In language faintly reminiscent of the early days of the Pan Motor

Company, Bouthinon then explained his statement that the present stockholders owned more in capital assets than their gross investment totaled. "The plan is to capitalize the new company at the gross value of the plant, and then exchange stock in the new company for stock in the old, giving stock equal in value to the original gross investment of each stockholder for the shares which would be called in by the sale. Then the state Securities Commission would no doubt permit the sale of additional stock, the proceeds of which would be put into additional needed equipment. The new company would then be on a sound financial basis."

Bouthinon would get no help from Charles Schwab in financing the new company. The Farmers State Bank had closed, and although a reopening in October was hinted, Charles Schwab, last president of the Pan Motor Company, was also the last president of the Farmers State Bank. In fairness, it was agreed by all that the bank's failure was not directly connected with the motor plant, by whatever name it was called; Schwab had put his bank heavily into real estate at a bad time.

On August 5, the second meeting of the Mutual Motors stockholders was held at "the old Pan plant," as it was coming to be known. Again, not enough shares were represented to make the meeting official, only 88,000 being on hand. But the Bouthinon forces had picked up strength; they now had 68,000 proxies, while Hubbard's share had dwindled to 17,000. The informal group, most of them now favorable to Bouthinon, again heard heated discussion on the merits of the reorganization plan. Most of Hubbard's objection, apart from his antipathy to Bouthinon, centered on what he called "the merger" with Diamond Steel Products Company. Bouthinon denied that the Minneapolis firm, of which he was also president, would gain any great advantage at the expense of Mutual stockholders. He said the plan was to reduce the capitalized value of the plant on paper to achieve the actual physical evaluation. Then, he said, the Securities Commission would allow the sale of more stock.

Bouthinon was backed in his arguments by St. Cloud attorney James J. Quigley, Sr., who went over the plan in detail for the assembled stockholders.

Bouthinon and Quigley told the audience that other companies similar to Diamond Steel Products Company, which manufactured a single line of replacement parts for cars, were doing well. "Car manufacturers are selling cars as fast as they can make them," Bouthinon said, "and they can't keep up with the demand for parts. This is the business to be in. Now! I want to equip the plant here to manufacture not one but 15 different lines of parts."

At the conclusion of Bouthinon's and Quigley's presentation, Hubbard was asked to present his plans for the company. He proposed investigating the possibilities of manufacturing the Kernan Insect Destroyer, an invention of stockholder Thomas Kernan, and said he did not trust the present management and would block any attempt they would make at refinancing.

Another meeting was set for August 15.

On that date the quorum figure still eluded management and they went on into September seeking the proxies that would constitute a legal meeting. Finally it took the threat of another receivership to stir the reluctant—or apathetic—stockholders into some action. On September 15, Bessie V. Milne, Martha Fraser, and F. E. Ellis, represented by Emery Swenson, filed a complaint in Judge John Roeser's court asking that an injunction be issued restraining any sale of the plant. The court was also asked to place the corporation in the hands of a receiver pending the outcome of the litigation. The complaint named George Bouthinon and Paul Ramstack as defendants and claimed they were attempting to sell the plant, appraised at $750,000, to Diamond Steel Products Company for $215,000. The complaint stated that the Diamond Steel company, valued at only $136,307.08, would then be worth close to a million dollars after spending only $215,000 to buy the Mutual stock.

The language sounded so much like Hubbard's contention that it was freely believed he was behind the suit. If he was, it was poor strategy. Judge Roeser heard the plaintiff's case and set a future date for hearing the defendant's rebuttal. Three days later it was announced that the management of Mutual Motors had at last secured the endorsement of the stockholders for their reorganization. The complaint was never acted upon.

Bouthinon's group began the reorganization and made plans for the sale of stock in the new company. By the end of September 1924, the new $500,000 corporation, known as the Diamond Motor Parts Company, was ready to sell the stock remaining after the exchange had been made with Mutual Motors stockholders. After a little more than a year, Mutual Motors & Manufacturing Company passed out of existence, or rather, metamorphosed into Diamond Motor Parts.

The Federal Trade Commission, with their ruling against the "Pittsburgh-plus" practice, had proved to be a boon to Bouthinon. Now Pandolfo wanted to explore the possibilities the commission opened to him. Early in December 1924, he won the right to offer evidence in support of an application for a *writ of habeas corpus* on the ground that he was illegally imprisoned. It was an interesting proposition. He claimed that evidence read into the record of his trial had come from a statement he had made to the Federal Trade Commission after his indictment but before his trial. As such, his statement had been extorted from him by the commission, and therefore he should have statutory immunity from the sentence.

Pandolfo's *writ*, demanding his release, was objected to by government attorneys on the grounds that his statement was voluntary. Judge John C. Pollack, in Kansas City, agreed and denied the motion.

Early in 1925, there were rumors that the Pandolfo Manufacturing Company plant, empty since the foreclosure of the bonds, might be sold and reactivated. J. C. Crever of St. Joseph, one of the trustees, verified that he had received at least four offers and that sale might be negotiated in the spring. One offer came from Thief River Falls, Minnesota, one from Minneapolis, one from Chicago, and a fourth from a company to be organized locally. Beyond saying that one offer was from a firm contemplating a radio parts factory, Crever would give no more information.

In March 1925, plans to consolidate the Minneapolis Diamond Steel Products Company into the St. Cloud unit depended on the ability to sell the stock. This would be no easy feat in view of the history of the company, but with strong effort by both Bouthinon and Quigley the sale proceeded briskly.

There was a small shock of apprehension when, shortly after the stock sale started, local police began to get requests for a description of A. Egbert Pandolfo. It appeared that someone had been visiting various sections of the country claiming to be S. C. Pandolfo's son and saying that he was engaged in promotion of a motor parts company. In Butte, Montana, the man, accompanied by a younger man who declared he was Samuel Junior, passed a check that bounced. But neither description tallied closely enough to either of the Pandolfo half-brothers, and it appeared someone was attempting to take advantage of Samuel Pandolfo's name and reputation.

In June, James J. Quigley said that as soon as new machinery could be installed in the old Pan plant and a production quota of 7,000 wrist pins a day maintained, the Diamond Motor Parts Company would start up the St. Cloud plant. Between the Minneapolis and St. Cloud plants a production of 14,000 a day would be maintained, Quigley said.

A month later Quigley had further news concerning other business property in western St. Cloud; the Pandolfo Manufacturing Company plant was sold by the trustees to the Glide Road Machinery Company of Minneapolis. Charles N. Beyhan had been involved in getting a Minneapolis firm interested in the local plant. The *Journal-Press* of Monday, July 20, reported that the Glide Road Machinery Company, whose president and major stockholder was Henry G. Foote of the Foote Lumber Company and the Foote Oil Company of Minneapolis, had received a "bonanza offer" for its Minneapolis plant at 2601 Fourth Street Southeast, an offer so attractive that they were unable to refuse it. They were looking for another location and Beyhan, who was to be the general superintendent of the company in St. Cloud, brought the Pandolfo plant to the attention of George C. Andrews, plant manager. The Glide Road Machinery Company was described as exclusive manufacturers of patented road surfacing devices: graders, drags, shapers, and scrapers.

The story was premature, at the least. Only one more mention of the company, implying that negotiations were still proceeding, was made. Then Glide Road quietly slid from sight.

The announcement that Diamond Motor Parts would begin production soon was a bit premature, too. On Thursday, September 24, at the annual stockholders meeting, Bouthinon revised his original plan about keeping both plants in operation; he now intended closing the Minneapolis plant as soon as local production, not yet started, could be maintained at a "high level." The stockholders toured the plant and saw the new machinery and tempering ovens that had been installed. Thomas Kernan, inventor of the Kernan Insect Destroyer, was reelected vice president, James Quigley was made secretary, and Paul Ramstack treasurer. With President Bouthinon and Charles Tanner, these men constituted the board of directors, and they were given a vote of confidence by the stockholders.

By late October, several Minneapolis employees of Diamond Motor Parts, including Bouthinon, had rented houses in Pan Town, and it was promised that work in the plant would start November 16. On October 22, a luncheon was held in the Breen Hotel, and Mayor J. Arthur Bensen welcomed the new industry to St. Cloud. Bouthinon disclosed that Diamond Motor Parts Company, claiming to be the largest auto parts company in the world, was capitalized at one million dollars. (Hubbard had been right about that!)

It was December before the Minneapolis plant, which had produced a surplus of 250,000 piston pins on overtime to tide the company over during the move, was closed down. The St. Cloud plant was now the only producing unit of Diamond Motor Parts. Of the 81 people employed in the Minneapolis plant, all but two moved with the company to St. Cloud.

The delayed startup notwithstanding, once the company was in operation in St. Cloud it developed rapidly. In February 1926, Diamond Motor Parts absorbed the National Bushing Company of Minneapolis. The addition of the 25 new employees to Diamond's work force—it had grown from 75 to 150 in two months—brought it up to 175; the payroll increased to $17,000 a month.

But the prime news came when Bouthinon and Quigley announced that Diamond Motor Parts was declaring a quarterly dividend on the basis of eight percent per year. In the nine years of its existence, no occupant of the Pan Motor plant had been able to pay its own way; here was one paying a return on investment. The *Journal-Press* paid proper tribute to the team that had produced this record:

> George Bouthinon, the president, and James J. Quigley, the secretary, are primarily responsible for the success. Mr. Bouthinon is a living example of what persistent, well-directed effort can do. He not only has sold his company to the big men of the country, but he makes a study of the financing of this rapidly growing organization and is a buyer of raw materials with no mean ability.
>
> He relies on the counsel of Mr. Quigley for administrative policies, and these two men, with the assistance of their associates, have been instrumental in bringing about this remarkable growth.
>
> St. Cloud is beginning to take an interest in the new company, and it is freely predicted that it is destined to become the largest single industry here.

Another prediction! But the company was shipping 1,000 pins to Detroit every day, in addition to supplying 360 domestic and 80 foreign jobbers.

In January 1926, E. F. Meyer, of St. Cloud Laundry, was attending a convention in Kansas City and drove up along the Missouri River to visit Pandolfo in Leavenworth. He was the first visitor Pandolfo had from St. Cloud. Meyer reported that the once-plump promoter was now emaciated, a result of stomach trouble, and was firmly convinced his death was only a short time away. He was genuinely bitter when he remarked that no one seemed willing to help him secure a pardon. "No one from St. Cloud even remembered me with a Christmas card last month." He was as much puzzled as hurt. "I honestly tried to do a lot for St. Cloud. I would appreciate just a little kindness from my friends back there. I still hold many of them in high regard and want you to extend them my warm regards."

Meyer disclosed that Pandolfo no longer had the job as clerk in the hospital; he was now in charge of cutting the lawn in the summer and cleaning the walks in winter. The inactivity bothered Pandolfo less than the inconsequence of the work; a man of his restless energy required meaningful work, and he was not getting it in prison.

Meyer's report triggered some action. A collection was taken up, and W. E. Quigley, a Minneapolis lawyer, went to Washington, D.C., to institute action on a pardon for Pandolfo. The Department of Justice informed Quigley that any action on a pardon would have to come before the federal parole board's next meeting in May. Quigley was led to believe, however, that a pardon would be looked on with favor. In May the favor had soured somewhat. The federal parole board turned down the request despite the fact that it was accompanied by the signatures of hundreds of St. Cloud citizens and medical statements concerning the state of Pandolfo's health.

If it was any consolation to Pandolfo, the denial was made with the stipulation that it was not to prejudice a later hearing that would soon be held in Leavenworth. At that hearing, in early June, the parole board felt it needed additional data and a decision was again postponed.

In the fall of 1926, the courts began to take final action on the property covered by the Pandolfo bonds. The bondholders had held the property since July 1924, and had not been able to sell any of the houses in Pan Town or the property downtown. The Pandolfo Manufacturing plant had been empty and idle all the while. The bondholders now filed a petition in district court asking for reappraisal of the property. They were hoping a more realistic valuation might result in sales, and the new appraisal did drop the total valuation from $350,000 to $275,000. Judge Roeser set the hearing for October 14. He thought the property could be auctioned on the basis of the new appraisal; he also expected some objections from the bondholders.

At the hearing, Roeser reviewed the history of the bonds and the property. "When Mr. Pandolfo severed his connection with the Pan Motor Company, he and Mrs. Pandolfo decided to devote their full time to other endeavors. To do this they needed a considerable amount of money. They proposed to raise it by bonding the many tracts of property in the present list. When Mr. Pandolfo's business failed, and he could not make the interest payments on the bonds, a receiver was appointed to protect the bondholders' investment. Up to the time the receivers took the property, Mr. Pandolfo was entitled to all income from it; but thereafter his income was cut to 40 percent. He agreed that this was just. But even 60 percent was not enough to keep the properties in repair, and the receivers spent $15,000 of their own money before they took full title to the property in July 1924.

"At that time the property was appraised at $350,000, equal to the amount of the bonds outstanding. When John Crever and Anton Schmidt were appointed in place of Ralph Olson and Frank Hinze who resigned, they replaced, for instance, 2,000 panes of glass to get the houses in rentable shape. Bathroom fixtures, furnace parts, and other property had been stolen from the empty houses and had to be replaced. As it now stands, the unpaid taxes due—which amount to about $15,000 a year—will wipe out any value the bondholders have left unless the property is disposed of instantly."

Lawyer Joseph B. Himsl asked the bondholders to remember they had made a bad investment. Their problem was not how to save their investment; it was too late for that. Their only chance was to minimize their losses. "If Pandolfo had been allowed to go ahead," Himsl said, "there might not have been a loss. But that is past argument now. We have only to salvage what we can."

Himsl explained how much the losses might be. In the new appraisal, houses in Pan Town were rated from $1,800 to $6,500; these changes meant little to most bondholders until Himsl made a sharper comparison. "The property of the Pandolfo Manufacturing Company was insured for $90,000, but was carried at $100,000. This is now revalued at $32,000, with back taxes of $12,000 due." There were more than a few injured looks

A committee, consisting of Reverend Raymond Basil, O.S.B., of St. John's Abbey, Herman Terhaar of New Munich, and Martin Schroeder of St. Joseph, was appointed to study the new appraisal. When they recommended its acceptance and an auction of the property according to its assigned values, Roeser agreed, but he emphasized that since this would be a convenience sale and not a forced sale, the court or the trustees could reject any bid they felt was unrealistic.

There was considerable discussion about the sale. Abbot Alcuin Deutsch, of St. John's Abbey, Ripley B. Brower, among other bondholders pressed for quick action. Roeser agreed again, saying that the sooner the sale could be held the better since taxes could only accumulate if they waited. They agreed to hold the sale on October 25.

Four days before the property was to go up for sale, there was news from Leavenworth: PANDOLFO RELEASED FROM PRISON! After serving three-and-a-half years of his ten-year sentence Pandolfo was released on parole and headed for Minnesota.

Shortly before being paroled, Pandolfo had written to Bishop Busch: "I am out of funds. Did not have enough money the other day to pay for a telegram and a collect message came in to me and I did not have the money to pay for it. . . . If ever a man in this life needed financial help at once, I am that man. . . . I hate to appeal to you and others for help in my distress, but I have always made good with you personally, and you know how things are with me. . . . I have never called upon you to help in so worthy a cause, and it seems to me impossible to imagine how one could ever be more deserving of your best and most favorable consideration."

In Minneapolis, where he stopped a short time, he denied intentions of bringing suit against anyone. "There are persons over the country against whom I could take some sort of action, but I have no inclination to make trouble for anyone. I am not myself right now. The experience I have been through has shattered my health, and I am under a physician's care. My first consideration is to regain my strength.

"I have no plans for the future right now. Until I am well again I shall not make any. First, I have several personal matters that require my attention here. When they are disposed of I will go to St. Cloud. Then I am going back to Virginia to visit my mother, Mrs. Kate Pandolfo. What I shall do next is uncertain. I am planning on coming back to the west to enter some sanitarium. Perhaps I shall return to St. Cloud for that purpose. I have a warm feeling for the city and its people, and if their attitude is what I hope it will be, I will make my home there. After I am well I intend first to repay personal loans made by friends who stood by me during my long legal fight. Whether I will reenter business in St. Cloud is up to the people of St. Cloud. I would like to go back there. I would like to justify the faith of so many of my friends there. You can tell the citizens of St. Cloud for me that words cannot express my gratitude to them."

While the imminence of Pandolfo's return could not alter the necessity for the sale of property that once was his, it certainly affected the attitude of some of the people prepared to bid on it. On the morning of October 25 the bids were opened by Judge Roeser. The Pandolfo Manufacturing Company plant, erected at a cost of $90,000 and given a reduced valuation of $32,000, was bid in at $850 by Capital Iron and Wrecking Company of St. Paul. Judge Roeser immediately rejected the bid, which was the highest of three received from wrecking firms. "I will allow the property to revert to the state for the $12,000 due in taxes rather than have it wrecked for that price," Roeser said heatedly.

The first house sold, at 839 30th Avenue North and appraised at $3,500, went for $1,600. The back taxes on it amounted to $600, which left the bondholders with an equity of $1,000. Other houses, however, did come closer to appraised values. One, at 3001 8th Street North valued at $5,000, sold for $3,000. Another, at 829 30th Avenue North valued at $3200, sold for $1,600.

The downtown property received no bids at all.

When one disgruntled bondholder registered an objection to the low prices the property was receiving, Roeser said it was a little late for such talk. He asked Crever and Schroeder for a summary of their trusteeship. Crever said $40,000 had been received in rents and that it had all been spent on repairs, insurance, and debts incurred before their receivership took over. According to the records, the receivership started out $14,000 in debt and now had $134 cash on hand. In all, bids totaling $105,830 were received in the sale that morning. When the taxes and assessments of $45,000 were paid, the bondholders had a little over $60,000 left.

The day before the sale, Homer McKenzie, a friend and former employee of Pandolfo, received a telegram from Pandolfo stating that he would be arriving in St. Cloud on the Great Northern train at 1:37 p.m. the next day. Plans were made for a welcome at the depot and another later at the Miner Theatre where movies of the Pan Motor plant in operation would be shown for an admission charge of 50 cents, the receipts to be turned over to Pandolfo. Friends who had seen Pandolfo in Minneapolis said his appearance, usually dapper and fashionable, was extremely poor. His clothes were ill-fitting and his health was bad.

Still discussing the sale that had taken place that morning, people began to gather at the Great Northern depot at one o'clock Monday afternoon, October 25, 1926. By 1:30, between 500-600 people were standing about in groups. When the whistle heralded the approach of the train, conversations died. The train neared the silent, anxious gathering and slowed to a stop in the hissing of steam. There was a long wait, some people drifting away with the quiet comment, "He'll probably come on a later train." Others remembered the confusion about his departure for prison almost three years earlier. Then Samuel Junior stepped down from the rear of one of the coaches and turned to help his father. A cheer came from those nearest Pandolfo, and they shouted to the others, "Here he is!"

He was perhaps 50 pounds lighter, and his face, gaunt and pale, mirrored the past three-and-a-half years. But the Pandolfo "twinkle" was still present. Julius Adams, representing St. Cloud's mayor who was out of town, reached Pandolfo's side and welcomed him back on behalf of the city. Tears rolled down Pandolfo's cheeks, and he continued to grip Adams' hand and shake it long minutes after the short greeting. The crowd pressed in on him, reaching through to pat his back and shake his hand, and to each who said they were happy to see him he replied, "I'm mighty glad to be back, too."

When he was asked what his plans were, he said, "I would rather not say anything right now. I'll save it until tomorrow night when I've rested. Thank you for coming. But I think I'd like to go home now."

He wiped his eyes with a handkerchief and walked away, holding on to his son and Homer McKenzie. As they made their way through the crowd, someone shouted, "Three cheers for Pan!" As the responding "Hip, hip, hoorays!" rang out on the bright October afternoon, Pandolfo's were not the only eyes filled with tears.

To reinforce the welcome at the depot, Monday's newspapers carried a full-page ad of welcome signed by 44 businesses and individuals, including "A Friend."

Pandolfo spent Wednesday morning talking to friends in his room at the Breen Hotel and visiting casually on the streets during the afternoon. By 7:15 that evening the Miner Theatre was packed with 1,000 people with the first showing of the motion pictures scheduled for 7:30. Pandolfo and a few friends entered the theatre shortly before the appointed time and took seats reserved for them near the front. At the conclusion of the six reels, George Miner introduced Pandolfo, and many in the audience remarked how like old times it was to see the former Pan president up on a stage in front of an audience. But they also noted that his voice was softer and his delivery less forceful than it had been.

He began by explaining that the films they had just seen had been taken in 1918, that there were later ones, in Washington, D.C., taken in 1919, that would surprise even those who thought they had followed the progress of the company day by day. He thanked them all for their warm welcome, at the depot yesterday and last night. They had all expressed their sincere regard for him and their hope that his health would mend. "This has given me a feeling that cannot be bought by any man's money."

"There is one thing that grieves me greatly, however. That is the false propaganda that some of my friends have told me was in circulation. Some said I was a good promoter, a good organizer, a good stock salesman, but that I was lacking as a business manager, that I was not conservative enough.

"Back in 1916 I quit the insurance business. I wanted to build an industrial business, one that would be a monument to myself and one that my children could look at after I had gone and take inspiration from, beyond the inspiration of other children. That was my dream. And the Pan Motor Company was the result."

He described the condition of the Pan Motor Company when he had resigned as president and how it had faltered and died when he left. "I want to say right now, particularly for the benefit of those responsible for news being spread on the wires of the press, that Pan did not go down fair! I did not cause one penny loss to a single human being during the course of my management. There is only one thing in particular in my heart right now. That is to regain my health and get back into fighting trim, face the future and build anew. I look forward to the future with the hope of building along lines that will be successful in the end."

"It will take four or five months for me to get into condition. I have always been frank with you, and I'm going to tell you my troubles. A little over a year ago I developed a rupture. A few days later I got another. An operation will probably be necessary to cure this. I have some abscesses on the roots of my teeth, and I'll have to have them all pulled and some new ones set in. And I have indigestion. What I need is a few months at Battle Creek or some place like that."

"I will see you again in five or six months. And I'll never forget St. Cloud or my friends here, and I'm going to make good with every one who has believed in me and trusted me."

While Pandolfo was still in town, Judge Roeser ordered the successful bids on the Pan Town property approved, and the deeds were presented to the new owners.

On November 4, Pandolfo left St. Cloud, and the newspapers graciously offered space for his statement:

> To the people of St. Cloud and vicinity:
>
> Till further notice my address will be Roslyn, Virginia.
>
> You have been wonderful to me. I appreciate your kindness; your confidence in me will inspire me and stimulate me to do all I can to achieve something worthwhile in due time.
>
> You have given me something which money cannot buy and for which many a rich man will gladly give much of his wealth.
>
> It behooves me to live and operate among friends. I shall be with you again. For the information of all, when I die I desire to be buried here. I want my dust to mingle with yours.
>
> Your friend,
> S. C. Pandolfo

Although he still had not told even his closest friends what he intended to do—perhaps because he himself didn't yet know—there were rumors that Pandolfo had arranged to place a bid on the Pandolfo Manufacturing plant when it would again be placed for sale on November 13. But the day arrived and the property failed to attract a bid. The purchasers of homes in Pan Addition entered bids on the vacant lots next to their homes, paying one dollar over the delinquent taxes due, and the bondholders were able to derive some small additional return on their investment. The house across from Empire Park, at 30 Fifth Avenue North, was sold to A. Lommell for $2500, but the other downtown property did not receive a *bona fide* bid.

Early in December, Pandolfo, in a letter to friends in St. Cloud, revealed that he and Miss Agnes C. Kulla, a former maid in the Pandolfo household in St. Cloud, had been married on November 17 in Clarendon, Virginia, by Rev. Frederick P. Lackey, pastor of St. Charles Catholic Church.

Before Christmas, Pandolfo and his new bride moved back to the Beverly Apartments in St. Cloud. He had spent some time in a sanitarium in Battle Creek and appeared to have regained much of his strength. In a Christmas letter to Bishop Busch, whose episcopal residence was only a block or two away, Pandolfo wrote: "I am broke—and through no fault of my own—and cannot give you a Christmas present; but I am thinking of you and the future. My thought is that we must live a clean, simple life—and help one another and be more comfortable and happier, and, especially so, since this is the only life we can ever hope to live in our present form and consciousness."

He now had the motion pictures that had been made for the Chicago trial but never shown, and he began to exhibit them. At a preview of the pictures for several friends at the Grand Theatre, Pandolfo gave a running commentary, often citing the cost of a particular piece of machinery as it was pictured in operation. When the lights came up at the conclusion, he leaned back in his seat. "To think that all is gone. It is a shame. A shame!"

He made arrangements to use the Institute building to exhibit the films, charging a small admission and giving a running commentary about the past, present, and future.

"When these pictures were taken, the plant was employing about 700 workers with a payroll of 180,000 dollars a month. St. Cloud needs a big industry as does every town that wants to keep on the map and build up solid prosperity. My idea is to find out the extent to which St. Cloud people are willing to assist in an effort that will be of direct benefit to the community. It goes without saying that nobody can build a business concern with only wind, faith, and sympathy. I hope to learn that St. Cloud people will be willing to furnish something else."

He meant money, of course. Posters around the Institute auditorium proclaimed:

PANDOLFO WANTS—Money
Confidence of people
An opportunity to "Make Good"
Fair consideration in placing responsibility for downfall of Pan Motor Company
An industry in St. Cloud that will eclipse even the gigantic motor company which he promoted
Sole control and management of business
To reinstate himself in the good graces of the people
To let the world know he is not licked
To show his old foes and enemies they erred in denying their confidence

PANDOLFO DOES NOT WANT—
A board of directors

PANDOLFO HAS—
Nothing (of monetary value)
Ability
Put three old line life insurance companies on their feet

Built the gigantic Pan Motor Company and its plant
Confidence in the future of St. Cloud

As the weeks went by, Pandolfo warmed to his audiences. And as he warmed, the comments he made got more personal. As a result, the audiences grew with each performance. The movies of the plant at the height of its activity bolstered the impression that "everything certainly was humming along" when Pandolfo was president. As soon as he resigned, he said, the gutting and dismantling took place. He had little confidence in the board of directors who had asked for his resignation. "I carry no grudge against them for that; they thought they were doing their duty," he repeated several times. But if he had no grudge to carry, he did have a deep and abiding antipathy.

"I owned 40,000 dollars' worth of stock in the Pan Motor Company, more than four times what the other directors had combined. I had dreams of a city of 75-100,000 people, all living and working together. Just when I could see in the future the realization of my aims, I was forced to step down. I can do it again. This time I'll avoid the mistakes that I made in the past. I believe that honesty is the best policy. Lay all of your cards on the table, face up, for the people to see, and they will give you financial support.

"I'm asking all who believe in my honesty and integrity to call me or write to me. And, if possible, loan me some money. If I can get sufficient capital pledged, I will announce plans for an industrial undertaking that will again set the world to stare and draw attention to St. Cloud."

These words alone were enough to shiver the spines of many St. Cloud citizens. But Pandolfo had more.

"I promise you this: I will not be hampered by a board of directors. I have lost all confidence in such bodies. Even Christ, when he chose 12 apostles, found one Judas and seven others at times were not one in faith with him. I want to run this business alone.

"I will give my personal notes, to run 14 months, for what money is lent to me. And I don't want anyone to come across unless he feels he can kiss the money goodbye. I'm sure the investment will succeed and be a safe one if I am not interfered with, but I don't want to ask anyone to take such a risk with me who can't afford it."

Late in the week he returned to his attack on the Pan Board of Directors. "Why, they tried to cut my throat at the trial. In 1919, when machines and material were coming in and there wasn't ready cash to pay for them, I turned over my commissions, amounting to over 72,000 dollars, without taking a note. When I resigned as president, I asked for a settlement. I finally got it in 1922, a note for $35,000!

"I cleared those birds at my own expense at the trial in Chicago. That trial cost me more than $100,000, and I paid it all—even the hotel bills until the break, when they moved to their own hotel. When I got back, one of the Directors loaned me ten dollars, and I paid him back. Another loaned me 15 dollars, and I'm going to pay him back tomorrow.

"The Pan Motor Company was a solvent, going concern when I left it. The directors collected about $800,000 of the outstanding stock money and even sold more preferred stock. And with all this money, they still couldn't make it go."

He was warming to his subject, and some of his old power and fire returned. "I built a hotel," he shouted, "and homes for the workers to keep them happy. It hurt me to see all of that go and have them blame it all on me. There is no better businessman in the world than Pan! I'll build you a big city if you want it. You can't keep a good man down!"

Finally, on Thursday, January 13, the last night of the series, it was thought, Pandolfo dropped some hints about what he had in mind. He suggested that his plans might center around the vacant Pandolfo Manufacturing plant, but the reference was brief and unclear. "I can and will create another industrial empire here or elsewhere. I prefer to do it here. The buildings of the old plant are lying idle. They are going to wrack and ruin through lack of use, and taxes are accruing against them constantly. Something should be done."

But the 200 men and women in the audience heard no further details of the planned industry. In fact, people talking with him later could not get him to identify which buildings he had been referring to.

Then, when the meetings were supposedly over and the industrial empire still not clearly outlined, Pandolfo scheduled one more meeting for early February at Cathedral High School auditorium. Eight hundred people showed up to hear his plans. What they heard—or rather, didn't hear—must have disappointed them. "There are ten millions of dollars in currency in Stearns county right now," Pandolfo said. "The investment of a part of that amount with me will mean another industrial enterprise for St. Cloud of which you can be proud. I am through with businessmen. They have no money. The working man and the farmer have enough money to back a great business and do something for themselves and their community. The Kiwanis, the Rotary, the Chamber of Commerce won't do it. If anything is done it should be done by the combined efforts of us common people."

He referred to patents he had on various items and said the idea for a great local enterprise had come to him. But whether the backing he sought did not materialize, or his plans required further maturing, nothing came from the meeting beyond another look, via the motion pictures, into the past of the Pan Motor Company in its heyday.

Perhaps there was no connection, but early in February, Hugh Evans, a director of the old Pan Motor Company, after being in business 27 years, sold his wholesale grocery business to Nash Finch Company. He may have been trying to get beyond Pandolfo's reach.

INCORPORATED UNDER THE LAWS OF THE STATE OF SOUTH DAKOTA

NUMBER 1877 SHARES

Mutual Motors and Manufacturing Company

CAPITAL $1.500.000

ST. CLOUD, MINNESOTA

This Certifies that A. W. LYSLO is the owner of ***TWENTY-THREE*** Shares of the Capital Stock of Mutual Motors and Manufacturing Company transferable only on the books of this Corporation in person or by Attorney upon surrender of this Certificate properly endorsed.

In Witness Whereof the said Corporation has caused this Certificate to be signed by its duly authorized officers and its Corporate Seal to be hereunto affixed this 5TH day of DEC. A.D. 1923

SECRETARY PRESIDENT

SHARES EACH.

Mutual Motors & Manufacturing Company barely had time to issue stock and get a letterhead printed (still using the Pan Motor Company logo) before they were "absorbed" by Diamond Motor Parts.

George Bouthinon, president of Diamond Steel Products of Minneapolis, saw the advantages of the empty Pan plant and brought his company to St. Cloud. Within a short time it was being called the "General Motors of Replacement Parts," but this business, too, eventually was sold and the Pan plant lay idle once more.

Pandolfo had started the Pandolfo Manufacturing Company to manufacture his patented Combination Compartment Tank shortly after arriving in St. Cloud. Almost immediately his plans outstripped the building he had first used in St. Cloud and he erected the office and factory buildings across the tracks south of the Pan plant. With his resignation from the Pan Motor Company he devoted all the time he could spare from his appeal of his sentence to the manufacturing company. A few of the products are pictured below and on the following page.

A Luggage carrier and Made-O-Metal wheels are here installed on a Model T Ford Roadster.

Folding chairs advertised to "make a seven passenger out of five."

The Coffee-maker from Sunny Italy.

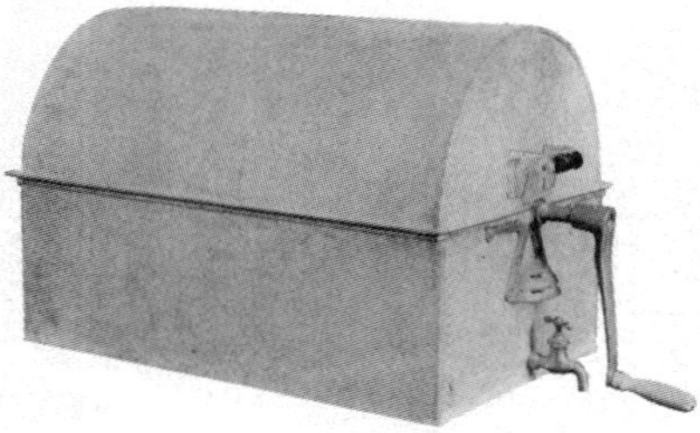

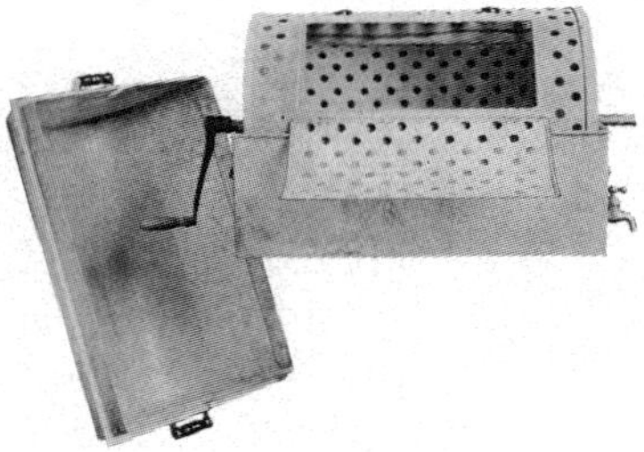

"The Made-O-Metal Washing Machine now being developed." The hand-powered clothes washing machine certainly was easier than hand scrubbing on a washboard.

(Left) Advertised as "A Table of More Than Ordinary Usefulness," this was the precursor of the later ubiquitous TV tray. *(Right)* Fenders for the Fordson Tractor.

The Simmons "Wheel of Steel" made by the Pandolfo Manufacturing Company.

Pandolfo continued to use the "pan shape" for his logo in this company and many of the products were identified as "Handy-Pandy" items.

A "Made-O-Metal" Drafting Board Stand.

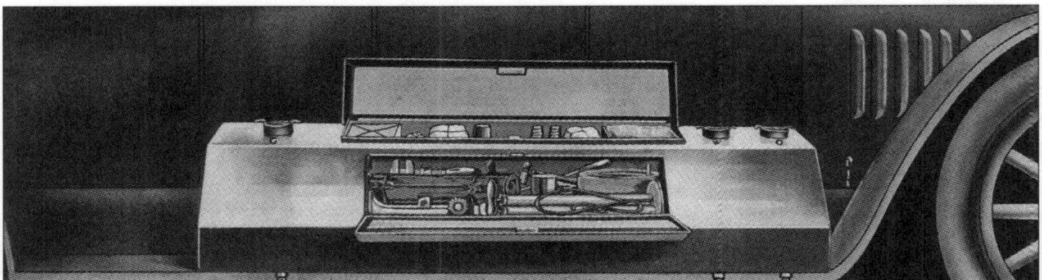

The Pandolfo Combination Compartment Tank was no longer used on the Pan car after Pandolfo resigned from the company, but he maintained the rights and continued manufacturing it for use on other automobiles, showing it here mounted on a running board. But it appears the car door could not be opened in this application and may have meant the death of his product.

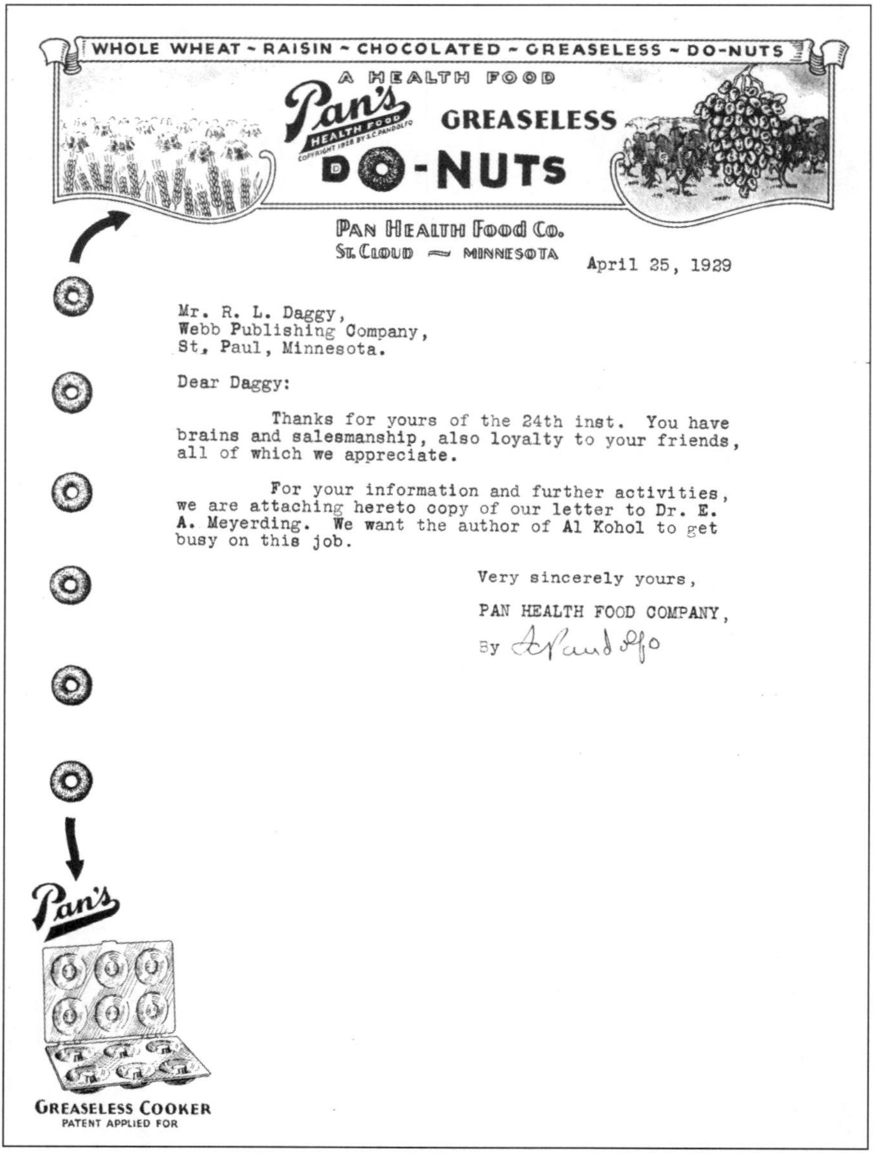

WHOLE WHEAT ~ RAISIN ~ CHOCOLATED ~ GREASELESS ~ DO-NUTS

A HEALTH FOOD

Pan's HEALTH FOOD GREASELESS DO-NUTS

PAN HEALTH FOOD CO.
ST. CLOUD ~ MINNESOTA

April 25, 1929

Mr. R. L. Daggy,
Webb Publishing Company,
St. Paul, Minnesota.

Dear Daggy:

Thanks for yours of the 24th inst. You have brains and salesmanship, also loyalty to your friends, all of which we appreciate.

For your information and further activities, we are attaching hereto copy of our letter to Dr. E. A. Meyerding. We want the author of Al Kohol to get busy on this job.

Very sincerely yours,

PAN HEALTH FOOD COMPANY,

By

Pan's

GREASELESS COOKER
PATENT APPLIED FOR

This letter was written to Richard L. Daggy, the printing salesman from Webb Publishing in St. Paul, the company that had printed the lavish *Pictorial Proof of Progress* book Pandolfo hoped would silence those critics who were saying the company had not done anything with the money they had taken in. He was now as enthusiastic about "do-nuts" and health foods as he had been about insurance and automobiles.

The "Masterbilt" Six—a car designed by Victor Gauvreau, with body design by Edgard DeSmet, built for a group of investors in Minneapolis/St. Paul. The car had an air-cooled engine and had much promise, but the consortium ran out of funds after the prototype and no production models were ever built.

(Far Left) Victor Gauvreau retired to Tucson in 1948. He was the last surviving member of the mechanical team that produced the Pan car. *(Above, right)* Edgard DeSmet, former body designer at Pan, at the press showing of the new Willys. While at Willys, DeSmet worked on the Jeep. *(Left)* Ed Carlson shows his Pan car to Samuel and Agnes Pandolfo in 1956, on Pandolfo's last visit to St. Cloud on his way to Alaska. Eddie Lommel, who had been a driver for Pandolfo, also visited with the still sprightly Pandolfo.

Reo executives and the first 1934 Flying Cloud coming off the Lansing final assembly line. Second man on left is Ray A. DeVlieg, works manager; on the far right is Ray J. Fitness, chief engineer. Both men had worked at Pan Motor in St. Cloud. *(Photo courtesy John Conde, American Motors)*

This airview, taken several years ago, shows the nucleus, Factory No. 2, of today's enlarged facility. The buildings in the background were all that remained at that time of the Drop Forge complex. The remains of the foundation of the Drop Forge Building and the Coal Bunker were removed when the overpass over the rail line was completed.

The Pandolfo Family at home.

(*At left*, Florence Coleman.)

Mrs. Anna Pandolfo relaxes with the *Saturday Evening Post*.

A different arrangement of furniture in the same room as the photo above.

The bedroom in the Pandolfo home.

Formal portrait of Mrs. Anna Pandolfo.

Mrs Pandolfo with Vivian and Sammy Jr.

(Left) Sammy Jr. and Vivian. Mrs. Pandolfo left her husband sometime after the Chicago trial, but came back to care for the children after her husband's appeal of his sentence was denied.

The camera captures a tender moment with Sammy Jr. and his mother on the steps of the Pandolfo home in Pan-Town.

CHAPTER XII

PANDOLFO HAS ARRIVED!

THE DIAMOND MOTOR Parts Company, humming along quietly in the old Pan Motor plant, surfaced infrequently in the newspapers. In April 1927, Bouthinon presided at a sales meeting during which the managers of the New York, Chicago, and 20 other regional offices gave their sales figures. Bouthinon was optimistic about the future of the company and said, "We now produce over 600,000 piston pins, machine bolts, bronze bushings, and water pump parts every month and are the largest replacement parts plant in the world."

During that summer little was heard of Pandolfo and his plans for the industrial empire he was attempting to create.

Then in August the local newspapers carried a strange item that appeared to be a news story until the reader came to "—adv." at the conclusion.

> Pandolfo today received a letter from C. H. Wagner, San Antonio, Texas, one of his former insurance agents:
>
> Well, how is your family? I hope well and that you will put all your original plans over yet regardless of all the dirt you had dished out to you. Do not let the troubles you had take that old fighting spirit out of you that you always had but come right on up as you used to tell us that defeat was only found in those that had no guts. So stay right in there, old top. My heart and hand is with you.
>
> If you get ready to start something where you can use an old true pulling horse who will do his darndest and think you can use me, let me hear from you at once as I am ready to pile it on them.
>
> What has happened to your auto factory? Do you still control it and if so are you going to start it up again? You should if you can see your way through to do so. There are still some Pan cars running in the valley but around here I have not seen any lately. But, say, Pan, I talked to an owner of one in the valley and he said I will run this one till Pandolfo builds some more and then I will trade this one for a new one and guarantee that I will drive it back to St. Cloud where it was originally built and hang it over the front entrance with a sign on it, They defeated me but I came back.

> I asked him what he will take for it and he said it is not for sale. But when Pan builds his new car I will get another Pan car sure as I am living.
>
> Now, listen, Pan, let me hear from you at once and bear in mind that you have lots of friends here and as I was out at Marfa I met lots of good men that are your friends and all said I hope Pandolfo comes out all okay and then he gives it to them good and proper.

Within a week Pandolfo called another meeting at the Institute and revealed his plan . . . or plans. He had two ideas. His first suggestion, an extension of his earlier remarks about financial support coming from "us common people," sounded something like a cooperative bank or credit union. "In eastern cities," he said, "large financiers put up the money to attract industry. But here in the middle west this isn't done. So the money has to come from another source. Where?" Before he could answer his own rhetorical question, a few members of the audience, seeing the point of his remarks, quietly made for the exits.

"None can benefit himself without benefitting everyone in the city, and by the same token, everyone should aid programs designed to attract industry to the city. For this reason I am proposing a working man's industrial club."

There were many perplexed looks until Pandolfo filled in the details. "The laboring man himself should bear the cost of attracting industry to the city. For example, a man earning less than five dollars a day would contribute 50 cents a month to the club; those earning over five dollars a day can contribute one dollar a month. Those earning less than ten dollars a week would pay only 25 cents per month. But everyone will pay an initial fee of one dollar."

A huge fund would be created, Pandolfo said, "which would be used to attract manufacturing plants to this area. It would also finance the enlargement of existing plants and give St. Cloud the impetus for a growth never before witnessed, even greater than the Pan Motor Company."

His own place in this venture was identified when he offered to serve as promoter of the program. But beyond this brief outline, Pandolfo never mentioned the project publicly again.

Several metal objects on the speaker's table had aroused the curiosity of some members of the audience when they first entered. Pandolfo now picked up one of the products. "One of the uses of a fund like this would be to manufacture an item like this. The donut is in universal demand, with but one objection to it as a delicacy—the grease. Eliminate the grease and you will have a food item that millions will pay good money for. And this greaseless pan does it!"

The cast iron pan, the size of a large book, was hinged and opened like a book. In each half were depressions for six donuts. The donut batter,

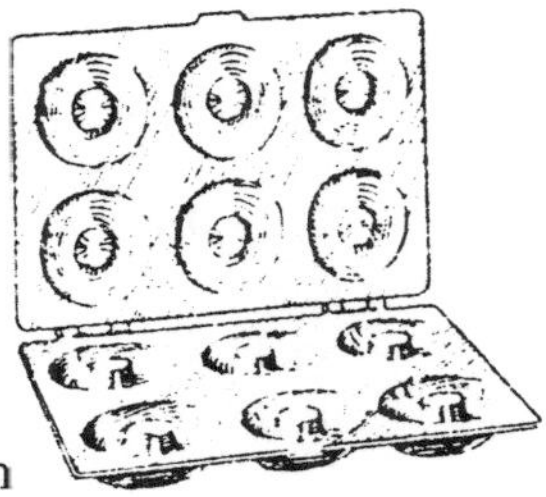

Pandolfo explained, was poured into the deeper half, the pan was closed and placed in an oven or on top of a stove. Delicious donuts could be made without grease, a half-dozen at a time.

But the greaseless pan was only part of his plan. He would sell the pans for five dollars each. This would finance a plant which would manufacture the pans. (They were now being made for him in Chicago.) The funds realized from the sale of the pans would also finance a nationwide string of donut kitchens dispensing greaseless donuts and other health foods.

When the meeting broke up, several ushers distributed promissory note forms and took orders for the donut pans.

In early September, Pandolfo leased property at 14 Sixth Avenue North—next door to Fred Schilplin's *St. Cloud Daily Times*—and carpenters began to remodel the building to Pandolfo's specifications. And they were unique. The building, inside and out, would be totally white, an indication of the standard of cleanliness to be maintained. The Donut Shoppe, as he called it, would not only sell over-the-counter but would distribute through other retail outlets as well.

Donuts and donut pans, however, were not his only irons in the fire. In late October, another offer was placed before the public in a newspaper ad.

A CHANCE THAT RARELY COMES
IN A LIFETIME

You Have It Now!

> I will sell 1000 acres of land in 10- and 20-acre tracts. This is all the land of this kind anyone needs. The land is situated in sunny New Mexico. The soil is from ten to 15 feet deep, it is level, there is no timber on it. So there is no clearing problem.
>
> I am acquiring over 18,000 acres of this land but I do not wish to sell over 1000 acres now at the price and on the terms offered. I intend to colonize this land and build a town on it and develop a hydroelectric plant near it and give more or less employment out of season to the people on it.
>
> Prunes, grapes, head lettuce, cauliflower, English walnuts and many other things grow remarkably well on this kind of soil and in this climate. This land can be made to yield from 500 to 15,000 dollars per acre per year, after prunes come into bearing, and also up to 1,000 dollars per acre on celery and head lettuce. Cauliflower and head lettuce grown in this section bring a premium on the Chicago and New York markets.

Over 300 days of sunshine per year. The winters are mild. You can work comfortably every day in the year out in the open. It excels California for healthfulness. The air is bracing, and the clear skies and sunshine are stimulating. No hail and no storms. The summers are cool and pleasant. Bees, poultry, dairy cows, hogs and other things thrive and four to five cuttings of real alfalfa per year. A prosperous farm community is within about three miles of this tract.

This land can be made to grow 60 bushels of wheat, 120 bushels of oats, 100 bushels of corn, and two bales of cotton per acre if you want to waste it that way. But prunes, grapes, celery, head lettuce and English walnuts are the crops to go after. The county agent and the A. and M. College will cooperate.

I will not sell anyone more than 20 acres because that is enough. There is an abundance of good water from about 40 to 60 feet under the surface. This land will have to be irrigated, therefore you can put the moisture as and when needed. It will cost very little to put down a shallow well and build a surface dirt tank and use an electric pump. I will furnish the power in due time at not to exceed 2¢ per kilowatt. I intend to develop a fruit and grape farm for myself on part of this land and expect to spend part of my time on it each year.

I will sell the first 1000 acres in 10- and 20-acre tracts at $30 per acre, and I assure you that nobody will ever get any of the balance for so low a price. After the prunes and grapes come into bearing it should be worth $100 per acre or more. If desired, I will accept as down payment only $5.00 per acre and one dollar per acre a month. There can be no question about the title because the title is from the United States government to the state of New Mexico and will be from the state to me and then to you after you pay for it.

I can also give employment the year round to a few good men who buy and pay for land because I intend soon to commence development work on this land. This tract is about 100 miles on the South Pacific Rock Island mail line northeast of El Paso, Texas, and the altitude is about 4400 feet. Ultimately it is planned to have a central cooperative marketing agency so that the best prices may be obtained for all products raised on the land.

It is better than I have explained. If you want to make money and have good health, better get in while there is a chance at the bottom price. It is better than words can convey, and if it is good enough for me, it is good enough for you.

S. C. Pandolfo

It was the only time this Eden of the western world was ever mentioned in print.

Meanwhile, the rosy future that Diamond Motor Parts had talked about in April seemed to have faded by November. It was now time for the successor to the Pan Motor Company to plead, "A bit more capital is required." Diamond had merged with the Gill Manufacturing Company of Chicago, manufacturers of piston rings. (A third company, Fulton, was sometimes mentioned as a partner in the merger.) The directors of the merged companies were listening to an offer from the business community of Kokomo, Indiana, an offer that included a plant site and money to finance the move.

Stock sales, in the amount of $50,000, would keep the industry in St. Cloud; it was suggested. Diamond had been paying six percent dividends on its stock and planned eight percent for the current year. This, they were quick to point out, was from earnings, not from the proceeds of additional stock sales.

A "Committee to Keep Diamond Motor Parts in St. Cloud" was formed and began to canvas the city for support. The loss of the company would mean several things to St. Cloud, the committee claimed:

> Loss of the $300,000 annual payroll and loss of another $125,000 distributed in the city in various ways;
> One hundred fifty vacant homes and the loss of the tax revenue from these homes;
> St. Cloud would get the reputation for being a "dead one" and will suffer a business depression that will take years to overcome.

Not the least of the committee's support came from a source they might not have expected—Samuel Pandolfo. He urged immediate and large purchases of stock as "the only thing that St. Cloud citizens could rightfully do under the circumstances. There is no chance of loss to anyone, and there is everything to gain."

The Kokomo offer was a difficult one to refuse; not only would the company have a new plant free of charge, it was reported, but the St. Cloud plant could then be sold for cash. Somehow, after a week of talking in Chicago, Bouthinon and Quigley were able to convince the directors that the St. Cloud location was best. Bouthinon then revealed the name of the third company involved in the merger: the Schleider Valve Company of Detroit. The name had been given as the Fulton Company for two reasons, he said. Schleider had a contract with a large automobile company, and the contract might have been canceled before the location was decided; secondly, another company, a competitor of Diamond, had been trying to effect a merger with Schleider and the news might have set off new efforts.

"Schleider produces what is considered one of the best valves in the industry," Bouthinon said. "They have made valves for Chandler, the

Cleveland tractor, Waukesha Motors, and for Chevrolet until recently, when Chevrolet decided to make their own."

The merger meant new officers for the company. Bouthinon remained as president, Elmer J. Smith became vice president, F. B. Moxham treasurer, and Vern Schleider secretary. Bouthinon explained the further duties of the officers. "Mr. Moxham will remain as plant superintendent; Mr. Smith, who was president of the Gill Company, will be general sales manager; and Mr. Schleider will be in charge of sales to automobile manufacturers. This merger means that our company will now have outlets with over half of the 2,500 jobbers in the nation," Bouthinon said proudly.

Coincidental with the Diamond-Gill-Schleider merger, Pandolfo, on a more limited scale, was starting the promotion of the greaseless donut. The first ad appeared in a special edition of the *Daily Times*, published to express appreciation to the Great Northern Railroad.

The New Ford Will Be a Good Car . . . But Cheap!

> Henry makes the Lincoln, but not at the Ford price, because of the difference in quality. You get what you pay for. Your Chevrolet is made by General Motors. So is the Cadillac. And there is no comparison on quality or price.
>
> So it is with Do-Nuts. From now on Pandolfo will make and sell whole wheat, greaseless, raisin Do-Nuts, the real health food, and the price will be 30¢ a dozen.
>
> In Do-Nuts, as in all other things, you get what you buy and pay for. You need the food value and iron and roughness in this palatable health food.
>
> Buy some every day and do your bit in helping a new industry on the GREAT NORTHERN line go over big. They will give you more health, pep and strength and bring home the bacon. On sale at all Grocery stores and eat shops from and including November 26 on.

This first ad, mentioning the long-awaited Model A Ford that Henry was just releasing to dealers, was followed by a week-long series of small ads for the Pandolfo Company, as it was first called. All of the ads stressed the health aspect of greaseless donuts and used such catch-lines as **THE BODY AND MIND MUST BE FIT FOR EVERY DEMAND,** and **GOOD HEALTH PRODUCES MORE PEP AND IT CLEARS YOUR MIND,** and **SICKNESS IS CAUSED BY THE FOOD YOU EAT OR THAT YOU FAIL TO EAT.**

One, titled simply **KEEP FIT,** summed up the health message:

> There are more food value and medicinal properties in one dozen of Pan's whole wheat, raisined, greaseless Do-Nuts than

> in two pounds of choice beef steak and far better for the digestive organs.
>
> Every element of food value and tonic will be found in these wonderful health Do-Nuts. One every morning for each of your family will keep the doctor away and put iron in your blood and clean the digestive tract of all foul, decayed matter and will brighten your eye, clear the skin and put more life in your step. They will give you pep.
>
> Demand them at all grocery stores and eat shops. They are 30¢ a dozen. If necessary, call at my business place at 14 6th Avenue North for them.

Another ad promised "If every family in St. Cloud will use these wonderful health Do-Nuts daily, in two months I will have a health food factory going here that will put the town on the map." Another made a unique offer: "Pan's whole-wheat, raisin, greaseless Do-Nuts will keep you well or will correct many troubles. Try Them. If you will eat one a day and do not feel better at the end of the month, I will pay a cash bonus if you make affidavit to that effect."

It was clear that Forsyth's deft touch in the Pan advertising was lacking in these blunt, rambling messages.

In December, chocolate-covered Do-Nuts, at 55¢ a dozen, were added to the product line just in time for Christmas.

At Diamond Motors, the stockholders increased the company's capitalization from two million to three million dollars, and the board of directors was increased from five to seven. Elmer J. Smith and Vern W. Schleider joined Bouthinon, Thomas Kernan, F. B. Moxham, Charles F. Wilbert, and M. F. Murray on the board. Ben Forsyth returned to the old Pan plant as advertising manager for Diamond in January, 1928. (He had left St. Cloud three or four years earlier to join the advertising department of International Harvester Company in Minneapolis and later had moved to the Bureau of Engraving in St. Paul.)

By mid-February, the machinery from Gill's Chicago plant had been installed at St. Cloud, and production was started with an initial order for 100,000 piston rings.

Meanwhile, a sometimes strange and often mysterious interlude was taking place in the Pandolfo Manufacturing plant. In December, 1927, John Crever, the trustee for the Pandolfo bondholders, made overtures to city and county officials concerning a reduction of the back taxes that had accrued on the property. Both the city commission and the county commissioners had tentatively agreed to a 50 percent reduction on the taxes, subject to the approval of the state tax commission, if it could help get the property sold and back in production.

In May, 1927, practically every person in the world who could be reached by the news waited while a thin, boyish young man took a silver monoplane down a muddy runway at Roosevelt Field in New York and disappeared into the rainy dawn, headed for Paris. Lindbergh and the Spirit of St. Louis—"We"—made it. And in the rush of sudden interest in aviation, St. Cloud, next door to the Little Falls, home of Lucky Lindy, did not want to be left behind.

So, in February 1928, Crever disclosed that the company on whose behalf he had been seeking a tax reduction on the Pandolfo plant was Midwest Aircraft Corporation. Not so strangely, the spokesman for Midwest Aircraft Corporation was the ubiquitous Charles N. Beyhan, who had also been spokesman for the Glide Road Machinery Company, for a Pan Motor Company stockholder group, and, unofficially, it seems, for several granite companies in the area. Midwest Aircraft, Beyhan said, had been "sponsored" (whatever that meant) by officers of the Consumers Home Oil Company who, with some other Minneapolis and St. Paul people, had bought all the stock in the company. The fact that local people were not being asked to support the company financially—except by the cancellation of 50 percent of the back taxes—was a novelty. Beyhan's first approach to Crever had been on the matter of the taxes, and it was agreed that an offer of $20,000 for the property would be made by Midwest and accepted by Crever and Judge Roeser if the $14,000 tax load could be halved. Midwest also bargained for 36 acres adjoining the property, hoping to use it for an airport and an aviation school. The taxes due on the acreage were greater than the appraised value the court had placed on the land, and the property had been available to anyone who would pay the delinquent taxes.

Later, Midwest made an offer of $10,000 to cover all back taxes and to pay $30,000 in cash to the city and bondholders whenever an agreement was reached. But, according to Beyhan, the city, instead of accepting this offer, asked for $23,000 in payment of back taxes. Midwest then began receiving offers from other cities, Fargo, North Dakota, among others.

"I have discussed this with A. F. Bonzer, Junior, the president of our company," Beyhan reported, "and we can better afford to accept the other offers. We have no St. Cloud stockholders to be beholden to, and we're free to locate anywhere."

Then Beyhan casually mentioned his better mousetrap. "The demand for airplane engines has grown so much that the manufacturers of the OX-5, the most popular engine, cannot meet demand, and they have engaged Victor Gauvreau, the man who designed the magnificent Pan car, to design an engine for us. He is now the president of his own consulting engineering company, the Govro-Nelson Company in Detroit, and he has been retained as a designer and consultant by our company."

No one had mentioned this to Gauvreau. After two years with the St. Cloud Hudson Essex dealership, Gauvreau had sold out to W. J. Hornibrook and had moved back to Detroit. With Joseph Nelson, the experimental engineer at Pan, he had formed the Govro-Nelson Company in

1923. The closest business association their company had back in Minnesota after starting their Detroit business was a commission, in 1924-25, from a group of Minneapolis businessmen to design a car called the Masterbilt. It featured an air-cooled engine, and Gauvreau's friend and former Pan co-worker, Edgard DeSmet, had designed the body. One experimental model was built in Detroit, but the group backing it ran out of money and the project was abandoned.

It was Victor Gauvreau's last association with Minnesota-based backing. But he was now being touted as the designer of a new aircraft engine, some specifications of which were cited by Beyhan. It was to be a seven-cylinder radial design, air-cooled, producing 115 horsepower. Beyhan said airplane manufacturers from the middle states had shown great interest in the engine.

On February 28, 1928, the St. Cloud city commission, in a generous and hopefully far-sighted move, agreed to eliminate all but $800 of the back taxes due on the Pandolfo Manufacturing plant. It left to Midwest Aircraft and the Pandolfo bondholders to decide who would absorb the $800.

Early in March, before that decision was reached, there came to St. Cloud a man who rivaled even Pandolfo in getting attention: Captain W. Hoseas Mohlar, recently of the Lafayette Escadrille of World War I fame. Mohlar, who preferred to be called "Flying Hoseas," came to St. Cloud to negotiate with Midwest Aircraft for the construction of his plane, the *Spirit of Kansas City*, designed by the American Eagle Company of Kansas City. It was a huge, three-engine design, and it was to be used by George Haldeman on a flight from London to New York in the summer. Within a few weeks, though, Haldeman was no longer mentioned, and Flying Hoseas had joined Midwest Aircraft as designer and engineer. He was drawing plans for the remodeling of the Pandolfo plant, and Beyhan announced that Midwest Aircraft would sign a lease on the building with Crever. "Workmen will start remodeling tomorrow."

Then Midwest Aircraft Corporation, like Glide Road Machinery Company before it, flew quietly out of public sight.

But not Flying Hoseas. Mohlar remained in St. Cloud, and in May 1928, incorporation papers for the North Star Aircraft Corporation of St. Cloud were filed in St. Paul listing Hoseas Mohlar as one of the incorporators. (Other incorporators were Aloys Zierten, Merrill Firebaugh, Marlin Barker, Frederick Heinzel, all of St. Cloud, and Ben J. Korte of St. Rosa.) The capitalization of the company was fixed at $50,000, and in June they moved into the Schoener Building in St. Cloud, south of St. Germain street, between Ninth and Tenth Avenues, just west of St. Mary's Grade School. They had, it was claimed, orders for "dozens of machines as designed by Captain Mohlar." Mohlar called the plane he was designing the *Liberty Belle*. Sadly, for it held much promise, the *Liberty Belle*, flown by a test pilot, crashed near Albany, Minnesota, on its maiden flight. The crash was the end of Mohlar as well, who, it turned out, had never been with the Lafayette Escadrille.

In December, after introducing chocolate-covered donuts, Pandolfo found he had flooded the St. Cloud market for his donut pans. He left for an extended tour of the Dakotas and Montana. Clarence Brinkman, a young baker, was hired by Pandolfo to accompany him.

As they traveled through the rural areas, Brinkman said, a routine soon developed. "In the small towns, Pandolfo would rent or somehow arrange for the use of a country schoolhouse or something similar. I would move in my equipment and start making greaseless donuts as fast as I could. Pandolfo went around and told everyone he saw to come for a free show and food that evening. He would show the movies of the Pan plant in operation and tell how he had started it up from nothing. Then he would show them the donut pan and tell how he was going to build a business to make the pan. We would start serving the donuts and coffee then, and when they had tasted those donuts he would take orders for cookers as fast as he could write. He also borrowed money on his personal note to invest in the company."

Later, Pandolfo hired out-of-work entertainers—circus acts and vaudeville performers—and put together a variety show with enough appeal to attract an audience. He charged 50 cents admission, which was supposed to cover the costs but never did. When the entertainment was over, Pandolfo made his sales talk. One of the North Dakota papers described the operation:

> Samuel C. Pandolfo spent from Thursday until Tuesday in Wilton, North Dakota, with his traveling show, the main purpose of which was to raise capital to promote the Pan Health Food Company. Mr. Pandolfo has invented a cooker to make greaseless donuts and is asking people to help in this project and also to place before the public a chocolate-covered donut in the form of a candy bar.
>
> He is a great believer in advertising and plans on using unlimited resources in boosting his products. Mr. Pandolfo carries with him statistics on the amount expended on advertising by similar articles and uses these for arguments on the success of his greaseless donuts.
>
> The show went from here to Washburn Tuesday, with a few of the organizers remaining in Wilton for a few days.

Pandolfo had determined on a unique method to borrow money for this new venture. He would give his personal note, paying seven percent interest, on any money loaned to him. The note was renewable as long as he continued to pay the interest. It was, in effect, a perpetual note. In addition to the interest, those lending money were promised first chance on stock in Pandolfo's company when—and if—he ever incorporated. Quite often he would accept a personal note in exchange for his interest-bearing note. These would be discounted at local banks for cash. He was, in essence, repeating the method he had used in financing his insurance business.

Obviously this complicated financing required complicated accounting procedures, at least more than the attention Pandolfo was able to give it while traveling. An office staff was recruited in St. Cloud to remove such plebeian tasks from the shoulders of the president. In Washington, D.C., Pandolfo had met Captain Beverly J. Chew, an Army man whose service career had been cut short by an unfortunate misunderstanding, never clearly explained. Pandolfo had invited "Cap" Chew to join him in St. Cloud. Chew had been fascinated by Pandolfo, and only many months later, after seeing one opportunity for solvency after another slip away as Pandolfo's plans outstripped the ability of the business to support them, did Chew realize that his only opportunity with Pandolfo would lie in observing how not to run a business. William C. Wenker, from Freeport, Minnesota, came to the Pan Health Food Company to work in the office at about the same time.

An ad for an auditor, placed in the local papers, was answered by Philip Lemm. Lemm had been working at a local bank but was looking for a change. He had been getting $170 a month at the bank and when he asked Pandolfo what his pay would be at the Pan Health Food Company he was told he would get $125 a month.

"Is that the best you can do?" Lemm asked.

Pandolfo tipped back in his chair and hooked his thumbs under his suspenders. "No, young man, it isn't the best we can do, but until you prove yourself, that's what you're going to get."

"Well, where are the books?" Lemm wanted to know. Pandolfo pointed to a collection of suitcases, boxes, cartons, and file folders stacked against a wall.

It took Lemm two weeks, working ten or 12 hours a day, to sort out the invoices, receipts, notes, way bills, and various bank accounts Pandolfo had scattered all over the west when he was "out in the field." As the sorting-out process went on, Lemm discovered something that could not have been determined until the audit was made: Without the infusions of money from Pandolfo's field trips, the Pan Health Food Company would be unable to operate. As an example, Pandolfo had priced a dozen donuts at 55 cents with the costs based on Brinkman's figures. But Brinkman was a careful man, a trained baker who measured his ingredients precisely and wasted nothing. In addition, Pandolfo had added nothing to the cost figure for office overhead and the other items that were part of his costs. Lemm found, when he had all the accounts in order and proper books set up, that the dozen donuts selling for 55 cents were costing Pandolfo 58 cents to produce. While Lemm explained his figures to Pandolfo, the look of doubt was slowly replaced by one of mild shock. Pandolfo took "Cap" Chew and Willie Wenker to lunch that noon and asked their opinion of Lemm. When they told him that Lemm had sorted out the affairs of the company in admirable fashion, Pandolfo agreed to let the three men run the business while he went "out in the field."

But this solution raised problems too. The 15 or 20 salesmen Pandolfo had sent out—selling his notes, not his donuts!—were authorized to take 25 percent commission on any money they took in. They frequently accepted only a small portion down, but kept their full 25 percent commission on the whole amount. It was the familiar story that Pandolfo never seemed to learn from.

When Pandolfo joined them in the field, he "gingered them up," as he had done for his Pan Motor stock salesmen, and the money would flow into the offices in St. Cloud. Lemm saw his books go out of the red and start to show a modest profit because he was now able to pay invoices on time and take advantage of buying opportunities. Then word would come from Pandolfo that he had just purchased 3,000 pounds of chocolate and had written a check for the full amount. Shortly thereafter the bank would notify Lemm that the account was again overdrawn.

From one of his field trips Pandolfo returned with notes amounting to $400,000. He had taken in $70,000 in cash but retained only $4000 after the expenses were paid. When he was in the office he was apt to buy beyond the company's ability to absorb either the cost or the supplies.

A seedless raisin salesman called at the office one day and Pandolfo, eager to impress, waved aside the usual price discount the salesman quoted. "Now, you sharpen your pencil, young man, and give me your best price on ten thousand pounds." The salesman figured furiously, quivering with delight. Despite desperate wig-wagging from Lemm, Chew, and Wenker behind the salesman's back, Pandolfo placed the order. When the office staff asked him where they would store that many raisins, Pandolfo said the more pressing problem was how to pay for them. And he left them to figure out the storage problem while he went "out in the field" to raise the money.

In spite of a parade of similar incidents, the three office men were making headway. They figured they could get the cost of the donuts down if they could control Pandolfo's urge to buy anything and everything. Keeping him in the field seemed to solve one side of the problem, at least.

Pandolfo was doing so well raising money that in April 1928 the Securities Commission of North Dakota, claiming that Pandolfo had raised some $20,000 in Ward County alone, conducted an investigation to determine if he was in violation of the state's blue sky laws. They discovered he was raising money on his personal notes alone and therefore did not come under their jurisdiction.

By May, Pandolfo was predicting that his donut business would soon be making profits of $500 a day. His wife Agnes had developed a variety of small fruit pies, and these were added to the line. Lemm, Wenker, and Chew now had several salesmen—for the food line, not the notes—and the accounts they were opening throughout the state soon began to flood the small bakery with orders. The word was out that Pandolfo, as he did in every enterprise, produced a superior product. The Pan Health Food Company was soon shipping their donuts to other bakeries to be sold by their route men. Pandolfo was not talking in specifics yet, but he mentioned some property he had in east St. Cloud where he might put up a plant. But the summer passed, the plant was not started, and in October he headed west again to raise more money.

While the Pan Health Food Company marked time for the moment, Diamond Motor Parts was expanding. With the successful completion of the Gill and Schleider mergers, Bouthinon announced the purchase of the Security Muffler Company of Utica, New York. Diamond was growing so rapidly that Bouthinon could report at the stockholder meeting in September that sales had increased 650 percent over the year before. At the National Standard Parts Association exhibition in Cleveland that November Diamond Motor Parts had the largest exhibit at the show, occupying seven booths and featuring an enlargement of a page from the new "E-Z Find Parts Catalog," designed by Ben Forsyth, and an eight-foot-long model of the Diamond plant in St. Cloud. The company was being referred to as the "General Motors of replacement parts."

The recognition coming to the occupant of the former Pan Motor plant stirred Pandolfo to activity. He was back in town for the winter, and he announced he had leased the Peters Building, on the north side of St. Germain Street between Fifth and Sixth avenues, and had plans for a cafe that would serve coffee, donuts, and "Pan Health Pies" at five cents each. His campaign began with a full page ad in the local papers on December 6.

PANDOLFO'S MOTTO IS
A Quitter Cannot Win, and a Winner Never Quits
Also - Any Dead Fish Can Float Downstream,
But It Takes a Live One to Swim Up.

Who is Pandolfo? Well, he is the man who organized and built the Pan Motor Company, and it was always growing and in good condition when he got out of it.

Many people in and out of St. Cloud say that Pandolfo put St. Cloud on the map. Also Pandolfo built Pan-Town-on-the-Mississippi. There are monuments of achievement here in St. Cloud to the credit of Pandolfo, and St. Cloud has been profiting by them for 11 years.

Many people in the United States want to know what Pandolfo is doing now. The Answer follows:

Pandolfo is building the Pan Health Food Company. It is a manufacturing concern. It is concentrating on the greaseless, whole wheat, raisin, chocolated do-nut. It is running three shifts 24 hours a day in making this do-nut. This do-nut will keep fresh indefinitely. It is a health food and also a delicious confection. It is rich in iron and has a special iodine content. It embodies all the food elements required by the parts of the human body.

It is a perfect food. It is very palatable. It retails for 5¢ each or 55¢ a dozen. An expert of one of the biggest manufacturers of drugs in the world writes from Detroit, Michigan: "Let me first say that your do-nuts are most delicious and I am wondering if they can be obtained in Detroit."

Also a big manufacturer in Illinois who had them analyzed in his laboratory writes: "Your interesting baked samples were also received and samples were duly tested by us as suggested, and we have inside information that they are all you claim for them."

Premature death, untimely old age, and sickness are caused more from improper eating and unsuitable foods than from any other one thing. One or two of Pan's greaseless, whole wheat, raisin, chocolated do-nuts a day may "keep the doctor away." Eat them every day.

The Pan Health Food Company is now shipping these do-nuts to many states. The company will soon be marketing two other kinds of do-nuts, namely, the greaseless, whole wheat, raisin, and also the plain. The company will also have on the market very soon three kinds of five cent individual pies sanitarily wrapped: the raisin, the apple, and the peach.

It is also the company's plan to bring out a special health bread in the near future. There are many other unique products to follow as rapidly as the company can get to them.

The company is also marketing its greaseless do-nut cooker which can be used in any stove or oven and it retails for only $5.00.

The company recently leased the granite building on St. Germain Street from the Cold Spring Brewing Company and in the front part of it is putting in the most up-to-date do-nut, coffee, and sandwich parlor in existence. It will be a thing of art and efficiency. There is no other place in the world like it. It will be open to the public about Christmas time. Watch St. Cloud papers for announcements about the opening date.

It is the company's intention to put in a chain of do-nut, sandwich, and coffee parlors all over the United States patterned after the one now being established in St. Cloud. The company has placed orders recently for about $17,000 in additional equipment which should be received this month.

Some famous writers commenting on life have said:

"Nature to each allots his proper sphere."
-Congreve
"They who forgive most shall be forgiven."
-Bailey
"Riches have wings and grandeur is a dream."
-Cowper
"The paths of glory lead but to the grave."
-Gray
"What is ambition? 'Tis a glorious cheat."
-Willis
"The way to bliss lies not on beds of down."
-Francis Quarles
"How long we live, not years but actions tell."
-Watkins
"For live we may, yet die we must."
-Shakespeare

Life is a very complex thing. When the end comes we can take nothing with us. But the big question is, what have we left behind? Pandolfo wants to leave behind him a memento of success and usefulness to others. What is ambition? 'Tis a glorious cheat. Yes, it is. It also leads to chains and prison. Or on a lonely isle in exile. Or to an untimely grave. But it also leads sometimes to improvement and betterment of mankind. Pandolfo wants to be of service to his fellow man. And be the means of creating opportunity and better living and employment to many.

"And man, whose heaven-erected face the smiles of love adorn, Man's inhumanity to man makes countless thousands mourn." How true! and how unfortunate that statement is.

Would it not be better this way? "If cruel words were kisses and every scowl a smile, a better world than this is would hardly be worthwhile. If purses would not tighten to meet a brother's need, the load we bear would brighten above the grave of greed."

Pandolfo believes in "Do It Now," by Grellet, who said, "I expect to pass through this world but once. Any good thing that I can do therefore or any kindness that I can show to any fellow human being, let me do it now. Let me not defer nor neglect it for I shall not pass this way again."

Therefore Pandolfo has given the world the Pan Health Food Company and its products and the opportunity it will create. Everybody is invited to come and see the

PAN HEALTH FOOD COMPANY
14 6th Avenue North St. Cloud

The jumbled mixture of hard sell, information, popular philosophy, and maudlin poetry contained everything but white space. But it was only the opening gun. Three weeks later, in another full page ad, the poets and philosophers were replaced by pens and pencils, and the hard sell had the upper hand again.

THREE PAN'S DO-NUTS A DAY
KEEP THE DOCTOR AWAY

Pandolfo Comes Back! He conceived, organized, and built the Pan Motor Company. Under his leadership it grew, expanded and was in good condition. When control was wrested from him, it was in good condition.

PAN'S GREASELESS DO-NUT
Is America's Greatest Health Food!

PANDOLFO HAS ARRIVED!

An Optimist and Pessimist,
The Difference is Droll;
The Optimist Sees the Do-nut,
The Pessimist—the Hole!

SANTA CLAUS IS COMING!

Combination Pen and Pencil Set—lever self-filling all-metal Fountain Pen, gilt finish, fancy shaped design fitted with gilt ball pointed pen and safety clip. Pencil in gilt with standard fine lead and safety clip—all in new plush case.

ONE DOZEN OF PAN'S GREASELESS, WHOLE WHEAT RAISIN, CHOCOLATED DO-NUTS
America's Most Nourishing Health Food and a Most Delicious Confection

—AND—

America's Greatest Pen and Pencil Value in One Christmas Package for Only One Dollar!

Postage Prepaid
THIS LIBERAL OFFER IS FOR
INTRODUCTION PURPOSES ONLY
PAN'S PEERLESS GREASELESS
DO-NUT COOKER

1. It absolutely revolutionizes the cookery of do-nuts, muffins, and all individual cakes.

2. It eliminates the grease that ruins digestions, fills doctors' offices, and clutters hospitals.

3. Its tight construction creates the vacuum which retains the aroma and flavor otherwise lost.

4. It provides six absolutely perfect holes pleasing to the eye and economical of material.

5. It does away with the drudgery of cleaning grease from the cooking utensil.

6. It cooks perfectly in any stove or oven, heated with any fuel.

7. It saves the enormous cost of grease heretofore used in the cookery of do-nuts, muffins, individual cakes and the like products.

8. It is made of a high grade, special patented aluminum alloy which renders it practically indestructible under ordinary usage.

9. By reasons of lightness, small space and ease of cleansing, it is the ideal cooking utensil.

10. It enlarges the menu of food preparation in the do-nut form, such as graham, bran, whole wheat, and kindred products.

11. It is an ideal equipment for households, hospitals, restaurants, cafeterias, and diet kitchens.

12. It is an essential part of the equipment of every commercial bakery.

13. It is the most suitable Christmas gift for wife, Mother, sister, or daughter.

14. It rids you of grease, gives days of peace and nights that are free from pain.

For your own health's sake, stop stomach ache and you'll be yourself again.

A coupon at the bottom of the ad allowed the reader to order (1) one dozen do-nuts and one pen and pencil set for $1.00; (2) one Pan's Peerless Greaseless Do-Nut Cooker for $5.00; (3) one Vest Pocket Flashlight for 45¢; (4) or all four items for $6.45.

Pandolfo had purchased thousands of the pen and pencil sets at 30¢ a set and was advertising them in the rotogravure sections of the Minneapolis and St. Paul Sunday papers as well as local papers. The ads proved, however, that even a master promoter could have an occasional failure; less than 30 of the pen and pencil sets were sold.

The seesaw effect that seemed to exist between Pandolfo's enterprise and the Diamond Motor Parts Company came into play once more that winter. Diamond was now operating under a threat of investigation by federal agents. A claim was made that the company was, of all things, using false statements in the sale of its stock. The charge was pointed more at several stock-selling agents the company had employed than at the management, but for George Bouthinon, who had worked tirelessly to make a success of Diamond, it was the final shock. Bouthinon had been extremely fatigued, mentally and physically, by his work on the mergers and by the threat of moving from St. Cloud. The news that the company would now be subject to investigation broke his precarious health, and he entered the hospital with what was charitably called nervous exhaustion. He never completely recovered his health. The investigation disclosed that the company, although doing well in sales, was not substantially financed, and creditors became worried.

Diamond Motor Parts closed down in December 1928, and in early February 1929, the court appointed receivers for the disjointed company: Malcolm D. Chandler, later a vice president of Northwestern National Bank of Minneapolis; Frank E. Saterlee of Minneapolis; and Elmer J. Smith of St. Cloud. Once again the Pan plant was the center of litigious turmoil. In this case, however, the receivership was to preserve a prosperous and operating company, not to preside over the dissolution of a battered and profitless business. The company began operations again on a small scale in February, after a bleak, cheerless Christmas for the employees. By March, an offer to buy the Diamond Motor Parts Company was made by Aluminum Industries of Cincinnati. Distinct, again, from the receivership of the old Pan Motor Company, the Diamond receivers had the pleasure of seeing the company's sales double over those of the previous year.

Comparing several offers made for the company, the receivers petitioned the court to accept the offer of Aluminum Industries. On April 1, 1929, when no objectors to the sale appeared in Judge John B. Sanborn's court in Minneapolis, the judge ordered acceptance of the offer. (Not only was the April 1 date coincidental, but this was the same John Sanborn who, as a member of the Minnesota Securities Commission, had conducted hearings on the Pan Motor Company's license to sell its stock in Minnesota in May, 1918.)

As a result of the sale to Aluminum Industries, the unsecured creditors of the company would now realize less than 50 percent of their claims, and the equity of the Diamond stockholders was wiped out by Sanborn's order. Many of these stockholders were originally stockholders in the Pan Motor Company.

Later in April, Aluminum Industries, to raise the capital for their St. Cloud move, marketed a new issue of stock in the amount of $2,500,000. The issue was sold on New York and Cincinnati exchanges and was oversubscribed ten times before it was opened, testifying not only to the character of Aluminum Industries but also to the interest and activity of investors in those early days of 1929. Aluminum Industries, started in 1920, specialized in aluminum castings. At the time they bought out Diamond, they had a five-acre plant in Cincinnati. Their Permite brand pistons had been used in one million cars in 1928. H. J. Hater, vice president and general manager, and F. J. Glennon, sales manager, came to St. Cloud to inspect the plant during April. They brought a new general manager, Richard Lewis, but retained much of the office staff from Diamond; Charles Wilbert remained plant superintendent; Max Murtagh was made production manager; and Selmer A. Ramsey was chief engineer.

By June, employment at the plant was over 500—as high as it had been under Diamond—with day and night shifts working. But two months later the number had dropped to 300.

During that summer of 1929 another milestone was passed in the long-lived story of another element from Pan Motor's heyday: the Pan sewer. The city had been all but coerced into construction of this facility, made super-size to serve what it hoped would be the future and rapid expansion of Pan Town. When the assessment had been announced in January 1920, it had been the largest single project the city had undertaken. Now, in June 1929, the city commission voted to refuse to pay the warrants, forcing investors to take the matter to court for a decision. The decision of the city commission was made well in advance of the October 1 date when the warrants would come due.

The city contended that the warrants were in reality liens against the benefitted property, not on the city itself, and the looming legal entanglements looked insurmountable. The warrants, including interest and penalties, would have a value of $411,000 when they came due later in the fall, and their legal status was in doubt. John B. Pattison, city attorney, attempted to have a bill passed by the state legislature empowering the city to issue new bonds to pay off the old warrants, assuming the new bonds as a general obligation of the city. During the debate on the bill the members of the legislature could not agree concerning the city's liability. They preferred to leave it to the courts.

St. Cloud citizens were divided. One group held that refusal to pay the warrants would injure the city's credit in the future and force higher interest rates on future municipal issues, if not make it impossible to sell them. It would also put the city on record as refusing to pay a debt it once promised it would pay.

Others felt that the purchasers of the warrants should be bound by the letter of the purchase agreement. They argued that the general credit of the city would not be affected if it followed the letter of the law. Besides, they insisted, the city had no right to shift the burden of payment onto property generally that was not benefitted by the improvement.

Mayor James Murphy said the commission felt the state supreme court was the only body properly qualified to decide the issue. Rather than have the city take on the burden of payment and have some taxpayer bring an injunction to stop it, the holders of the warrants should take the initiative and try to enforce their claim, Murphy suggested.

Only a few of the home-owners in Pan Town had kept up payments on their assessments; the majority allowed them to lapse. The tax titles were not even taken in many cases, and the entire sum, together with interest and penalties for ten years, was unpaid.

The question did not bother Samuel Pandolfo. He now had his cafe in operation and had hired Cordelia Klock, nutritionist from the nearby Veteran's Administration Hospital, to oversee the management. On one of his money-raising trips in the field he talked to the manager of the Miller Bakery in Denver who told him that the bakery, together with a cafe in Fort Collins, Colorado, owned by the same company, was making a profit of 5,000 dollars a month. Pandolfo saw a chance to branch out in his "home territory." He began to press hard in the field, and in July 1930, Willie Wenker, "Cap" Chew, and Phil Lemm got the word to close down the Pan Health Food Company offices in St. Cloud and move to Denver.

As Pandolfo began promoting this new enterprise, a once familiar word began to creep back into his literature—incorporation. He had considered this legal form a one-way ticket to failure since the day of the Pan Motor Company failure, but now he found the burgeoning business of health food, bakeries, cafes, and do-nuts too complicated without it. In the fall of 1930 he gathered all the property he owned or held into one corporation. The Pan Health Food Company, Incorporated, now encompassed S. C. Pandolfo, Trustee of Pan Health Food Company; Pan Health Food Company, unincorporated; The Pandolfo Company; Pan's Do-Nut Shoppe; Pan's Pure Food Restaurant; and Pan Health Food Parlors.

He wanted to acquaint the public—especially the stock-buying public—with the opportunities he was making available, and he printed a new brochure with the following description of his greaseless do-nuts:

> Pan's 50% Whole-Wheat, Raisin, Chocolated, Greaseless Do-Nut is NOT a doughnut, in any sense, except in shape. It is one of the most nourishing foods on the market. It is a delicious confection. It—above all—is a health product. It is rich in all the elements required by the human system. It is especially rich in

> iron, iodine, mineral salts, natural fruit sugars, and vitamins. There is no animal fat in it—but there are four kinds of oil. Eat one a day and keep the doctors away. They will give you vim, vigor, and vitality.

He was now making three kinds of greaseless do-nuts: the 50% whole-wheat, raisin, chocolated do-nut; the same without the chocolate coating; and a straight flour do-nut. He described his other products with equal force in the brochure:

> Pan's Potato Chips are different. They are the best on the market. They are not cooked in animal fat or stagnated juice from sweat glands. They are cooked in Crisco, and the Crisco is kept fresh. That is why we get more for our Chips than others do.
>
> Pan's Grandma Cookies are in a class all their own. The Honey Macaroons, the Malted Milk Special, the Fruit Bar, the Dainty Fill, the Cocoanut Bar, the Favorite, and the Oatmeal are going over big. Thousands of merchants are selling them every day. They are put up in neat cellophane packages. That makes them appeal to the eye—sanitarily packed.
>
> Pan's 10-cent Fruit Pies are a knock-out. Fruit is good for anyone, because of its natural fruit sugars, iron, mineral salts and vitamins. Nobody ever went wrong by eating a good fruit pie. There is 20% whole wheat in our pie crust. There is no animal fat in our pie crust. These wholesome fruit pies are individually and sanitarily packed in neat glassine bags.

As usual, he was presenting a superior product, and as usual he was taking everyone into his confidence. He reserved the back page of the brochure for his personal message and report. It was titled *PROGRESS! - Facts by Pandolfo, What we are doing.*

> THE PAN HEALTH FOOD COMPANY is making progress. BUSINESS IS GOOD WITH US.
>
> People have to eat, and we are supplying them with food. The Company was incorporated on September 2, 1930, under the Corporation Laws of Colorado. We are capitalized for Five Hundred Thousand (500,000) shares of no-par, fully paid, non-assessable stock.
>
> The State Securities Commission of Colorado, on September 3, 1930, issued to us a permit to sell our stock at not less than Ten Dollars ($10) per share.

We have a large fleet of trucks working out of the Denver factory. We are covering most of Colorado, and portions of New Mexico, Nebraska, Kansas and Wyoming in these trucks.

Our trucks call upon merchants, take their orders, deliver, and collect—all at the same operation. We get, practically speaking, a weekly turnover on all of our products. In other words, we plant, cultivate, harvest, and market at least fifty-two (52) crops in the year. That is better than any farmer or ranchman can do.

In our Cookie Department, we are running two (2) shifts—16 hours per day.

We have started our Pie Department. We put out a very fine line of 10 cent fruit pies. They are sanitarily packed, each one in a glassine bag—and the label on the bag tells its own story. We put 20% of whole wheat in the pie crust. There is no pie crust on the market like it, or in its class.

We are adding two new trucks to our fleet of trucks—and-soon we will be putting on more new ones. Yes, sir, the Pan Health Food Company is growing by leaps and bounds.

Our St. Cloud, Minn., Cafe—Pan's Cafe—is doing a nice business, and is making money. We have approximately Sixteen Thousand Dollars ($16,000) invested in Pan's Cafe in St. Cloud, Minn. Our net profits last month on this one place of business were $772.09. If we averaged this for the year, that would be $9,265.09 per annum—and we should do better than this. On this basis, we are earning at St. Cloud approximately 10% or over $90,000—and with a capital investment of only about $16,000 at that point.

Pan's Cafe at Fort Collins, Colorado, is improving right along—but it is not doing so well yet as the one in St. Cloud; but we feel very sure that it will show a satisfactory profit, and, in time, may excell [sic] Pan's Cafe at St. Cloud.

Pan's Cafe at 1060 Broadway, Denver, was opened for business on August 30, 1930, and we are more than satisfied with the results, and we are exceedingly optimistic concerning its great success. It is a winner.

The restaurant business—properly managed—is a good and profitable business. In the cafe game we get 365 crops in the year, and 3 harvests every day. It is a cash business. A cash business, efficiently managed, is the safest kind of business.

We believe the Pan Health Food Company has made one of the most remarkable progresses in America in the past two years, if and when you consider all the conditions. Many old established businesses have gone down—the farmers and ranchmen have suffered on account of tumbling prices—labor had been penalized on account of reduced wages and unemploy-

> ment—seasoned stocks and other securities have gone to the "bow-wows"—but the Pan Health Food Company, under the leadership and management of S. C. Pandolfo, has been going onward and upward.

Pandolfo then described the incorporation process in great detail and concluded:

> We believe you will agree that our stock certificate is the most attractive and most beautiful thing that you ever saw in the nature of a stock certificate. It will not be very long now until the stock certificates will be issued and delivered to those entitled to receive them.
>
> We wish every one of our investors and friends could come to Denver and go through our factory, and see just what we are doing, and what we are trying to do, and what we are working to.
>
> If all our friends and investors will give us the support that we believe they will and that we should receive, there is no limit to the degree of our success.

Pandolfo was predicting the future with the same bravado he had had when the Pan Motor Company started. Still, the business might have been able to survive the depression; many businesses did. But the combination of the depression and Pandolfo's habit of starting out at top speed was too much. The business was barely able to pay its own overhead, much less make payments on the fleet of trucks, the new equipment he was ordering, and the candy factory he bought and was remodeling in Denver. At a time when every other business in America—and most throughout the world—were marking time, hoping only to ride out the depression, Pandolfo "put his hand to the throttle and poured on the steam."

Pan's Café in St. Cloud suffered a different fate. Cordelia Klock had no problems turning a profit for the corporation—as long as Pandolfo remained away from the business. But when he visited St. Cloud she found it impossible to keep accurate records of the cash receipts. She finally insisted that he notify her when he was taking cash out of the register. He told her it was his business. And she told him he could run it. She went across the street and opened another cafe in competition, Klock's Tick Tock Café.

Klock's Café was soon out-drawing Pan's Café, and Pandolfo fought back in typical fashion. It was out of proportion to the situation, but Pandolfo decided to give away a Plymouth car. Everyone coming into the café got a chance on the car, even those who bought no more than a cup of coffee. When the big day came and the winner—Mary Schroeder, a local girl and the niece of Fred Schroeder, the receiver of the Pandolfo bonds—was announced, Pandolfo didn't have the money to buy the car he was giving away. Otto Brothers, the dealers who were to have supplied the car, told

Miss Schroeder Pandolfo had paid nothing down on the Plymouth, and they were not able to give her the car until Pandolfo would demonstrate some ability to make regular payments.

Pandolfo's first offer to Miss Schroeder was a book of tickets, good for meals at Pan's Café. When she refused them, he took off on another field trip armed with his pad of personal note forms. By the time he reached Minot, North Dakota, he had raised $500, and he returned to St. Cloud to offer it to Schroeder. Heeding her uncle's advice, Miss Schroeder took the money. (She deposited the money in a St. Cloud bank; the bank later closed and she lost her prize for good.)

Following the embarrassment of not being able to deliver the car as promised, business at the café dwindled. The waitresses, who hadn't been paid for some time, were ready to quit and stayed on only when arrangements were made to pay them day by day. But even this stratagem lasted only a short time. Pan's Café was unable to make ends meet and closed. Pandolfo's last business connection with St. Cloud—the home of the Pan Motor Company, Pan-Town-on-the-Mississippi, the Pandolfo Manufacturing Company, the Motor Hotel, and the Pan Health Food Company—was ended.

At the closing of the St. Cloud café, Phil Lemm left the company in December 1930, but "Cap" Chew and William Wenker, even knowing what the probable future was, stayed on. Privately Chew explained to Lemm, "I'd like to see how it's going to end."

Pandolfo, in a short autobiography written years later, gave his version of how it ended. "When I was absent from Denver in 1931, a few creditors for small amounts, not over $2,000 or $3,000, were ribbed up to throw the company into receivership. I was in Texas on business for the company and did not know until it was too late. I hurried back and did my best to raise enough money among the subscribers to clear the thing up and pay off what little indebtedness we had against so many assets—but they just did not have the money and had no way of raising it."

Pandolfo's assessment of his assets requires some explanation. He considered the unpaid stock subscriptions as good—almost—as money in the bank. He was still using the measuring stick he had cut for his insurance business in the Southwest 15 years earlier. And it gave him the same answer.

As he had in every previous venture, Pandolfo had spread his abundance around—when he had it to spread. He had taken only his expenses during the promotion of the health food and café business, and, although he had lived well enough and traveled extensively, he had no money saved from commissions or salary to fall back on when the business went under.

Phil Lemm described a typical Pandolfo arrangement. "When he bought the fleet of delivery trucks, he made a down payment and then never paid another penny on them. No wonder they were foreclosed."

The old Pan plant, now known as Aluminum Industries, was in full swing, but Diamond Motor Parts had not yet passed into complete oblivion. In February 1930, Frank O. Ecklund of St. Paul, chairman of a stockholders committee, sent a long letter to all Diamond stockholders urging concerted action in their efforts to "smoke out the entire affair." Ecklund claimed that Diamond's business had been good, that the company was not bankrupt but rather had gone into voluntary receivership because of difficulties that, he felt, could have been overcome with a little effort.

"In June, 1924," Ecklund wrote, "the Diamond Motor Parts Company did a $30,000 business; four years later they did $140,000 for the same month. Business for all of 1928 amounted to a million-and-a-quarter dollars. The business for 1929 would have been even greater," Ecklund claimed. Even though the company may have been a bit short of cash, Ecklund said they had many orders on hand that could have been used as security for short term bank loans. "Or the officers could have appealed to the stockholders for a little bit of capital to tide the company over." Obviously he was ignorant of the history of that phrase in connection with this business. "Instead," he charged, "the officers built themselves a beautiful lodge on the shores of Grand Lake and enjoyed themselves on our money!"

Ecklund denied or disputed many of the claims that had been filed against Diamond in the receivership proceedings. But he saved his best argument for the last. "The company which bought our plant has increased its business from 35 to 65 percent since acquiring the property, which goes to show that our business is just as sound today as it was in January."

Well, not exactly.

The threat of an investigation was too much for George Bouthinon. He had not completely recovered from his breakdown; when news of the argument reached him in California, he slipped away from his wife and nurses and drove to a lonely stretch of beach where he ran a hose from the exhaust of his car into one of the windows.

No investigation of Diamond's receivership was ever conducted; at least the results never appeared in a public record. But the threat of the investigation provoked Malcolm Chandler, one of the receivers of Diamond, into action. In October 1931, in Spokane, Washington, attorney E. H. Belden, representing Chandler, filed suit to collect 100 percent assessments against the stockholders in the Diamond Motor Parts Company. Suits against 50 stockholders for amounts totaling $26,882 were filed in superior court in Spokane, while 30 more, for amounts less than $100 each, were filed in justice court. (One of those being sued was Robert Harper Hutchinson, the man whose efforts had resulted in Mutual Motors and Manufacturing Company, which had merged with Diamond Steel Products to become Diamond Motor Parts.)

The suits were the first steps in a legal give and take that went on for the next two years. Hutchinson organized the defense and responded to the suits with vigor. At a meeting of 25 of the stockholder/defendants in his office in the Hyde Building in Spokane on the evening of October 17, 1931, Hutchinson explained how the suits came about. "In 1923, I helped raise 200,000 dollars to buy part of the Pan Motor plant when it was placed in the hands of receivers. Eventually it was turned over to George Bouthinon, who had a small plant in Minneapolis. Bouthinon moved his facility to St. Cloud in 1924 and took over Mutual Motors and Manufacturing Company, as we had called our company. The name was changed to Diamond Motor Parts Company, which operated successfully until 1929, when it was put into the hands of receivers. A firm of certified public accountants showed that at the time the company went into receivership it had $706,080.23 in assets above liabilities.

"This assessment is a surprise, to say the least. It is taken under a clause of the Minnesota state charter providing that corporations doing a banking business are subject to a double liability for stockholders. There was nothing about our business partaking of the nature of a banking business. Therein lies our grounds for a fight.

"If this goes to a trial, we have a number of questions to ask of our own. To date the receiver has made no accounting of the more than 700,000 dollars in assets above liabilities. Also he had asked for a salary of 25,000 dollars, which amounts to about 1,000 dollars a month! Frankly, I don't think he has done more than ten minutes' work a day."

When the suits came before Judge Huneke in superior court in Washington in November, two of the assessments were singled out for action by E. D. Weller, the attorney representing the defendants. He claimed that the Minnesota law under which the assessments were made required that the stockholders be given a specific time during which payment could be made; in this suit the Minnesota court had ordered payments be made "forthwith."

Judge Huneke sustained the claim, and the opposing sides retired to plan further strategy.

In December, Judge Huneke sustained another defense claim on two points. The first was a restatement of the previous objection: no sufficient time had been given the defendants. The second point was based on the fact that stock purchased by Fred McCullock was never transferred on the company books to Mary Ellen McCullock, his widow, who was now being assessed $2,940.

In his opinion regarding the first point Judge Huneke ruled: "The Minnesota statute provides that when an order has been made by the court requiring payment of a stockholder's super-added liability, the stockholder shall have a stated time within which he may pay such assessment to the receiver before an action may be begun to enforce its collection. The complaint shows that this was not done, but on the contrary, the order directing the payment of such assessment also directed the receiver to commence actions forthwith against any and all stockholders. The Minnesota court in the case at bar was without power to make the order; hence it is void."

The defendants would not have to pay the assessments.

But in February 1932, Chandler had attorney Belden appeal one of the cases to the Washington State Supreme Court, and on July 6, Judge Huneke's ruling was reversed.

The defendants *would* have to pay the assessments.

In October 1932, the cases were presented to Judge Huneke again. With the "stated time" defense stricken by the supreme court, the defendants claimed the stock was simply non-assessable. Chandler and Belden had come prepared for this defense, and they indicated that Minnesota had a statute permitting the assessment of stock even though it is identified as "non-assessable." They cited a United States Supreme Court decision upholding their view.

Judge Huneke, in the face of this high-powered decision, issued a memorandum decision advising the stockholders they were "deprived of the non-assessable defense." A few days later, Belden, arguing his brief before the judge, insisted that the United States Supreme Court had held that the stock could be assessed by a receiver in Minnesota, although not by the company issuing the stock. The defense argued that because the stock had been plainly marked "non-assessable" and the state of Washington had permitted its sale with that understanding, the attempt to assess it now constituted a fraud.

The way was now cleared for the case to go to trial, and the judge ruled that the Pan Motor Company investors were entitled to an opportunity in court to sustain their allegation of fraud. He would permit the stockholders to testify as to representations made to them at the time they bought the stock in Diamond Motor Parts Company as well as Pan Motor stock.

Despite this ruling, favorable to the defense, Chandler and Belden won their case. The defendants would have to pay the assessments.

Some of the defendants gave up and paid. But Brown and Weller, defense attorneys, appealed the decision to the state supreme court once more. The supreme court upheld the lower court's verdict. Brown and Weller asked for a rehearing; it was denied in May 1933.

Several more of the defendants gave up and paid. But a small knot of 28 fought on. On December 21, 1933, they got a Christmas present from Judge Lindsley in a superior court. They heard the judge declare that fraud had indeed been committed upon the State of Washington by not stating on the stock certificate, submitted to the Secretary of State with the application to sell stock, that the stock was liable to assessment. He also upheld that "the methods of the stock salesmen who operated here between 1926 and 1929 resulted in fraud upon the stockholders, and that this fraud was participated in and made possible by the State of Minnesota not requiring a warning on the stock as to its liability for assessment in the case of insolvency."

Finally—the defendants would not have to pay!

If H. S. Wigle were still living in Spokane he must have found the whole proceeding amusing.

Sam Pandolfo and his dog.

CHAPTER XIII

Can anybody get a fair trial . . .

IN 1930, SAMUEL C. PANDOLFO, although he never would have admitted to it, could have been called a failure. He had organized several businesses—two, possibly three, large enterprises (his insurance agency in the Southwest, the Pandolfo Manufacturing Company of St. Cloud, the Pan Health Food Company), and one potentially gigantic undertaking: the Pan Motor Company. He had, through his own initiative, caused the erection of enough homes, buildings, power plants, water works systems and miscellaneous structures to found a substantial town. By a conservative estimate he had raised and directed the expenditure of 15-20,000,000 dollars. Despite the initial success of each of these businesses, little if any of this money remained with Pandolfo, not only because of the expensive litigation in which he became involved but also because of his generous habits in equipping his projects and paying his employees . . . when he could. The monument of a thriving business that he longed to leave to his children, as an object of pride if not in their actual possession, never materialized.

In the early 30s, with the depression spreading across the nation, Pandolfo found that his usual sources of capital had dried up. The farmers of the northwest and the ranchers and stockmen of the southwest had no money to invest even if Pandolfo had created some grand new proposition for them. He returned to what had made him his first real wealth: selling life insurance. From 1932 to 1938 he bided his time, waiting for the economy, and potential investors, to recover.

As the dust bowl slowly greened, watered by the pump priming through the Roosevelt administrational alphabet, and life came back to stagnant businesses, Pandolfo, with the instincts of the born promoter, came to life, too. On April 1, 1938—the date recurs with almost calendar-like regularity throughout Pandolfo's history—the Old Line Insurance Shares Corporation filed papers with the Corporate Commission of the State of New Mexico at Santa Fe. (The name was not original with Pandolfo; the Old Line Life Insurance Company of America has been in business in Milwaukee since 1910, and there was an Old Line Insurance Company in Lincoln, Nebraska. Pandolfo's new venture had no connection with either of these.)

The home office of the new corporation was Albuquerque, and the officers were Samuel C. Pandolfo, president; Agnes Pandolfo, vice president;

O. J. Nesbit, M.D., secretary; and Chester A. Rader, treasurer. Dan A. McPherson was the legal agent, and the company assets were said to be $25,000 in capital stock. The business of the company was described as buying, selling, and lending money on premium notes for insurance, and dealing in real estate and personal property. Pandolfo had been doing something like this all his adult life, but now he was incorporated for the particular purpose.

The early days of the business seem to have been uneventful by the usual Pandolfo standards; that is, there were no giant barbecues or nationwide stock-selling drives. But there was some similarity between this and Pandolfo's other enterprises: eventually some of the directors and officers became disenchanted and left the company. Later, although Pandolfo remained president, his wife Agnes was made secretary-treasurer, and new officers were taken on to replace those who had left. W. P. Cater, a merchant from Cerro, New Mexico, became first vice president; R. E. Zellers, another merchant from Dixon, New Mexico, became vice president; C. W. Williams was made vice president and general manager; F. H. Wilson, a retired Indian Agency employee from Tularose, New Mexico, became another vice president, as did C. H. Muchmore, a state highway engineer from Socorro, New Mexico; Max Uhlig was made manager of the small loan department and assistant secretary-treasurer.

Some of these same officers were also members of a group Pandolfo called the Advisory Directors.

Three years after the inception of the company, some of the new officers and employees left. Max Uhlig resigned as an officer, Pandolfo explained, because he wanted to sell real estate for the corporation on commission, an activity forbidden to salaried officers by the corporation bylaws. R. E. Zellers said his banker, among others, had laughed at him for buying into the Old Line Insurance Shares Corporation. (Did Pandolfo then remember H. C. Ervin, who had resigned from the Pan Motor board for similar reasons?) Zellers stock was returned to the company.

Many of the Advisory Directors also resigned or were "eliminated." In Pandolfo's words, "We eliminated Munson [a stock farmer from Weed, New Mexico] and Jones [an apple farmer from Roswell, New Mexico] because they were old and getting too feeble to attend meetings. We eliminated Fitzgerald [a Roswell rancher] and McPherson [an attorney and former probate judge, and later a district attorney] and Fitch [Mrs. Allie Fitch, manager of the Fitch Corporation, and member of the Board of Regents for the State School of Mines in Socorro] at their requests, because they had been urged by my enemies to get off. We left Mr. Beck [Joseph E. Beck, a cattleman and farmer of West Cliff, Colorado] off because he lived too far away, and we could not get him to come to stockholders' meetings or any other kind, and because he lived out of the state."

Pandolfo took a salary of $250 a month from the company, while his wife, as secretary-treasurer, got $100 a month. He received no commission on the stock sold by agents, but by a curious coincidence his company, whose capitalization was listed at $25,000, paid out approximately $25,000 in commissions to stock-selling agents during the two years and two months before its president was indicted for using the mails to defraud. (Although the company had been incorporated on April 1, 1938, Pandolfo said the office hadn't opened until December, and they began active business only in January 1939.)

The indictment, brought in March 26, 1941, charged Pandolfo with eight counts of mail fraud and four counts of violating the security and exchange laws. It had been sought after a complaint, filed by several stockholders, charged Pandolfo with mismanaging company funds.

Pandolfo immediately called in all directors of the corporation and as many of the advisory directors as would come. At the meeting, the directors discussed the indictment with Pandolfo and then asked him to leave the room so they could continue their discussion more freely. When he was called back, Pandolfo was handed a resolution passed by the board members expressing their confidence in him and assuring all other stockholders that Mr. Pandolfo had done no unlawful act. (Although 13 people were listed as present at the meeting, only eight actually signed the resolution.)

The beleaguered president found himself in the same situation he had been in with the Pan Motor Company; the loyalty exhibited by the people he was supposed to have cheated must have been as comforting as the loyalty of the Pan stockholders had been in asking him to be president again as he was on his way to prison.

However, problems arose when this resolution was made public. "That caused alarm," Pandolfo recalled later. "The prosecutors and investigators got very busy and threatened the signers, or most of them, with prosecution for contempt of court and other things. That scared some of them stiff."

Whether the signers openly repudiated their signatures or just tacitly ignored the resolution is not clear, but for Pandolfo to be convinced they were working against him it was only necessary for them not to speak out strongly in his behalf.

In early April 1941, Pandolfo was arraigned and pleaded not guilty. He was released on $5,000 bond until the trial, set for June 24 in Santa Fe, then the headquarters for the district court. The trial, presided over by Judge Colen Neblett, took seven days compared with his Chicago trial, which had taken almost seven weeks.

Evidence was introduced showing that Pandolfo frequently bought stock in insurance companies at one price and then entered it on the company's books at another, higher price. Pandolfo explained the practice. "Let me emphasize that the difference between what these securities were bought at and set up on the books at represented company deficits in operation during its developing period and also costs and expenses in raising capital. Such costs are ordinarily capitalized as assets anyway, and such procedure is proper. I did not personally profit by any of it. The corporation got all the benefit from it."

It was true he did not personally profit from such entries, but it made the corporation's books reflect a situation that was not truthful.

He was accused of making similarly inflated entries involving what was called the War Mothers' Memorial. In 1925, in New Mexico the mothers of soldiers in World War I had organized a bond-selling drive to build a hospital or hospitals for veterans. After land was purchased but before a building program was initiated, the government elected to build a Veterans' Hospital in the area of Albuquerque. The bonds the War Mothers' organization had sold—about $71,800 worth—reached maturity in 1931 and were defaulted; the property was placed in the hands of a receiver and eventually sold to the Old Line Insurance Shares Corporation for $30,000. However, Pandolfo, using the same bookkeeping practice he used with insurance company stock, had entered the property on the books of the corporation at $60,000 because, as he said, "We believe that we can work out of it anywhere from between $75-100,000. We intend to sell the property in small parcels."

This arbitrary determination of the value of the land came under heavy attack by the prosecution at the trial. Although Pandolfo might not have realized it, it also reduced the profit he could have shown if and when the property was actually sold.

The trial itself was a confusing barrage of charge, countercharge, and complicated bookkeeping entries. At one point, evidence that had been accepted without question by Pandolfo's attorney actually referred to stock transactions made by his son Samuel C. Pandolfo, Jr. But Pandolfo discovered this only after the trial and made it one of the points on which he based his application for pardon.

In the course of the trial, the prosecution introduced 117 exhibits, the defense 82. Most of these were the voluminous, complicated records typical of investment transactions. As a result, the trial record required one-half cubic foot of storage space on the shelves of the National Archives and Record Services of the Federal Records Center at Denver.

Regarding the record's size and complexity, Pandolfo made an interesting and valid point in his pardon application written July 15, 1944. "On July 1, 1941, at 4:15 p.m., my case was submitted to the jury. At 8:40 that evening they returned the verdict. The difference between those two periods is four hours and 25 minutes. The jury had to walk approximately a third of a mile or more to supper and the same distance back. They were out about two hours for supper. Therefore, they had only about two hours to consider my case. The following were submitted to the jury: 58 printed pages of indictment; 15 printed pages in instructions; 118 Government exhibits; 82 defense exhibits.

"There are not 12 men in Congress, or in the English parliament, or anywhere else on earth, who could have read, analyzed, discussed, and understood all these things under 20 to 40 hours. But this jury of seven Mexicans, more properly called Spanish Americans in New Mexico, and five white men, more properly referred to in New Mexico as Anglos—all averaging in education not over the fifth grade, and none having any knowledge about, or experience in, the matters involved—did it in about two hours."

The verdict they reached in two hours was "Guilty."

The next day, July 2, 1941, Judge Neblett sentenced Samuel Pandolfo to ten years imprisonment and imposed a fine of $800. Pandolfo immediately began another long, costly appeal procedure. Because of his record in the Pan Motor case, however, this fight was more uphill than ever. On March 16, 1942, before any decision had been reached in his appeal, Pandolfo prepared to attend the annual stockholders meeting of the Old Line Insurance Shares Corporation. He had resigned his position in the company after the trial, just as he had done 22 years earlier in the Pan Motor case. Now, as he sounded out the stockholders concerning the coming meeting, Pandolfo felt he may have been hasty in following his attorney's advice to resign. He began to count proxies, contemplating regaining control of the company.

Déjà vu ended for Pandolfo here, however.

When word of Pandolfo's appeal to the stockholders reached Judge Neblett, he let it be known that if the stockholders gave Pandolfo such a vote of confidence after what had happened, he would support Pandolfo's efforts in his appeal. Pandolfo's opponents redoubled their efforts to defeat him, and by limiting him to three minutes of explanation at the stockholder meeting, they succeeded.

In May 1942, the Tenth Circuit Court of Appeals affirmed the judgment of the District Court; Pandolfo's attorneys got an order extending the time one month for filing a petition for rehearing to June.

Pandolfo's appeal for a new trial was heard in Oklahoma City by Judges Alfred P. Murrah, Samuel Bratton, and P. Phillips. Judge Murrah wanted to refuse the new trial; Judge Phillips, a Denver jurist, wanted to allow a rehearing, saying "It is my opinion that the testimony of the witness Fisher was incompetent and that we cannot say on this record that it was prejudicial. . . . It is my conclusion, therefore, that the rehearing should be granted, and that the judgment should be reversed with instructions to grant the appellant a new trial."

The deciding vote was cast by Judge Samuel Bratton.

Twenty-six years earlier, in Clovis, New Mexico, Pandolfo's debate with Alex Shipley had resulted in law suits, and they had finally signed an agreement promising to refrain from further action. Shipley's lawyer at that time was Samuel Bratton.

Pandolfo's petition was rejected, and his only recourse was the United States Supreme Court. On June 22, 1942, another petition for a *writ of certiorari* was filed with the Supreme Court on Pandolfo's behalf. It was denied on October 21, 1942.

When he had initiated his appeal, Pandolfo had been refused bond by Judge Neblett; later, Judge Phillips fixed bond at $7,500, and four business acquaintances in Albuquerque signed the bond for Pandolfo. Pandolfo later explained what happened after he was released on bond.

> While this case was on appeal, subterranean and clandestine influence was exerted on the bondsmen to throw me overboard, without notice or warning, or a chance to make another bond so as to release them. The plot was designed for an evil purpose to give me adverse publicity, and to hamstring me in my efforts to carry on my fight.
>
> These bondsmen submitted to Judge Neblett a motion or application to vacate my bond and to direct the U. S. Marshal to apprehend and surrender me.
>
> Each and every allegation set forth as a reason for vitiating my bond was a clear-cut misstatement of fact. In other words, the statements were just plain lies—and sworn to.
>
> I WAS IN ALBUQUERQUE THE DAY THAT THE ORDER WAS GRANTED.
>
> I was both disappointed and surprised to learn what they were doing. I then called in person upon two of them, and begged them to let matters remain status quo for a few days to give me time to see my friends so that I could make another bond and thereby release them. THEY REFUSED. The marshal's deputies were looking for me then. I had spent most of that day with them, before I learned what was going on.
>
> Since Judge Neblett had nothing to do with the bond in the first place, and was already prejudiced against me—I thought he was exceeding his authority or at least taking undue advantage of me. Furthermore, the bondsmen themselves could have taken possession of me and delivered me to the marshal—but they were too ashamed of themselves to do that, or did not have the nerve to pull such a dirty trick on me with no cause for it, and were hiding behind an order by the court granted on false statements, sworn to by them, and knowing that they were false.
>
> I had every reason to believe that I should win on appeal, and could not see the necessity of being bottled up in prison during the months to come while the case was on appeal. I could do more to help my wife and myself to carry on my fight in the open.
>
> Seeing the unreasonable attitude confronting me, and realizing that they would have to remain on my bond till the case was disposed of on appeal if they could not surrender me by the foul methods employed—I deliberately drove out of the state.
>
> At no time did I intend to hurt them financially, but only to protect myself against a foul blow below the belt.

The *Denver Post* saw the story in a slightly different way. On Monday, November 16, 1942, they ran the following story:

S. C. PANDOLFO, NOTORIOUS
CON MAN, ARRESTED

Reward Traps Swindler Once
Convicted of 5-Million Fraud

S. C. Pandolfo, 69, described by the authorities as "the most infamous confidence man of the western United States," was in the city jail here Monday on his way to Santa Fe, N.M., where he faces a ten-year prison sentence imposed for using the mails to defraud.

T. W. Hanna, an Albuquerque N. M., bondsman, and Ernest Salazar, deputy United States marshal, took Pandolfo into custody in Miles City, Mont., where he had been arrested after a circular offering a $500 reward for his retention was sent there by Hanna.

STARTED OPERATIONS 26 YEARS AGO

Pandolfo came to public notice, according to Hanna and Salazar, in 1916 when he formed the Pan Motor Car corporation in St. Cloud, Minn. On Feb. 1, 1919, he was indicted by a federal grand jury in Chicago for using the mails to defraud.

The indictment alleged the company had started "on nothing and had never been on a productive basis, altho it had taken over 5 million from 50,000 working people who had bought stock in it."

Pandolfo was convicted, fined 5 millions and given five years in Leavenworth prison. [Obviously Hanna, Salazar, or the Denver Post got something confused!]

In 1927 he formed a company to promote the sale of a greaseless donut frying machine and is alleged to have sold $20,000 worth of stock before the company dissolved.

JUMPS BOND PENDING APPEAL

"After that," Hanna said, he came to New Mexico and formed the Old Line Insurance Shares Corporation. Again the federal government investigated his activities and he was convicted of using the mails to defraud and sentenced to ten years in the penitentiary.

"He appealed to the circuit court and the conviction was upheld, but he had jumped the bond of $7,500 which I and three other businessmen had furnished. We had 3,500 circulars

> printed and circulated to all parts of the country. It was thru them that he was arrested in Miles City.
>
> "There he was using the name of W. H. McFarlen and had already formed another company for the sale of stocks and bonds."
>
> Hanna and Salazar will leave here with their prisoner Monday night.

Pandolfo had been arrested in Miles City by Charley Allen, Custer County sheriff. He was taken into custody on November 9 and gave his occupation as salesman. He had been using an alias, although he readily admitted that he was S. C. Pandolfo. He had come to Miles City in late June, to the best recollection of the sheriff, and he was immediately recognized as a "man about town." According to Sheriff Allen, he "dressed like a prince, was accepted in all the clubs, had a wonderful personality, and seemed to be an excellent salesman." There were rumors that a well-to-do widow was quite taken with Mr. McFarlen, but these activities were not part of the sheriff's investigation. On November 14, Pandolfo/McFarlen was released to Ernest Salazar, United States marshal from Denver.

Strictly speaking, Pandolfo's only offense had been to leave the state without informing the court. He was not avoiding imprisonment, technically, because he had not been directed to surrender to the court until November. However, Hanna couldn't be blamed for getting anxious. No one had seen or heard from Pandolfo since June; at least, no one who would admit it. United States Marshal Felipe Sanchez y Baca had wired other marshals in the Southwest to detain Pandolfo if he appeared in their territories, but he was being actively sought by the bondsmen only.

Sanchez y Baca delivered Pandolfo to the custody of the warden at Leavenworth on November 20, 1942, where he became neither McFarlen nor Pandolfo, but No. 59594. And immediately he began seeking a pardon.

On July 15, 1944, a 196-page booklet titled, APPLICATION OF SAMUEL C. PANDOLFO TO THE PRESIDENT OF THE UNITED STATES FOR A PARDON OR SUCH OTHER RELIEF DEEMED PROPER, was sent through channels on its way to the President. It is divided into 38 sections, and the opening lines of Section 1 almost guaranteed that no action would be taken: "CAN ANYBODY GET A FAIR TRIAL ON A CRIMINAL CHARGE IN A FEDERAL COURT? Observation and personal experience have convinced me that he cannot."

The application is a wide-ranging compendium of Pandolfo's opinions, from his appraisal of his own motives in his enterprises ("I was only trying to make some money for friends who had invested with me") to his view of the trend in prison population:

> Since 1910, the Federal prison population has grown, year by year, until today it is 15,000% of what it was then. Who is to

> blame? People are no worse than they used to be.... SOCIETY is to be blamed for these evils. Society has been passing increasing [numbers of] laws to make more and more good people criminals every year, building more prisons to put them in, creating an ever-increasing salaried personnel to run them, and requiring a larger and larger prison population to work, as slave labor, in mounting prison industries in competition with free labor and free enterprise. All of this is developing into a growing parasitical octopus—detrimental to human liberty, freedom of enterprise, and harmful to producers and taxpayers. Society is thus planting and cultivating the seeds that will ultimately destroy itself.

It was a unique explanation.

After a recitation of his reasons for the miscarriage of justice in his case, Pandolfo based his final appeal on his age, and he gave evidence that he had not been completely out of touch with insurance actuarial tables.

> At best, I have only a few more years to live. The average expectation of life at my age is only 8.43 years. More will die much sooner.
>
> I am too old to try to build another business by promotion or otherwise.
>
> I am convinced that the powerful invincible super government of organized interests will not permit me to sell stock to build any future business, regardless of age or merit, and what I now desire is to be able to make a modest living and live in peace.
>
> I crave some spot, in a pleasant climate, where fishing and hunting are fine, and where, in quietude and enjoyment with my faithful wife, and loyal dog, I may calmly cover my last lap over life's highway to a peaceful end.

In his search for anyone he felt might have some additional influence in Washington, Pandolfo turned to John L. Connolly, the St. Paul attorney who had represented him in his tax case in the early 1920s. Connolly had left the private practice of law and was the secretary and general counsel for Minnesota Mining and Manufacturing Company (3M) in St. Paul. He offered to do what he could to help secure Pandolfo's release, but he warned that the efforts would most probably not be successful.

Pandolfo asked Connolly to hand out copies of his application, which would be supplied by his wife Agnes, who was working at Pratt & Whitney in Kansas City, to every senator and congressman he knew, particularly Minnesota Senators Joseph H. Ball and Henrik Shipstead and Congressman Harold Knutson. Connolly pointed out that such a

Republican delegation would hardly have much influence with President Harry Truman. Connolly did, on a trip to Washington in March 1945, call on David M. Lyons, the pardon attorney in the Attorney General's office, and point out discrepancies in the record of Pandolfo's trial; how Judge Phillips, in a dissenting opinion on a petition for a new trial, had called the testimony of one witness incompetent. Lyons said it was not within the province of his office to re-try the case. So Connolly's efforts had to be confined to helping Pandolfo find people who would write letters to the parole board on his behalf.

A year after he submitted his application, Pandolfo was transferred to the Federal Correctional Institution at Seagoville, Texas, outside Dallas. He arrived on July 18, 1945, and almost immediately he was given the task of instructing other inmates in elementary mathematics and Spanish. At Seagoville, Pandolfo intensified his efforts at seeking a parole if not a pardon. Through his own efforts he got some help from what might have seemed an unexpected source.

Pandolfo had corresponded with his old friend, Bishop Joseph F. Busch of St. Cloud. Late in 1945 he wrote to Busch: "You know that I was guilty of no criminal offense in the Pan Motor case. I just got in the way of entrenched and organized interests. The same facts apply in general to my present predicament. . . . At my suggestion, my wife sent you a printed copy of my application for executive clemency. This was about a year ago. If you received it, you will know what I now am in prison for. I should not be in any prison." Pandolfo pleaded with Busch to write a letter on his behalf to the parole board.

Ever willing to come to the aid of someone in trouble, the bishop replied: "From the printed copy of your appeal, I concluded that you were now on parole, and tho I laboriously plowed through about one half of said copy, when I noticed all the local endorsements from St. Cloud, I considered them sufficient. I'm very sorry to know of your situation and hope the enclosed copy of my letter to the Pardon Board will bring the desired and requested results."

Bishop Busch on November 16, 1945, sent the parole board a letter which stated, in part:

> Mr. Pandolfo is very well known to me, as I had very close association with him, while he resided in our city of St. Cloud. When he was sentenced for alleged irregularities in connection with his promotion of the Pan Motor Company, our community considered the sentence as unduly severe, if not entirely unjustified. His prosecution was believed due mainly to the hostility of rival interests.
>
> Personally, I believe that any mistakes he may have made were due more to fault of judgment, rather than any conscious criminal intent.

At his age, and after the severe experience he has undergone, I believe it would be a humane and Christian act to grant him an absolute pardon, rather than mere parole.

I am therefore appealing to your human sympathy and Christian sentiments to grant Mr. Pandolfo an absolute pardon.

Connolly's own letter to the parole board saw to it that the errors in the record were part of the material to be heard by the board in December.

Whether Pandolfo's age—he was then 71—or his long fight, or a résumé of his application sent to Attorney General Tom Clark, or Bishop Busch's letter—or a combination of all these—was responsible, the parole board did not indicate. But on March 15, 1946, 16 days after becoming eligible, Pandolfo was released from Seagoville on parole to run to October 20, 1952.

He returned to Colorado, settling in Montrose. Six days after his release he was back at work, selling for Bankers Union Life Insurance Company. He hadn't lost his touch; near the end of January 1947 he wrote to his old friend Congressman Harold Knutson: "I have written approximately half a million of issued and paid-for business since I returned to work. Am doing very well." Well enough, in fact, to undertake another task. His letter continued: "This summer I am going to get a Pardon, or at least a commutation of sentence to time served. Of course, as you must know, I am still a prisoner. . .while on parole." The letter closed with these instructions to Congressman Knutson: "Take care of yourself. Keep up your courage to fight on for a reduction in taxes, more economy in government, less government in business, and more sanity and business in government."

Whatever Pandolfo did to get his pardon, he did it quietly. And it might have stayed quiet if, on November 9, 1947, his name had not appeared in a by-lined story in the *Chicago Sunday Tribune*. The story by James Doherty told of the activities of the House Committee on Expenditures in the Executive Department. A subcommittee, whose chairman was Congressman Clare E. Hoffman, Republican from Michigan, was investigating the prompt paroles that had been given to four notorious Capone gangsters from Chicago. Hoffman, who was in Chicago to confer with another committee member, Congressman Fred E. Busby, Republican from Illinois, said that the records of 233 criminal cases in federal courts that had resulted in sentences of ten years or more had been checked. "We find," Hoffman was quoted as saying, "that few of the 233 persons received the quick pardons given to Paul Ricca, Louis Campagna, Charles Gioe, and Phil D'Andrea. Of the 233 cases, 104 of the convicts were eligible for parole prior to September 1, 1947, but only 20 received this lenient treatment. The 20 included the four Chicago men and John Roselli of California, their codefendant [convicted on a charge of extorting $1,000,000 from motion pictures producers on threat of violence and strikes]. Of the other 15, three were released so they might be deported; others had no previous record and may have deserved leniency."

Hoffman then gave the records of the others whose paroles were under inquiry. "The first one is Samuel C. Pandolfo, sentenced July 2, 1941, in the United States District Court of New Mexico to ten years for a postal fraud case. He was eligible for parole February 27, 1946, and was paroled 16 days later. His prior record included a conviction and ten year sentence in 1919 for conspiracy to use the mails to defraud, on which he was paroled after serving no more than three years."

If Pandolfo was aware of the committee's interest and followed its investigation, he would have found justification for some of the accusations he had made in his application for pardon. The subcommittee's ostensible purpose was to investigate "the manner in which the United States Board of Parole is operating and as to whether there is a necessity for a change in either the procedure or basic law."

The report, No. 2441, was submitted to the second session of the 80th Congress, and the concluding paragraph read:

> The hearings have not been concluded. The Department of Justice has refused to permit the Federal Bureau of Investigation to advise the committee as to the result of its investigations. The committee members are in possession of information which tends to show that if subsequent hearings are held, there is a possibility that the source of the funds used to influence the granting of these paroles, the identity of the recipients of that fund and the manner in which it was used, may be discovered. For that reason, no hearings have been scheduled for the immediate future. Future hearings, if any, will be held when called by the subcommittee or the chairman of the full committee.

No further hearings were held.

Apparently, in checking further, Hoffman learned that Pandolfo's age must have been the determining factor in his release, for no further mention of Pandolfo's name appears in the record of the committee.

For more than a year, interest in Pandolfo was confined to his vicinity in Colorado, where he continued selling insurance. Then, in the latter part of 1949, the trial of Preston Tucker in Chicago on a fraud charge sent reporters digging for background information. Max Sonderby, of the *Chicago Sun-Times*, found the Pan Motor case and brought it up to date. Benjamin Epstein, one of the prosecuting attorneys, was by then a circuit court judge, and Sylvester Rush, another of the prosecution team, had returned to a judicial bench in Omaha. Sonderby neglected to trace any of the other participants in the case; it might have presented a more balanced view of the Pan Motor Company if he had. It would have shown, for example, that Pandolfo had survived his prison sentence with his enthusiasm and his sales ability unimpaired; that he had built a sizeable health food and restaurant business until his old nemesis, deficit spending, had combined with the depression to bring him down; how he had launched another financial enterprise, the Old Line Insurance Shares Corporation, which fell victim to his habits of effusive enthusiasm committed to paper and "future entry" bookkeeping; how he had survived a second prison term; and how he was still able, at the age of 75, to make a living selling insurance.

Reporter Sonderby would also have found that Fletcher Dobyns, one of the defense lawyers, had been appointed special assistant attorney general of the United States in 1921, 1922, and 1926. Dobyns had written two books: *The Understanding of American Politics* in 1932, and *The Amazing Story of Repeal* in 1940, in which he attempted to explain that Prohibition had failed because newspaper reports were slanted to show that the law was being ignored when in reality it wasn't. Dobyns had retired from the law firm of Dent, Dobyns and Freeman in 1925 and moved to Pasadena, California.

The careers of some of the technical staff of the Pan Motor Company might have made interesting reading for those like Judge Kenesaw M. Landis, now the commissioner of baseball, who thought the Pan Motor Company had been a fraud from start to finish.

Ray J. Fitness, purchasing agent for the Pan Motor Company in 1919, had left St. Cloud for Kalamazoo, Michigan, where he had become chief designer for the newly-formed Handley Motors. When Checker Car bought the Handley interests in 1923, Fitness left. He went to Reo Motor Car Company in Lansing, holding several positions including works manager; he was chief engineer for the passenger vehicle side of Reo in 1936 when the company discontinued building passenger cars. Fitness worked for other manufacturers, including Chrysler, later on. He died in May 1971 in California.

Ray A. DeVlieg, methods engineer at Pan Motor Company, left St Cloud to join Maxwell Motor Company in 1922, and by the time Walter Chrysler, who was running Maxwell, acquired the company and changed the name to Chrysler, DeVlieg was general works manager for all Chrysler plants. He joined Reo around 1930, and from 1933 to 1936 was a director and vice president in charge of manufacturing. When Reo terminated passenger car production, DeVlieg joined an old friend from Chrysler days, George Mason, at Kelvinator Corporation. Mason was then working on a merger between Kelvinator and Nash Motors Company of Kenosha, Wisconsin. DeVlieg was made works manager for Nash at Kenosha, where he modernized the plant facilities and supervised production. Within a few years he was back at Detroit in charge of all production at Nash-Kelvinator.

During World War II, DeVlieg headed N-K's war production, principally Pratt & Whitney aircraft engines, Hamilton Standard propellers and Sikorsky helicopters. Following the war, N-K, in the tough years for auto independents, merged with Hudson Motor Car Company to become American Motors Company. DeVlieg had worked on some of the details of this merger, which was completed in May 1954, but he had retired in September 1953.

From his father and mother, who met at a school for deaf mutes in Rotterdam, Holland, DeVlieg inherited a personal philosophy best indicated by some advice he gave his step-son when the young man got his first job. "Show up for work an hour early and work an extra hour after everyone else has gone." That work ethic may explain why, two weeks after his retirement, Ray DeVlieg had his second and fatal heart attack and died October 15, 1953.

Edgard DeSmet, Pan body designing engineer, left St. Cloud for Handley-Knight in Kalamazoo, and later worked for Hudson as chief body engineer and at Chrysler before coming to Willys-Overland on September 1, 1936, as a body designer. At Willys he became, successively, assistant chief engineer (1939), chief engineer of the aircraft division (1942), and executive engineer (1944). On January 1, 1947—the year in which he was one of five men nominated by the readers of *Automotive Engineer* magazine as "Automotive Engineer of 1947"—DeSmet was appointed assistant to the vice president of engineering at Willys.

He had first worked on the 1937-38 Willys sedan and the 1939 Overland sedan at Willys. When World War II halted civilian passenger production, Willys turned to military vehicles, and DeSmet contributed to the body design of the Jeep, which Willys was developing for the Army. Following the war, when Willys adapted the Jeep to civilian use, DeSmet worked on all the various versions of the ubiquitous Jeep. He also contributed to the design of the Willys Aero car. When Kaiser purchased Willys in 1953 and dropped the Aero line, DeSmet retired, 20 years and 20 days after starting at Willys.

He continued to serve Willys as a consultant after his retirement, but he began to devote more time to a project that had gained him more renown within the automotive industry than even Pandolfo could have predicted for him. Perhaps during his last years at Pan, possibly even earlier, DeSmet had started developing a system, or science, he called Planography. It is best described as a non-mathematical system for reproducing graphically on a board or paper or aluminum sheet a non-geometric surface that had been developed by a stylist and a clay modeler. The system consisted in drawing a car's primary body lines, which picture the body as a solid mass. Using these lines as a foundation, the entire surface is graphically developed with mathematical precision by following what DeSmet called "certain uniform and scientific principles." As his associates watched him work with his system in the early days and saw the results, they asked for instruction in Planography. DeSmet finally agreed to teach three fellow engineers at Hudson. He never advertised his system nor his course in it, but by word of mouth his graduates did, and the number of engineers asking for instructions finally grew to where he had to limit the class to 60 students a year.

In 1936, the graduates of DeSmet's course, with his approval, formed the DeSmet Alumni Association, principally to help him screen the growing number of applicants for the course.

From the time he retired in 1956, DeSmet continued to refine Planography and taped his lectures for future use. DeSmet died in February 1969, but his system was still being taught years later by his chosen successor, George Dolengowski. Only in later years, when computers took over many of the repetitive chores of body designing, did Planography fall into disuse.

When Victor Gauvreau, chief automobile designing engineer, saw that no new design would be forthcoming at Pan Motor, he joined Willard Hornibrook in taking over the dealership for Hudson and Essex cars in St. Cloud. Gauvreau also commuted between St. Cloud and St. Paul to teach a course in machine design and automotive engineering at the University of Minnesota. In 1923, Gauvreau sold his interest in the car agency to Hornibrook, and he returned to Detroit to form the Govro-Nelson Company with Joseph Nelson, his assistant at Pan. The consulting engineering firm started in a plant on Trumbull Avenue in Detroit, but by 1928 they required additional facilities. They were making the engine for the Aeronca aircraft (which may explain why Charles Beyhan found it so easy to involve Gauvreau with the Midwest Aircraft Corporation, although Gauvreau had no knowledge of the Minnesota venture), and a second plant at 1931 Antoinette Street was built. Gauvreau, whose engine for the Pan car had been compared so favorably with the Liberty airplane engine, was also involved in making improvements in the basic Liberty engine.

As the Aeronca business declined, the Govro-Nelson Company (Nelson had left the company by this time) began to make engine components for the Warner Aircraft Corporation of Detroit. This precision work led to the development of their own drilling units, and the company was granted patents on the units in the late 1930's. More precision work, in the development of fuel injection pumps for the Eclipse Division of Bendix Corporation, for American Bosch Corporation, and others, followed.

Gradually, in the 1950's, the company phased out of prototype work and into machining production quantities of aircraft parts; more recently the major share of its business was the production of its own air-hydraulic automatic drilling and tapping equipment.

In 1948, with his son-in-law, Orvil R. Aronson, now president of Govro-Nelson, Gauvreau retired and with his wife Elizabeth went to Tucson to live. In retirement, he took up painting, an art he had given up when he started technical school in France as a young man. His wife died in 1959, and, on December 29, 1971, Victor M. Gauvreau, the last surviving member of the technical team that produced the Pan car, died at Tucson Medical Center at the age of 83.

None of these men, nor Pandolfo, were mentioned in the story written at the time of Preston Tucker's trial in 1949. But if reporter Sonderby had dug deeper into the careers of both Pandolfo and Tucker he would have found a series of curious parallels:

Both men, presidents of automobile companies bearing their name, were neither engineers nor designers nor particularly astute businessmen. They were, principally and outstandingly, salesmen—salesmen who knew instinctively the advantages of eye-catching features: Pandolfo with his sleeping car body and compartment tank, and Tucker with his more sophisticated rear-engined car and Cyclops headlight. While Tucker had a longer history of association in the automotive field, starting as an office boy at Cadillac in 1916, (about the same time that Pandolfo was beginning to organize the Pan Motor Company) it was as a salesman, regional manager, and owner of a car agency that he gained his experience, not in the production end of the automotive industry.

Tucker's difficulties began when he was caught between the War Assets Administration and the Reconstruction Finance Corporation in a departmental squabble that eventually involved the Securities and Exchange Commission as well. Pandolfo's first brush with state securities commissions later also involved the Capital Issues Committee of Congress and the Federal Trade Commission.

Both men were respected by many people, and both were also attacked vigorously as "charlatans and crooks, smooth-talking promoters who will give you a flashy song-and-dance while they take your money with beautiful promises." Obviously, both men were also extreme optimists.

They both went on trial in Chicago, in the same great, grey Federal Building, in October, 30 years apart. (Tucker's first trial began in early October and, because inadmissable evidence was introduced, it was declared a mistrial and the second one began on October 18; Pandolfo's trial started on October 23.) Both men were charged with conspiracy to defraud. As in Pandolfo's trial, testimony showed that Tucker's first car was made of parts from other manufacturers, rebuttal testimony pointing out that this was standard practice in new cars.

There is an eerie echo in other testimony from Tucker's trial. Lee Treese, an expert on mass production methods, said that the Tucker Corporation had tried hard, that its die program was more than 90 percent complete in June 1948, and that it would have succeeded in producing a good car except for outside interference. The same argument by the same kind of expert witnesses was given at Pandolfo's trial.

Where Pandolfo had been attacked by Colorado Congressman Edward T. Taylor among other, Tucker's trial produced testimony to the effect that Senator Homer Ferguson of Michigan would have liked to see Tucker closed down.

Pandolfo's defense attorneys had claimed that post office investigators had misrepresented themselves in securing information from witnesses; SEC and Internal Revenue agents were similarly accused by Tucker's counsel.

Both trials were burdened with hours of testimony from accountants who piled detail upon detail in giving evidence on the companies' financial affairs. When the details were all finally in the record, the information in both trials pointed to much more money being spent on promotion and advertising than on development and production. The final government witness in Tucker's trial, an SEC accountant named Joseph Turnbull, testified that Preston Tucker had netted more than $500,000 from his automobile enterprise; Pandolfo's earnings from the Pan Motor Company had been given as "at least $500,000" by the final government witness, accountant Wesley Bennett.

At Pandolfo's trial the defense attorneys surprised everyone by not making a final statement to the jury. Tucker's attorneys rested their case without calling a witness! "It is impossible to present a defense," attorney Daniel Glasser said, "when there has been no offense."

At this point the trails of the trials diverge for a moment. Where Judge Landis' charge to the jury seemed to pre-suppose Pandolfo's guilt, Judge Walter LaBuy's instruction, delivered in 45 minutes, was precise and impartial. "The fact that the defendants and those associated with them failed to mass produce an automobile and accomplish what they undertook is not of itself proof of fraud. Erroneous judgment may be as consistent with good intentions as with bad intentions. Good faith is a complete defense." In contrast, Judge Landis had told the jury at Pandolfo's trial that "a large and operating factory is no proof of good intent. One of the biggest swindles [in Chicago] involved a meat-packing company who had invested $300,000 in good buildings."

Not surprisingly, Tucker's jury found him not guilty.

Then the similarities between Tucker and Pandolfo begin again.

Litigation involving Tucker stockholders dragged on for 13 years, as did litigation involving Pan Motor—and Diamond Motor—stockholders. Pandolfo had instituted libel suits involving five million dollars in damages after his first indictment; Tucker started damage suits for a total of 19 million dollars. Neither one of them collected a penny.

Preston Tucker died in 1956. That same year, Pandolfo, 81 years old, found the pace of life in Montrose, Colorado, too routine. There is a possibility that his past was occasionally intruding on his present. For whatever reason, he sought broader opportunities and fresh territory. Passing through St. Cloud on his way to Alaska in March 1956, Pandolfo said, "I'm still thinking in terms of tomorrow and the day and the week and the month after that."

With years of experience telling him what to expect in his future home of Alaska, he spent some time, both in St. Cloud and in Washington, D.C., collecting letters of recommendation from congressmen, senators, and other influential citizens. All, of course, recommended him as an individual of high honor, tremendous industry, and great vision.

Despite his age, Pandolfo did not go to Alaska to rest. On November 18, 1958, the corporation section of the Department of Commerce of the State of Alaska issued corporation papers to the Alaska Reserve Underwriting Corporation. Something new was added to—or rather subtracted from—what was to be Pandolfo's final enterprise: In the list of incorporators neither his name nor his wife's appeared. Listed were John E. Clarke of Auburn, Nebraska; William B. Witteman of Mohall, North Dakota; David K. Brower, Thomas P. Brower, Forrest M. Solomon, John F. Connery, Lee Suvlu, Fred K. Ipalook, and Ned Nusunginya, all of Point Barrow, Alaska.

The company was capitalized at $1,562,500, divided into three million shares of Class A common stock, 100,000 shares of Class B common stock, and 25,000 shares of Class C common stock; all classes had a par value of 50 cents a share. The company's principal place of business was given as Fairbanks. But three or four other items in the record tell more of the story. Thomas Brower was listed as the registered agent for the stock, and the registered office was given as "Brower's Store in Point Barrow." The purpose of the business was "to form all kinds of insurance companies, purchase real estate, everything." When the Department of Commerce asked the planned duration of the business, Alaska Reserve Underwriting Corporation blithely replied, "Perpetual." The Department reports that the record on Alaska Reserve Underwriting was stricken January 2, 1962.

Perpetuity in this case had lasted a little over four years.

The Pandolfos, by January 1959, were living in Fairbanks, in apartment 534 in the Northward Building. With his usual foresight, Pandolfo issued during that year two booklets giving his background. Possibly he felt it was wisest to present his side of his story before others could embarrass him with the details told by an unfriendly writer. One of the booklets was a reprint of his 1920 catalog from the Pandolfo Manufacturing Company titled "Our Family Album." With a few pages added on, it brought some of his history up to date and added his opinion of some of the verdicts that had been returned against him. A second booklet, titled "Brief History and Background of S. C. Pandolfo," went into greater detail. Much of it was picked up from his application for pardon sent to the president from prison in 1944; it too was brought up to date. He was factual in both booklets but also very selective; his idea of the charges brought against him in 1919 ignored the items in the indictment and concentrated on such things as his letterhead and one line used in advertising the Pan Tank Tread Tractor.

His last paragraph in the "Brief History" booklet—perhaps the last paragraph he ever wrote for public view—should be the one by which he is remembered. At the conclusion of 56 pages of explanation, history, quoted correspondence, and reproduced letters, in all of which his life is somehow conjured up, he states simply:

> It is sincerely hoped that the review of some of the activities of my life which I have set forth on the pages of this pamphlet will serve to provide basic information to all interested persons. Without the review it can be understood that the whispered word, the rumor or innuendo could result in misunderstanding and distrust. All may be sure that I am not proud of nor pleased about the two convictions that have been outlined here, but I have taken for myself a full measure of consolation, and may I say pride, in the knowledge that had the two described ventures been permitted to continue, all present evidence in my opinion, points to the conclusion that investors would have been well rewarded.

Early in December 1959, at the age of 85, Pandolfo required a doctor, and Dr. Daniel E. Tatum was called. Pandolfo's condition was not serious enough at that time to prevent him from making plans for "tomorrow and the day and the week and the month after that," and later in December he telephoned Robert Sis, a young friend in St. Cloud, and asked him to come to work in Alaska. Sis asked what his duties would be, and Pandolfo said that he needed someone to chauffeur him; he was getting too old to drive for himself. (Pandolfo, the man who had been driving since his first Jeffrey-built Rambler, who had worn out, by his own count, 37 cars before starting his own car company, who had used Fords almost continually after that, was now driving a made-in-Sweden Volvo!) Sis' duties in St. Cloud were such that he could not give a definite answer then, and it was decided to wait until after Christmas for the final decision. With a cheery seasonal greeting, Pandolfo promised Sis he would call back "next year."

Shortly before Christmas Pandolfo suffered a cerebral hemorrhage and was taken to St. Joseph's Hospital in Fairbanks. His age mitigated against recovery, but for the first two and a half weeks of 1960 he held on. Then, around January 20, Dr. Tatum diagnosed bronchial pneumonia, and Pandolfo's condition deteriorated.

The last week of January had been extraordinarily cold, even for Alaska. Nights were getting down to 40 degrees below zero, and the temperature during the daytime barely reached zero. It was unlikely weather for a man from the Southwest, one who liked "warm days and soft nights," who had complained more than once about Minnesota's "frozen winters," and who had said in his application for pardon, "I crave some spot, in a pleasant climate. . . ."

Pandolfo's remarkable vigor, the strength evident 40 years earlier that had allowed him to recover his health quickly in 1926 and in 1946, fought off this last attack on his life for a week. But the years had accrued, and even Pandolfo's strength and will had limits. At one o'clock on the cold afternoon of January 27, 1960, Samuel Conner Pandolfo died at the age of 85. His wife Agnes was with him. His other immediate survivors were his sister Lena in Arlington, Virginia, his son Samuel in Denver, and his daughter Vivian in El Paso.

Services were held at ten in the morning on February 1 at the Fairbanks Memorial Chapel. Then Samuel Pandolfo, the man who had wanted "my dust to mingle with yours in St. Cloud," was buried in the Birch Hill Cemetery in Fairbanks. The weather, under increasing cloudiness, had warmed a bit.

The Pan 1919 Three-Passenger Roadster, planned but never built.

This cover on the Pan house organ sent to its salesmen featured the sign designed and built by the Fox Sign Company of St. Cloud. The photo was taken with Miss Laura Ward in the "Pan car" before the sign was hung on the northeast corner of Factory No. 2.

This machine is digging the trench for the sewer lines connecting Pan-Town to the municipal sewer system; apart from the buildings, this was the longest-lasting involvement of the city with Pandolfo.

Mrs. Pandolfo and her driver stand beside the family Packard, not the Pierce Arrow printing salesman Richard Daggy thought Pandolfo was using before Pan cars were available. The photo appears to have been taken at the rear of the Pandolfo home, with the water tower of the Pan plant in the background. The driver appears to have been prepared for deeper snow; there are chains on the back wheels.

Pandolfo family members identified as *(standing, l. to r.)* Samuel Pandolfo III, Egbert Pandolfo; *(seated, l. to r.)* Samuel C. Pandolfo, great grandson, Rodney Pandolfo, great grandson, Samuel Pandolfo, Jr.

These are the last known portraits of Samuel Conner Pandolfo. The one on the right was taken to be used on his last printed *apologia*, A BRIEF HISTORY AND BACKGROUND OF SAMUEL PANDOLFO, printed in Alaska.

EPILOGUE

THE LEGACY THAT Samuel Conner Pandolfo and the Pan Motor Company bequeathed to St. Cloud was, as his presence was at various times, both a blessing and a curse. The physical properties of Pandolfo's enterprises remained for a time as liabilities to the city as well as to the individuals who had invested money in them. They were also constant reminders of what might have been.

The Pandolfo Manufacturing Company buildings, so long unused and derelict, were finally taken over by Megarry Brothers road construction company. In the fall of 1972, the premises were vacated again when Megarry closed down. But both the office building and the factory are presently in use.

The buildings of the Pan Motor Company, except for the main assembly building, fared much worse. In the drop forge group only one building remains standing and in use at this writing: the Heat Treat building. At one time it was flooded and used as an indoor skating area by a local figure-skating group headed by Lloyd Tenvoorde, son of Steve Tenvoorde, who was both a Pan Motor stockholder and Pandolfo's nemesis from his bus-line days. Stearns county eventually took over the building, bricked up the glass walls, and used it as a maintenance and storage facility for highway maintenance equipment. It now serves a private business.

The large hammer shop, with its tempting targets of glass windows, succumbed early. Its special construction features made it fit for little else but a drop forge plant. In the early 30s, when Holy Angels Catholic Church was partially damaged by a fire, part of the hammer shop roof was utilized to replace the burned roof of the church. The remaining walls of the shop became a hazard and were removed; today the foundations, once visible on the ground, are buried under the overpass crossing the railroad tracks.

The main assembly building remained in almost constant and productive use. Following the demise of Diamond Motor Parts, it was shared for a time by at least three concerns: a soft-drink bottler, a printer specializing in advertising materials, and a frost-shield manufacturer (which maintained for the building some tenuous connection with the automotive industry). And during this occupancy it was partly damaged by an explosion.

During World War II, the plant was purchased by Charles Johnston, and as the Char-Gale Company it turned out ailerons and fuselage sections for the Curtiss-Wright Commando airplanes. With the conclusion of war work, Char-Gale began manufacturing prefabricated furnace fittings and ducting. In June 1945, the property was sold to Franklin Manufacturing Company, a private label manufacturer, and chest freezers, under several brand names, emerged from the factory originally built to produce automobiles. For a short time the property was again remotely connected with the automotive industry when Franklin Manufacturing was purchased by Studebaker Corporation, but on January 1, 1968, Franklin became a wholly-owned subsidiary of White Consolidated Industries. The plant, a little over 100,000 square feet in 1917, has grown to eight times its original size under WCI. During its peak production year, WCI's 1,200 employees annually produced more than 500,000 freezers and refrigerators in 320 different models for ten different customers. During 1991-92, much of the remaining original structure's east façade of the Pan Motor plant building was remodeled and a new structure erected. At the present time, the plant is owned by Electrolux Home Products, and used by its Frigidaire Freezer Division.

The houses in Pan-Town-on-the-Mississippi remain. They survive today as sturdy reminders of the excitement that was a part of those days before 1920. One of the longest lasting items of Pandolfo's legacy is concerned with the houses in Pan Town; in fact, it is literally connected to them: the Pan sewer and the litigation it spawned.

It began in the early days of the Pan Motor Company when Pandolfo, pressing hard to complete homes for his employees, persuaded (!) the City of St. Cloud to spend more money than it had ever spent for a single improvement. Assessments for the sewer were to be spread over a large area, what was considered the "benefitted property," consisting of, in addition to Pan-Town, many vacant lots and unimproved tracts of land. Warrants, issued and sold by the city to finance the construction of the sewer, were to be retired solely out of assessments on the benefitted property. But many, in fact most, of the owners of the assessed lands defaulted in their payments, and the title to much of the property was forfeited to the state. The forfeiture wiped out the liens on the property, and with no source of revenue for their payment, the city's warrants were not redeemed.

As of December 1930, the outstanding and unpaid amount on the Pan sewer warrants totaled $337,575. A suit on behalf of 70 individual warrant holders was brought in St. Cloud by Ernest S. Judd of St. Paul, Arthur Regan and George Bleecker of Minneapolis, George M. Martin of Duluth, and Leo M. Rosenberger and Charles F. Ladner of St. Cloud. District Judge Anton Thompson ruled that the city was not obligated to pay the warrants from other income sources. The Minnesota Supreme Court, in May 1936 and again on rehearing in April 1937, stated that the city had done everything required of it in attempting to provide for the payment of the warrants by levying assessments against the benefitted property. The court concluded, "The city's obligation under these warrants were [sic] not, and under its charter could not be, its general obligation."

Back in 1931, a statute was enacted by the state legislature which provided that upon acceptance of its terms by the city of St. Cloud, the state tax commission would abate all general taxes against the forfeited land and would deed the property back to the city. The city was to set up a trust fund for the warrant holders, and it was to use proceeds from the sale of the property to retire the warrants of the Pan sewer and the interest due on them. The city accepted the terms in May 1931, and the deed which conveyed the property to the city was executed April 1, 1938. (Coincidentally, on this same date Pandolfo's Old Line Insurance Shares Corporation was incorporated in Santa Fe, New Mexico.) The city thus became trustee of the Pan Sewer Trust Fund and was required by law to devote the proceeds from sale of the land in the "benefitted area" to retirement of the warrants plus the interest due.

As cash accumulated in the trust fund from year to year, payments in the form of dividends were made to warrant holders and to the city itself. Dividends, ranging from five to 20 percent, were declared by the city in the years from 1941 to 1961 totaling 100 percent. Most of this amount had been realized from sale of the property in the newly platted Centennial Addition.

In 1962, the city requested a report from the state public examiner's office concerning the financial affairs of the Pan Sewer Trust. The report, submitted on May 18, 1962, listed all of the income and disbursements of the Pan Sewer Trust Fund to that date and concluded:

> The actual cash dividends paid on the principal during the past 20 years amounted to . . . $347,347.97 as compared with the amount due of $360,746.79. The balance of $13,398.82 was due warrant holders at December 31, 1961. The principal reason for the unpaid dividends is the fact that the persons entitled thereto have failed to present their trust certificates for endorsement by the Trustee.
>
> Laws 1957, Chapter 9, authorized the Council to plat any of the unplatted lands and to install essential improvements, such as sewers, water mains, curbs and gutters, and street improvements in the area. The cost of the platting and the improvements was to be paid from the proceeds of the sale of the land or from special assessments levied for the improvements.
>
> Because of these improvements a great number of lots were sold. This enabled the city, as Trustee, to pay substantial dividends to the holders of the trust certificates.
>
> Beginning with the year 1941, participating trust certificates were issued to permanent improvement revolving fund warrant holders involving improvements numbered 368, 369, and 370, because of the Trust created by Laws 1931, Chapter 156. Such certificates were only issued at such times when the original warrants were surrendered by the holders thereof to the City Clerk.

The final chapter in this last item of Pandolfo's legacy was written, appropriately, in a district court room in St. Cloud in March 1974, by Judge Paul Hoffman. Through the city's acceptance of the responsibility in the trust fund, warrant holders received full payment plus interest. The city was now attempting to determine if warrant holders were entitled to interest on the warrants beyond October 1929, the due date of the original bonds. A court-appointed attorney, Michael Donohue, represented the warrant holders, and attorney Gerald Thoreen argued the case for the city. The court ruled that the city's obligation was discharged; the original bonds had not provided for interest beyond October 1929, nor had the statute setting up the trust fund.

Money left in the fund was later used by the city to adapt the Central Junior High School building into quarters for city offices, which had been getting crowded in the old building, the former post office that had been moved from the corner of Eighth Avenue and St. Germain to the corner of Fourth Avenue and St. Germain.

The matter of the Pan sewer and the Trust Fund necessitated by it are finally no longer a part of the city's financial responsibility—52 years after the fact! However, some additional recognition was given to the instigator of the project; one of the streets in the newly platted Centennial Addition is named Pandolfo Place.

Perhaps the most insidious, elusive legacy the Pan Motor Company bequeathed to St. Cloud was an attitude. It may be unfair to attribute it all to Pan Motor, for certainly if the attitude was engendered by the death of Pan Motor, it was also fostered by the failure of the successors to Pan Mutual Motors and Diamond Motor Parts. There can, though, be no denying that the crash of the Pan Motor Company, however slowly it came, accompanied by national publicity of a kind few people locally felt it deserved, drew a pall over the initiative of the city. For years, every venturesome business plan, every new project of breadth and scope, was haunted by the memory of the whole-hearted effort that had been the hallmark of the city's participation in Pan. There was extreme reluctance to get involved, if not an outright denial or abandonment of every projected enterprise.

The generation that had lived through "the Pan Motor debacle" was gun-shy in the same way a person who has once been shot at will ever after regard a sharp sound in the light of that experience. The scars remained. In the civic attitude the scar may have been manifest in a blanket denial, for some years at any rate, of grandiose plans for civic or business improvements.

As members of the community who had participated directly in Pan Motor eventually retired from the scene, the memory of it faded until it could be discussed in jocular terms, even to recounting how much money one's father or grandfather or uncle had lost in Pan stock. As the years passed, the discussions nostalgically turned to "what might have been." Local newspaper stories about the Pan Motor Company or people principally connected with it always referred to "the time when St. Cloud rivaled Detroit." There is today a tendency on the part of many who have had only second-hand contact with Samuel Pandolfo—through a father, mother, relative, or friend—to spring immediately to his defense when some outsider refers to "the Pan Motor swindle."

It would have gladdened Pandolfo's heart. For he gave his own description of himself in 1956 to a St. Cloud reporter too young to have known him in his heyday. He was describing his return to St. Cloud from prison in 1926. "Why, there must have been 400-500 people at the depot to greet me," he said, and there were tears in his eyes at the memory. "Now, you don't meet a crook with a brass band!"

APPENDIX
EMPLOYEES
of various local Pandolfo enterprises

The following lists were made from St. Cloud City Directories for the years noted. (The employers listed were either directly formed by Samuel C. Pandolfo, or were industries which stemmed from his efforts. The dates given usually reflect employment for the year before; that is, Peter Anderson was working at the Pan Motor Company in 1917, when the data was collected. The year listed is the year of the publication of the directory.)

Pan Motor Company

1918

St. Cloud

Anderson, Peter
Atzersdorfer, Miss Mary
Bachmann, Mrs. Blanche M.
Barritt, John
Becker, Harmon E.
Benson, Miss Mamie
Bertness, Oscar M.
Bethel, Miss Zula M.
Beutler, Miss Olga
Bishop, Mrs. Eleanore D.
Booth, George
Campbell, E. Frank
Campbell, Miss Mary
Carpenter, Guy A.
Claringbole, Harry
Clausen, Arthur
Cohn, Arthur
DeSmet, Edgard C.
Diamond, William
Donohue, John
Dubruiel, Omer F.
Eastling. H. C.
Fitness, Ray J.
Fowler, W. H.
Gauvreau, Victor M.
Gorman, Edward J.
Gustafson, T. A.
Guthrie, George R.
Hamilton, Alex P.
Hanson, Olof H.
Holm, Nels
House, Bryan E.
Hutson,William B.
Jeffery, Everett M.
Jewell, Henry H.
Johnson, Lawrence H.
Kershaw, Mrs. Edith
King, Cosby
Kremer, Miss Christena K.
Kruschel, William A.
Kuepers, Bernard H.
Lahr, Miss Florence
Lambert, Harry E.
Larson, Nels
Larson, O. C.
Leonard, Miss Frances
McGolrick, John B.
Martini, Peter J.
Miller, Floyd S.
Minette, Miss Helen
Morrison, Miss Irene
Murphy, Miss Lucy
Nemec, Frank L.
Nichols, Leonard
Norgon, William J.
Norwak, Cahsimer
Nowak, Herman P.
Olson, Miss Claire A.
Orcutt, Miss Uena
Pandolfo, Egbert
Pandolfo, Samuel C.
Parent, Miss Annie E. L.
Peck, William W.
Redman, Miss Aileen
Rengel, Miss Irene
Reuter, Paul
Richardson, Miss Pearl B.
Risch, Charles L.
Robinson, Abraham
Rodlun, Troy M.
Schmit, Miss Marie
Schmitz, Miss Loretta
Selden, Charles W.
Sherry, Emanuel
Smith, Adelberr R.
Smith, Leroy W.
Sykes, Wallace S.
Walden, Albert
Walter, William W.
Ward, Miss Laura A.
Wayman, William H.
Weimer, Miss Elva L.
Wilder, Lucien W.
Wolden, Albert
Zierden, Miss Margaret H.

Sauk Rapids

Bolinski, Henry
Hoskins, William R.
McManus, Lawrence P.
Morrison, Miss Elizabeth I.
Mowan, Clarence L.
Murphy, Miss Lucy E.
Robatzek, Fred W.
Seltenheim, Miss Emma
Welk, Paul H.

Waite Park

Pelarske, Miss Clara

1919-1920

St. Cloud

Accardi, Michael
Adams, Arthur E.
Adams, Miss Nell B.
Adams, Robert
Akervik, Otto
Ambrosich, Miss Elizabeth
Anderson, Albin M.
Anderson, Arthur M.
Anderson, Carl
Anderson, Emmitt S.
Anderson, Peter
Anderson, Ray
Anderson, Robert
Anderson, Miss Ruth
Anthony, Perry H.
Atzersdorfer, Miss Mary
Barker, Charles W.
Barnisky, Frank
Barritt, John
Barthelemy, Arthur
Beattie, A. J.
Belanger, Joseph B.
Benjamin, Cyrus A.
Benjamin, Willard J.
Benn, Walter J.
Bergendahl, George
Bernick, Miss Anna G.
Bettenberg, Michael
Biganeck, John
Birch, Edward T.
Birks, Mrs. Rossie M.
Bloomer, Frank
Boock, Albert C.
Booker, Harry W.
Born, Arnold
Boyden, Horace A.
Boyle, John D.
Bratter, Benjamin
Brazee, V. H.
Brick, August C.
Brown, Leroy
Brown, Warren W.
Bruenner, Miss Cecilia A.
Brutger, Mathew
Buckman, Frank A.
Budd, Lewis S.
Buehring, Miss Emaline
Burgmeier, Thomas Jr.
Burnham, Miss Launie B.
Callahan, Albert
Callahan, Leo J.
Campbell, E. Frank
Carlson, Wallace
Carney, Charles
Casey, Michael T.
Casey, Robert
Cater, Herbert J.
Chambers, Charles
Chandler, T. R.
Chase, Oscar L.
Chirhart, John T.
Chmiel, Anthony
Claringbole, Harry
Clark, H.. L.
Clow, George A.
Cobb, George
Coleman, Mrs. Florence E.
Connell, Vergne
Cook, Miss Bertha
Cook, Louis H.
Cooley, F. N.
Cooper, James C.
Cotton, Freeman
Cotton, John E.
Crapau, J. H.
Crawford, C. Lewis
Czaika, Miss Gertrude
Czaika, John L.
Czaika, Raphael M.
Dagley, Russell
Dahl, Hans M.
Degolier, Paul
DeSmet, Edgard C.
DeVlieg, Ray A.
Dezurik, John
Didlake, Roy P.
Diedericks, Joseph
Dierbeck, Eugene L.
Dimler, Louis
Dingmann, Edward H.
Dombovy, Vincent J.
Dombrovsky, Miss Alma T.
Dreis, Haney N.
Dressling, Wilfred W.
Dullum, Olaf J.
Ebel, Arthur
Eckenod, Lloyd P.
Egan, Herbert G.
Erickson, Gust
Erickson, Victor
Fark, Miss Esther L.
Fiereck, Joseph T.
Figge, William
Finlayson, John J.
Finley, John
Fitness, Ray J.
Fitzgerald, J. R.
Flannery, Raymond R.
Folger, David A.
Forsyth, Benjamin F.
Forsyth, L. B.
Foster, Thomas
Froelich, Carl
Fruhner, Fred
Furlong, William
Fyhr, Oscar
Galarneau, O. W.
Gallipo, Fred W.
Gauvreau, Victor M.
Gebecke, Miss Catherine M.
Germann, Jacob
Ginstrom, Anton L.
Ginzel, Charles
Gisler, George
Gliszinski, Edward
Goblirsch, Joseph B.
Goblirsch, Michael
Goff, Lester
Golobich, Matt
Gorman, Edward J.
Gorski, J.
Graper, Harry
Gregory, Cristo
Griebler, F. William .
Gutt, Traugott J.
Hackett, L. E.
Hagedorn, Will
Hageman, William F.
Hahn, Lawrence
Hall, Miss Ruth
Hallberg, William
Hammer, Paul
Hanson, Arthur T.
Hanson, Olof
Harder, Edward F.
Harper, William H.
Harris, Clarence
Hartle, Curtis
Hathaway, Fred
Haugh, Ralph
Hedman, Leo
Hefflefinger, William
Hein, Albert A.
Hemmerling, Peter
Hengel, Paul P.
Henke, Harold
Hill, E. M.
Hillman, Luther O.
Hissem, Charles I.
Hjelm, Miss Ellen V.
Hogan, F. J.
Holland William R.
Hoover, Irvin B.

Hornibrook, Walter L.
Hornibrook, Willard
House, Bryant
Humbert, Charles C.
Humphrey, Hiram F.
Imholt, Miss Emma
Jackson, Miss Hilda
Jacob, Frank
Jacobs, C. Lawrence
Janochowaki, Joseph
Janski, Miss Helen
Jarpe, John
Jeffery, Everett M.
Jenderseck, Stephen P.
Johnson, Arthur L.
Johnson, Clarence R.
Johnson, E. Richard
Johnson, Edward B.
Johnson, Floyd
Johnson, Henning W.
Johnson, Oscar
Jones, Elmer E.
Jones, Milton J.
Juhl, Emil
Karstens, Walter R.
Keene, Jeremiah
Kegerries, June
Kelley, George
Keppers, Joseph B.
Kern, Leo F.
Kernan, Miss Mary
Kershaw, Mrs. Edith
Kiklas, Miss Marie M.
Kiklas, Miss Rose
Kivley, Ray
Kline, Joseph
Klinkhammer, Alex J.
Klinkhammer, John P.
Klobas, Frank
Knapp, R. M.
Knightinger, Terrell
Koenig, John
Kolles, Thomas
Kollmann, Miss Olivia B.
Koralenski, Joseph
Kost, Miss Estelle
Kraemer, George
Krall, Elmer
Krieg, Alfred
Kruschel, William A.
Kuenzel, George E.
Kuenzel, Victor C.
Kuffel, Miss Rosalie M.
Kujawa, Frank
Lacher, Eugene T.
Lacher, Quirinus, J.
Lafferior, Ollie L.
Lahr, Frank
Lambert, Harry E.
Lang, Frank
Langen, Charles
Langer, Miss Anna
Langworthy, Burton E.
Larsen, Juul
Larsen, N. William
Larson, Oscar
LeClair, Loyal
Leim, John P.
Lentz, H.
Lentz, L. M.
Lepinski, Emil H.
Lepinski, Joseph B.
Lepinski, Raymond H.
Lies, Mathias P.
Lillebak, Karl
Lindquist, William
Lindstrom, Carl L.
Lorentsen, Christ
Lossing, Clarence A.
Ludwig, A. W.
Luhring, Oscar E.
Lund, Axel
Lund, Walter
Lundin, Worth
McGee, James
McGolrick, John B.
McKenzie, Angus D.
McQuerry, John
McVeety, Miss Mamie L.
McVeety, Miss Sadie E.
Maihs, Miss Martha A.
Malikowski, John
Martini, John F.
Matson, Albert J.
Matson, Miss Eva I.
Merchlevich, Joseph L.
Mergens, George P.
Merker, Paul O.
Meyer, Robert C.
Middleton, George
Mielke E.
Milberg, Franklin S.
Miller, Peter A.
Miller, Roy
Monroe, Miss Grace C.
Mooney, E. L.
Moore, Fred W.
Moore, Orrin A.
Morris, James
Morris, John
Morrison, John A.
Moth, Robert H.
Munsinger, Melvin N.
Murasko, Joseph
Murphy, Miss Addie
Myers, Eugene
Nagushefski, Miss Augusta
Nagushefski, Miss Mary L.
Nelson, Joseph
Neutzling, Frank L.
O'Malley, Miss Mary A
Olson, Fred
Omundson, Ole
Opsahl, Hans
Orren, Miss Hazel E.
Orth, John J.
Osterhoff, Edmund
Packard, Edward A.
Page, Ray
Pawli, Michael
Peck, William W.
Perry, L. E.
Person, Anton
Peterson, Clayton
Peterson, George A.
Petters, Alfred E.
Pierce, Sydney
Pograba, John J.
Porter, Harley R.
Porter, Lynn R.
Preuss, Alfred
Rader, Miss Genevieve
Rasmussen, Richard E.
Rayfuse, William A.
Raymond, Fay E.
Ready, David E.
Reed, Ivan
Reinardy, Peter M.
Rengel, Miss Irene
Reuter, Paul
Richardson, Miss Pearl B.
Rimelspacher, Carl
Risch, Charles L.
Robartz, Joseph
Roberts, Harland H.
Robinson, Abraham
Rozmarek, Felix
Rucks, C. William
Ryan, John
Salgy, John
Salter, Ray
Salzbrumm, Paul
Samboll, Gabriel
Sand, Peter S.
Sandmeier, Mrs. Lydia M.
Sauer, Alphonse J.
Schaefer, Miss Charlotte
Schaefer, Ursus I.
Scheibel, Frank
Schellinger, Albert
Schepers, Miss Florence M.

Schepers, Miss Loretta
Scherin, Carl
Scheron, Michael
Schieferstein, Roy H.
Schiller, John C.
Schmid, Leo
Schneller, Richard
Schnettler, Frank
Schnettler, Mark
Schriver, Michael
Schroeder, Miss Frances A.
Schroeder, Joseph A.
Schueler, Richard
Schuler, Andrew B.
Schumacher, George S.
Seger, Verne C.
Segerstrom, Miss Evelyn
Sharrer, Lee E.
Shen, John
Sherry, Manuel
Shocker, Charles H.
Sinclair, Bert A.
Skarnes, R. F.
Slonezysnki, S.
Smart, George
Smith, Forrest
Smith, Herbert
Smith, L. C.
Smith, William
Soltow, Oliver C.
Soukup, Anton Jr.
South, Lester F.
Spence, F. B.
Stafford, William A.
Stans, Henry J.
Statz, Bernard
Stauffacher, Warner
Stee, Ole E.
Stensrud, Hans M.
Stewart, Ray
Stickney, Charles J.
Stiles, Ora J.
Stone, George N.
Stowe, Harry E.
Straub, William F.
Stromborg, Carl B.
Sullivan, Hugh W.
Swanson, Isadore
Swanson, Miss Lena
Tamreck, Nicholas
Taylor, Arthur E.
Tenvoorde, Miss Cressie
Terry, Michael V.
Then, Eugene
Then, Gregor
Thimell, C. M.
Thomas, Frank O.
Thompson, George E.
Tibbets, Harold
Todd, W. Roy
Tomczik, Lawrence J.
Trumbell, Eugene
Vanden Heuvel, Anthony
Van Emster, Florentin T.
Vicj, Sverre
Villaume, Charles V.
Vogt, C. J.
Voll, John A.
Waite, Henry
Walker, Harry
Walter, William W.
Wandel, Samuel A.
Ward, Miss Laura A.
Washburn, Miss Lottie H.
Webb, Frank J.
Wegler, Frank X.
Weis, Frank
Welz, Stephen J.
Wendt, G. H.
Wengert, Alfred W.
Wengert, Frank M.
West, Henry
Wilcox, Orrin
Williams, C. W.
Wilmot, Isaac G.
Wilwerding, Thomas
Witt, John J.
Witzmann, Miss Anna
Wold, F. E.
Wolf, Miss Emily M.
Woodard, David
Woodbery, Charles
Woods, Bernard A.
Woodward, Francis E.
Wruck, Mathew J.
Youngman, H. Leroy
Zachmann, Clemens N.
Zak, Simon
Zeidler, Albert H.
Zenz, Peter A.
Zesbaugh, L. G.
Zierden, Miss Hildegard
Zimmerman, Walter
Zinken, Miss Adeline G.
Zins, Michael
Zojdel, Henry
Zolldan, Hubert A.
Zopff, Hans
Zorn, Frank

Sauk Rapids

Elwell, Frank E.
Johnson, Carl A.
Leas, Loren R.
Morrison, Miss Irene E.
Olson, Harry
Schindler, Arthur C.
Sitko, Miss Freda C.
Sodergren, Herbert
Sorenson, Samuel A.
Stullich, Carl
Walstedt, Ralph
Wilkins, William

Waite Park
Bahe, Otto
Mrozek, John M.

1921-1922

St. Cloud

Anderson, Abijah M.
Anderson, Albin
Behrmann, Henry H.
Bossoni, Batista
Callen, Arthur
Dahl, Hans M.
Davis, Harry B
Diethart, Ferdinand A.
Emmel, Joseph
Fitzgerald, James E.
Hoover, Irvin B.
Hornibrook, Willard J.
Johnson, Charles
Johnson, Harry L.
Johnson, Henning W.
Kiklas, Miss Marie M
Kiklas, Philip J.
Kiklas, Miss Rose F.
Kremer, Miss Christena K.
Larson, Oscar
Lauer, Miss Eleanor M.
Maihs, Miss Martha A.
Martini, John F.
Monroe, Miss Grace C.
Naguschefski, Miss Augusta
Omundson, Ole
Paulson, Miss Lelia G.
Ramstack, Paul J.
Risch, Charles L.
Rosenberger, Florian G.
Salgy, John
Schnettler, Frank V.
Speechly, George F.
Sullivan, Hugh W.
Tomczik, Lawrence J.
Wagner, Mathias H.
Wegler, Frank X.
White, Volney
Witzmann, Miss Anna
Zierden, Miss Hildegard

1923-1924
St. Cloud
Birk, Emil S.
Kiklas, Philip J.
Kremer, Miss Christene K.
Lahr, Miss Florence A.
Omundson, Ole
Ramstack, Paul J.
Schnettler, Frank V.

1925-1926

Omundson, Ole
Sanderson, David

Pandolfo Manufacturing Company

1919-1920

St. Cloud
Blattner, Christ J.
Dorrsey, George C.
Dreebin, Harris
Dreyer, Henry
Kelly, Oscar C.
Lambert, Anthony
Schoener, Edward
Underferth, August F.

1921-1922
Baker, Arthur W.
Birk, Miss Alvina
Birk, Emil S.
Budd, Miss Minnie J.
Carley, Walter
Cisar, Edward
Coleman, Rollie F.
Dreebin, Harris
Forsyth, Benjamin F.
Gilbert, G. Newport
Gisler, George D.
Goblirsch, Joseph B.
Harris, Clarence E.
Henke, Erwin C.
Lahr, Miss Florence A.
Mack, Frank J.
Myers, Eugene
Nelson, Joel W.
O'Malley, Miss Mary A.
Pelowski, Miss Augusta H.
Petters, Alfred K.
Schulz, William H.
Stafford, William A.
Youngman, Hjalmer L.
Zimmermann, Walter

Motor Hotel & Cafe

1919-1920
Bishop, John
Johnson, Cordelia
Johnson, Mrs. Elizabeth
McLean, Robert E.
Zellner, Edna

1921-1922
Gross, E. A.
Hall, Miss Mabel
Kortuem, Miss Lena M.
Love, William L.
McLean, Robert E.
Oakley, June
Oakley, Marian
Richardson, Charles E.

1923-1924
Brumas, Harry
Brumas, Nicholas
Kampa, Miss Rose
Weatherford, William A.

Pan Realty Company

1919-1920

Cooke, Paul F.

Pan Mercantile Co.

Hammer William A.
Morris, Glenn H.

S. C. Pandolfo Home

1918
Katchezenski, Marie

1919-1920
Carlet, Walter
Czaika, John L.
Hillman, Arthur O.
Lahr, Jacob
Van der Lende, Peter

Pan Health Foods & Café

1929-1930

Brinkman, Chester
Brinkman, Clarence
Brinkman, Della
Brinkman, Lawrence
Daniels, Edgar W.
Dibblee, George D.
Dibblee, John J.
Froelich, Celestine
Lemm, Philip J.
Marshall, William H.
McCormick, Mrs. Hattie
Moran, Lucille
Newman, Jeanne
Roering, Verena
Sniezek, Loretta
Sniezek, Mrs. Mary
Steil, Mrs. Anna
Stockard, Margaret
Wenker, William J.
Wizman, Rose

1931-1932
Loehrer, Bernard
Loehrer, Clara
Loehrer, Helen
Sarff, Ethel

Diamond Motor Parts

1925-1926
Kiklas, Philip J.
Ramstack, Paul J.
Schnettler, Frank V.

1927-1928
Abfalter, Charles
Adkins, W. Hale
Adrian, Cyrilla
Allen, Raymond
Anton, John
Banach, Anthony A.
Barry, Charles S.
Barthelemy, Ruth
Bauman, Donald
Becker, Peter
Behrmann, Henry H.
Bennett, Edward
Benvit, Una M.
Bergman, Elsa
Bergman, John
Bergstrom, John G.
Bisenius, Clarence
Bitner, Richard
Blommer, L.
Bolz, Charles
Bonin, Arnold
Boos, Helen
Bormes, Richard
Bouthinon, George G.
Breen, Richard

Brinker, Anton
Brust, Nicholas
Busse, Hilda
Cadwell, Donald
Cannon, James H.
Casper, Benjamin A.
Casper, William E.
Clayton, Millard A.
Danzl, B. V.
Danzl, Roman
Delmonico, Frank
Diederichs, Joseph B.
Eickenbrock, Thomas
Eklund, Edward J.
Eklund, John E.
Eklund, Stein
Engel, Alphonse H.
Erickson, Paul
Eveslage, Joseph B.
Folsm, Chester
Fortmeyer, Henry M.
Fritz, Harold
Forelich, Leonard
Froelich, Walter
Gronning, Odele W.
Hahn, Theo
Hanson, John
Hanson, Merle
Harmann, Fred W.
Hendry, John W.
Hennessy, John H.
Heqrkle, William
Holen, Adolph B.
Hoskins, Raymond
Inman, Lewis A.
Isaacson, Elmer
Isaacson, Oliver T.
Johnson, Cyrus
Johnson, Jensena
Johnson, Stanley
Jones, Elmer E.
Junceski, Joseph
Kennedy, Eleanor
Kernan, Leonard G.
Kernan, Thomas F.
Kiklas, Philip
Kingen, James B.
Koerner, Alphonse A.
Koprek, A.
Koprek, J. A.
Kortner, Conrad H.
Krebsbach, Esther C.
Krebsbach, Rosella
Lremer, Christian K.
Kudla, John
Kuenzel, George
Kuffel, Alf
Lahr, Edward
Lahr, Florence
LaMar, Edward
Larson, Ole H.
Larson, Oscar
Larson, Roy W.
Lenner, Harvey J.
Lepinski, John
LeRoy, Benedict
Lindblom, Elsie
Loulan, William F.
McKinney, Ralph
Macho, John
Magnuson, Harvey
Malikowski, Vincent
Maness, Custer
Manger, Marjorie
Marshall, Leo
Martini, Gerald
Mathiesen, Ervin
Mechenich, John
Medich, Arthur
Mehr, Aloys
Meiers, Mack
Meiner, Joseph D.
Meline, Fritz G.
Mercer, Ruth J.
Messersmith, George W.
Meyer, Bert
Meyer, Louis
Meyron, Hans O.
Minnette, Al
Moline, Henry
Munson, Borghild
Munson, Gertrude
Murtaugh, Max D.
Nadeau, Henry
Nahan, Francis
Nash, Kenneth
Nissen, Claude J.
Noga, Agnes
Noga, Veronica
Nohner, Veronica
O'Dowd, Anthony
Oelschlager, Lillian L.
Oelschlager, William H.
Oos, Joseph C.
Orth, John
Osborn, Lyle
Otto, Clarence
Peck, Charles
Perry, Earl
Peters, Robert
Peterson, George
Peterson, Sven H.
Poulot, Donald
Presse, Joseph W.
Prow, Ervin
Ramsey, S. A.
Rassier, Nicholas E.
Reed, Howard
Reed, Omer
Reidesel, Hubert
Robillard, Leo
Rothstein, Clemens
Rucks, Carl W.
Sauer, Victor
Schave, Edward
Schmid, Hilda A.
Scholtes, Theo
Schomer, Clarence
Schroeder, Frances A.
Schwartz, Andrew
Schwartz, Reeves R.
Secord, Gilmore
Secord, Karl
Skinner, Walter
Skoog, Donald E.
Smith, Max
Smolnik, Walter
Stillman, Laurel
Surowski, Anthony
Sweet, Frank L.
Telschow, Alvin
Thomey, Nicholas
Thompson, H. A
Thorsland, Sherman
Unke, R. F.
Vogel, A.
Wachtler, S. F.
Walstedt, Erwin
Walz, Ernestine
Warnert, Elmer
Wegler, Frank X.
Wenker, Albert W.
Wenker, Johanna
Wenker, Raymond
Wenker, Robert
Wicks, H. J.
Wilbert, Charles P.
Wilwerding, Thomas M.
Wimmer, Harold
Zierden, N. G.

1929-1930

Adkins, W. Hale
Adrian, Clarence
Ahles, Robert C.
Alexander, Sarah
Armstrong, John
Banach, Anthony A.
Barry, Charles S.
Bartz, Elmer G.
Basil, Lester

Becker, Peter
Benedict, LeRoy
Bennett, Donald A.
Bennett, Edward
Benoit, Mrs. Una
Bergman, John
Bergstrom, John A.
Betz, Bernard
Brean, Richard J.
Brummer, Benjamin A.
Cadwell, Donald
Casper, William E.
Chaika, Jerome
Clayton, Millard
Collins, Warren
Cordie, Edward
Cotton, Leo
Crow, Erwin
Danzl, Bernard V.
Danzl, Clarence
Danzl, Roman
Delmonico, Frank
Diedrich, Albin
Doty, Milo C.
Ebnet, Arthur
Ebnet, Joseph
Eickenbrock,Thomas J.
Eklund, Edward J.
Eller, William
Engelhart, Elmer
Ervin, Mathieson
Eveslage, Fred
Eveslage, Joseph
Fahrentholz, Evelyn
Finn, Lester
Finn, Lloyd
Flick, Fred
Forsyth, Benjamin F.
Fritz, Harold J.
Garwell, Willard G.
Hansen, Louis
Hansen, Merle
Hanson, Glenn
Hanson, John
Harmonn, Fredrick
Harrington, Bessie
Hartfiel, Elmer
Hartman, Arthur
Heisick, Roman R.
Henkemeyer, Walter
Hennessy, John H.
Herkle, William
Hurst, Robert
Jahns, Samuel
Jensen, Hans
Jernberg, Elizabeth A.
Johnson, Carl J.
Johnson, Sylvester
Jones, Elmer E,
Junceski, Leo
Kennedy, Eleanor
Keppers, Leo
Kernan, Leonard G.
Kiklas, Philip J.
Knafla, Charles
Knaus, Paul
Kock, Eleanor
Koerner, Alphonse A.
Kollmann, Katherine
Koprek, Al
Korte, Isabel
Kortner, Conrad H.
Kramer, Albert
Krebsbach, Esther
Krebsbach, Rosella
Kretlaw, E.
Kuffel, Alf
Lacher, Eugene T.
Lahr, Edward
Lahr, Elmer
LaMar, Edward
Larson, Ole H.
Larson, Orrin H.
Lauer, George
Leicher, Mrs. Jensena
Lenner, Harvey J.
Lepinski, John
Lepinski, Rudolph
LeRoy, George G.
Lindahl, Ella
Lindblom, Elsie
Lomatz, Philip T.
Lufkin, Dorothy
Macho, John C.
Malikowski, Helen
Malikowski, Pauline
Malikowski, Vincent
Mallinger, John P.
Marchand, Maurice A.
McConnell, Ira J.
Medeck, Arthur W.
Mehr, Aloys
Meier, Mark F.
Meinz, Selma
Meixner, Joseph D.
Mercer, Ruth J.
Merrifield, Bert F.
Meuleners, Bernard T.
Meyer, Bert
Meyers, Julia
Meyers, Louis
Mihelich, Cecelia
Mihelich, Frank J.
Minnette, Aloysius
Mullally, Roy J.
Murphy, Francis
Murtaugh, Max D.
Myron, Hans
Nelson, F. V.
Noga, Aloys
Noga, Thomas
O'Dowd, Anthony
Oelschlager, Lillian
Osborn, Lyle C.
Osgood, Forrest T.
Otto, Edward P.
Pallies, Richard
Palmersheim, Henry P.
Pandolfo, Samuel C.
Pappenfus, Winslow
Peck, Charles E.
Peterson, Hugh H.
Pozarski, Helen
Pull, Albert
Randall, Arthur
Rassier, Mrs. Lucille
Rassier, Roman
Rau, Arthur
Rau, Clarence
Reed, Howard E.
Reed, Omer
Riedesel, Hubert
Riley, Edward
Roering, H. Joseph
Rothstein, Clements
Rucks, Carl W.
Scherber, Leo J.
Scherer, Ethel
Schleider, Vern W.
Schmidt, Nicholas
Scholtes, Theodore
Schuler, Lucy
Schulte, Catherine
Schwartz, Andrew
Scott, Evelyn B.
Seibert, Elmer A.
Skinner, Walter
Skoog, Viola
Smuda, Edward
Sparrow, Julia
Sprague, Elsie
Stafford, William
Steffes, Veronie
Stiko, Earl
Stommes, Bernard P.
Surowski, Anthony
Swan, Rueber
Terwey, Andrew
Theide, Fred
Thomey, Nicholas
Tindle. Gretta

Trossen, Alfred C.
Twist, George
Twist, Gerhardt, G.
Ulrich, Lawrence J.
Unke, Reinhold
Urbaniak, Celestine
Vogel, Aloys
Wegler, Frank X.
Weis, Alphonse J.
Weller, Martin
Wheelock, R. B.
Wilbert, Charles P.
Wilmerding, Thomas
Wintermeyer, John
Wochnick, Anna
Ziebol, Harry F.
Ziebol, Robert
Zierden, Norbert J.
Zimmer, Emma

Aluminum Industries

1931-1932

Adams, James
Biksen, Dorothy
Bormes, Theodore H.
Casper, William E.
Chirhart, John T.
Collins, Warren
Cotton, Leo A.
Duea, Daisy W.
Eller, William F.
Emmke, William W.
Engelhard, Elmer M.
Fharenholtz, Evelyn
Fritz, Harold J.
Grovender, William H.
Hansen, Gertrude
Hansen, Gladys
Hansen, Glenn J.
Heddens, Bano J.
Hennessy, John H.
Herkal, William
Hinz, William A.
Honer, Harold L.
Johnson, Inez
Juneski, Leo E.
Kennedy, Eleanor
Kiklas, Michael A.
Koch, Eleanor C.
Lagergren, Laura
Lewis, Richard B.
Kindbloom, Dorothy
Lindbloom, Elsie
Mangner, Marjorie
McKenzie, J. Donald
Mullally, Roy J.
Murtaugh, Max D.
Nelson, Frank V.
Paquin, Norman J.
Patka, Delia
Peck, Charles E.
Peterson, Hugh A.
Rau, Arthur E.
Rausch, Mathilda
Reed, Howard E.
Riedesel, Hubert
Scales, Merwin
Scholtes, Theo C.
Skinner, Walter
Taylor, Darwin M.
Teicher, Mrs. Jensena
Tindle, Gretta
Ulrich, Liola
Wachtler, Stephen F.
Walstedt, Ervin

"An Achievement"

ACKNOWLEDGMENTS

A book concerned with as much detailed information as this cannot be the work of one person. Help, and in abundance, came from many people, some of whom have died in the time it took to complete this manuscript and find a publisher. To all of them, living and dead, I wish to express my gratitude.

Without the encouragement, advice, and help of Bill Moline, who went a good distance down this same road of research and reporting, I would never have had the confidence to begin or the will to continue. Roy Bernick, and Bob Sis, of St. Cloud; Damie Gruber, of Webb Publishing Company in St. Paul; Terry Kohner, then Editor of *Northern Automotive Journal*, St. Paul; John L. Connolly, St. Paul; Douglas Forsyth, of Edina, and Frank Forsyth, of Rochester; William Keleher, of Albuquerque; William Waldeck, of Grand Junction, Colorado; Peter and Robert Neis, of St. Cloud; Stanley Francis, of Denver; D. D. Schendel, of St. Paul; Henry Sniezek, Charles Richter, Maurice O'Link, Warren Hull, Carl Fritz, and Richard Egerman, all of St. Cloud, provided much information or pointed me to convenient access to it.

To Fred Barry, then of WJON; to Melvin Synhorst, Secretary of State of Iowa; Jacques Daringer, manager of the LaSalle Hotel, Chicago; Robert Dortch, Director of Records, Birmingham Southern College; Dr. Marcus West, Archivist of the Diocese of Richmond, Virginia; Earl Nunn, Superintendent of Schools, Las Cruces, New Mexico; Marvin Krause, Chapel of Chimes, Fairbanks, Alaska; Mark Lohmann, Miles City, Montana; the Honorable George Romney, Secretary of HEW, Washington, D.C.; Clark Hunting, Minneapolis; Linda Phillips, Denver; Congressman John Zwach, Washington, D.C.; Mrs. William Fleet, Denver; Fred Thielman, St. Cloud; Russell T. Wing, Excelsior, Minnesota; Raymond T. Logue, Vice President, Ford Motor Company, Detroit; John Simon, Styling Office, Chrysler Corporation, Detroit; Fred W. Grant, Pioneer Engineering & Manufacturing, Warren, Michigan; Paul Doerner, Stearns County Attorney; John Streitz, St. Cloud City Clerk; Postmistress Dorothy Parsons, Johns, Alabama; and to Gary Gordon, Minneapolis, who did legal research on the appeals; to each and all of them my thanks for their efforts on my behalf.

For information about their relatives I thank John Kulla, Elmdale, Minnesota; S. C. Pandolfo III, Denver; William P. Hahn and Mrs. Paul (Vivian Pandolfo) Croff, El Paso; Mrs. Hannah Putnam, Safford, Arizona; Ms. Lucy (DeSmet) Travis, Toledo; and Mr. and Mrs. Orvil Aronson, Detroit. A special debt is owed Victor Gauvreau, Tucson. Despite his age and aversion to talking about himself, he gave generously of his time and mementos with patient kindness. My disappointment in not having this book completed before he died is far outweighed by my sorrow at the loss of his warm friendship.

To the following who gave or lent photographs, magazines, and other special material, my thanks:

Mrs. Carl Cummins, St. Paul; Joe Haftreiter, Anthony, New Mexico; Sidney Blakeway, Fargo, North Dakota; David K. Bausch, Allentown, Pennsylvania; Mr. and Mrs. Charles Wilbert, St. Paul; Mrs. Al Wengert and Mrs. Arwood Waldrup, Cold Spring, Minnesota; Mrs. Peter Dinndorf and Mrs. Walter Andrews, Robert Thyen, Mrs. Barney Bachman, John Schreder, Mrs. Mark Schnettler, James Gammell, and Richard Manthey, all of St. Cloud.

The following associations and departments supplied information for which I am grateful: William E. Naviaux, Executive Secretary of the Omaha Bar association; Norman Carlson, Director of the Bureau of Prisons, Department of Justice, Washington, D.C.; National Weather Record Center, Asheville, North Carolina; State Climatologist, Champaign, Illinois; Amy R. Jennings, Librarian, Federal Trade Commission, Washington, D.C.; E. E. Greeson, Clerk of Court, district of New Mexico, Albuquerque; Robert Svenningsen, Chief of Archives, Denver branch of the Federal Records Center, Denver; Colonel Earl E. Browning, Jr., Deputy Director of the Office of Information for the Armed Forces, DOD, Washington, D.C.; Office of the Attorney

General, Montgomery, Alabama; Office of the Attorney General, Austin, Texas; W. O. Sanders, Manager of the Texas State Board of Insurance, Austin, Texas; Laura M. Miura, supervisor of licenses, and Lee R. Elling, Supervising Insurance Investigator, Colorado Commission of Insurance, Denver; Department of Insurance, Lincoln, Nebraska; Department of Insurance, Pierre, South Dakota; Michael Cox, Assistant Archivist, State Records Center and Archives, Santa Fe, New Mexico; Securities Division of the State of Minnesota, St. Paul; Automobile Manufacturers Association, Detroit; Monte Irvin, Office of the Commissioner of Baseball, New York City; Joseph Gilbert, General Manager, Society of Automobile Engineers, New York City; American Society of Mechanical Engineers, New York City; Arizona Bankers Association, Phoenix; Department of Education, Macalaster College, St. Paul; Records Office, University of Minnesota, St. Paul.

For advising me where to look I am particularly indebted to Glanville Smith, Cold Spring, Minnesota; Gertrude Gove and Ruth Cadwell, both of St. Cloud; and J. Richard Heinzkill, Eugene, Oregon. For technical knowledge and historical help my thanks to John "Pete" Schmauch, Tamaqua, Pennsylvania; Robert F. Scott, Croton-on-Hudson, New York; John Conde, assistant director of Public Relations, American Motors Corporation, Detroit (who also supplied several rare photos); Ralph Dunwoodie, Harrah's Automobile Collection, Reno, Nevada; Keith Marvin, Troy, New York; Jan P. Norbye, Jackson Heights, New York; Sidney Strong, Early American Museum, Silver Springs, Florida; Dr. Alfred S. Lewerenz, Hollywood, California.

For their help, and in many cases their photographs, I want to thank Joseph Justad, Hennepin County Historical Society, Minneapolis; the Stearns County Historical Society, St. Cloud; Caroline Dunn, Indiana Historical Society, Indianapolis; the State Historical Society of Wisconsin, Madison; the Milwaukee County Historical Society, Milwaukee; the State Historical Society of Colorado, Denver; the Nebraska State Historical Society, Lincoln; Miss Barta Letovsky of the Greater Omaha Historical Society, Omaha; Mrs. Paul Rhymer, curator of prints at the Chicago Historical Society; Herman Moncus of the Tucumcari Research Institute, Tucumcari, New Mexico; Mabel Turner, assistant Librarian of the Eastern Washington State Historical Society, Spokane. Special gratitude is owed the library and newspaper staffs of the Minnesota Historical Society in St. Paul.

Industrial information was obtained from many Chambers of Commerce, and I thank their research staffs in Minneapolis; Cincinnati; Detroit; Chicago; Tucumcari (New Mexico); Indianapolis; Grinnel (Iowa); San Antonio (Texas); Phoenix (Arizona); Denver; and—not the least, but last—St. Cloud.

Many libraries were valuable sources and I thank Miss Mary Cattie, Free Library of Philadelphia; James J. Bradley, Automotive History Collection of the Detroit Public Library; the University of Iowa Library, Iowa City; New York Public Library; Milwaukee Public Library; Spokane Public Library; Martina A. Brown, of the History Department of the Minneapolis Public Library; Miss Marguerite Donnellan, Cataloguing Librarian of the Chicago Bar Association Library; the Library of Congress, Washington, D.C.; and the staff of the Great River Regional Library in St. Cloud.

The libraries and morgues of many newspapers gave material that was necessary to establish the chronology of events in this record. I thank Roy Swanson and Roman Baltes of the *St. Paul Pioneer Press*; William W. Sannwald of the *Chicago Sun Times*; the *Omaha World Herald*; the *Grand Junction* (Colorado) *Sentinel*; C. W. Snedden of the *Fairbanks* (Alaska) *Daily News-Miner*; the *Chicago Tribune*; the *Denver Rocky Mountain News*; Robert Inman of *The Denver Post*; the *Milwaukee Journal*; the *San Antonio Express and News*; *The New Mexican*, Santa Fe; the *Spokane Daily Chronicle*; the *Western Banker* Magazine; and the *Automotive News*.

A number of people gave freely of their time to talk to me, many of them for several hours at a time and some on more than one occasion. I would like to thank Richard Daggy of St. Paul; Bill Bettenberg of Sartell, Minnesota; Mrs. Paul Ahlmer, Al C. Petters, Clarence Brinkman, Eddie Lommel, Philip Lemm, Mrs. Robert Koehn, and Lillian Oelschlager, all of St. Cloud. Special thanks to Leo Croteau of Tucson who recorded his interview with Victor Gauvreau for me. And to John V. McMillin II of Iowa City, Iowa, whose genealogical research of his family also provided a "lost link" to this narrative, a grateful thanks for his help and his interest.

Finally, a special thank you to Dick and Roy Bernick. Roy's purchase of a Pan car and his granting me unlimited access to it provided answers to many questions I would otherwise have been unable to resolve.

John J. Dominik

BIBLIOGRAPHY

While there was no attempt to make this book a formal, annotated history, all of the information in it has been documented in one way or another. Thus, while no annotated bibliography was utilized, several books did provide background information. From Clark E. Hunting's fifth-year paper, written in 1962 principally on the Pan Motor Company, and to which I hereby acknowledge a large and fruitful debt, I obtained not only a filled-out chronology but the titles of several books that provided information on the early automotive industry: *THE AUTOMOBILE INDUSTRY; Its Economical and Commercial Development*, by **Ralph C. Epstein**, Ph.D., published in 1928 by A. W. Shaw & Company, New York. *THE STORY OF THE AMERICAN AUTOMOBILE*, by **Rudolph E. Anderson**, published in 1950 by Public Affairs Press, Washington, D.C. *THE POWER TO GO, The Story of the Automotive Industry*, by **Merrill Denison**, published in 1956 by Doubleday & Company, Inc., Garden City, NJ. *THE AUTOMOBILE INDUSTRY—The Coming of Age of Capitalism's Favorite Child*, by **E. D. Kennedy**, published in 1941 by Reynal & Hitchcock, New York.

Several other books were used, either for the information they provided about their subject or their author: *JUDGE LANDIS AND TWENTY-FIVE YEARS OF BASEBALL*, by **J. G. Taylor Spink**, published in 1947 by Thomas Y. Crowell Company, New York. *THE AMAZING STORY OF REPEAL*, by **Fletcher Dobyns**, published in 1940 by Willett, Clark & Company, Chicago. *HISTORY OF STEARNS COUNTY*, by **William Bell Mitchell**, published by H. C. Cooper, Jr & Co., Chicago, in 1915. *HISTORY OF THE UPPER MISSISSIPPI VALLEY*, by **Winchell, Neill, Williams,** and **Bryant**, published in 1881 by the Minnesota Historical Company, Minneapolis.

Finally, other publications—magazines, brochures, and reports — were used: *Pan Siftings*, *Motor World*; *Automotive Trade Journal*; *Automotive Engineering*; *Horseless Age*; *Pan Stock Sales Record*; *Associated Advertising*; *Monte Vista Journal*; *Merchant, Banker, and Manufacturer*; *World's Work*; *The Banker's Journal*; and the last and best source—*Pictorial Proof of Progress*, the lavishly illustrated publication of the Pan Motor Company.